St. Martin's Uncovered

St. Martin's Uncovered

Investigations in the churchyard of
St. Martin's-in-the-Bull Ring, Birmingham, 2001

Megan Brickley and Simon Buteux

Josephine Adams and Richard Cherrington

*With contributions by Helena Berry, Lynne Bevan, Marina Ciaraldi, Rowena Gale,
Michael Hodder, Annette Hancocks, Emma Hancox, Cathy Patrick, Stephanie Rátkai,
Michael Richards, Simon Wallis, Penelope Walton Rogers and Gaynor Western*

Principal illustrations by Bryony Ryder. Studio photography by Graham Norrie.

Oxbow Books

Published by
Oxbow Books, Park End Place, Oxford OX1 1HN

© Megan Brickley and Simon Buteux, and the individual authors 2006

ISBN 1-84217-201-8

A CIP record of this book is available from the British Library

This book is available direct from

Oxbow Books, Park End Place, Oxford OX1 1HN
(Phone: 01865-241249; Fax: 01865-794449)

and

The David Brown Book Company
PO Box 511, Oakville, CT 06779, USA
(Phone: 860-945-9329; Fax: 860-945-9468)

or from our website

www.oxbowbooks.com

Front cover: The spire of St. Martin's Church with the roof of Selfridges, Bullring, behind.
Back cover: (above) 'Thomas Martin' gold mourning ring;
(below) 19th-century advertisement for funerary transport.
Cover design by Bryony Ryder

Printed in Great Britain by
Arrowsmith, Bristol

Contents

Contents of CD

Summary

The archaeological excavations at St. Martin's church-yard, Birmingham uncovered 857 burials dating to the late 18th century and the 19th century. The majority of the burials (734) were in simple earth-cut graves but the remainder were buried in a large chambered vault, ten family vaults and 24 brick-lined graves. The burials represent a cross-section of Birmingham's population during the period of the Industrial Revolution, with those from the earth-cut graves broadly representing the working classes and those from the burial structures the middle classes.

Detailed anthropological analysis has been carried out on a sample of 505 of the skeletons, investigating aspects of demography and health. Over the last ten years there have been significant advances in the development of diagnostic criteria for pathological conditions in human skeletal material and the range and type of pathological lesions recorded in the investigation are far greater than those found in previous investigations elsewhere in Britain. Compared to the modern British population the analysis revealed a high prevalence of metabolic diseases, such as scurvy (vitamin C deficiency) and rickets (juvenile vitamin D deficiency). The results for these and other pathological conditions reveal that there were very real links between the prevalence of diseases and the socio-economic status of the individuals under investigation. This is most striking in the patterns of various types of trauma, which graphically illustrate the hard lives led by working-class women. Overall, the anthropological study provides ground-breaking new insights into the health of a population living through a period of intense social and economic change.

The investigations also provide insights into burial practices and the funerary trade, with detailed reports on the structure and use of the vaults, the coffins and coffin furniture, funerary attire and other textiles, jewellery and other personal items. At no other site has such a range of burial types been investigated in comparable detail. New evidence of social bias in burial practices, notably the under representation of females and infants in the vaults, is discussed. Documentary research on named individuals from the vaults provides information on family histories which complements and informs the anthropological and archaeological analyses. Most of the families investigated are representative of typical Birmingham trades of the 19th century, including ironworking and brassfounding, and the documentary research traces the changing fortunes of these families. This research also enables the social context of the building and use of the burial structures to be explored.

Throughout the report an attempt is made to place the findings in the context of their social, economic and religious background, in order to provide an integrated analysis. The report concludes with contrasting reconstructions of two funerals at St. Martin's, one of a wealthy iron merchant and the other of a butcher's wife.

Foreword

The Birmingham Alliance

Throughout history Birmingham has been a leading centre of trade and market innovation. One of its earliest known transformations, in the 1100s, turned it from a village into a thriving market town. Later, in the 18th century, it was described as 'the first manufacturing town in the world' and in the 19th century its industrial greatness earned it the soubriquet 'the city of a thousand trades'. In the 1960s it became one of the country's most celebrated examples of revolutionary urban planning, which brought with it the opening of the old Bull Ring shopping centre. At the time, it was one of the world's largest shopping centres outside America and an exemplar of shopping centre design.

Today Birmingham is undergoing yet another transformation. The city is seeing billions of pounds of new investment, and the opening of the new 110,000m² Bullring in September 2003 has been a major milestone in reviving the city's status as a leading European retail capital.

The opening of Bullring has brought over 130 different retailers together in a new central focus of shopping, leisure and entertainment. Its creation is part of a long continuum of Birmingham's history as a major trading centre. Not only has the archaeological work confirmed the site as the historic heart of the city – but through Bullring it will continue to be so.

Sited beneath the spire of St. Martin's Church, this historic centre for market trading began life in 1166 when the city was awarded a charter giving it the right to have its own market. Since then, the site's existence as a market has continued to the present day. The opening of the old Bull Ring shopping centre in 1964 brought the location international prestige as one of Europe's largest and most modern shopping complexes. Almost forty years on, the 26-acre site is again the centre of innovation, this time as the home of the largest retail-led urban regeneration project in Europe: Bullring.

The construction of this latest manifestation of Birmingham's transformation has brought startling and exciting discoveries. New evidence, unearthed during archaeological digs commissioned by The Birmingham Alliance over three and a half years as part of Bullring's regeneration, has provided new perspectives on the city's history.

This volume is concerned with the excavation of St. Martin's Churchyard to create St. Martin's Square, a focus for the development placing the ancient church once again at the heart of the city's thriving commercial life. The sensitive excavation of vaults and graves in the former churchyard has shed fascinating new light on the lives and deaths of a sample of Birmingham's population, rich and poor, during the 18th and 19th centuries, the time of the city's rise to international stature as a centre for manufacture and commerce.

The Birmingham Alliance is privileged to have been part of the process which has allowed so much more knowledge of the city's history to become known. The dedication of the team of archaeologists from The University of Birmingham during their time of discovery has been outstanding. Special thanks must be made to Mike Hodder, Birmingham City Council's planning archaeologist, the Rev'd Canon Adrian Newman of St. Martin's-in-the-Bull Ring Church and also to Cathy Patrick, of CgMs Consulting, the archaeological consultant to The Birmingham Alliance. It is their efforts which have brought about this book – another vital chapter in Birmingham's fascinating history.

Jon Emery, Hammerson; Neil Varnham, Henderson Global Investors; Bob de Barr, Land Securities

Foreword

The Leader of Birmingham City Council

The 857 residents of 18th- and 19th-century Birmingham whose mortal remains were excavated at St. Martin's lived during a time of change; a time when Birmingham was becoming a major commercial and manufacturing centre whose products reached throughout the British Empire and beyond. They would have witnessed massive building work in the busy city centre and the development of suburbs. The archaeological excavation of St. Martin's churchyard took place in another time of change in which Bullring and other developments reflect the European and international status of 21st-century Birmingham.

The Birmingham Alliance and its archaeologists rose to the challenge of the excavation of St. Martin's churchyard in advance of the creation of a new public square in Bullring. Excavation procedures and subsequent analysis had to respect the understandable sensitivities of dealing with human remains while ensuring that the maximum information was retrieved. Unlocking this information in a sensitive way has respected the individuals buried there, and their remains have subsequently been reburied.

Careful excavation and subsequent detailed study of the human remains ensured that, in addition to the part they played in the prosperity of the city while they were alive, the people buried at St. Martin's have contributed, as they could never have imagined, to our understanding of the city at a crucial period in its history. Far from being morbid or ghoulish, examination of their remains has revealed fascinating and nationally significant facts about what it was like to live in Georgian and Victorian Birmingham. These results complement our knowledge of life and work derived from other archaeological excavations in the Bullring and elsewhere in the city centre.

Careful planning and partnership with the City Council has again ensured that, in addition to delivering high quality development worthy of the city's renaissance, information about the city's past has been properly recorded. At St. Martin's, as well as the publication of this detailed report, an interpretation panel in the new square describes the results to the shoppers of today.

Councillor Mike Whitby
Leader of Birmingham City Council

Acknowledgements

The investigations in St. Martin's churchyard and the subsequent analysis and report were funded by The Birmingham Alliance, the developers of Bullring. The excavation team from Birmingham Archaeology would like to thank all at The Alliance who helped to make the project a success. The work was monitored on behalf of The Alliance by Cathy Patrick of CgMs Consulting and on behalf of Birmingham City Council by Mike Hodder, the Council's Planning Archaeologist. The support and perseverance of Cathy and Mike throughout the project is appreciated.

David Lowe, George Harbutt and colleagues monitored the removal of human remains on behalf of Birmingham City Council Environmental Services.

Thanks are due to the staff of the on-site contractors, Sir Robert McAlpine, notably Andy Brown, Neil Doherty, Graham Dodds, Mark Durham, Manus Ferry, Chris Illsley, Tom Kelly and Paddy McBride. The advice of Kimber Heath, Benoy Architects, Astorre Marinoni, Waterman Partnership, and Mike Nisbet, Gardiner and Theobald Management Services, is also gratefully acknowledged.

Thanks are also due to the Rev'd Canon Adrian Newman and the team at St. Martin's, together with members of the congregation, for their cooperation and patience in often disruptive circumstances.

The fieldwork was managed for Birmingham Archaeology by Gary Coates, and the initial stages of the post-excavation programme by Gary Coates and Annette Hancocks.

The fieldwork was initially supervised by Chris Patrick and subsequently by Richard Cherrington, with the assistance of Andy Rudge and Chris Hewitson. The excavation was carried out by Sue Beighton, Sabina Belim, Susie Blake, Bob Bracken, Alison Dingle, Mary Duncan, Nathan Flavel, Paul Harris, Emma Hancox, Mark Hewson, Maurice Hopper, Loz Jones, Richard Lee, Ruth Leak, Phil Mann, Helen Martin, Gynfor Morris, Michelle Morris, Emily Murray, Charlotte Neilson, Ed Newton, Russell Norris, Dave Priestley, Sally Radford, Barrie Simpson, James Taylor, Sarah Watt and Steve Williams. The assistance of Malcolm Hislop and Steve Litherland with the building recording is gratefully acknowledged.

Processing of artefacts and human remains was initially supervised by Jan Jackson and then by Emma Hancox, with the assistance of Lydia Bird, Sarah Blewer, Lyn Cassells, Priscilla Guzman, Malcolm Hislop, Rebekah Judah, Cat Orchard, Lisette Piper, Martin Smith and Sarah Weatherall.

The illustrations were prepared by Bryony Ryder, John Halstead and Nigel Dodds. The studio photography was undertaken by Graham Norrie.

The authors are very grateful to Dr Simon Mays of English Heritage and Dr Julian Litten, who kindly read and commented on parts of a draft of the report. Dr Mays read Chapter 4, on the physical anthropology, and Dr Litten read Chapters 1–3, 5, 6, 8 and 9. Their detailed comments and advice have improved the report greatly, and several errors have been corrected, although it was not always possible to adopt every suggestion made. Drs Mays and Litten are not of course responsible for the content or the errors that remain. In addition, Dr Litten kindly drew our attention to, and provided a copy of, the unpublished 1837 trade catalogue issued by CW&Sons of Birmingham, held in the Linford-Bridgeman Collection at Lichfield.

Megan Brickley also wishes to thank the following:
The Arts and Humanities Research Board (AHRB) who awarded her a grant for research leave, allowing her to undertake the analysis of data obtained from the human bone and write up the results of this research (award RL:APN: 16822 AN: 9280).

The Natural Environment Research Council (NERC) who funded the research on vitamin D deficiency conditions (award reference NER/A/S/2002/00486). Data from this research has been included in this report.

Dr Jonathan Reinarz, Centre for the History of Medicine, University of Birmingham, who kindly supplied information regarding early hospitals in Birmingham. Professor Sue Black who supplied the recording form for infant skeletons used during skeletal analysis.

Lydia Bird, Rachel Ives and Sean Carter for entering data from the recording forms into the database and for typing up the Individuals Catalogue, which forms Appendix 5 of this volume.

Staff at the London School of Hygiene and Tropical Medicine, in particular Dr Hamidou Traore and Dr Mike Taylor of Imperial College, who helped out with the hybridisation of the PCR products for the MTB DNA tests.

Jo Adams would like to thank the following:
The staff of Birmingham Archives and Birmingham Local Studies; Rev'd Canon Michael Blood and Rev'd D. H. Raynor for their help in religious matters; John Harris from Cribb & Sons; Richard Jones from St. Martin's bell ringers for the loan of books; and the National Meteorological Archive.

Annette Hancocks wishes to thank:
Roxanne Fea, Curator of the British Dental Association Museum, for her assistance.

Emma Hancox gratefully acknowledges:
the assistance of the staff at the Print Room and The National Art Library in the Victoria and Albert Museum, and also John Harris at the National Funeral Museum.

Cathy Patrick of CgMs would like to pass on her especial thanks to the following people:
Jon Emery, Mel Evans, Vic Michel and Simon Wallis at The Birmingham Alliance; Mike Nisbet at Gardiner & Theobald Management Services, Kimber Heath at Benoy, Sara Boonham at Gardiner & Theobald, Astorre Marinoni at Waterman Partnership; all at Sir Robert McAlpine; the Rev'd Canon Adrian Newman at St. Martin's; David Lowe, George Harbutt and their team at Environmental Services, Birmingham City Council; Andrea Haines and her team at Quinton Cemetery. Thanks also to Mike Hodder, Planning Archaeologist, Birmingham City Council, for his support throughout the scheme; to Megan Brickley at the University of Birmingham and to all at Birmingham Archaeology.

The authors are grateful to Val Lamb, Clare Litt and Sarah Monks at Oxbow Books for their advice and help, and for skilfully steering the manuscript through to publication.

Illustration acknowledgements
We are grateful to The Birmingham Alliance who provided the photographs used on the cover and for Figs 3 and 26, and to Myra Dean who supplied the photograph used for Fig. 13. The illustrations comprising Figs 15, 20, 24, 164 and 173 were kindly supplied by the Local History Department of Birmingham Archives.

Overview: Excavations in St. Martin's churchyard and the archaeology of burial grounds in Birmingham

Michael Hodder
Planning Archaeologist, Birmingham City Council

The excavation of St. Martin's churchyard was the first, and at the time of writing is still the only, extensive archaeological excavation of a burial ground of any period to have taken place in Birmingham. It amply demonstrated the range of information provided by burial grounds on various aspects of the city's past and how, when the need for their excavation arises, this information can be retrieved. This overview looks at the results of the St. Martin's excavations in their wider city context, first in terms of the archaeological resource itself, second in terms of the management of that resource, and finally it very briefly summarises the overall achievement of the excavation and its significance for future work.

The burials investigated in the excavation had been made at a time when Birmingham was becoming internationally famous, and the methods of analysis of the human remains and their results are themselves of international significance. This overview is written from the point of view of the management of Birmingham's archaeology in the context of new development, but many of the issues raised here apply equally to other parts of the country and indeed to the treatment of human remains throughout the world.

Human remains and the history of Birmingham

Despite the wealth and variety of archaeological remains in Birmingham, human remains are so far absent from most periods of the city's past (Hodder 2004, 170). No human remains of prehistoric, Roman or Anglo-Saxon date are yet known in Birmingham, although they have been found in other parts of the West Midlands. Intact and securely datable graves have been archaeologically recorded in Birmingham for the post-medieval period only, and all of these were in urban locations. The burials

excavated at St. Martin's are contemporary with those recorded at St. Philip's Cathedral (Patrick 2001), those from the Park Street Burial Ground exposed in Albert Street (Krakowicz and Rudge 2004), and those excavated in the churchyard of Holy Trinity in Sutton Coldfield (Leach and Sterenberg 1992).

The only intact Birmingham burials likely to date from before the 18th century are those found in the Park Street excavations in the Bull Ring (Buteux 2003, 38–41; Buteux and Rátkai forthcoming). These are probably medieval in date but even if they were more recent, possibly 17th century, they would still be the oldest datable burials from the city. The undated burials in Bull Street mentioned by William Hutton (Hutton 1783, 189) might have been medieval or earlier (Bassett 2001, 20; Hodder 2004, 92–93), and other medieval inhabitants of Birmingham are represented by disarticulated remains and contents of charnel pits at St. Martin's, and by many unmarked graves and fragments in the graveyards of parish churches of medieval origin.

In addition to disturbance and dispersal of earlier burials in intensively used churchyards by later interments, the absence of earlier remains is partly a result of acid soil conditions in the north and west of the city, in which unburnt bone does not survive for more than a couple of centuries. In the Sutton Coldfield area, for example, even the bones of 18th- and 19th-century burials at Holy Trinity church were in poor condition, and hardly any bone was found in excavations along the line of the M6 Toll motorway (Booth 2001). The lack of human remains is also, and perhaps mainly, a reflection of the locations in which archaeological excavation has taken place.

The information provided by burials and burial grounds also relates to other aspects of the archaeological record of recent centuries, and like these it augments and sometimes challenges the documentary record. The analysis of the human remains at St. Martin's and study of their coffins, coffin furniture and the method of interment, together with the documentary record for the individual people and their families, tells us not only about individual lifestyles and society's attitudes to death but also about other aspects of 18th- and 19th-century Birmingham, such as industries and the consumption of their products. For example, most if not all of the coffins and coffin furniture are likely to be Birmingham products. The coffin fittings were made of several different metals, reflecting the range of Birmingham's metalworking industry: cast iron grip plate fittings, grip plates of brass, other copper alloys, lead, tin and nickel. As well as metal for fittings, the coffin cases used a large amount of timber, mainly elm. Where did this come from? It presumably formed part of the traffic of raw materials along the canals and was offloaded at one of the many canalside timber yards and sawmills marked on 19th-century maps.

In the coffins, their fittings and the objects accompanying the bodies inside them, we are seeing artefacts in use, albeit a rather special type of use. This contrasts with the objects and materials usually found on other excavated sites such as Park Street: items that have been lost or discarded because they were broken or no longer required, and the waste products from manufacturing. Other objects in the burials at St. Martin's, particularly jewellery, pins, buckles, and buttons made of bone and copper alloy are, like the coffins and coffin fittings, likely to have been mainly Birmingham products, and many of them might have been made not far from St. Martin's.

Managing the resource

Pressure on land in the city centre and elsewhere for new development means that even former burial grounds are not necessarily regarded as areas to be preserved forever. St. Martin's is not the only burial ground in the city to be affected by recent development, but it is the only one in which burials affected by the development were archaeologically excavated and fully analysed. At St. Philip's the archaeological recording accompanied rather than preceded the development and the analysis of excavated remains was not carried out to the same level of detail as at St. Martin's. At Holy Trinity in Sutton Coldfield a single trench was archaeologically excavated in the area affected by the development, and burials in the part of Park Street Burial Ground now under Albert Street were recorded following their exposure in trenches for new services. In retrospect, in the light of the information recovered from St. Martin's, more stringent requirements for archaeological work should perhaps have been imposed by the City Council and the ecclesiastical authorities at St. Philip's and Holy Trinity. However, at least there was some archaeological work at these, which was not the case at St. Bartholomew's chapel in the 1960s (Neilson and Duncan 2001) and Key Hill,

part of which was affected by the construction of the Metro in the 1990s, although at both of these burials were removed in advance of development and reburied, and a record was made of the monuments at Key Hill.

Now that we recognise the information resource offered by the city's burial grounds, how is this managed when they are affected by development proposals? Three particular, and linked, characteristics of burial grounds as archaeological sites stand out: they attract much public attention; they potentially contain a huge amount of information; and they cannot be examined satisfactorily by sampling.

Human burials in Birmingham are the remains of those who walked the city's streets before us, so they are naturally going to be the subject of much interest. Too often, however, the human remains themselves attract attention, often macabre, that detracts from appreciation of the information provided by them and by other archaeological remains. It is essential to make it clear that it is the combination of detailed examination of the human remains themselves with study of accompanying objects and information from other contemporary sites, that contributes to our understanding of the past.

The amount of information that can be obtained through detailed examination of human remains is far greater than would have been possible just a few years ago and we can be sure that in the future new techniques will tell us even more. Out of respect to the people whose remains we are excavating, as well as best archaeological practice, it is essential to maximise the information return from them, but it is inevitably costly and time consuming to obtain this information. The St. Martin's project was fortunate in obtaining additional funding from other sources for some pieces of work but even more could have been done than was possible with the resources available. Where do we draw a line? This raises three questions: the potential retention of remains for future examination, the application of a sampling strategy, and the potential for preservation *in situ*.

Retention and storage of human remains for future study is currently the subject of debate at a national and international level, so will not be further discussed here. The human remains excavated at St. Martin's were reburied following analysis, as agreed at the outset of the excavation.

Although only a percentage of archaeological features such as ditches and pits, like those found on the Park Street site near St. Martin's, would normally be excavated, the complexities of burials and burial grounds mean that neither can be satisfactorily sampled in this way. At St. Martin's, the horizontal and vertical extent of excavation were both determined by the extent of earthmoving required for the new development. The extent of analysis was determined by the time and budget available; the cost was estimated before the excavation started and a date for re-interment was agreed as part of the post-excavation programme.

It is difficult, if not impossible, to achieve total preservation *in situ* on an urban site through design of a new development which is likely to include major structures and landscaping, particularly for an archaeological site as big as a graveyard. Even so, human remains, coffins, coffin fittings and other objects left buried are still subject to biological and chemical decay, the rate of which may be affected by the development itself. Preservation *in situ* also means that the information contained in the site is locked in rather than released.

Total excavation, i.e. the entire burial ground and all its individual burials, and total preservation, i.e. a design for the new development that ensures that the burials are preserved for at least the lifetime of that development, are two extremes. The achievable reality, determined by the details of the development, may actually be somewhere between the two, as at St. Martin's.

In the real world of 21st-century Birmingham, what is both realistically achievable and a reasonable requirement as part of the development process when burial grounds are affected? The answer, and one which is of course equally applicable to any piece of archaeological work, is to establish rigorous and justified research aims at the outset, with reference to national and regional research frameworks.

Excavations at St. Martin's: the achievement

Alongside the broader significance of the information derived from the human remains excavated at St. Martin's, three features of particular importance to the archaeology of Birmingham and its management stand out: the relationship of the archaeological remains of the resting place of the dead to those of the places where people lived and worked; the practical on-site solutions to excavation of a burial ground as part of new development; and, addressing the question posed above, the contribution of the results in formulating research priorities and strategies for the future.

The combination of the information from human remains with that from 18th- and 19th-century deposits, structures and objects excavated on other sites in the city centre, especially those at nearby Park Street and Edgbaston Street as part of the Bullring development, with the documentary evidence related to individuals and their families and other written, illustrative and cartographic sources, and with surviving buildings and structures, provides a rounded picture of this period of Birmingham's past.

A pragmatic and practical approach to the excavation of St. Martin's that included the active involvement and cooperation of other professionals alongside archaeologists demonstrated that, despite logistical challenges, this type of site can be excavated in such a way that detailed information can be extracted from it. The same outcome can be achieved on other Birmingham burial grounds affected by development.

Before the St. Martin's excavation took place, archaeological information of sufficient detail to assess the place of Birmingham's burial grounds in research priorities and strategies was simply not available. With the benefit of this new information, we can now identify unanswered questions and suggest how they might be answered. This is not an introverted process: it informs and guides the response, through the planning process, to development proposals.

1 Introduction

Simon Buteux

This volume concerns archaeological excavations which were undertaken in the former churchyard of St. Martin's Church, Birmingham, England (NGR: SP073866), between May and November 2001 (Figs. 1 & 2). The excavations were carried out in the context of a landscaping scheme that involved lowering the level of the churchyard and creating in its place a new square, St. Martin's Square, in front of the church. During the excavations 857 burials were recorded, in simple earth-cut graves and more elaborate brick-lined graves and family vaults, dating mainly to the earlier part of the 19th century. The majority of the skeletons have been scientifically analysed and documentary research has been undertaken on those individuals who could be identified from surviving coffin plates, and on other members of their families buried with them in the vaults.

The creation of St. Martin's Square was part of the redevelopment of Birmingham's medieval centre, the Bull Ring, a market place which has existed since at least the 12th century. This involved building a bold and exciting new shopping destination, 'Bullring' – the largest commercially-led urban redevelopment project in Europe – on this historic site. Bullring swept away the 1960s redevelopment (the 'Bull Ring Centre') that had preceded it and has fundamentally changed the face of Birmingham's historic centre. Two iconic buildings, however, were preserved: the Rotunda, a circular office-block tower and a vestige of the 1960s redevelopment, which has become a major Birmingham landmark (and is now a Grade II Listed building of architectural and historical importance), and St. Martin's Church, the oldest church at the heart of Birmingham (Fig. 3, colour).

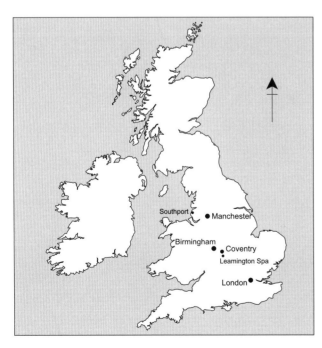

Fig. 1: Location of Birmingham and other towns and cities mentioned in the text.

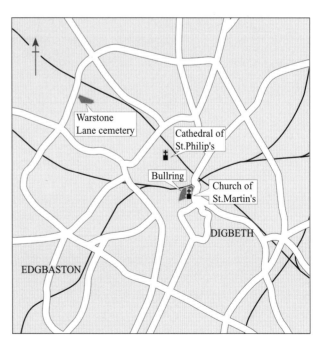

Fig. 2: Location of Bullring and St. Martin's Church in Birmingham City Centre.

The redevelopment project managed to reunite St. Martin's Church with the retail centre of the city, which it has always served, but from which it had been cut off by the road systems of the 1960s development. Today, from the Bullring shopping complex a flight of steps (overlooked by a statue of Admiral Lord Nelson, one of the first to be commissioned by a grateful nation) leads down to the expansive St. Martin's Square and the church itself, cleaned and restored (Fig. 4). Although the present church of St. Martin's dates almost entirely to 1872, when the church was rebuilt in the Gothic style, there has been a church on this site since the 12th century – fragments of Norman architecture were uncovered during the Victorian rebuilding and the excavations described in this volume recorded parts of the foundation of the medieval west tower (Appendix 3, CD). Members of the de Birmingham family, the medieval lords of the manor, were buried in the church, and several impressive memorials of these aristocrats are still preserved within

the Victorian church. Of more interest in the present context, however, is the fact that in the churchyard which surrounded the church the 'ordinary' people of Birmingham's central parish have been buried for more than 30 generations.

It was these burials that were the focus of the archaeological excavations and which are the subject of this report. Due to the intensive use of the graveyard from the 12th century down to the middle of the 19th century, only the latest of the thousands of burials which had taken place over the centuries were preserved. These surviving burials dated predominantly to the late 18th century and the earlier part of the 19th century. The earliest burial uncovered that could be securely dated belonged to the 1720s, whilst documentary records show that very few burials took place after 1863; the last burial, in a family vault, took place in 1915.

The burials which survived in St. Martin's churchyard thus span the period of the Industrial Revolution, perhaps

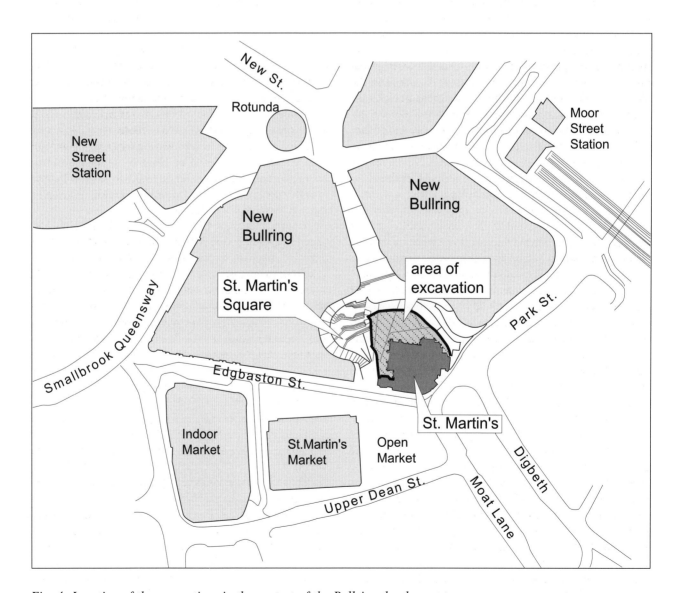

Fig. 4: Location of the excavations in the context of the Bullring development.

the most significant period of social transformation in British history. It is, of course, impossible to put dates on a complex phenomenon such as the Industrial Revolution, but most historians would define it as the period from around the middle of the 18th century down to about 1840. The 857 burials excavated in St. Martin's churchyard are thus a sample of the men, women and children who lived through the world-changing events of the Industrial Revolution. It would be little exaggeration to say that those who died at the beginning of this period and those who died at its end lived in different worlds. Furthermore, we know both from the archaeology and the documentary sources available to us, that those buried in the churchyard encompassed almost the whole of the social spectrum in Birmingham. There are burials of the working classes in simple earth-cut graves (the vast majority) and there are burials of the middle classes in more elaborate brick-lined graves and family vaults.

These facts make the burials from St. Martin's churchyard a very important group. We can ask of them a range of questions which documentary sources can only partially answer, or answer with their own particular bias. For example, what was the impact of the Industrial Revolution on patterns or mortality and health? What differences were there between rich and poor, and the children of rich and poor? These and other questions are addressed in Chapter 4, which describes the scientific analysis of the skeletons, and forms the core of this report. Other questions which can be asked relate to the social and symbolic significance of burial itself. How does the variety of burial practices represented – the choice of burial clothing, the sort of coffin, the type of tomb – reflect social structure and social change and the aspirations of those buried at St. Martin's? Most of the evidence relevant to these questions relates to the middle classes. This was a period in which a new middle class was defining itself relative to other strata in society. Many of these were self-made men of relatively humble origins (it would be anachronistic to add 'and women' to this statement, at least as a generality, although the role of women was no less transformed). How did these people choose to represent themselves and their families in death? These and related questions are addressed from various perspectives in Chapters 5 to 9.

There is a greater significance yet to the men, women and children who were buried in St. Martin's churchyard. Arthur Young described Birmingham in 1791 as 'The First Manufacturing Town in the World'. Hyperbole perhaps, but there is no denying Birmingham's pivotal role in the Industrial Revolution in Britain and thus, by extension, in the world. The people who drove the Industrial Revolution were mainly of the 'middling sort' – anonymous, or at least largely unknown today. Individually their achievements were often small and undramatic, but cumulatively, for better or for worse, they changed the world. Some of these people were buried in St. Martin's churchyard and Joseph Warden (unknown

until now to history but a central figure in this report) is emblematic of them.

Mention of a specific name brings us to another aspect of this report. On the one hand, the skeletal remains from the churchyard provide a database for the objective analysis of patterns of mortality and health, and patterns of burial ritual. On the other hand, each of the skeletons excavated was once an individual. One aim of the excavations was to try and identify insofar as possible each individual – from the details preserved on the coffin plate – and research their life history. The histories of these individuals would not only be interesting and important in themselves, but they would inform (and act as a 'control' upon) the analysis of the skeletal remains. In the event, as the excavations progressed it rapidly became apparent that there was an extreme bias in this evidence. There was not a single case where the identity of a burial in a simple earth-cut grave (i.e. the graves, it is presumed, predominantly of the working class) could be determined; the soil conditions were such that the coffin plates, where these survived at all, had corroded beyond legibility. The elitism and precautions of the middle class, who buried their dead apart from the masses in brick-lined graves or family vaults had won out – they quite often survived as identifiable individuals whereas the remains of the lower classes were destined to complete anonymity.

Nevertheless, the lives of those buried in the brick-lined graves and family vaults, more than quarter of whom could be identified, provide fascinating insights into some of the men and women – manufacturers, traders, professionals – who, it could be said with some justification, 'made' the Industrial Revolution. These lives are explored in Chapter 6.

A further aspect of the excavations is the light that they have shed on the funerary industry in Birmingham. This industry was big business. Not only were there the undertakers themselves, but all those who supplied the trade – for example, the makers of funerary attire, coffins and coffin furniture. During the 19th century Birmingham came to supplant London as the centre of the funerary trade in England, and it can be safely assumed that the great majority of the coffins and other 'impedimenta of death' were made or supplied locally. Various aspects of this trade are explored in the specialist reports in Chapter 5, while Chapter 8 provides an overview of the funerary industry.

Trade and industry were, of course, what 18th- and 19th-century Birmingham was all about, and this aspect of the St. Martin's excavations provides a link to the wider archaeological investigations of which the St. Martin's excavations were a part. Integral to the development of the Bullring shopping complex was a series of archaeological excavations around the old Bull Ring market place, within which St. Martin's Church was situated. Both the market place and the church go back at least to 1166 when Peter de Birmingham, the lord of the manor, obtained a royal charter to hold a market here. In addition to the excavations in St. Martin's churchyard, there were large-scale excavations at Edgbaston Street, Moor Street and Park Street, all streets surrounding the Bull Ring market place, together with a number of smaller-scale investigations (Fig. 5). These excavations, which are published in *The Bull Ring Uncovered*, a companion volume to this one, chart aspects of the development of Birmingham from the 12th century through to the 19th century. In particular, the excavations provide archaeological evidence for the development of industry from the medieval period, when tanning and pottery manufacture are documented, through to the 18th and 19th centuries, when the evidence for metalworking industries grows in importance. At the Park Street archaeological site especially there was evidence for iron and copper alloy working in the 18th century, and it is not difficult to imagine that some of the products of this industry, in the form of coffin fittings and furniture, found their way into St. Martin's churchyard, only a stone's throw away.

Thus the archaeological excavations undertaken in advance of the construction of Bullring and the creation of St. Martin's Square provide new insights into both life and death in 'The First Manufacturing Town in the World'. Indeed, these excavations are the first large-scale archaeological investigations to have taken place in Birmingham's historic centre. Chapter 2 provides a summary of the historical and archaeological background to the Parish of St. Martin's and the church itself, while in Chapter 7 an attempt is made to provide a sketch of life in the parish in the 19th century. Finally, in Chapter 9, there is a brief description of what two funerals which took place at St. Martin's in 1856 might have been like, using the documentary and archaeological information available to us. One was of Joseph Warden, a wealthy and successful iron merchant, whose family vault was one of the most interesting and informative uncovered at St. Martin's. A considerable amount has been learnt about his life and that of his family. The other is of Ann Cockayne, a butcher's wife. Little is known of her

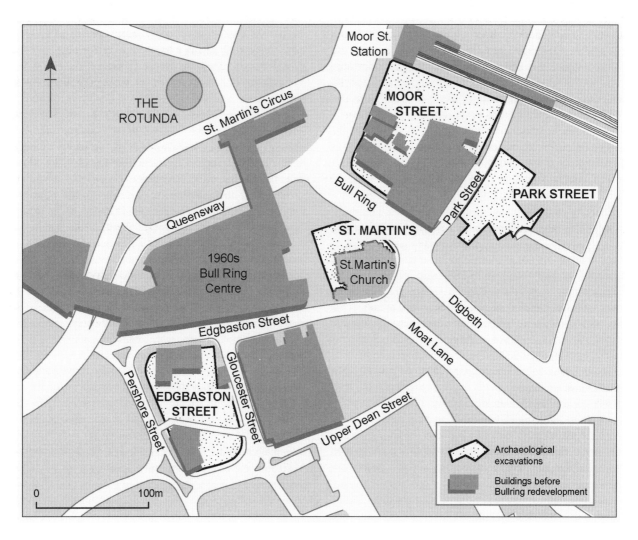

Fig. 5: Principal archaeological excavations undertaken in advance of the Bullring development, showing the old Bull Ring Centre.

life, and the location of her grave is unknown, although it was almost certainly one of the simple earth-cut graves.

This volume, therefore, should be of interest to readers with a wide range of interests. First and foremost it provides a detailed scientific analysis of a major assemblage of skeletons from the period of the Industrial Revolution – the first such analysis of an assemblage from the English Midlands and one of only a handful from the country as a whole. This scientific study will be an important source for all those concerned with patterns of past human health, especially as derived from the techniques of physical anthropology; it contains much significant new research in terms of both methodology and results. Second, the volume provides new evidence relating to funerals and the funerary industry in the 19th century in their wider social context. Third, it provides fresh insights into the social history of 19th century Birmingham and into the life and work of some of the people of 'the town of a thousand trades'.

This report aims to be relevant to both the academic and to the general reader, and different chapters of the report have different readerships primarily in mind. For both the specialist and general reader, Chapter 2 provides the necessary background. For the general reader, Chapters 6 to 9 give the family and social history, and aim to summarise and put into context the fascinating subject of funerals and the funerary industry, with specific reference to St. Martin's in the late 18th and 19th centuries. Much of what is presented in these chapters is anchored in the more technical descriptions and analyses presented in the central chapters of the report, Chapters 3 to 5, where more detailed discussions of many of the themes will be found.

The planning background and reburial of the human remains by Cathy Patrick and Simon Wallis

The planning permission for the Bullring development included conditions covering landscaping works in St. Martin's churchyard. These required details of landscaping of public open spaces to be submitted for approval and an agreed programme of archaeological investigation and mitigation to be carried out ahead of works being undertaken.

The churchyard was owned by Birmingham City Council, having been previously appropriated from St. Martin's. Sections 238 to 240 of the Town & Country Planning Act 1990 applied to the removal and reinterment of human remains and exempted St. Martin's churchyard

from the provisions of the Disused Burial Ground Act 1884 which often apply. The Birmingham Alliance, developers of Bullring, were required under the Act to apply to the Home Office for 'Directions' in respect of the removal of human remains from the churchyard ahead of the landscaping works.

Prior to the Directions being confirmed, there was a period of notification by advertisements in the local press and site notices setting out the intention to carry out removal and reinterment of human remains and inviting relatives of those people buried within the churchyard to come forward. Relatives had the right, according to the Act, to arrange exhumation and reburial of their relatives prior to the landscaping works starting.

No relatives responded to the advertisements and, following completion of the period of notification, the Home Office granted permission, subject to the Directions, for the works to commence; the Directions were further supplemented by written guidance from the Diocesan Registrar. Essentially, these stated that all human remains were to be treated with dignity and respect and that the excavation area should be screened off to ensure that no member of the general public was subject to any distress by witnessing removal of human remains. Environmental Health Officers from Birmingham City Council represented the Home Office on site throughout the excavation to ensure that the work complied with the Directions.

CgMs Consulting, as archaeological advisors and project managers to The Alliance, liaised with Mike Hodder, Planning Archaeologist for Birmingham City Council, to ensure that work within the churchyard met the requirements of the archaeological conditions required by the planning permission. CgMs commissioned Birmingham Archaeology (formerly Birmingham University Field Archaeology Unit) to carry out the archaeological excavation and post-excavation analysis which is reported upon here.

Following completion of the excavation and post-excavation analysis of the human remains, CgMs co-ordinated reburial of the remains. Those remains which could be named, and those which formed part of an identified family group, were reburied in one of the vaults within the churchyard, accompanied by any personal items with which they had originally been buried. A service, led by the Rev'd Canon Adrian Newman, was held in May 2003. The majority of remains could not be identified and these, along with the disarticulated remains, have been buried in Quinton Cemetery (as with the named remains, any personal items were reburied with the person they originally accompanied).

2   The Parish, the Church and the Churchyard

Josephine Adams

The parish

From medieval times through to the 19th century, St. Martin's churchyard served as the principal burial ground for the Parish of St. Martin's. A parish can be defined as a sub-division of a diocese, an area having its own church and incumbent. Today, their role in civil administration is minimal. In the past, however, a parish served more than just an ecclesiastical function, it was a fundamental unit in the administrative framework of England in both town and country. The Parish of St. Martin's was the Ancient Parish of Birmingham, comprising 2,996 acres in Warwickshire. It was bordered by Handsworth to the north, Aston to the east, Edgbaston to the south and to the west by the Staffordshire parish of Harborne.

As the burials excavated in St. Martin's churchyard dated no earlier than the 18th century, the medieval origins and growth of Birmingham are beyond the scope of this volume. It is sufficient to say that the roots of Birmingham's prosperity in manufacture and trade reach well back into the medieval period, and that by the 18th century the industrial character of the town was fully established. The industry of primary importance was metal working. Birmingham manufacturers produced a huge variety of articles in iron, brass and steel, such as swords, knives and cutting tools of all types, nails, wire, utensils, household fittings, buckles, buttons, snuff boxes and all kinds of trinkets (Fig. 6). By the 19th century a substantial part of this industry was involved in the making of 'coffin furniture', the metal fixtures and fittings on coffins (Chapter 8). There were some large establishments, such the Soho Manufactory of Matthew Boulton, built at Handsworth in 1764 and employing up to a thousand workers, but much more common were small, family-scale workshops.

A series of enterprises of importance to Birmingham revolved around cattle. Birmingham was a major cattle market and there were many butchers in the town. There was also a range of industries which were based on the 'secondary products' of cattle – hides, bone and horn. There were many tanners, who convert hide into leather, and leather workers such as saddlers, whip-makers and glovers, together with bone and horn manufacturers, and glue-makers. The metal and leather based industries were accompanied by others employing a variety of materials: cloth-making, rope-making, button-making (using shell and bone), glass-making, potting and the manufacture of clay pipes, to name just a few. Along with those directly engaged in manufacture, there were those who worked in the necessary 'service industries': market-stall holders and shopkeepers, inn keepers, and those involved in the transport of goods and people – by packhorse, wagon and coach, and later by canal (from the late 18th century) and railway.

Although by the beginning of the 18th century Birmingham's industrial character was firmly established, the layout of the town still reflected its medieval

Fig. 6: Typical Birmingham metalwork products (from an advertisement in Wrightson's New Triennial Directory of Birmingham, 1818).

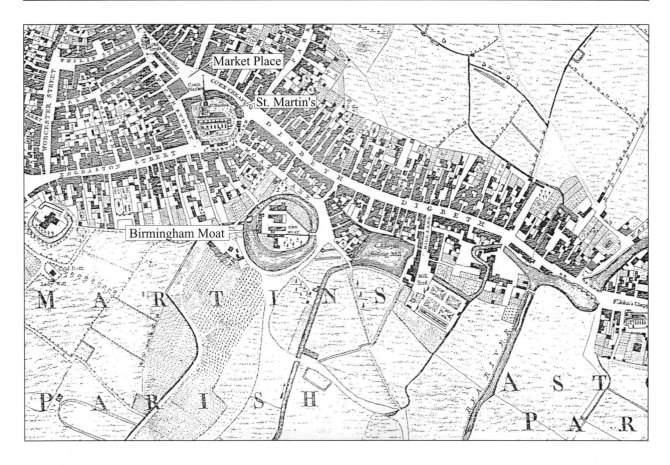

Fig. 7: Samuel Bradford's map of 1750. At this time the centre of Birmingham still preserved much of its medieval layout.

origins. This fact is important for understanding the development of the church and churchyard at St. Martin's. The town's principal market was in the market place that surrounded the church to its north, while to the south of the church was the manor house – in medieval times seat of the de Birmingham family, the lords of the manor – still encircled by its medieval moat (Fig. 7). In the streets that approached the church and market place, almost all of the industries noted above were practiced, very close to the centre of the town. The excavations undertaken in advance of the Bullring redevelopment have revealed much evidence for these (Buteux and Rátkai forthcoming, Buteux 2003, Hodder 2004). At Edgbaston Street, for example, there is extensive evidence for leather tanning, as well as bone-working, button-making and glass-making, while at Park Street there is evidence for both iron smithing and the working of copper alloys (Fig. 5). Even the buildings within the Lord of the Manor's Moat were, by the latter part of the 18th century, largely given over to industry, principally an iron works. The Moat House was occupied in 1785 by John Francis and Son, coffin-nail makers (Watts 1980, 25), a business conveniently close to the churchyard where many of its products must have ended up.

By the 18th century, contemporary descriptions,

illustrations and maps provide a good impression of what Birmingham's market place was like (Fig. 8). The area of the market immediately around St. Martin's, to its north and west, was called the Bull Ring. The name first occurs in 1550 and may relate to the practice of baiting bulls prior to slaughter in order, so it was believed, to tenderize the meat (Skipp 1980, 36). Corn Cheaping was the corn market, and cattle, horses and sheep were sold along High Street. Dairy produce was sold at one end of the Bull Ring and all other products, including linen, woollen cloth, iron, steel and brass were sold at the Wednesday and Thursday markets (Skipp 1980, 35–36).

The growing prosperity of the town, together with increasing immigration into the area, resulted in a huge increase in Birmingham's population in the 18th century. In 1700 Birmingham's population was probably in the order of between 5,000 and 7,000 but by 1750 the population had at least trebled in size to 23,688; it may have been the fastest growing industrial town in the country (Hopkins 1998, 20). This put enormous pressure on the market, on the church and on the churchyard, the latter having to accommodate the dead of an increasingly populous parish.

Over the years, what had presumably begun as temporary market stalls in the medieval period had by the

Fig. 8: The Bull Ring market place in the later 18th century. In the foreground is the Old Cross; behind is St. Martin's Church, which is surrounded by timber-framed shops that had encroached onto the market place.

18th century transformed into more permanent buildings. Birmingham's first historian, William Hutton, described the problem: "The space now used as our market was in 1769 completely choked with buildings and filth; the shambles [butcher's shops], the round house and the cross nearly filled the area" (quoted in Upton 1993, 15). The area in the immediate vicinity of St. Martin's was becoming increasingly congested, with a growing number of people crowded into existing properties. Any new building was on the back of the existing houses and shops facing the street, resulting in the creation of narrow alleys or 'entries' giving access to small houses and workshops (V.C.H. 1965, 7). A row of houses had been built around the perimeter of the churchyard, partly obscuring it from view. There were many small shops in the crowded streets immediately around the church, some of which backed on to the churchyard itself. They included mercers, drapers, ironmongers, saddlers, grocers and outfitters, many of whom had their wares spilling out on to the footpaths. All this, together with the crowded stalls of the market that centred around the Old (or High) Cross, made the area a vibrant place, where many people gathered together and conducted their daily business (Dent 1894, 55). Contemporary illustrations (Fig. 8) and maps, such as Samuel Bradford's map of 1750 (Fig. 7) show very clearly the buildings surrounding the church and churchyard and occupying much of the market place.

As the population of the central area of Birmingham grew it became apparent that St. Martin's alone could not serve the whole area. In 1731 St. Philip's Church was built in the north of the town and St. Martin's Parish was reduced in size. Hanson's map (Fig. 9) shows the extent of Birmingham in 1778, when most of the town, apart from the area in the immediate vicinity of St. Philip's, was within St. Martin's Parish. Subsequently the parish boundaries were altered again as St. George's (1812) and St. Thomas' (1829) Churches were built. The 1847 Scholastic and Ecclesiastical Map of the area indicates that by this time, while there were still some vestiges of the parish left in outlying areas of the ancient boundary, the main focus of St. Martin's parish was now the immediate area around the church.

Throughout the later part of the 18th century and into

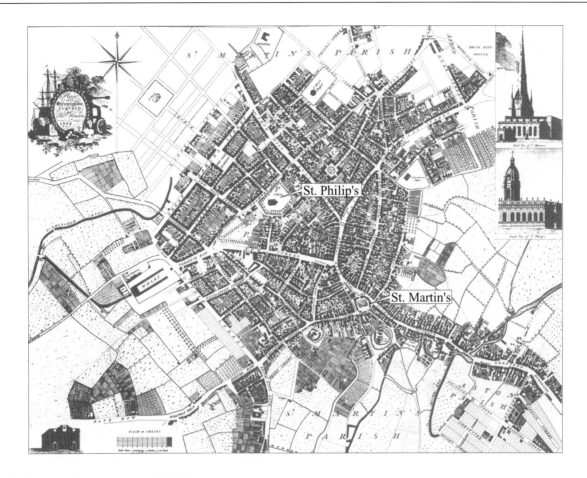

Fig. 9: Thomas Hanson's map of 1778.

	1801	1811	1821	1831	1841
Population	60,822	70,207	85,416	110,914	138,215
Inhabited houses	12,044	13,652	17,323	22,532	27,272

Table 1: Population and inhabited houses in Birmingham Ancient Parish, 1801–1841. Based on Census Reports 1801–1841 (V. C. H. 1965, 9).

the 19th century the population of Birmingham continued to grow dramatically (Table 1).

From the late 18th century onwards, an attempt was made to deal with Birmingham's hopelessly congested market place and inadequate market facilities. This work was undertaken by the 'Street Commissioners', established by a local Act of Parliament in 1769. The Commissioners were responsible for the planning of streets, lighting and housing in the town, and for the control of pollution and crime. The various buildings choking the market place were pulled down, the Old Cross in 1784, the Shambles and Roundabout House. The old timber-framed shops and houses which encircled St. Martin's church were also demolished, a process that was complete by 1810. This not only recreated an open market

place, but transformed the appearance and setting of the church and provided an opportunity to extend the churchyard (see below). In 1809, a statue to Admiral Lord Nelson, England's greatest hero of the day, was erected on the site of the Old Cross, looking over the market place and churchyard towards the church (Fig. 10).

As well as clearing the market place, new market facilities were provided, including a new market for the sale of live cattle and horses on the site of the Lord of the Manor's Moat. In 1812, Thomas Francis, coffin-nail maker, is still listed as living at Moat House, while John Ainsworth, whipmaker, was living at the Moat (Watts 1980, 25). John Ainsworth died in 1815 at the age of 29 and was almost certainly amongst the burials excavated in the vault (Vault 23) built by his father, Isaac, at St.

Fig. 10: The Bull Ring in 1812. The statue of Nelson is in the middle ground with St. Martin's behind.

Martin's in or shortly after 1810 (see Chapter 3). However, in 1812 the Commissioners began negotiations for the purchase of the land and buildings 'called the Moat and Moat House', and over the next few years the moat was filled in and Smithfield Market built, the new beast market opening in 1817 (Fig. 11).

Next the Commissioners turned their attention to getting the bulk of the retail marketing off the streets. This led to the demolition of many of the buildings fronting onto the west side of the old market place and the erection of the Market Hall, opened in 1835. At the time it was claimed to be 'the finest building of the kind in the kingdom'; 600 stalls could be 'accommodated in the body of the hall, and space left for four thousand persons to perambulate' (Skipp 1983, 105–6). In the following years, in the area around the market place and church, a wholesale butcher's market, St. Martin's Market, was built (1851), together with a wholesale fish market (1869) and a covered vegetable market (1884).

This piecemeal redevelopment, spanning a century from the demolition of the Old Cross (1784) to the construction of the vegetable market (1884), may be considered the first Bull Ring redevelopment. This century also encompassed the majority of the burials investigated in St. Martin's churchyard, and almost all of those buried in vaults.

Although much of the area around St. Martin's was transformed, and the church and churchyard were also transformed, as will be described below, the church still stood at the commercial heart of Birmingham as it does today. The old open market running from New Street down to the Bull Ring outside St. Martin's church still thrived, and during the 19th century the area was renowned not only for its markets, but for the street preachers and entertainers, barrow boys, and soap-box orators, who all contributed to produce something of a fairground atmosphere around the church (Fig. 12).

However, events were not always peaceable. Violent and drunken behaviour were not uncommon in the streets around St. Martin's, as newspaper reports of the period testify. Rioting broke out from time to time. In May 1810, for example, a dispute in the Bull Ring between shoppers and stall holders over the price of potatoes developed into a full-scale riot (Upton 2003, 18). That the price of potatoes could spark a riot is testimony to the extent of real poverty amongst many of those who lived in the parish, and is reflected in the evidence for malnutrition and vitamin deficiency revealed in the analysis of the skeletons from St. Martin's churchyard (Chapter 4). Much more serious were the Chartist riots of 1839, which saw hand-to-hand fighting in the Bull Ring between the campaigners for universal

Fig. 11: The Birmingham Moat and Manor House c.1815, shortly before their destruction to create Smithfield Market.

Fig. 12: The Bull Ring on a market day, early 19th century.

manhood suffrage and the police, much damage to shops and other property, and the burning of the market (Upton 2003, 18–19). Although it is not supposed that much of it occurred as a consequence of rioting, the number of injuries that may be attributed to interpersonal violence is one of the significant findings from the analysis of the human remains from the churchyard (Chapter 4).

The conditions of life and work in St. Martin's Parish during the late 18th and 19th centuries were often hard, and contrasts between the lives of the poor and those better off were stark. Many amongst the working classes inhabited over-crowded and unsanitary 'court' housing and worked long hours in generally small and sometimes dangerous workshops. Some aspects of life and work in the parish are further explored in Chapter 7, as a necessary context for the interpretation of both the different modes of burial (fundamentally those of employer and employee) and of the human remains themselves.

The population of Birmingham continued to grow rapidly as the 19th century progressed. In 1837, the year of Queen Victoria's accession, it was about 170,000 and by 1901, the year of Victoria's death, it was over 500,000 (Skipp 1983, 7). However, Birmingham did not become a Borough until 1838 and the growth of the town and its industrial importance were only belatedly acknowledged in 1889, when it was granted the status of 'City', and this was recognised by the Church in 1905, when the City of Birmingham became a separate diocese. It was St. Philip's, however, not St. Martin's, that became the cathedral church, although the latter retained its status as the parish church of a fairly small area in the centre of the city (Crowe 1975, 34). The crowded streets and high density of building resulted in high population levels, with 96 people per acre in 1931, compared to an average of 20 people per acre for the rest of the city. This was then to decrease sharply between 1931 and 1951 as a result of slum clearance and the post-war re-building of the area around the church, which had suffered heavy bomb damage during the Second World War (V.C.H. 1965, 12).

In the 1950s and 60s the area was completely re-developed as a new road system encircled the central area of the city and the Bull Ring Centre was built, and although the Bull Ring retained its markets, St. Martin's became somewhat cut off from the main shopping and administrative areas of the city. The population that it served had been 80,000 in 1830, before dropping to 2,100 in 1938 and to only 500 in 1975, vividly illustrating the change in the use of the area as the houses were demolished and small factories and warehouses took their place (Crowe 1975, 37).

New life was breathed into the Parish and Church of St. Martin's at the opening of the 21st century, when the Bullring redevelopment reunited the church with the retail centre of Birmingham.

The church

St. Martin's-in-the-Bull Ring is for many one of the most enduring symbols of the City of Birmingham, with its distinctive Victorian architecture prominent in the constantly changing city skyline (Fig. 13, colour). This abiding quality creates the impression that the building has remained unchanged over the centuries. However, St. Martin's has undergone many alterations in its long history.

Whilst it is impossible to say precisely when the first church was built, there is evidence to suggest that there has been a place of worship on the site since the 12th century. In 1872 demolition of the old building in preparation for the construction of the existing church revealed some stonework with chevron decoration that indicated Norman origins (Holliday 1873). This suggests that the church existed in the 12th century, close to the market place and the Lord of the Manor's Moat.

The earliest documentary evidence of a church on the St. Martin's site seems to be in the 'Pleas of the Crown', when sanctuary was claimed within the walls of the church in 1285. Then in 1330 Walter de Clodshale, the Lord of Saltley, founded a chantry at St. Martin's so that a priest could perform a daily service for himself and his wife. Richard de Clodshale founded a second in 1347, and a third was founded by the Gild of the Holy Cross, that was later to found a school that became the present King Edward's (Trott 1992, 10). This patronage of chantries continued until Henry VIII's Reformation, when the priests were dispossessed and the land went to the crown (Dent 1894, 7).

An early description of the church building in *The Making of Birmingham* by R. K. Dent suggests that it consisted of a nave and chancel, north and south aisles, and a tower at the western end of the building. It had elaborate stained glass windows and there may have been paintings on the walls and ceiling (Dent 1894, 7). This early church was made of red sandstone, which weathered over the years necessitating many alterations to the fabric of the building. The churchwardens seem to have had considerable influence over these alterations, and in 1690 Thomas Gisburne and Edward Est were blamed for encasing the building in brick. Whilst this was considered necessary in view of the deterioration of the sandstone, opinion varied as to the result (Fig. 14). Dent considered "the glaring new brickwork in which St. Martin's has recently been entombed as ugly" (Dent 1894, 55), while Hutton says "the bricks and workmanship are excellent" (Hutton 1795, 331). In 1763 George Birch and Richard Hicks added a vestry, and in 1772 Thomas Salt and Richard Gooden removed the font and made themselves a sitting room (Bunce 1871, 15).

As the town of Birmingham developed it became apparent that St. Martin's could not accommodate the rapidly growing population. In the late 17th century pews were at a premium, with a charge of 4d per seat levied in 1676 (Bunce 1873, 74). In an effort to alleviate the problem various alterations were made to the interior of the church in the 1730s so that more pews could be added. This involved stained glass windows being destroyed and tombs removed. In the old side chapels staircases were built to new galleries, so that "every recess capable of only admitting the body of an infant, was converted into a seat" (Hutton 1795, 332).

As a result of this light was restricted, so in 1733 the middle roof of the chancel was taken off and the side walls raised by about nine feet to accommodate more windows (Hutton 1795, 332).

The increase in the number of pews was again organised by the churchwardens, who were allowed to make the alterations themselves and sell the seats to minimise their costs (Dent 1894, 79). The unsold seats were then let for an annual rent. Some pews were labelled with their owner's name and locked to prevent anyone else using them. The location of a pew in the church was also important and usually an indication of a person's status. This is illustrated by an advertisement in the local paper of 1812:

St. Martin's Church – To be let (on lease, if desired) the most distinguished Pew in this Church, late in the occupation of S. T. Galton Esq., in front of the gallery directly opposite the Pulpit (quoted in Bunce 1871, 16).

By the 1860s this practice was revoked, and all parishioners were in theory given equal rights to most of the seats in the church. However, up to 1954 a few remained that could be booked for a nominal rent (Crowe 1975, 30). In social terms, the practice of exclusive rights to the use of pews, of payment to secure the best ones, and even of locking them to prevent use by others, is almost perfectly reflected in the organisation of burials in the churchyard (Chapter 3).

In 1781 there was concern about the safety of the spire of the church and a Mr John Cheshire was paid £10 to build scaffolding to examine its condition. He subsequently rebuilt 40ft of the spire using stone from Attleborough, near Nuneaton, and further strengthened it with a 105ft spindle of iron running up its centre. Part of his payment on completion of the job was that he could keep the ladders that he had used (Hutton 1795, 331; Bunce 1871, 15).

Nearly 70 years later, in 1849, rumours about the safety of the spire returned, prompting a proposal that the whole church should be rebuilt. Designs were drawn up by an architect, Philip Hardwicke, with a projected cost of £12,000. A public appeal was launched but only £5000 was raised and the project was abandoned. The money raised was, however, used in 1855 to re-case the tower and rebuild the spire, making it safe (Bunce 1871, 17).

St. Martin's, which had been described by the Rector, Dr Wilkinson, as a "brick barn abomination" (Crowe 1975, 31) was eventually rebuilt in 1872. All parts of the building, apart from the tower and spire, were demolished (Fig. 15) and a new church, 50ft longer than the old one,

Fig. 14: St. Martin's Church in 1835, from the north. Due to decay of the sandstone the nave was encased in brick in 1690.

was built in the Gothic style (Fig. 16). It was designed by J. A. Chatwin, a Birmingham architect. The enlargement of the church, principally to the east, would have involved the destruction of many graves and vaults in the churchyard.

The church was affected by the events of the Second World War. The railings were taken down for the war effort, and then, in 1941, a bomb landed outside the west door damaging the roof and windows. Temporary repairs were carried out to enable services to continue, and the church was finally restored after the war in 1947. In the 1950s and 1960s building work was carried out on the south side of the church to construct a new church hall and vestry (involving more removal of burials) resulting essentially in the building as it is to be seen today.

The church bells have, since the 17th century, been an important part of church life (Jenkins 1925, 58–60). The earliest records suggest that a peal of six were in existence prior to 1629 and they were replaced by a peal of ten in 1758, with two more added in 1772. The present peal of 16, one of only three with this number in the world, was

Fig. 15: Two views of St. Martin's during demolition of the medieval church in 1872.

installed in 1991. The ringing chamber, accessed by 47 steps in the tower, is thought to be one of the best-appointed compartments for ringers in the country. The walls of the room are covered by commemorative boards celebrating the accomplishments of the ringers as far back as 1820, when one of the churchwardens listed at the time was Isaac Ainsworth, a saddler, whose family vault (Vault 23) was amongst those investigated in 2001 (his son, John Ainsworth, a whipmaker, has already been mentioned above as living at The Moat in 1812).

Fig. 16: St. Martin's Church in 1875, shortly after rebuilding in the Gothic style.

Fig. 17: Medieval stone effigies of members of the de Birmingham family from St. Martin's church.

The churchyard

St. Martin's churchyard has undergone many changes over the centuries. Its location near the market areas and manorial moat and at the intersection of important roads meant that the boundary was altered several times, both to accommodate the needs of the church and the re-development of the surrounding area. These changes have involved both the expansion of the churchyard and the removal of burials on various occasions, until finally the western and northern parts of the remaining churchyard were landscaped to create St. Martin's Square as part of the Bullring redevelopment (the context for the 2001 excavations).

Burial records for the church begin in 1556 but documentary sources suggest that both the church and churchyard had been used for burial since at least the 13th century, although the various structural changes that took place over the years destroyed the many ledgerstones that covered the floor of the church (Jenkins 1925, 33). Beneath the chancel was a crypt that was used for burials, and during the 1872 rebuilding vaults full of crumbling coffins were discovered under the church floor (Jenkins 1925, 36). Burial in a church ('intramural burial') is the most high-status location – the nearer to the altar the better – with burial in the churchyard ('extramural burial') generally coming a poor second. Various members of the de Birmingham family, the lord's

of the manor, were buried in the church throughout the medieval period, along with other local notables, and were commemorated with stone effigies, a few of which survive and are on display in the church today (Fig. 17). Other tablets in the church suggest that rectors and their families may also have been granted the privilege of intramural burial, together with parish clerks and others who had made special bequests to the church (Jenkins 1925, 53–57). Parish records note that as late as 13th April 1811 the practice of intramural burial continued, with one Joseph Guest being listed as 'buried in the church'. A scale of charges for burials at St. Martin's of 1848 (see Chapter 8), provides details of the fees both for the building of a vault in the church and for each fresh interment in the same, implying that the practice – at least in theory – continued up to this date. These fees were the most expensive that could be incurred for a burial at St. Martin's.

For the less exalted burial took place in the churchyard. Given the growth of Birmingham's population from the 17th century onwards, the pressure on the churchyard was relentless. As early as 1665 the churchyard was found to be too small to bury all the victims of the plague so many were buried in a large pit in Ladywood Green (Jenkins 1925, 22). In the 1800s the number of burials grew dramatically, resulting in a gradual increase in ground level. An early engraving illustrates the problem, with a view of St. Martin's Lane showing the very high wall which was necessary to revet the southeast corner of the churchyard (although the natural topography of the site, which slopes down from north to south, also contributed to the need for a wall of this height here) (Fig. 18). Hutton (1835, 244) remarked that:

> the dead are raised up, and instead of the church burying the dead, the dead would in time, have buried the church.

In 1781 the serious consequences of this gradual increase in the height of the churchyard became apparent as:

> the ancient walls thereof on the south side and south east sides had in several parts bulged and given way and became dangerous to such as passed along a certain street or land adjoining the said churchyard (uncatalogued document in Birmingham Archives, Box 6).

So under the auspices of the Act for Lightening and Cleansing the Streets, it became necessary to:

> take down and rebuild the Ancient Wall with the Buttresses or supporters thereof and to strengthen the said wall by widening the same and make it substantial and durable…three feet and six inches or thereabouts in breadth (uncatalogued document in Birmingham Archives, Box 6).

Several of the houses in St. Martin's Lane had out-buildings and yards that actually encroached into the churchyard, and this land was purchased in 1781 to enlarge the area available for burials in the southern part of the churchyard (Bunce 1873, 77). This new area was then enclosed by a new boundary wall, which was topped with iron railings.

A more substantial measure to create more space for burials was the purchase in 1807 of 2½ acres of land in nearby Park Street, which was to become a detached burial ground for St. Martin's (Allen 1849, 38) (Fig. 19). After the necessary preparations had been made to the area the first burial in Park Street was recorded in the parish burial records:

> On Saturday the 16th day of June 1810 was interred in the new burial ground in Park St by the Rev Edward Hill, John Sims, being the first for whom a grave was opened after the consecrating of the land which took place on the first day of June preceeding.

However, proximity to the church is a frequent indicator of the prestige of a burial place (and within the church proximity to the altar), and in time the Park Street burial ground came to be seen as a very undesirable location:

> By degrees the ground came to be looked upon as only fit for the poorest of the poor, until after being divided by the railway, this 'God's Acre' was cared for by none, and was well called the 'black spot' of the town (Showell's Dictionary of Birmingham 1885, 32).

As the number of burials continued to increase, a further extension was made to the churchyard itself. On 2nd May 1810, a faculty was granted to enlarge the

Fig. 18: St. Martin's Lane in 1840. The churchyard wall can be seen on the extreme right.

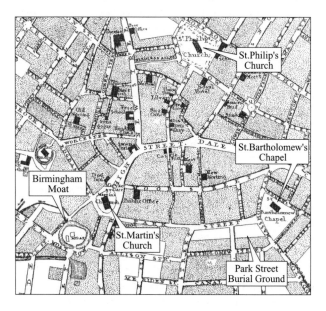

Fig. 19: Kempson's map of 1808 showing the location of the Park Street Burial Ground and St. Bartholomew's Chapel, a 'chapel of ease' to St. Martin's.

churchyard by the purchase of land in Spiceal Street that was "abutting on the back part thereof to St. Martin's Churchyard" (uncatalogued document at Birmingham Archives, Box 6). This extension is of particular interest here as it involved the northern part of the churchyard which was the subject of the 2001 excavations. It also needs to be understood in the context of the work of clearance of old buildings from the market place and from around the church which was described earlier in this chapter. It was the clearance of the buildings from around the perimeter of the churchyard, through the actions of the Street Commissioners, which provided the space that made the extension possible.

Prior to the clearance of these buildings, the churchyard was very tightly hemmed in on its eastern, northern, western and much of its southern side. A plan of 1801 shows this clearly (Fig. 20). Figure 21 is an enlargement of the relevant portion of Hanson's map of 1778 superimposed on an overall plan of the excavated burials in St. Martin's churchyard. The extremely constricted space for burials is very evident, as is the high density of intercutting graves in the northern part of the churchyard. (No burials are shown in the eastern or southern parts of the churchyard as these were built over during the rebuilding of the church in 1872, which extended the church 50ft to the east, and by the construction of the church hall and vestry on the south side of the church in the 1950s and 1960s.)

Prior to their demolition, the existence of these buildings will have determined much of the character of the churchyard. Illustrations of the 18th century (Fig. 8) show them to have been timber-framed shops and houses, two stories high. Given the height of the church and the surrounding buildings and the smallness of the space available for burial, the northern part of the churchyard in particular, where the church cast its shadow, must have been very gloomy. With the number of burials that were taking place by the 18th century it cannot have been pleasant and almost certainly posed a health hazard.

Many of the finds which were made in the churchyard in the course of the archaeological excavations are likely to be refuse from the occupation of the buildings that surrounded it. A total of 921 sherds of pottery was recovered (Rátkai, this volume, Appendix 1, CD). There were 29 medieval sherds but the majority of the assemblage was made up of blackware and coarseware dating to the 17th and 18th centuries, with a strongly utilitarian aspect. There was little 19th century pottery and what there was largely dated to the first half of the century and represented the lower end of the market. The dating of the pottery is thus consistent with it having derived from houses and shops demolished at the beginning of the 19th century, and the character of the pottery gives some indication of the status of the inhabitants of these buildings. Many of the other finds from the churchyard, such clay tobacco pipes, coins, bottle and window glass, window leading and lead shot (Bevan, this volume,

Chapter 5) also probably relate to the occupation of these buildings.

The otherwise continuous ring of buildings surrounding the eastern, western and northern sides of the churchyard was broken in the middle of its northern side by a wide passageway that lead out into the Bull Ring. In Figure 21, this passageway is shown as occupied by a large vault (Vault 10), which was indeed built under the passageway in or shortly before 1785 (see Chapter 3). The need to build a vault in this location – a project apparently initiated by the church and not private enterprise (Chapter 3) – is testimony to the intense pressure on space within the church in the later 18th century.

The demolition of the buildings surrounding the churchyard, which began with those on the south side in 1781 (above) and was finished by 1810, will have transformed the appearance of both the church and churchyard. Figure 22 shows the extent of the churchyard in the middle of the 19th century, following the extension, and Figure 24 shows a view of the church and churchyard of about the same date. The view is taken from the Bull Ring market place over the northern part of the churchyard (and also shows the new spire completed in 1855). The churchyard on this side of the church is now surrounded by a low stone wall surmounted by iron railings, and where the passage through to the Bull Ring once had been there is an elaborate iron gate. In the middle ground, the church and churchyard are overlooked by the statue of Nelson. The extent of the transformation can hardly be exaggerated, and several wealthy families now took the opportunity to build vaults in this part of the churchyard, as is described in Chapter 3.

The parish burial records show that in the years following the extension to the churchyard burials took place at a rate of between 300 and 800 per year, but the records do not specify as to whether they were buried in the churchyard or in the overflow burial ground in Park Street. In 1863 the numbers dropped dramatically to single figures, which coincided with the opening of Witton Cemetery, an out-of-town Town Council amenity built to serve the whole community. It is unclear whether a decision was made to cease burials in the churchyard after that date because it was full, or because it became the vogue to patronise the newer cemeteries. In addition to Witton Cemetery, a private Anglican cemetery was opened at Warstone Lane in 1848 (a private cemetery for nonconformists had already been established on adjacent land at Key Hill in 1836). Warstone Lane Cemetery was very grand (Fig. 25) and catered for those who could afford it. Certainly after 1863 the majority of burials in the churchyard took place in the family vaults, suggesting that some sort of restriction had been brought in to limit burials at St. Martin's.

During the rebuilding of the church in 1872 the churchyard was disturbed again, and the Bishop of Worcester wrote:

Fig. 20: Plan of St. Martin's and the Bull Ring in 1801.

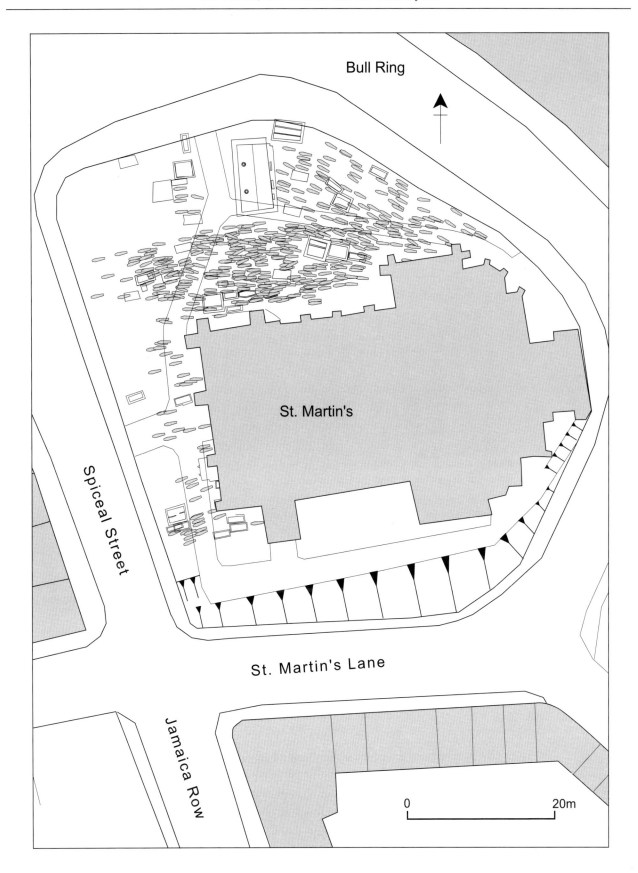

Fig. 23: Plan of St. Martin's and its churchyard in 1912 (enlarged from Ordnance Survey map) with burials and burial vaults excavated in 2001 superimposed.

Josephine Adams

Fig. 24: Two views of St. Martin's in the mid-19th century, from the north. The view on the left shows the new spire, completed in 1855, under construction. The statue of Nelson, erected in 1809, is in the middle ground.

that when it shall be found necessary in carrying out this work to interfere with any graves or vaults the coffins and remains therein deposited shall be carefully and decently removed and forthwith re-interred without being more exposed than is absolutely necessary (BDR/DI/13/9a).

In 1873 the Secretary of State issued an Order in Council stating that burials should be discontinued at churches throughout the city, including St. Martin's, except in vaults and walled graves with an air-tight coffin (Cox 1892, 87). All the graveyards were becoming over-crowded, creating some public health concern, and with the opening of the council-owned cemeteries slightly further from the centre of the town, more people chose to be buried in these. At St. Martin's, the burial records show that this trend in fact began rather earlier: 544 burials took place in 1863, in sharp contrast to the total of 52 for the whole of the following period up to 1915.

The health of Birmingham residents was again a cause for some concern in 1873, when it was decided that more urban open spaces were needed for recreation. Since the burial grounds that were no longer used for interments were becoming neglected and overgrown the Corporation obtained an Act, with the consent of the Bishop of Worcester, to acquire the land and turn them into parks.

A notable example of this was the Park Street burial ground, the detached graveyard of St. Martin's, that was transformed into Park Street Gardens and opened to the public in 1880.

At the same time the churchyard around St. Martin's was landscaped, with new trees planted and turf laid, and the surrounding iron railings renovated. The total cost of the improvements to the two sites was £10,263. In 1879, just prior to this work in the churchyard, a plan was drawn up (MS 943/13/2) illustrating the location of vaults and grave markers. This, used in conjunction with a contemporary vault record book (MS 943/13/1), gives some indication of the surviving grave markers that may have been moved during the renovation.

The churchyard became even more accessible to the public in February 1927, when the City Council passed a new by-law stating that St. Martin's churchyard, together with other closed burial grounds in the city, would be open to the public. The churchyard then became a public park that linked the markets to the other city centre shops.

In 1960 an Act of Parliament was passed to allow removal and re-burial of human remains from the south side of the churchyard to an existing area of consecrated ground within the churchyard. This was to accommodate

Fig. 25: Warstone Lane Cemetery, opened in 1848.

the construction of the new church hall and vestry. The order was issued in retrospect, having been overlooked when the building work took place in 1953 (MS 661948).

During the redevelopment of the Bull Ring in the 1960s the surrounding roads were altered again, encroaching on the churchyard, and many monuments and remains were transferred to Witton Cemetery (Crowe 1975, 50).

In 1998 the churchyard became the subject of an appropriation order by the Birmingham City Corporation, under the Town and Country Planning Act 1990. This meant that the Church no longer exercised any control over the land, which was then deemed the property of the Corporation. The churchyard remained undisturbed until 2001 when the archaeological excavation took place in advance of the landscaping works for St. Martin's Square (Fig. 26, colour).

3 The Excavations

Simon Buteux and Richard Cherrington

Introduction

The appearance of the churchyard prior to the archaeological excavations represented the cumulative effect of several episodes of landscaping and redevelopment since the major rebuilding of the church in 1872 (see Chapter 2). With one exception, none of the funerary monuments and gravestones that had once stood above the graves survived in position. The churchyard had been comprehensively landscaped as a public open space, grassed and crossed with paths. Grave markers had generally been laid flat, and were found on the surface or in the topsoil, many in a fragmentary state. As they had been moved they could not be related to the graves revealed by excavation. The access corridor of a large 'chambered vault' (Vault 10) had been filled with a large quantity of fragmentary gravestones, pushed in through the air-vents. Some complete gravestones did survive, but these had either been used in the construction of pathways through the graveyard, or had been used to cap brick-lined graves. Forty gravestones with legible or partially legible inscriptions were uncovered during the excavation; the memorials were photographed and the legible details recorded (Appendix 2, CD). The earliest gravestone recorded commemorated a death in 1698 and the latest a death in 1862; the vast majority dated to the first half of the 19th century.

The only gravestone (ST 16) which could be related to burials uncovered during the excavation commemorated the deaths of Sophia Warden in 1860 and Edwin Warden in 1861. This stone was associated with the Warden family vault (Vault 5), which is discussed in detail below.

In this chapter the results of the excavations are described, beginning with the excavation methods, before proceeding to description of the earth-cut burials, the burial vaults and the brick-lined graves (Fig. 27, colour). An opportunity to record the medieval and Victorian foundations of the church and the brick foundations of the Victorian churchyard wall was also provided by various aspects of the groundworks; the results are presented in Appendix 3 on the CD.

Excavation methods

The landscaping of the churchyard for the Bullring development required that the site was cleared of archaeological deposits, burials and burial structures to two different, finished, reduced levels. These were depths of 800mm (Zones A & C; Fig. 28) and 1500mm (Zone B; Fig. 28) below the ground level prior to the excavations. The development team provided on-site guidance as to where and when these depths were achieved. For archaeological reasons, it was sometimes necessary to excavate and record deposits below these levels.

The former topsoil and modern landscaping deposits were removed by a 360° excavator, fitted with a toothless ditching bucket, under the supervision of an appropriately qualified archaeologist. Surviving grave markers were recorded on *pro-forma* recording sheets and photographed, before being removed. Where necessary, exposed archaeological features and grave cuts were mechanically reduced in depth to facilitate further excavation by hand. The overall site plan (Fig. 28) was produced using a total station theodolite incorporating the *Fastmap* system. Archaeological deposits and burials were recorded using *pro-forma* record cards, supplemented by measured drawings, colour slide, colour print and monochrome photographs.

Brick-lined graves and burial vaults were exposed by the mechanical excavator. Variations in the construction of the burial structures meant that differing dismantling techniques were employed, based on the individual characteristics of each structure. The most common method was to hand reduce the structure to a safe, workable level using lump or sledge hammers with bolster chisels. Once the burial structures were uncovered and hand cleaned they were recorded using *pro-forma* vault record cards, context cards, building recording sheets and skeleton record sheets. Vaults and their contents were planned at a scale of 1:10.

An official from Birmingham City Council Environmental Services was present on site at all times to ensure that the conditions of the Home Office directions for the

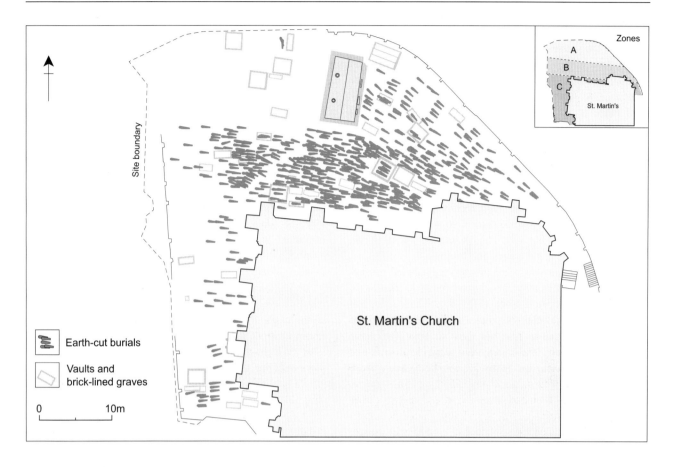

Fig. 28: Overall plan of the excavations, with inset showing zones of different excavation depths.

removal of human remains were adhered to (see Chapter 1). The human remains were screened from public view at all times and treated with due care and attention to decency. Most of the excavated human remains were transferred to the University of Birmingham for detailed analysis. In a few cases, due to the state of preservation of the remains, it was not deemed possible or appropriate to remove the human remains from the site. Such remains were reburied in the churchyard in a vault designated for the purpose. Full details of the procedures followed for the excavation and recording of human remains are provided in Chapter 4.

Fifty-seven lead coffins, that is coffins of composite lead and wood construction, were encountered within the burial structures, but only those deemed to be 'compromised' were opened and fully investigated and recorded. Lead coffins were deemed compromised if the lead shells were punctured or damaged in any way. The final decision on this matter lay with the on-site representatives of Birmingham City Council Environmental Services. In the majority of cases, human burials in lead coffins were excavated *in situ* with the skeletal remains transferred to the University of Birmingham for analysis in the normal manner. For logistical and health and safety reasons, a few lead coffins were removed to a specially prepared on-site unit for detailed investigation and recording.

Earth-cut graves

A total of 857 burials was recorded during the excavations at St Martin's. Of these, the large majority, 734 or 86%, were uncovered in simple earth-cut graves. The burials were in a variable state of preservation, with some only represented by a few bones (for a full analysis of skeletal preservation see Chapter 4). A large amount of disarticulated human remains was also recovered from charnel pits and archaeological layers.

Dating

Broad dating of the burials was achieved through the associated coffin furniture, although this was in a very decayed state, and occasionally other associated finds (see Chapter 5). Relative dating of burials was provided by the stratigraphic relationships of grave cuts to features more securely dated, principally the burial vaults. About 60 graves lay within the area of the churchyard extension which was created in 1810 (see Chapter 2), so are obviously later than this date. From this evidence it would appear that the majority of the burials date from the later

18th century through to the middle years of the 19th century. Only one burial could be directly dated to the 18th century, a burial of the 1720s dated by means of lettering on the coffin lid (see below). Documentary sources (see Chapter 2) indicate that very few burials took place at St. Martin's after 1863, which provides a likely terminus for the burials in earth-cut graves (those in vaults and brick-lined graves continued).

Burial types and preservation

There were several varieties of burials in earth-cut graves at St. Martin's. The most common was a single inhumation in a supine posture buried in a wooden coffin with metal fittings (Fig. 29). The intensity of burial meant that many of the graves were intercutting.

The coffins survived in varying degrees of preservation, ranging from barely visible stains to pieces of quite well-preserved timber (Fig. 30). There was not enough wood left in most instances to tell if they had been single or double case but they all appear to have been single break, becoming very narrow around the ankles. Wood samples from 28 of the graves were

examined, of which 19 were identified as elm, six as oak, two as pine, and one as hazel or alder (Gale, this volume, Chapter 5). The coffin grips and plates were all very corroded. The grips were all made of iron, and were mostly too corroded to assess even the basic shape or decoration. There were generally only small fragments of plate surviving, none of which had any legible writing. The preservation of the human remains was variable and is discussed in detail in Chapter 4.

Exceptionally, one adult burial (HB 408) was recorded with copper-alloy lettering on the coffin lid (Fig. 31, colour). The lettering read [M?] [172?] [(A)GE] [85]. HB 408, dating to the 1720s, was the earliest datable burial at St. Martin's. This burial had cut an earlier charnel-pit filled with poorly-preserved disarticulated human bone.

In addition to the standard single burial, in some cases two or more burials were stacked on top of each other in a single grave cut (Fig. 32). There was one example of a double burial; here a child (HB 502) and an adolescent (HB 503) had been interred side-by-side in a shallow gave cut (Fig. 33). Both these individuals had their arms

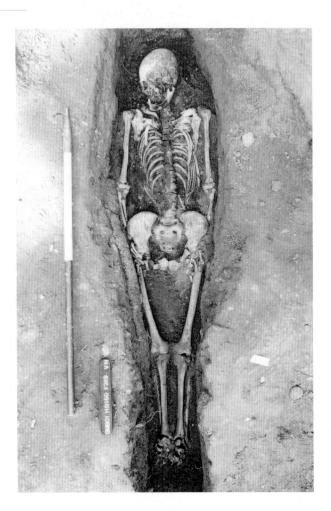

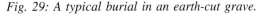

Fig. 29: A typical burial in an earth-cut grave.

Fig. 30: Burial in an earth-cut grave with disintegrated remains of wooden coffin.

crossed over their chests. This would suggest that they had been buried in funerary shrouds, or tightly wrapped in winding sheets. The use of funerary shrouds or winding sheets was evident from the numerous fastening pins recovered.

Infants were often buried with only a winding sheet (Fig. 34); in six cases an infant was buried with an adult, suggesting a mother and infant who had both died during child birth, although other interpretations are possible. In five instances foetal remains were recorded *in situ* within the womb area of female burials.

Small finds

Many small finds were recovered from the earth-cut burials and churchyard overburden (see Bevan, this volume, Chapter 5). The assemblage is varied, containing both personal items and residual discarded material. The preservation of these items is not particularly good when compared to those from vault and brick-lined grave contexts but still creates a picture of life and death in and around the churchyard. In addition to the pottery (see Chapter 2 and Appendix 1, CD), the finds included shroud pins, wig curlers, buttons, coins and tokens, fragments of clay tobacco-pipes, fragmented leather, and even a pair of scissors. Much of the material was 18th or 19th century in date and, with the exception of the shroud pins and possibly the buttons, probably originated in the main from the properties which surrounded churchyard until the early 19th century (Chapter 2). Some of the clay pipes, however, may have been discarded by grave

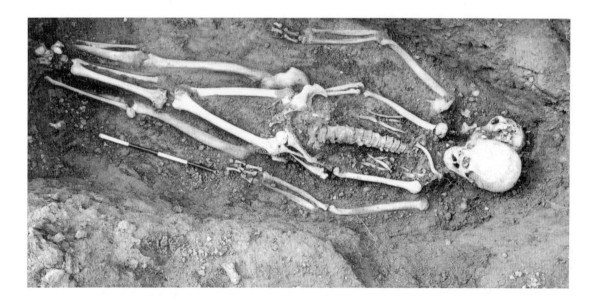

Fig. 32: Two burials superimposed in earth-cut grave.

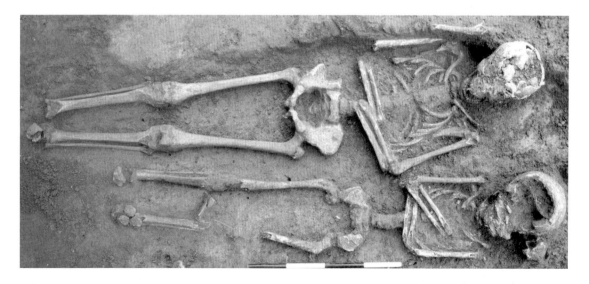

Fig. 33: Double burial of an adolescent (HB 503) and a child (HB 502) in a single earth-cut grave.

Fig. 34: Infant burial in an earth-cut grave.

diggers. Evidence for pipe-smoking is not just confined to the recovery of the pipes themselves. Eleven of the burials exhibit distinct 'pipe-groove' wear on their teeth, formed by the pipe-stem being clutched in the mouth (see Chapter 4).

Spatial patterning

The earth-cut burials at St. Martin's appeared to exhibit discernible patterns of spatial distribution. An obvious bias is introduced by the different depths of excavation carried out in different zones of the site. As explained above, two different dig depths, of 0.8m and 1.5m, applied to three separate areas of the site, referred to as Zones A, B and C (Fig. 28). Zone B had the deeper dig depth of 1.5m, and consequently a much higher density of burials was recorded here in comparison to Zones A and C, with shallower dig depths. However, in the eastern portion of Zone A, to the east of the large chambered vault (Vault 10), the depth of excavation exceeded 0.8m for practical

purposes, and this explains the fact that earth-cut graves were excavated in this area but not to the west of Vault 10. In the western portion of Zone A earth-cut graves were certainly present (the cuts for these graves could be seen) but the shallower level of ground reduction here meant that these graves could be preserved *in situ*.

Recovery bias apart, certain patterns are apparent. The density of graves in Zone A is less than in Zone B, with little intercutting of graves. Many of the graves in this zone lay within the area of the extension to the churchyard, to the north and west, that took place 1810 (Chapter 2), so the overall density of graves may have been less here, and the graves may have been deeper. The lack of earlier burials in the area of the churchyard extension may also have provided the impetus for the construction of the numerous burial vaults here after 1810 (see below). Furthermore, the orientation of many of the earth-cut graves in Zone A appears to be related more to the orientation of the boundary wall, burial vaults and former paths than to the orientation of the church (Figs. 22 & 23, Chapter 2).

Zone B was excavated to a depth of 1.5m and understandably shows a large number of recorded burials. The zone also largely coincides with the original area of the northern part of the churchyard, where burials had taken place for centuries (Fig. 21, Chapter 2). The orientation of the graves appears in the main to follow the orientation of the church. The general density of burials was high, with a great deal of inter-cutting. This high density of burials petered out at the western extent of Zone A; this area forms part of the westwards extension of the churchyard in 1810, but was also not excavated to the full depth of 1.5m. Few burials were recorded in a diagonal band running northeast-southwest across the zone. This gap in the burials corresponds to the line of a former path which led from the west doorway of the church to the gateway in the northern churchyard boundary wall (Fig. 22, Chapter 2).

Zone C exhibited a similar paucity of recorded burials to Zone A. There were very few burials recorded in the area of the westwards extension to the churchyard which took place in 1810; burials may have been deeper here. However, there did appear to be some grouping of burials, especially around Vault Groups I and II. It is noticeable that many of the recorded burials were located beneath the pathway surrounding the 1872 church but comparatively few elsewhere (Fig. 23, Chapter 2). The several landscaping episodes which took place in the churchyard following the rebuilding may have contributed to the uneven distribution of the burials.

Burial structures: introduction and definitions

Types of burial structures

A total of 35 burial structures were uncovered in St. Martin's churchyard (Table 2), although not all were fully excavated. For the purposes of this report a *brick-lined grave* is defined as a subterranean chamber lined with brick and closed with a barrelled roof or ledger stone. Brick-lined graves have the capacity to receive a single burial laid horizontally, or multiples thereof stacked one above the another. A total of 24 brick-lined graves of various designs was identified. *Family vaults* are defined as a brick-built chamber large enough in plan to house a minimum of two coffins side by side, and usually with provision for several layers of such burials. They are closed with a barrelled roof. Study of the burials from these vaults has shown they were used to house the dead of particular families. A total of ten such family vaults of various designs was identified. The term

chambered vault has been applied to one large and elaborate burial vault comprising four chambers opening off an access corridor (Vault 10).

All the burial structures – the brick-lined graves, the family vaults and the chambered vault – were allocated Vault Numbers, from 1 to 36 (one number, 29, was allocated to remains which proved not to be a separate burial structure so it is not used). To avoid confusion, the Vault Numbers applying to brick-lined graves are prefaced simply with a 'V' (e.g. V01, V03, V12) while those applying to the family vaults and chambered vault are prefaced with 'Vault' (e.g. Vault 2, Vault 4, Vault 10) (Fig. 35).

All three types of structures are collectively termed *burial vaults* or simply *vaults*. This is the sense in which

Structure type	Number of structures	Number of structures with recorded burials	Number of burials	Number of burials analysed	Number of burials identified from *depositum*	Total number of burials identified
Brick-lined grave	24	22	43	41	3	4
Chambered vault	1	1	20	17	2	3
Family vault	10	8	60	40	21	44
Totals	**35**	**31**	**123**	**98**	**26**	**51**

Table 2: Types of burial structures and numbers of burials.

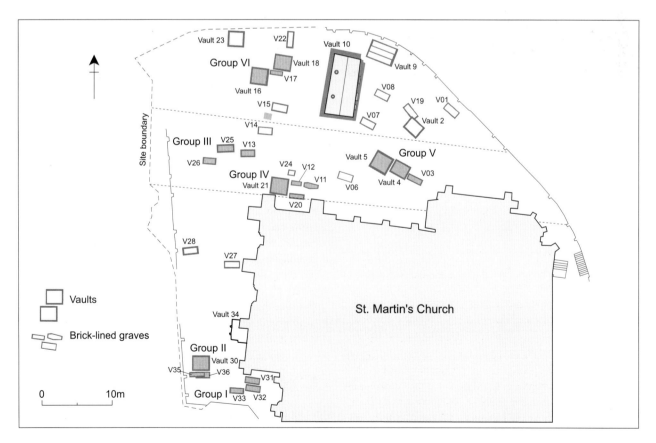

Fig. 35: Plan of excavated vaults and brick-lined graves (vault groups shaded).

'vault' is used in the analysis of the human remains described in Chapter 4.

Dating

The most direct means of dating the construction and use of burial vaults is through the names and dates inscribed on coffin plates – or *deposita* as they are called – found within the vaults. Unfortunately, the survival of legible *deposita* was uneven – comparatively good for the family vaults but poor for the brick-lined graves (Table 2). Five of the ten family vaults could be dated in this way (and the family identified) whereas only two of the brick-lined graves could be so dated. Furthermore, for these five family vaults it was possible to use burial records in combination with the archaeological and anthropological evidence to suggest, with varying degrees of probability, the names and date of death of many more people buried within them (Table 2), thus refining the probable date of use and construction considerably. Although only two partially legible *deposita* survived in the large chambered vault (Vault 10), documentary sources and burial records enabled the construction and use of this vault to be dated with considerable precision.

For the vaults as a whole, further dating evidence was provided by the nature of the brickwork and other building materials; the general character of the coffins, coffin furniture and any personal items found; stratigraphic, cartographic and documentary evidence; and the physical grouping of the vaults. None of this evidence, however, is as reliable or precise as that provided by legible *deposita*.

The specific evidence for the dating of the various types of burial structure is described in the appropriate sections below. For introductory purposes it may be noted here that the large chambered vault was probably constructed in 1785 or very shortly before and used for burial until at least the 1830s. The family vaults were probably mainly constructed in the period 1810 to 1830 but were used for burial through to 1915. The brick-lined graves are likely to have been constructed and used throughout most of the 19th century.

Grouping

Many of the burial vaults appeared to be grouped together, both spatially and structurally (see Fig. 35). Six possible groups are suggested in Table 3.

It is assumed from the spatial patterning, and often the structural similarities, of vaults in a particular group, that the vaults were built in sequence and not much separated in date. If this assumption is valid, then if one of the vaults can be dated directly by legible *deposita* or other means, a possible date range is achievable for the other structures. This analysis is presented in Table 4. Details of the inferred construction dates will be found in the relevant descriptions of the individual vaults below.

As there were no datable vaults in Vault Groups III and IV a date range cannot be suggested for these groups.

It is possible that the vault groups, or some of them, may reflect relationships between those buried in the various vaults, either relationships between individuals (in the case of brick-lined graves) or between families. Unfortunately there was insufficient evidence to address this question.

Function

Interment in burial vaults no doubt occurred for a wide variety of reasons, some of which may have been particular to conditions at St. Martin's. Burial structures reflect the socio-economic status of the occupants and serve to separate them from the 'rank and file' of the churchyard. Deposition in a burial structure may also express the wish to keep the family unit together. Associated monuments seen above ground would have given a focus for mourning and paying respects. The excavation of new graves constantly disturbed earlier earth-cut burials, while deposition in a burial structure largely prevented such disturbance. Interment in a burial structure further acted as a safeguard against the

Group	Brick-lined graves	Family vaults
I	V31, V32, V33	
II	V35, V36	Vault 30 (Haines)
III	V13, V25, V26	
IV	V11, V12, V20, V24	Vault 21
V	V03 (Sansom)	Vault 4, Vault 5 (Warden)
VI	V17	Vault 16, Vault 18 (Home)

Table 3: Possible groupings of vaults.

Group	Inferred construction date of vault	Inferred dates of other vaults in the group
I	V33: 1826–1831	V31 and V32 of similar date to V33 (very similar construction)
II	Vault 30: 1810–1816	V35 and V36 later than Vault 30
V	Vault 5: 1812–1842 V03: 1862	Vault 4 earlier in date than V03 and probably close in date to Vault 5
VI	Vault 18: 1810–1816	Vault 16 probably close in date to Vault 18. V17 later than Vault 18

Table 4: Inferred dates of construction in Vault Groups.

perceived or real threat posed by grave robbers, the so-called 'resurrection men' of the 19th century.

The question of the function of the vaults is explored more fully in the discussions of the individual vault types provided below.

Chambered burial vault (Vault 10)

Vault 10 was the largest and most elaborate burial vault at St. Martin's. It was situated towards the northern boundary wall of the churchyard and was the only example of what has been termed a 'chambered' vault. Essentially, the structure consisted of four east-west orientated vaulted burial chambers (labelled A, B, C and D from north to south) served by a north-south orientated access corridor, likewise vaulted, that ran the length of the structure (Figs. 36–38). The overall external dimensions of Vault 10 were 9.75m north to south by 5.50m east to west.

Vault 10 was the earliest of the vaults in St. Martin's churchyard for which dating evidence was available. Although no burials in Vault 10 were found with fully legible coffin plates, inscriptions (two on coffin plates and one over the entrance to a chamber) recorded the names of three individuals, Daniel Rowlinson, Samuel Wyer and James Cockle, who had been buried in the vault. Documentary research (see below and Chapter 6) has established, with a high degree of confidence, who these individuals were, and that they died in 1801, 1802 and 1833 respectively. It would be surprising if the burial of 1801 happened to be the earliest of the twenty burials found in the vault (and the coffin of Daniel Rowlinson was stacked on top of another, presumably earlier burial), so the construction of Vault 10 probably took place in the later part of the 18th century. A more precise date is provided by the minutes of a vestry meeting of 1785, which record a resolution that "Ten pounds to be paid for

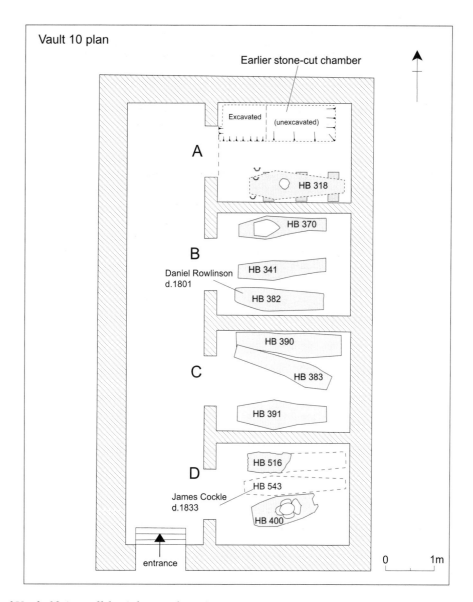

Fig. 36: Plan of Vault 10 (not all burials are shown).

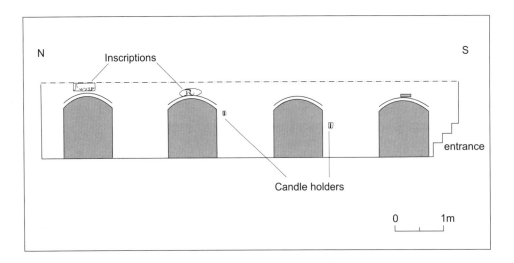

Fig. 37: Vault 10. Elevation of eastern wall of access corridor, showing entrances to chambers.

Fig. 38: Vault 10. View of access corridor, looking south towards the entrance.

every new vault situated in the Passage leading to the Bull Ring" (see Chapter 6). This is very likely to refer to Vault 10.

In 1785 St. Martin's churchyard was smaller than it was in the 19th century (see Chapter 2). On its east, north and west sides it was almost entirely enclosed by shops and houses. On the north side of the churchyard, however, a passage through these buildings provided access from the church and churchyard into the Bull Ring. This is clearly shown on contemporary maps and plans (Fig. 20, Chapter 2). When the position of Vault 10 is plotted onto an enlargement of the Thomas Hanson map of 1778 it exactly fits into and fully occupies the passage leading from the churchyard to the Bull Ring

(Fig. 21, Chapter 2). When the minutes of the Vestry Meeting refer to "… every new vault situated in the Passage …" they are presumably referring to the four individual chambers which comprise Vault 10, and this would indeed be a more usual usage of the word 'vault'. As the vaults were described as 'new' in 1785, they had perhaps been built in that year or only a year or two before. A note appended to minutes stated that "In consequence of this resolution Mr Edmd Tompkins paid Ten Pounds". Mr Tompkins perhaps purchased the use one of the four vaulted chambers which comprised Vault 10.

It is very probable, therefore, that Vault 10 was built in 1785 or shortly before and that use of the vault for burials started shortly after 1785. It is more difficult to establish for how long burial in the vault continued. The latest burial in the vault which could be identified was that of James Cockle, who died in 1833, although it could of course have continued in use for many years after that (the archaeological evidence suggests that there was at least one burial after James Cockle).

Entry to the vault was by means of steps that descended to the entranceway at the south end of the corridor. The build of the vault comprised multiple skins of clamped red bricks laid in header, stretcher and other decorative courses, and bonded with a limed mortar. The exterior brickwork was pointed in places, but most attention had been paid to the interior pointing. Inspection of the interior brickwork revealed that many of the bricks had been recycled from other contexts, such as chimney breasts. In contrast to the treatment of many of the brick-lined graves and family vaults, there was no evidence for whitewashing of the interior walls of Vault 10. However, there was evidence for the lighting of the corridor in the form of iron spikes towards its north end, which may have been fittings for lanterns, and what would appear to be six makeshift candle holders distributed unevenly along both sides of the corridor (Fig. 37). These consisted simply of dabs of mortar on the walls of the corridor into which a candle had been pressed, leaving its impression behind (Fig. 39).

Two circular openings in the roof of the corridor appear to have served as air-vents and light wells. The floor consisted mainly of the natural sandstone, but at the north end of the vault, in Chamber A, the vault builders had encountered an earlier rectangular chamber (2.3m × 1.1m), with neat vertical sides, excavated into the sandstone bedrock (Fig. 36). The soft fill of this rock-cut chamber had been floored over with dry-laid bricks placed flat, but these had partially subsided into the chamber. This chamber was partially excavated during the 2001 investigations, and it contained nothing but a fine sandy fill with occasional sherds of post-medieval pottery. It may have been an earlier rock-cut grave, but given its location it is more likely to be cellaring related to the buildings that once stood here.

The four burial chambers were entered through arched openings in the east wall of the access corridor (Fig. 37). These openings had been bricked up with a single skin of bricks, although at some point prior to the 2001 excavations the brickwork sealing each of the openings had been breached with a small hole, sufficient to see inside.

The entrances to each of the chambers were about 1m wide and about 1.2m high to the top of the arch. The four chambers were each the same size, with internal dimensions of 1.95m north-south by 2.65m east-west. This comfortably allowed space for three coffins side by side (or three stacks of coffins), orientated east-west, in each of the chambers. Generally the coffins had been placed with the head end to the west, although there were occasional exceptions, noted below.

Unlike the arrangement in the smaller family vaults

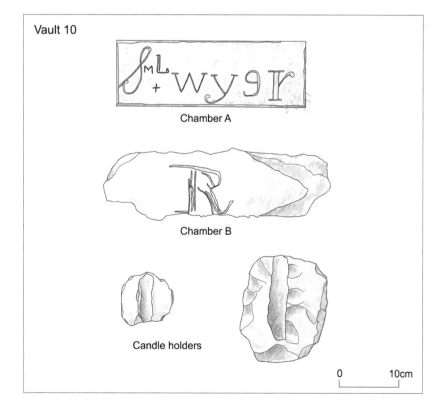

Fig. 39: Vault 10. Details of inscriptions above chamber entrances and mortar candle holders.

and many of the brick-lined graves, there was no provision for supports to create different levels or floors within the chambers, nor any internal partitions. Coffins were simply stacked directly one on top of the other, up to three stacks in each chamber. Generally the stacks were only two coffins high, with the maximum being a stack of four coffins. The lowest coffin in each stack was sometimes supported on brick coffin supports, to allow ventilation; these are described below.

The stacking of the coffins had exacerbated the effects of rotting of the coffin wood, with the upper coffins crushing those below. Generally the preservation of the coffins was poor and in no case had a fully legible *depositum* plate been preserved. In Chambers B and C the coffins were all of composite lead and wood construction. In Chamber D, however, the coffins were of wood construction only and the effects of the decay of the wood were particularly severe, such that it could be difficult to distinguish one coffin from another in a collapsed stack.

There were 20 burials in Vault 10 as a whole, of which 16 were fully analysed. Others were too fragmentary (or in one case too waterlogged) for analysis and were left *in situ*. All of the burials in Chambers A, B and C appeared to be adults, while the remains of three children were uncovered in Chamber D along with six adults. The number of burials in each chamber was variable, ranging from a single burial in Chamber A to nine burials in Chamber D. The burial details are presented in Table 5. The burials in each of the chambers are discussed in more detail below, where the question of the identity of individuals or potential family groups is also explored.

Chamber A

Chamber A contained a single adult burial (HB 318). The associated coffin survived only as fragmentary wood and metal fittings. The coffin had been placed at the south end of the chamber, raised on three brick-built coffin supports that ran outwards from the southern wall. The floor of the chamber was made of dry-laid bricks. This had been necessitated by the subterranean rock-cut chamber which was encountered below the floor in the northern half of Chamber A (see above), which the brick floor was intended to seal. Nevertheless, the brick floor had partially slumped into the soft fill of the rock-cut chamber.

Over the entrance to Chamber A a name had been carefully incised into a patch of render (wet when the inscription was made). It read 'SmL + Wy9r' (Fig. 39). The '9' is in fact a back-to-front 'e' and the inscription may be transliterated as 'Samuel Wyer'. The simplest explanation is that this was the name of the purchaser of the chamber. Whoever made the inscription would appear to have been illiterate or had difficulty with writing. Possibly it was written by a workman. The inscription would have served as a reminder of who was in the chamber, especially when the chamber was bricked up. Much more elaborate and detailed inscriptions were

associated with the family vaults in the crypt underneath Christ Church, Spitalfields, London (Reeve and Adams 1993).

Documentary research (Chapter 6) has identified a Samuel Wyer who was buried at St. Martin's in 1802, and he is very likely to be identified with the burial in the chamber. At the time of his death Samuel Wyer was a coach proprietor and Master of the Dog Inn in Spiceal Street, which was one of the streets bounding St. Martin's. Indeed he was buried just a few yards from his place of work and residence.

Chamber B

Chamber B contained six adult burials arranged in three stacks of two coffins each (Fig. 40, colour). All the coffins in this chamber were, as far as could be discerned, of composite lead and wood construction, and of fish-tail shape.

The lower burial in the south stack was not investigated. The upper burial (HB 382) was of an old adult male. The coffin, which used oak in its construction and retained traces of a black wool covering on the lid (Fig. 121, colour, Chapter 5), was distinguished by a lead shield-shaped *depositum* plate, which was partially legible and appeared to read 'Daniel Rowlin... Died March 30... Aged....'. Unfortunately the end of the name, the year of death and the age could not be read.

Contemporary obituaries record the death of a Daniel Rowlinson on 30th March 1801 (Chapter 6). Despite the fact that the last letters of the name on the coffin plate could not be read, the precise correspondence of the day and month of death leaves no doubt as to the identity of this individual. At the time of his death he was trading as a brass and cockfounder with his son. It is possible that Daniel's wife Ann, who died in 1817, and his son John, who died in 1831, were also buried in Chamber B and were amongst the other adult burials described below.

The lower burial of the middle stack (HB 376) was of an old adult female, whose coffin was distinguished by a lead coffin plate in the form of a cherub's head. Above this was the burial of a middle adult probable female (HB 341).

The lower burial in the north stack (HB 372), assessed to be a middle adult male, had a number of interesting features. It was raised off the floor of the chamber – the natural sandstone – by two large circular grinding stones (see Bevan, this volume, Chapter 5) (Fig. 41). Such coffin supports, more usually made of bricks (as in Chamber A), served to allow ventilation and delay the process of decomposition of the coffin. Whether the grinding stones had some symbolic purpose – relating, say, to the occupant's profession – or were merely conveniently to hand (which seems more likely) is a matter for speculation. The occupant of the coffin had worn, on his left hand, a gold 'mourning ring' commemorating one 'Mr THOS. MARTIN DIED 13 SEP 1808 AGED 53' (Fig. 135, colour, Chapter 5). This does not identify the burial but was a ring worn in commemoration of a dead friend or relative – the subject of mourning rings is explored by Bevan in Chapter 5. The burial above (HB 370) was of a young adult female, whose coffin included a wooden head rest. Two grooming combs of bone and shell were found by her head.

Over the entrance to Chamber B was an inscription, which had been incised into wet render in the same manner as the inscription over the entrance to Chamber A. The inscription in this case was simply a capital 'R' (Fig. 39). Given that one of those buried in this chamber has been identified as Daniel Rowlinson, the suspicion must be that the 'R' stands for 'Rowlinson' and that this was the Rowlinson family vault.

Chamber C

Chamber C contained four adult burials, arranged as two stacks of two coffins each. The lower burial in the south stack (HB 392) was not studied in detail and was left *in situ* but preliminary recording indicated an adult female. Fragments of a fabric coffin cover were noted on the coffin of the upper burial (HB 391). A notable feature of this burial, which was of a middle adult male, was the

presence in the coffin of a pinked and punched face cloth of wool textile (Walton Rogers, this volume, Chapter 5, Fig. 127).

Contrary to the usual orientation of the coffins in the vault, the coffins in the north stack were placed with the head end to the east. The lower burial of the north stack (HB 390) was of an old adult, probably male. The coffin had been raised on two brick coffin supports running out from the north wall of the chamber. The coffin had had a black wool cover ornamented with white metal coffin lace, fragments of which survived. The upper burial (HB 383) was of a middle adult female. The coffin, which had evidently been placed on top of the coffin of HB 390, had collapsed onto the floor of the chamber when the coffins had begun to rot. It had had a black wool coffin cover ornamented with metal coffin lace and held in place with decorative studs (Fig. 122, colour, Chapter 5).

It is possible (see discussion below) that one of the burials in this chamber was that of Edmund Tompkins, who is known to have paid ten pounds for a "vault situated in the Passage leading to the Bull Ring" in or around 1785 (see above). Edmund Tompkins died in 1824, aged 57. By extension, Chamber C could be the Tompkins

Chamber A

Human burial	Age group assigned	Sex assigned	Coffin details	Textiles/ personal items/notes
HB 318	Adult	Male	Wood (elm), very fragmentary, some studding on lid.	Samuel Wyer? d.1802.

Chamber B

Human burial	Age group assigned	Sex assigned	Coffin details	Textiles/ personal items/notes
South stack				
N/A	*Adult?*	-	Burial not examined.	
HB 382	Old adult	Male	Lead/wood (oak), fish tail, lead shield-shaped coffin plate that was partially legible, fabric covered top.	Daniel Rowlinson died March 30th 1801. Black wool coffin cover.
Middle stack				
HB 376	Old adult	Female	Lead/wood (elm), lead 'cherub head' plate.	Fragments of wool union textile.
HB 341	Middle adult	Prob female	Lead/wood	-
North stack				
HB 372	Middle adult	Male	Lead/wood (elm), fish-tail, large crest-shaped coffin plate, top edged with metal studs, fabric lined. Coffin supported on two grinding stones.	Wool union ?coffin lining edged with silk tabby ribbon. Ribbon around head from ?cap. Gold mourning ring commemorating Thomas Martin d.1808.
HB 370	Young adult	Female	Lead/wood, fish-tail, shield-shaped coffin plate, wooden head rest.	Two grooming combs of bone and shell.

Table 5: Vault 10 burial details (burials within the chambers are listed from the bottom to the top of the stacks. Where the age group and sex data are shown in italics these are based on preliminary on-site identifications only). Continued overleaf.

family vault, although this is very speculative. If this is the case then Edmund's wife Ann and two of his three children (son Edmund and daughters Eliza and Ann) may account for the three other adult burials in the chamber.

The 1809–11 trade directories list a Tompkins & Co of 5 Lichfield Street as "makers of ink stands, cruet & liquor frames &c", although this company cannot be definitely linked to the Tompkins family in question here (Chapter 6).

Chamber D

Chamber D contained nine burials. The coffins had evidently been arranged in three stacks. However, all the coffins in this chamber were of wood (elm where samples have been analysed) and had disintegrated very badly, so that in many cases all that remained were wood fragments, with the skeletons collapsed one on top of the other (Fig. 42).

The south stack comprised three adult burials, all in elm coffins. The lowest of the burials (HB 545) rested on a solid brick coffin support, 60cm wide, built up against the south wall of the chamber. The middle burial in the stack (HB 544) was of a middle adult female buried in a fabric-covered coffin ornamented with metal studs, which formed two rows around the border of the lid. The uppermost burial in the stack (HB 400) was not removed for full analysis but was identified as that of an adult.

The middle stack consisted of just two coffins. Although the coffin wood had disintegrated, the *depositum* plates survived, and for the lower burial (HB 543) could be partially read. The elaborate iron plate, with an oval centre and cherub and crown motifs (Fig. 118, colour, Chapter 5), appeared to commemorate one '[J]ames Cockl... Died Feby 20th 18?3 Aged 83 Years' (unfortunately the last part of name and the date could not be clearly read). The National Burial Index records a James Cockle, aged 83, who was buried at St. Martin's on 25th February 1833.

Chamber C

Human burial	Age group assigned	Sex assigned	Coffin details	Textiles/ personal items/notes
South stack				
HB 392	*Adult*	*Female*	Lead/wooden	Left *in situ*.
HB 391	Middle adult	Male	Lead/wooden (elm), enamelled coffin plate, fabric cover.	Pinked and punched face cloth of wool textile.
North stack				
HB 390	Old adult	Prob male	Lead/wood (elm), lozenge decoration on lead shell.	Black wool coffin cover with metal coffin lace.
HB 383	Middle adult	Female	Lead/wood (oak), fish-tail, rectangular coffin plate, studded pattern on lid.	Black wool coffin cover with metal coffin lace.

Chamber D

Human burial	Age group assigned	Sex assigned	Coffin details	Textiles/ personal items/notes
South stack				
HB 545	Adult	-	Wood (elm)	Resting on brick coffin support.
HB 544	Middle adult	Female	Wood (elm), fabric covering and decorative metal studs.	-
HB 400	*Adult*	-	Wood (elm)	-
Middle stack				
HB 543	*Adult*	*Male* (from coffin plate)	Wood, elaborate iron coffin plate with oval centre, cherub and crown motifs. Cherub-motif grips.	James Cockle died 20th February 1833 age 83.
HB 542	Adult	-	Wood, elaborate coffin plate.	-
North stack				
HB 516	Young adult	Male	Wood	-
HB 515	Child	-	Wood	-
HB 514	Child	-	Wood	-
HB 513	Child	-	Wood	-

Table 5 continued.

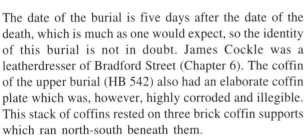

Fig. 41: Vault 10. Chamber B after excavation, showing the circular grinding stones which had supported the coffin of HB 372.

Fig. 42: Vault 10. Chamber D, view from chamber entrance prior to excavation. The wooden coffins had disintegrated badly.

The date of the burial is five days after the date of the death, which is much as one would expect, so the identity of this burial is not in doubt. James Cockle was a leatherdresser of Bradford Street (Chapter 6). The coffin of the upper burial (HB 542) also had an elaborate coffin plate which was, however, highly corroded and illegible. This stack of coffins rested on three brick coffin supports which ran north-south beneath them.

The north stack of burials had collapsed and the wooden coffins had almost completely disintegrated. The stack of coffins had been placed directly on the natural sandstone floor of the chamber. There were four burials, the lowest of which (HB 516) was assessed to be a young adult male, with three child burials (HB 515, HB 514 and HB 513) above.

Using James Cockle as a starting point, brief research was carried out using the National Burial Index, the International Genealogical Index and the parish burial records for St. Martin's into other members of the Cockle family who may have been buried in this chamber (Chapter 6). The results of this research are summarised in Table 6.

The parish burial records provide us with the name and date of burial (including the day and month although not shown in the table), sometimes with relationships and other information, but not always with the age. Thus while we know that six of those listed in the table were either the son or daughters of James Cockle and his wife Mary, we do not know their age at death. A maximum age of death may estimated on the assumption that none of the children were born earlier than a year after the marriage of James and Mary, which took place on 28th October 1781 (although it should be borne in mind that pre-nuptial conception was relatively common in this period [Cox 1996, 29]). Obviously, the births will in reality have been spread out over a number of years, so that the age at death given in Table 6 is a maximum and most will have been quite a few years younger when they died.

There are eight burials listed in Table 6 but there were nine burials in Chamber D, so at least one of the burials in the chamber is unaccounted for (and one coffin was stacked on top of that of James Cockle, so should be later than 1833). Furthermore, although three children were

First name(s)	Date of burial	Stated relationship	Other details	Age at death (see text)
Sarah	1783	'daughter of James and Mary'		<1 year
John	1789	'son of James and Mary'		<6 years
Not given	1793	'daughter of ...Cockle'		<10 years
Sarah Eliza	1802	'daughter of James and Mary'		<20 years
Catherine	1805	'daughter of James and Mary'	'vault, churchyard'	<22 years
Caroline	1807	'daughter of James and Mary'	'in a vault'	<24 years
Mary	1822	'wife of James'		65 years
James	1833			83 years

Table 6: Recorded burials of members of the Cockle family at St. Martin's.

identified from the anthropological analysis of the skeletons, there were no infants. Sarah Cockle, however, who died on 19th August 1783 will have been an infant at the time of her death, so she is not amongst the burials that were found in the vault. The simplest explanation for this is that at the time of Sarah's death the vault, which was described as 'new' in 1785, had not yet been built. The earliest burial which may possibly have been in the vault is that of John Cockle, who is assumed to have been less than six years old at the time of his death in 1789. He would thus be the earliest recorded burial in Vault 10 and indeed the earliest recorded burial in all of the burial structures at St. Martin's.

Given the inadequacies of the information available, it is fruitless to speculate further on the burials in Chamber D, other than to observe that the known children of James and Mary Cockle, together with James and Mary themselves, could account for seven of the nine burials in the chamber, comprising six adults and three children. This supposition is supported by the notes 'in a vault' and 'vault, churchyard' attached to the entries for Caroline and Catherine in the parish burial record. However, such notes are unusual, and the absence of this information in other cases (including that of James Cockle, identified from his *depositum*) cannot be taken to imply that a burial did not take place in a vault.

Whatever the problems with determining the precise identities of those buried in Chamber D, the fact that many of James and Mary Cockle's children died in infancy, childhood or adolescence is clear. This pattern is repeated in four of the five family vaults reported on below where comparable information is available.

The use of wood for the construction of the coffins in Chamber D, as opposed to the composite lead and wood coffins used in Chambers B and C, is an interesting difference of the burials here. It is certainly not a chronological difference (remembering that the coffin of James Cockle dates to 1833), as the other vaults at St. Martin's demonstrate the use of lead coffins throughout the 19th century. It would seem rather to be a 'cheap option' followed for all the burials in the chamber. In some of the other vaults (notably Vault 9) consistency in the form of the coffins and coffin furniture suggests the

use of one particular undertaker, favoured by the family. This may be the case for Chamber D of Vault 10 also, although at the cheaper end of the market, or the cheaper end of a particular undertaker's range.

Vault 10: Discussion

Tentatively, all four of the chambers in Vault 10 can be associated with a specific family: Wyer (A), Rowlinson (B), Cockle (D) and, by a process of elimination, Tompkins (C). The identification is obviously more speculative in some cases than others. It will be seen, when the other vaults at St. Martin's are considered below (each of which is essentially a freestanding version of the chambers of Vault 10 and generally of not dissimilar size), that in all five cases where the burials in a particular vault can be established, they all belong to the same family.

Irrespective of the correctness of the association of Edmund Tompkins with Chamber C, it is interesting to note that in 1785 Mr Tompkins paid ten pounds to the church for the use of one of the new vaults situated in the passage leading to the Bull Ring. In 1785, ten pounds was a very substantial sum of money. It is difficult to put this in today's terms but around the end of the 18th century £1 a week would be a good wage for a workman, and a small house would cost around £40 – £60 (wages and the cost of housing are discussed extensively in Hopkins 1998, e.g. 130, 152). Furthermore, this is unlikely to have been the only fee that needed to be paid as the church also made a charge for each individual interment – records of such charges go back to 1680 (Bunce 1875, 32). For 1848 a detailed list of charges is available (see Chapter 8, Table 136). At that time the total charge for a vault in the churchyard was £5 1s, and the charge for each new interment in a vault was £1 15s 6d.

The fact that Mr Tompkins paid nearly double in 1785 than somebody in a similar position would have had to have paid in 1848 suggests an important difference between what the two charges were for. In 1848 the fee (which was distributed between the rector, clerk and sexton, with the lion's share going to the rector) was evidently on top of whatever it would have cost to have the vault built. In 1785, it would appear from both the amount of the payment and the context of the reference to it that Mr Tompkins was paying for a vault that had already been built. It can be inferred from this that the church itself had paid for the vault to be built and that the charge to Mr Tompkins was intended to recoup the costs.

If the four chambers of Vault 10 are correctly identified with "….every new vault situated in the Passage leading to the Bull Ring" referred to in the minutes of the vestry meeting, then the total charge the church received would have been £40. This was about the cost at the time of building a small house (Hopkins *op. cit.*), to which the whole complex comprising Vault 10 may be broadly compared.

One of the motives behind building Vault 10 may have been profit. The extensive employment of reused bricks in its construction has been noted, which would have reduced the costs of materials considerably, so there was perhaps a margin for a fair profit. Another motive is likely to be the pressure on space for burials in the church at a time of growing population. The fact that the 'vaults' were situated not in the churchyard proper but in a passage leading out from the churchyard is in itself eloquent testimony to the pressure on space at the time. The historian of Birmingham William Hutton, writing in 1782, observed (amongst several other lively comments on the state of St. Martin's churchyard) that "A son not only succeeds his father in the possession of his property and habitation, but also in the grave, where he can scarcely enter without expelling half a dozen of his ancestors" (Hutton 1835, 97).

A vault in a passage leading between old shops and houses cannot be considered a prestigious location as the most prestigious location was a vault in the church, followed by a vault in the churchyard proper. That men were prepared to pay a very substantial sum for the privilege is further testimony to the desperate situation which prevailed with regard to space for burial at St. Martin's. From the little we know of them, these men – a brass and cockfounder, a coach proprietor, a leather-dresser – pursued trades that were typical of the emerging middle classes of industrialising Birmingham. In the following generation, men pursuing similar trades were able to construct for themselves family vaults within the churchyard itself.

Family vaults

Introduction

Ten examples of family vaults were identified during the 2001 excavations at St. Martin's. Although designs varied in minor respects, the construction of the family vaults all followed a similar pattern. A rectangular chamber was cut through the earth to the natural sandstone, which generally formed the floor. The builders of the vaults at St. Martin's were fortunate in that the bedrock appeared at about the right depth and was often level enough for

the purpose. The side or springer walls, generally two or three skins of brick thick, were then constructed. Wooden shuttering would then have been erected to support the brick-built barrel roof as it was constructed from the outside. Once the mortar had set the shuttering would have been removed and the two non-load-bearing end walls would have been built up from the inside, leaving provision for access.

The finished examples measured approximately 2.6–4.2m in length, 2–2.8m wide, and up to 3.5m in depth. Interior effects included the whitewashing of the walls to improve appearance or maximise any available daylight during the deposition of burials (it may also have served to cover up the employment of reused bricks). The interior brickwork features often included built-in putlocks to receive coffin supports and to serve as air-vents. Alternatively, putlocks were sometimes cut out of the existing brickwork.

Two examples (Vault 5 and Vault 30) had interior divisions formed by stone slabs laid both horizontally and vertically. Some vertical internal divisions were formed with brickwork. Iron braces and fixtures associated with coffin supports were also identified. As noted, flooring was usually formed by incorporating the natural sandstone into the design. In other cases, courses of dry-laid or mortared bricks laid flat formed the flooring. The barrel roofs were encountered in both an intact and a collapsed state.

As outlined earlier, the burial vaults contained two or more burials laid horizontally, or stacked multiples thereof. The preservation of the coffins and coffin furniture was good in comparison with the earth-cut graves. The majority of the vaults were uncovered in a structurally sound condition.

From the identifiable burials found within some of them, it is clear that these vaults were used for the members of particular families, so they are termed 'family vaults'. In five cases these families could be identified. In the other five cases this information was not available, either because no identifiable coffin plates had survived (3 cases) or because the burials were not investigated as the vaults could be preserved *in situ* (2 cases).

From the identifiable *depositum* plates and other sources of evidence, it is believed that the majority of the family vaults were built in the period from around 1810 to 1830, although burial in them continued through to 1915, with a peak in the 1870s. The dating evidence is reviewed in detail in the concluding part of this section. In the account of these vaults provided below, the vaults which could be assigned to specific families are described first, and in some detail. They are presented in what is believed to be the approximate order of their construction and use. A more summary account is given of the other vaults.

Vault 23: Ainsworth Family

This burial chamber was situated against the boundary

wall in a solitary position at the northern edge of the churchyard. Unusually, the vault was orientated north-south; that is, the barrel roof was sprung from the east and west walls, with timber coffin supports spanning between these two walls, on which the coffins had been placed on a north-south alignment. Thus the usual arrangement was rotated through ninety degrees. The reason for this is probably that it was designed to be one of a number of vaults laid out in a row against the northern boundary wall, and by adopting this orientation much better use could be made of space. Not only could more vaults be fitted in if their long axis was per-pendicular to the boundary wall, but access to the end to insert new burials would be easier. A brick-lined grave (V22) a little to the east and also on the boundary wall was orientated in the same way. Nevertheless, the vaulted roof had been strengthened to receive an above-ground monument, possibly a chest-tomb, orientated east-west, so that the inscriptions on the long side of the tomb would have been prominently visible.

The position of this vault in the 1810 extension to the churchyard (Chapter 2) provides a *terminus post quem* for its construction.

The vault measured 1.58m north-south by 2.42m east-west and was built of clamped red brick with a lime mortar. The flooring consisted of dry-laid bricks placed flat. The entrance was situated in the south elevation and comprised an arched opening that had been closed by a triple skin of brickwork (Fig. 43).

The vault contained nine coffins arranged in three levels (Table 7; Fig. 44). The upper two levels were supported on timber beams received by putlocks built into the east and west walls. However, the beams had rotted and the coffins had collapsed, leaving most in a crushed or fragmentary condition. The human remains were likewise mostly in a very poor state of preservation. Only two (HB 691 and HB 692) were subject to full analysis. For the others, basic preliminary identifications of age group and, where possible, sex were made on site but the bodies were not removed from the churchyard.

Two of the burials could be identified from legible *depositum* plates. These were Isaac Ainsworth (HB 702) and Hannah Ainsworth (HB 691), his wife. Husband and wife had been placed side by side in the middle level of the vault, their heavy lead coffins supported on three timber beams. There were no other burials on this level. Isaac Ainsworth, who died in 1837 aged 80, had been a saddler (see Chapter 6). Hannah died ten years before him, in 1827, aged 60.

Hannah was enclosed in an expensive coffin. The composite lead coffin had an outer case of oak and an inner shell of elm. Traces of a fabric covering survived, together with the remains of studding. The coffin grips were decorated with an angel/cherub motif. Hannah had probably worn a cap or bonnet tied with silk ribbons (Walton Rogers, this volume, Chapter 5, Fig. 130). Isaac's coffin was distinguished by having two coffin plates, each bearing the same details of his name, age and date of death. A plain rectangular lead plate was attached to the inner lead shell and an ornate metal plate to the outer wooden case.

The central position of Isaac and Hannah Ainsworth in the vault provides a clue to the possible identities of the burials in the levels above and below. The church

Fig. 43: Vault 23 (Ainsworth family). Bricked-up entrance from south.

Level 1

Human burial	Age/sex group assigned	Coffin details. *Textiles/ personal items*	Identified individuals	Date	Age
HB 697	*Child*	Wood (elm)	Isaac Ainsworth?	1811	< 4
HB 698	*Child*	Wood, fabric pins and coffin nails.	Emma Ainsworth?	1814	16mth
HB 722	*Adult male*	Lead/wood (elm), shield-shaped *depositum* with cherubs and crown, gold-coloured paint. Cherub-motif grips. Lozenge pattern on lead shell.	Isaac Ainsworth? or John Ainsworth?	1821 1815	28 29
HB 723	*Adult*	Lead/wood (elm), 'shadow' of shield-shaped coffin plate with cherubs. Cherub motif grips plates.	Isaac Ainsworth? or John Ainsworth?	1821 1815	28 29

Level 2

Human burial	Age/sex group assigned	Coffin details. *Textiles/ personal items*	Identified individuals	Date	Age
HB 691	Old adult	Lead/wood (oak exterior, elm interior), fabric covered, studded, rectangular *depositum*. Angel/cherub-motif grips. Lozenge patterning on lead shell. *Silk ribbons from ?cap.*	**Hannah Ainsworth**	**1827**	68
HB 702	*Adult male*	Lead/wood (elm), fabric covered, coffin plates on both lead and wood lids.	**Isaac Ainsworth**	**1837**	80

Level 3

Human burial	Age/sex group assigned	Coffin details. *Textiles/ personal items*	Identified individuals	Date	Age
HB 681	*Adult*	Wood (oak), very fragmentary. *Silk ribbon edging for wool textile. Sprig of box in coffin.*	John M Ainsworth? or Benjamin Ainsworth?	1845 1833	? 72
HB 692	Adult	Wood, slight fish-tail shape, stamped coffin plate, possible studding. *Silk ribbons and bow. Tortoise shell hair comb.*	Mary Ann Ainsworth?	1846	?
HB 676	*Adult*	Wood (elm), fabric covering, decorated plates (corroded).	John M Ainsworth? or Benjamin Ainsworth?	1845 1833	? 72

Table 7: Vault 23 burial details. (Age/sex categories assigned from preliminary inspection on site shown in italics. Burials identified from coffin plates are shown in bold.)

burial register reveals that only seven Ainsworths were buried in the churchyard in the period from 1810 onwards and these should correspond to the seven unidentified burials in the vault. The four burials in Level 1, the lowest level, comprised two children and two adults. These burials presumably predate those of Hannah and Isaac and may well include children of the couple who died young. Documentary research (Chapter 6) has indicated that two sons of Hannah and Isaac predeceased them. These were John, described as a 'whipmaker of Digbeth', and noted earlier as living at The Moat (Chapter 2), who died in 1815 aged 29, and Isaac, who died in 1821 aged 28. These were possibly the two adult burials in Level 1, HB 722 and HB 723. Both were buried in lead coffins of a type not dissimilar from that later used for their parents.

The younger children in Level 1 were buried in comparatively simple wooden coffins. These had been stacked one on top of the other in the northeast corner of the vault. The coffin of the upper burial (HB 698) had crushed the coffin of the lower burial (HB 697) when the wood had rotted. These burials were possibly the son and daughter of John Ainsworth, the whipmaker, and his wife, Elizabeth, and the grandchildren of Isaac and Hannah (see the family tree shown in Chapter 6). If the lower of the two coffins contained the earlier burial (not a watertight assumption as the coffins could have been stacked up at a later date to make space for the adult burials on this level), then HB 697 should be Isaac, who died in 1811 at an age of less than four and HB 698 should be Emma, who died in 1814 aged 16 months.

Taking account of the names listed in the church burial

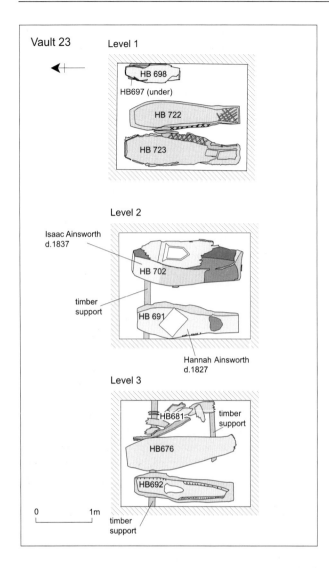

Fig. 44: Vault 23 (Ainsworth family). Plans of burials in vault.

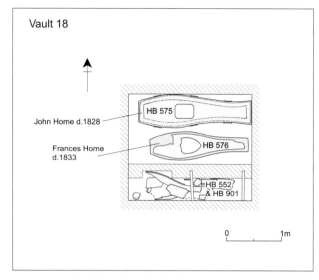

Fig. 45: Vault 18 (Home family). Plan of burials in vault.

register, it would seem that the three adult burials in the upper level (Level 3) of Vault 23 are possibly brothers of the Isaac (HB 702) who was buried in the middle level of the vault – Benjamin Ainsworth and John M Ainsworth, together with John's wife Mary Ann. If this is the case then Mary Ann, who died in 1845, should be HB 692, because a tortoise shell hair comb was found in association with this burial. Mary Ann's husband, John, who died in 1846, and his brother Benjamin, who died in 1833 aged 72, would account for the other two burials, HB 676 and HB 681. It should be noted that if this is the case then the vault was not filled up in strict sequence. Benjamin (d.1833), although dying before his brother Isaac (d.1837), was buried on the level above Isaac, leaving a space beside Isaac's wife Hannah (d.1827) for the burial of Isaac himself. Given the way that access to the vault was obtained and the different levels within the vault supported (i.e. 'open' timber beams rather than a 'sealing' floor) this was perfectly feasible, and it may be

noted from other vaults at St. Martin's that husbands and wives were placed together wherever possible.

The coffins on Level 3, which seem to have been only of wooden construction, were supported on just two beams. One was an oak coffin, which is comparatively unusual at St. Martin's (Gale, this volume, Chapter 5).

Amongst the mainly fragmentary coffin furniture from the vault was an isolated coffin grip stamped with the date 15th September 1842. This grip is presumably to be associated with one of the three coffins in Level 3, although none of the suggested burials correspond with this date. However, this evidence together with the likely dates of the earliest burials and the fact that the vault was built in an extension to the churchyard opened in 1810, suggest that the vault was built around 1810 and continued in use up to the 1840s. If it is reasonable to assume that the vault was built by Isaac Ainsworth for himself and his family, then Isaac, who was a church warden (Chapter 6), would have been in his early fifties at the time.

Vault 18: Home family

Vault 18 was also built in the 1810 extension to the churchyard, but being away from the boundary wall it was orientated in the usual east-west manner. It measured 2.56m north-south by 2.73m east-west (external). The entrance to Vault 18 was located at the western end of the vault and was formed by a bricked-in arched opening. The chamber was roofed with a barrelled roof in good condition. The interior walls of the vault had been whitewashed. Internal features included a single row of putlocks and a partition wall made of a double skin of bricks (Fig. 45 and Fig. 46, colour). The latter created a narrow compartment at the south end of the vault, barely wide enough for a coffin (indeed, the wall thinned to single skin of bricks at its west end, as if to accommodate the shoulder of a coffin). The partition wall was 1m high, and at its top was braced to the southern vault wall with metal straps bonded into the interior brickwork.

Vault 18 contained the remains of four individuals, two adults and two children. The burials were all on the floor of the vault, orientated east-west with the head to the west (Figs 45 & 46, colour). The two adults were found in the larger northern compartment and the fragmentary remains of the two children in the smaller southern compartment. The two adults have been identified from the coffin plates as John Home, who died in 1828 aged 50, and Frances Home who died in 1833 aged 53. John Home was a chemist and druggist and Frances was his wife (see Chapter 6). The burial details are shown in Table 8.

The two children identified from skeletal evidence are likely to be John and Frances' children. Five of their children died young; their deaths are recorded in the parish burial records and, in two cases, in obituaries (Table 9).

The fragmentary remains of the skeletons of two children were recovered from the southern compartment, where they were found amongst the disintegrated remains of coffin wood, with no trace of lead shells. The fact that there were two children represented (HB 552 and HB 901) only emerged when the skeletal remains were analysed. Analysis of these remains suggested that HB 552 was probably between 10 and 12.5 years old and HB 901 was between 7 and 9.5 years. This provides a good fit with Sophia Frances, who died aged 12 and Amelia, who died aged 9 (Table 9).

The remains of the infants do not seem to have been placed in the vault. It is apparent, as discussed below and in Chapter 4, that infant burials are underrepresented in the vaults in general and that for one reason or another it was often not considered appropriate to open up a vault for an infant burial. A similar phenomenon was noted in the intramural vaults at Christ Church, Spitalfields (Cox 1996, 20).

In the larger northern compartment were the coffins of John Home (HB 575) and Frances Home (HB 576). The particulars of the coffins and associated textiles are given in Table 10.

John Home (HB 575) had been buried in a fine coffin which was comparatively well preserved (Fig. 46, colour). Due to the presence of soft tissue, the remains of his body were not removed from the churchyard and were reburied in the vault designated for this purpose. The wooden outer case of the lead coffin appeared to be in a very good state of preservation but soon deteriorated when the vault was opened. This outer case was of elm wood covered in fabric and decorated with brass studs; on the lid the brass studs formed a double border around the edge. The rectangular brass coffin plate, coffin grips and grip plates were still intact. The inner lead shell was of a fish-tail design and had an incised lozenge pattern on the outside.

The coffin of Frances Home (HB 576) had an inner lead shell with an incised lozenge pattern on the outer surface. The degraded outer case was made of elm, with a shield-shape brass *depositum* on the lid (Fig. 46, colour). Fragments of the wool union coffin lining survived, together with animal hair, presumably from

Human burial	Age group assigned	Sex assigned	Identified individual	Date of death	Age
HB 552	Child	-	Sophia Frances Home?	1816	12
HB 901	Child	-	Amelia Home?	1819	9
HB 575	-	-	**John Home**	**1828**	50
HB 576	Middle adult	Female	**Frances Home**	**1833**	53

Table 8: Vault 18 burial details. Burials identified from coffin plates are shown in bold.

Human burial	Name	Date of death	Year	Age
-	Mary	8 May	1816	19 months
HB 552?	Sophia Frances	31 December	1816	12 years
-	Edward	6 March	1817	8 months
HB 901?	Amelia	23 February	1819	9 years
-	Alexander	12 December	1823	5 months
HB 575	John	27 October	1828	50 years
HB 576	Frances	20 November	1833	53 years

Table 9: Members of the Home family buried at St. Martin's.

Human burial	Coffin construction	Coffin shape	Wood type	Textiles	Notes
HB 552/ HB 901 *Child x 2*	Wood (fragments only). Flower-motif grips.	-	-	-	Sophia and Amelia Home?
HB 575 *Not analysed* (Left *in situ*)	Lead/wood, fabric cover, brass studs, rectangular brass coffin plate.	Fish-tail	Elm	Frags of poss wool union from around skull.	Tufts of human hair, grey. John Home d.1828
HB 576 *Mid adult Female*	Lead/wood, Shield-shaped brass coffin plate.	Fish-tail (slight)	Elm	Wool union coffin lining. Loose folds of wool union, trimmed with silk ribbon from ?winding sheet. Silk ribbon from ?cap.	Two copper alloy rings - ?eyelets Human hair, straight, grey Frances Home d.1833.

Table 10: Vault 18 coffin details. (The age group and sex of individuals assigned from skeletal analysis is shown in italic).

padding. Thick, loose folds of a wool union garment trimmed with silk ribbon were presumably the remains of a shroud or winding sheet (Fig. 126, Chapter 5). Silk ribbon from the head area, associated with straight, grey human hair, may be the remains of a cap. Two small copper-alloy rings found in the coffin may be eyelets from a garment.

Vault 18 was presumably built by John Home at some point between 1810, the date of the extension to the churchyard, and 1816, the date of what was probably the first burial in the vault, his daughter Sophia Frances. It is argued in the discussion below that it is likely to have been built in the earlier part of this range, when several individuals took advantage of the recent extension to the churchyard to build their family vault. John would have been in his early thirties at the time.

Although five of John and Frances Home's children died under the age of 13, and at least two of these were very probably buried in the vault, the couple may have had other children who survived into adulthood. Initially, the coffins of the children were presumably placed on the floor of the vault. Perhaps it was when John died that the vault was reorganised. A brick partition was erected at one end and in the small compartment thus formed, about 1m deep, the coffins of the children were stacked up. The iron tie bars between the top of the partition wall and the wall of the vault, as well as securing the burials, could have supported a wooden ceiling to the compartment, thus sealing it off completely. Space was now available for the adult burials of John and Frances.

Vault 9: Jenkins family

Vault 9 was the largest of the family vaults, belonging to the wealthy Jenkins family. It was located on the northern edge of the churchyard, in the area of the 1810 extension,

close by the churchyard wall and near to the imposing northern gate (Fig. 35). However, unlike the Ainsworth vault (Vault 23), it was not orientated north-south, to make the best use of space against the wall, but on the more usual east-west orientation. The construction of Vault 9 had caused slight damage to the large chambered vault (Vault 10), its southwest corner clipping the northeast corner of the earlier vault.

The evidence of a dated *depositum* suggests the vault had been built by the 1820s. However, for reasons of family history, given below, it is most likely to have been built in the period 1810 to 1816. Its use continued into the second half of the 19th century (the latest dated burial is of 1882), and it displayed clear evidence of major alterations and reorganisation late in its use, probably around the end of the 19th century.

At 4.8m long east-west and 2.4m wide, Vault 9 had the capacity to accommodate six or more coffins on any one level (Fig. 47). And at over 3m deep it would have been possible to have at least four levels of burials (compare Vault 5, below), so that the total potential capacity of the vault was upwards of 24 burials. However, only eleven burials were found, all confined to the eastern half of the vault.

The roof of the chamber was originally vaulted, a long barrel vault sprung from the north and south walls. Other than for its size it was of conventional construction, with a whitewashed interior. Entry would have been from the east and west ends, both the east and west walls displaying evidence of bricked-up entranceways. However, at later date the crown of the vaulted roof was demolished along its east-west axis, leaving just the haunches at either side (Fig. 48). Two steel girders were inserted lengthways, through the ends of the vault, to support the two sides of the roof. Stone slabs had been placed along the grooves

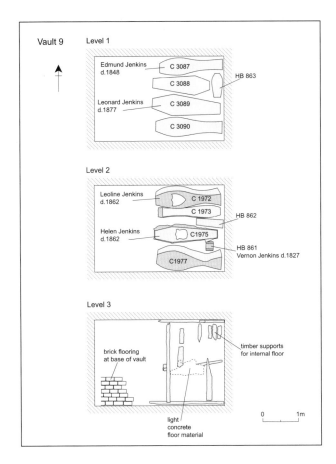

Fig. 47: Vault 9 (Jenkins family). Plans of burials in vault.

Fig. 48: Vault 9 (Jenkins family). The roof of the vault from the east.

of the girders to form a removable roof entrance (Fig. 49).

The evidence suggests that these major alterations to the roof structure were accompanied by reorganisation of the interior of the vault. When the vault was entered, through the roof entrance, two layers of coffins were visible, which had been carefully arranged at the east end of the vault. The west end of the vault was empty, where the brick ground floor could be seen (Fig. 47). However, the interior floors within the east end of the vault had rotted and collapsed, causing considerable jumbling and damage to the coffins. There appeared to have been two interior floors, the uppermost of which overlay the two levels of coffins but had not itself, apparently, supported any coffins. This floor had been supported on timber joists spanning north-south and further bridging joists running east-west (Fig. 47, Level 3). The floor itself was of a light concrete. When the timbers had rotted most of this floor had collapsed onto the coffins below, which were covered by a layer of debris.

Below this upper floor were two layers of coffins. The upper layer of coffins (Level 2) had evidently once been supported on another internal floor of similar construction, but this survived only as a layer of debris covering the lower layer of coffins (Level 1). The collapse

of the floor supporting the Level 2 coffins had caused these coffins to fall onto those below and most were tipped at an angle. One coffin of an infant (HB 861) had ended up standing on its end, and another (HB 862) had fallen on its side (Fig. 47).

It was decided at an early stage in the investigation of Vault 9 that it would be possible to cap and retain this structure during the landscaping works, so analysis of the human remains was limited to the three infants (HB 861, HB 862 and HB 863) whose coffins had been most severely damaged. Otherwise, only summary recording of the coffins of the eight adult burials was undertaken, and the burials were left undisturbed.

However, an interesting aspect of this vault was that the shield-shaped brass *depositum* plates of six of the eleven burials had survived well and were fully legible. This sheds much light on the date of the use of the vault, on the family to whom it belonged, and on the reorganisation of the vault which evidently took place at a late stage in its use. The data are given in Table 11. Note that human burial numbers were not assigned to those coffins which were left untouched, and in these cases the context number assigned to the coffin is given as an identifier.

From Table 11 it is apparent that the burials do not

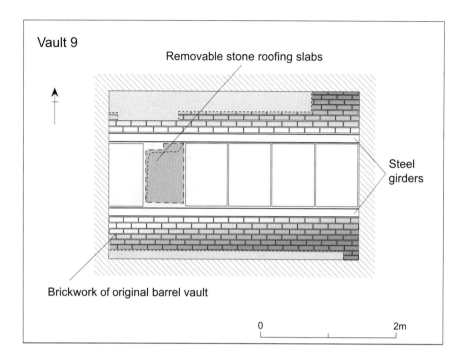

Fig. 49: Vault 9 (Jenkins family). Diagrammatic plan showing alterations to the roof structure.

occur in the logical sequence in which they were found, say, in Vault 5 (below), where the earliest burials occur on the lowest level and the burials on the levels above are progressively later. In some cases, an anomaly in the regular sequence of burials can be explained because a space is left for a particular burial, for example so a husband and wife can be together. A probable example of this was noted in Vault 23, where a space in the middle level of the vault seems to have been left for Isaac Ainsworth (HB 702) so he could buried by his wife, Hannah (HB 691), who died ten years before him, another member of the family dying in the interim.

In Vault 9, however, there is no evidence of any order in the sequence of burials. For example, the earliest dated burial, that of Vernon Jenkins (HB 861) in 1827, was associated with the upper level of burials (Level 2), although the coffin had collapsed on end into the lower level (Level 1). On the other hand, one of the latest of the dated burials, that of Leonard Jenkins (C 3089) who died in 1877, was on the floor of the vault in Level 1. Furthermore, it can be seen that there are two single-break coffins with straight sides in Level 1, including that of Leonard Jenkins. Coffins of this shape seem, on the evidence from St. Martin's, to have gradually replaced the older fish-tailed shape from the 1870s onwards (see also Vaults 5 and 30); Helen Jenkins (C 1975), who died in 1882, was also cased in a coffin of this shape.

It would appear, then, that the coffins in Vault 9 were thoroughly reorganised at some stage. Such reorganisation was no means uncommon in vaults, especially of the intramural (under the church) variety (Litten 1991, 195–226). A further indication of reorganisation in Vault

9 is provided by the way the coffins had been arranged. While most had the head end to the west, as was traditional, two (C 1973 and C 3088) had the head end to the east, and the coffins were evidently arranged to pack them into the smallest space possible. Infant burials were squeezed into the available space, as in the case of HB 863, which was orientated north-south to make the best use of space.

It is reasonable to suppose that this reorganisation of the burials took place at the same time as the major remodelling of the roof, probably around the end of the 19th century, and that the internal partition floors were constructed at the same time. It is interesting to note that concern for the traditional 'correct' orientation of a burial, i.e. with the head to the west so the risen body faced east, appears to have declined as the 19th century progressed – see, for example, several of the burials in Vault 30, described below. In general, however, the 'head-to-the-west' custom seems to have been a preference rather than a rule, to be adhered to only when practicalities did not demand otherwise; all the burials in Vault 23 were orientated north-south.

The effect of the remodelling and reorganisation of Vault 9 was to create more space in the chamber. There was space for four burials on the unused upper floor at the east end of the vault, and the whole of the west end was empty. It hardly seems credible that the effort and expense of this reorganisation and rebuilding took place without there being an intention to use the vault for a number of further burials. In the event, it appears, this did not take place, and one can only speculate as to the reasons.

Fig. 3: Modern view of St. Martin's Church framed by Bullring.

Fig. 13: St. Martin's and its churchyard in the 1960s. The Bull Ring Centre and markets are in the foreground (Photo: Myra Dean).

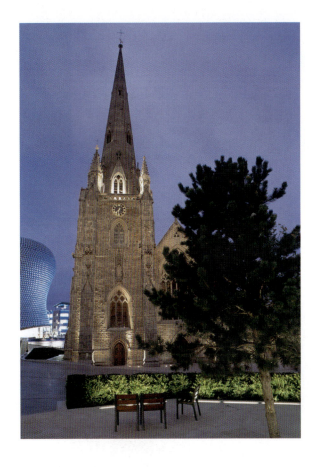

Fig. 26: St. Martin's Square today.

Fig. 27: View of the 2001 excavations, looking north, with the Rotunda in the background.

Fig. 31: Excavation of the earliest dated burial in the churchyard (HB 408). The copper alloy lettering on the coffin lid reads '[M?] [172?] [(A)GE] [85]'.

Fig. 40: Vault 10. Chamber B, view from chamber entrance prior to excavation, showing coffin stacks.

Fig. 46: Vault 18 (Home family). The well preserved coffins of John Home (right) and Frances Home (left). On the extreme left is the wall of the compartment containing the children, with the iron bracing straps visible.

Fig. 50: Vault 5 (Warden family). View of the vault from the west before excavation. The brickwork sealing the west entrance has been partially demolished.

Fig. 53: Vault 5 (Warden family). Burials in Level 2, from east. The coffin of George Warden is in the centre. In the compartment on the right is the coffin of Sarah Emma Warden.

Fig. 60: Vault 30 (Haines family). Burials in Level 1, north end of chamber. The coffins of Jane Lloyd Haines (left) and William Haines (right), from east.

Fig. 95: The arrow points towards the location of a possible healed blade injury on the skull of HB 270.

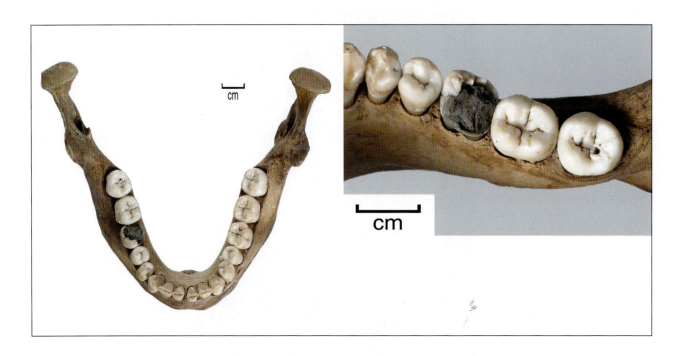

Fig. 105: Overview and close up of the mandible of HB 829, showing the filled first right molar.

Fig. 106: The Vulcanite dentures found with HB 297 (Ann Maria Browett).

Fig. 111: Coffin of HB 304, an adult female, from Level 4 of Vault 5 (Warden family). Late 19th century.

Fig. 112: Coffin of HB 321, a child, from Level 4 of Vault 5 (Warden family). Late 19th century.

Fig. 113: Grip plate with winged cherub motif from coffin of HB 723, Vault 23 (Ainsworth family) Level 1. Early 19th century.

Fig. 118: Iron depositum from the coffin of HB 543, James Cockle (d.1833), Vault 10 Chamber D. The elaborate plate is ornamented with a winged cherub motif and surmounted by a crown.

Level 1

Human burial	Coffin details/ *Textiles*	Age/sex assigned	Identified individual	Date	Age
C 3090	Lead/wood, fish-tail.	*Adult coffin size*	-	-	-
C 3089	Lead/wood, single-break, shield-shaped coffin plate.	-	**Leonard Jenkins**	**1877**	59
C 3088	Lead/wood, single-break, fabric cover, tin coffin plate.	*Adult coffin size*	-	-	-
HB 863	Lead/wood (elm), fish-tail.	Infant	Samuel Jenkins? or Frances Jenkins?	1816 1834	11 mths 10 mths
C 3087	Lead/wood, fish-tail, brass shield-shaped coffin plate.	-	**Edmund Jenkins**	**1848**	25

Level 2

Human burial	Coffin details/ *Textiles*	Age/sex assigned	Identified individual	Date	Age
C 1977	Lead/wood, fish-tail.	*Adult coffin size*	-	-	-
HB 861	Lead/wood, fish-tail, lead shield-shaped coffin plate.	*Infant*	**Vernon Jenkins**	**1827**	3 mths
C 1975	Lead/wood (oak), single-break, brass shield-shaped coffin plate, handles.	-	**Helen Jenkins**	**1882**	72
HB 862	Lead/wood (elm), fish-tail, cross-hatched pattern on lead shell. *Black wool coffin cover, frags wool union textiles, worsted 'coffin fabric', silk ribbon.*	Infant	Samuel Jenkins? or Frances Jenkins?	1816 1834	11 mths 10 mths
C 1973	Lead/wood, fish-tail, rectangular plaque engraved in lead lining.	*Adult coffin size*	-	-	-
C 1972	Lead/wood, fish-tail, brass shield-shaped coffin plate.	-	**Leoline Jenkins**	**1862**	37

Isolated coffin plate

Human burial	Coffin details	Age/sex assigned	Identified individual	Date	Age
C 1980	N/A	-	**Mary Jenkins**	**1861**	73

Table 11: Vault 9 burial details (Burials listed from south to north. Where no human burial number was assigned the context number of the coffin is given. Preliminary on-site age assignments in italics. Individuals identified from coffin plates shown in bold.)

Aspects of the history of the Jenkins family are briefly explored in Chapter 6. The central figure in the family was William Walker Jenkins, who probably had the vault built. William Jenkins, a brassfounder, was born *c.*1784 and died in 1846 at the age of 62. In 1833 his works employed 250 people, so he was a very substantial employer (Chapter 6). His coffin was not identified amongst those in the vault, but was probably one of the earlier ones of fish-tail design. In 1809, at the age of about 25, he married his wife Mary, whose shield-shaped brass coffin plate was found loose amongst the debris in the vault; it had probably become detached from one of the fish-tail coffins when the upper level of burials collapsed.

It was probably soon after his marriage in 1809 but before the death of his infant son Samuel (probably HB 862 or HB 863) in 1816 that William had the vault built. He may well have taken quick advantage of the space opened up by the extension to the churchyard in 1810 to build his vault. Given the size of the vault, William evidently had ambitious plans for the future. William and Mary had at least six sons: Samuel (d.1816 age 11 months), Vernon (d.1827 age 3 months), Edmund (d.1848 age 23), Leoline (d.1862 age 37), Thomas (d.1871 age 57) and Leonard (d.1877 age 59), and one daughter, Frances (d.1834 age 10 months). Of these, Vernon (HB 861), Edmond (C 3087), Leoline (C 1972) and Leonard (C 3087) were all buried in the family vault. The two unidentified infant burials in the vault (HB 862 and HB 863) are likely to be Samuel and Frances, and one of the three unidentified adult burials is likely to be Thomas. The relationship to William and Mary of the final identified burial in the vault, Helen Jenkins (C 1975) who died in 1882 aged 72, has not been established. From her age she could either be a daughter, born shortly after their marriage, or the wife of one of their sons.

Of the eight adult burials in the vault, five are accounted for from the coffin plates – Edmund, Mary, Leoline, Leonard and Helen. One of the unidentified adult burials is almost certainly William and another is very probably his son Thomas. Therefore only one adult burial is unaccounted for. The three infant burials are also accounted for, one definitely and the other two very probably.

Even with the incomplete information available to us, it is clear that the Jenkins family vault was used over only two generations, for William and Mary themselves and for their children. It is likely, however, given the major remodelling and reorganisation which took place towards the end of the 19th century (probably after 1882 when Helen was buried in the vault), that the intention was to use the vault for further burials. For whatever reason, it did not happen.

Vault 5: Warden family

In many respects, Vault 5 is the most informative and interesting of the family vaults, and it will be described and discussed in some detail. It was a very well-built, high-status burial structure, measuring 2.78m × 2.90m externally, which survived in an overall excellent state of preservation (Fig. 50, colour). It was abutted by Vault 4 to the east and was the only vault visible on the site prior to excavation. The build of the main structure comprised a triple skin of clamped red bricks laid in header and stretcher courses. A sturdy brick barrel-vaulted roof was sprung from the south and north walls. The interior walls had been whitewashed. The entrance to the chamber was at the west end, where there were clear indications that the central part of the west wall, which was not load bearing, was not part of the original build but had been dismantled and rebuilt – presumably on several occasions – to facilitate the insertion of burials (Fig. 50, colour). Any access through the east end would have been blocked by the construction of Vault 4.

The vault contained the remains of thirteen individuals; ten adults, an adolescent, a child, and one unassigned. These were arranged on four levels within the vault (Fig. 51). The unassigned burial was not removed from the vault for analysis but was preliminarily identified as an adult. The *deposita* survived well enough in five cases to enable these burials to be identified (Table 12).

The burials belong to members of the Warden and Browett families, which documentary research has shown were linked by marriage (Chapter 6). The earliest dated burial in Vault 5, on the lowest level (Level 1), was of Ann Maria Warden, who died in 1842 (the last part of the date was not clear on the *depositum* but is provided by the burial register). The latest dated burial, on the uppermost level (Level 4), was that of Ann Maria Browett, Ann Maria Warden's daughter, who died in 1894. The use of the burial vault thus roughly spans the period from the 1840s to the 1890s and contains the dead of at least two – and very probably three – generations.

A gravestone (ST 16) was found outside the vault, the only occasion during the excavations when a memorial could be associated with some confidence with a burial structure. The stone commemorated Sophia Warden 'second wife of late Joseph', who died in 1860 aged 68, and Edwin Warden, 'son of Joseph and Ann Maria' (Joseph's first wife), who died in 1861 aged 41. This suggests that Sophia and Edwin Warden were also buried in the vault, although this cannot be certain.

There is a strong presumption that Joseph Warden (1787–1856), although not identified from a coffin plate, was buried in the vault too. As is described in detail in Chapter 6, Joseph Warden was a successful iron merchant, who by the later years of his life owned several businesses. His first wife Ann Maria (HB 574, d.1842) and two of his children, George (HB 587, d.1863) and Ann Maria Browett (HB 297, d.1894), were definitely buried in the vault, as was Ann Maria's husband, Alfred Browett (HB 336, d.1869). Sarah Emma Warden (HB 598, d.1866), the wife of one of Joseph's sons, was also in the vault. Furthermore, Joseph's second wife Sophia (d.1860) was probably buried there, as was another of his sons, Edwin (d.1861). Given that so many of his close family were buried in the vault, it would be surprising if Joseph were not buried there also. It is possible that he is to be identified with burial HB 573, a 'middle adult, probably male' lying beside his first wife Ann Maria (HB 574) in the lowest level of the vault. Indeed, it seems likely that it was Joseph who commissioned the building of the family vault.

Burial	Name	Age	Date of death
HB 297	Ann Maria Browett	81	8th April 1894
HB 336	A(lfred) Browett		186?
HB 574	Ann Maria Warden	52	17th February 184?
HB 587	George Warden	33	26th November 1863
HB 598	Sarah Emma Warden	47	14th December 1866

Table 12: Vault 5, burials identified from deposita.

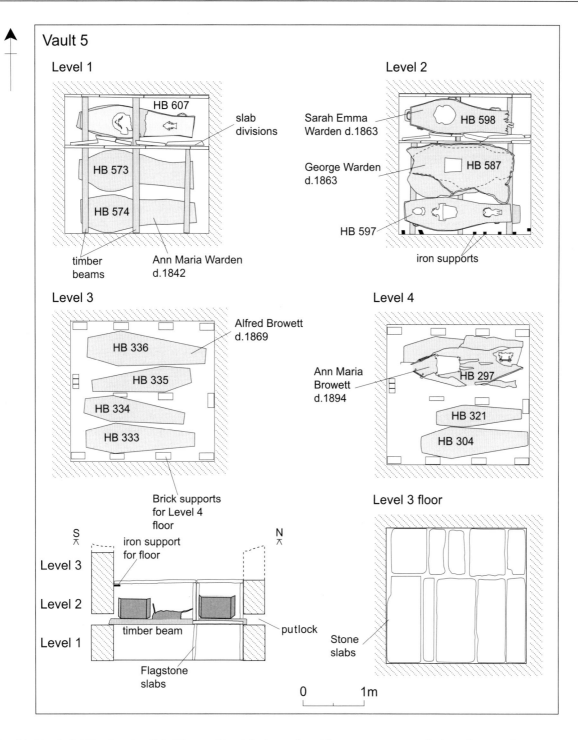

Fig. 51: Vault 5 (Warden family). Plans of burials in vault, with cross-section and plan showing floor construction.

The basic details of the burials in Vault 5 are given in Table 13. Individuals identified from legible *deposita* are shown in bold. The remaining burials have been tentatively identified using the church burial records (which give the name, age and date of death of all the Wardens and Browetts buried at St. Martin's), the sequence of the burials (which seem to progress from the south end of the vault to the north, as well as from the lower levels to the levels above) and the age/sex assigned to the individuals from anthropological analysis of the skeleton. The speculative nature of these identifications must however be emphasised.

The burials within Vault 5 were separated into four levels (Fig. 51). The three coffins in the lowest level (Level 1) had been placed on the floor of the chamber, which was formed of the natural sandstone (Fig. 52). The coffins were orientated east-west, with the head to the west. The northernmost coffin (HB 607) was separated from the other two by a partition of substantial sandstone slabs, two slabs thick, set vertically, which created a separate compartment or *loculus*. A set of similar slabs, but of a single thickness, had been erected against the inner face of the northern wall of the vault, giving the compartment a yet more distinctive appearance. These slabs also served to help support the two levels of coffins above.

The second level of burials (Level 2), also comprising three coffins, was supported on three substantial wooden beams, lodged in putlocks, running north to south (Fig. 53, colour); both sets of vertically-set stone slabs forming the northern compartment of Level 1 helped to support these beams. A second set of vertical slabs (double thickness across the vault and single thickness against the north wall), was erected directly above the slabs below, and was supported by them. This had the effect of continuing the separate compartment at the north end of the chamber through to the second level. These slabs also supported, at the north end of the chamber, the floor of Level 3. Along the south end of the chamber a series of iron floor supports, lodged in the brickwork, served to support the Level 3 floor.

The Level 3 floor was built of large stone slabs laid flat (Fig. 51). Five long slabs, each about 1.35m in length but of varying widths, spanned from the south wall (where they were held up by the iron supports) to the partition wall, where they were supported on the tops of the vertical slabs of the partition. Five shorter slabs spanned the northern compartment, being supported on the tops of the partition slabs and the slabs erected against the north wall. The floor slabs were mortared into place and the whole construction was sufficiently well built that the excavators (entering the vault from above, having carefully demolished the barrel-vaulted roof) did not initially realise that it was a 'false' floor to the vault.

The whole construction that created the lower three levels of the vault (Levels 1, 2 and 3) appeared to be 'of a piece' and planned from the outset. It may be concluded, therefore, that the vault was originally designed to take nine or ten burials: three each on the lower two levels and three or four on the upper level (Level 3), where the absence of a partition afforded a little more space. In the event, four coffins were placed in Level 3, although one

Level 1

Human burial	Age group assigned	Sex assigned	Identified individual	Date of death	Age
HB 574	Middle Adult	Female	**Ann Maria Warden**	**1842**	52
HB 573	Middle Adult	Prob male	Joseph Warden?	1856	68
HB 607	Old Adult	Prob female	Sophia Warden?	1860	68

Level 2

Human burial	Age group assigned	Sex assigned	Identified individual	Date of death	Age
HB 597	*Adult*	*Male*	Edwin Warden?	1861	41
HB 587	Young Adult	Prob male	**George Warden**	**1863**	33
HB 598	Middle Adult	Female	**Sarah Emma Warden**	**1866**	47

Level 3

Human burial	Age group assigned	Sex assigned	Identified individual	Date of death	Age
HB 333	-	-	Mary Elizabeth Warden?	1867	20/1
HB 334	Adolescent	-	Frederick Browett?	1870	16
HB 335	Adult	Female	Ann Maria Browett?	1868	22
HB 336	Middle Adult	Male	**Alfred Browett**	**1869**	58

Level 4

Human burial	Age group assigned	Sex assigned	Identified individual	Date of death	Age
HB 304	Middle Adult	Female	Mary Hannah Warden?	1871	50
HB 321	Child	-	Charles H M Warden?	1895	11
HB 297	Adult	Prob female	**Ann Maria Browett**	**1894**	81

Table 13: Vault 5 burial details. (Burials listed from south to north. Individuals in bold identified from coffin plates; other identifications are tentative. Preliminary on-site assignments of age/sex are given in italics).

Fig. 52: Vault 5 (Warden family). Burials in Level 1, from east. The coffin on the left is that of Ann Maria Warden. In the left hand wall the putlocks to support the Level 2 floor can be seen. On the right the slabs sealing the northern compartment are still in position.

of these (HB 335) was uniquely orientated with the head to the east, possibly because of the shortage of space.

Level 4, the uppermost level of burials, does not seem to have been part of the original design and its floor was a much more jerry-built affair. Stacks of machine-cut red bricks (contrasting with the clamped bricks of the main structure) were erected on the Level 3 floor, a line of four stacks each along the north and south walls and another line approximately across the middle of the floor (Fig. 51). These stacks supported the wooden floor boards of Level 4 (Fig. 54). This floor had not survived well, and it had partially collapsed onto the Level 3 burials below. There had been three burials on this level (Fig. 55).

Particulars of the coffins from Vault 5 and the associated textiles and personal items are provided in Table 14. The information on textiles is a selected summary only; the reader is referred to Walton Rogers' report in Chapter 5 for full details. Further details on the personal items are found in Bevan's report in Chapter 5.

The southernmost burial (HB 574) in the bottom level (Level 1) of the vault has been identified from the shield-shaped coffin plate as that of Ann Maria Warden, who died in 1842 at the age of 52. This is likely to be the earliest burial in the vault. Ann Maria was buried in a fish-tail coffin of composite lead and wood construction (Fig. 52); the excavators recorded traces of a fabric covering. She he appears to have worn a shroud decorated

with satin-covered buttons and ornamental satin ribbons and bows.

Ann Maria was the first wife of Joseph Warden (1787–1856) and provided the couple with twelve children. As suggested above, it seems likely that Joseph, who died 14 years later than Ann Maria, is to be identified with HB 573, in the coffin beside her. His coffin was similar; the undyed wool union coffin lining was arranged in concertina folds and held in place with copper alloy tacks (Fig. 124, Chapter 5).

The third and final burial in Level 1 (HB 607) was in the compartment at the north end of the vault. The fabric covering of the coffin was sampled and analysed and shown to be of black-dyed wool with metal coffin lace attached (Fig. 120, colour, Chapter 5). The 'lid motif' escutcheons, of which there were at least two, were fragmentary but clearly elaborate with an urn motif. The skeleton has been assigned to the category of 'old adult, prob female', and was found with two tortoise shell hair combs, one in position in the remains the hair. This may well be Sophia Warden, Joseph's second wife, who married him in her fifties and died four years after him in 1860, aged 68. Thus the burials in Level 1 would have been placed in the vault in sequence, from south to north, with Joseph Warden flanked by his first and second wives.

A similar south-to-north sequence of burials seems to

have taken place in Level 2 of the vault, with the first burial (HB 579) perhaps that of Edwin Warden, one of Joseph and Ann Maria's sons, who died in 1861 aged 41. Edwin was a builder by profession. The coffin, again of composite lead and wood construction, was fabric covered and ornamented with an iron *depositum* and escutcheons, painted black, with urn motifs (Fig. 53, colour, coffin on left).

The next burial to the north was definitely identified from the rectangular brass *depositum* as George Warden, another of Joseph's sons, who died in 1863, two years after Edwin. George was only 33 when he died, apparently of an opium overdose (see Chapter 6); a cranial autopsy was performed (see Chapter 4).

The third and final burial in Level 2 was that of Sarah Emma Warden, who died in 1866 aged 47; she was identified from the inscription on her shield-shaped *depositum* (Fig. 53, colour, coffin on right). All those buried in this level were therefore relatively young. Sarah Emma was the wife of one of Joseph Warden's sons, like his father an iron merchant and also named Joseph.

In Level 3 there was only one identified burial, that of Alfred Browett (HB 336), who died in 1869 at the age of 58. Alfred Browett, a tallow chandler, was the husband of Joseph and Ann Maria Warden's first daughter, whom they also named Ann Maria (see Chapter 6). Ann Maria Browett (HB 297) outlived her husband by 25 years, dying in 1894, and was also buried in the vault, in the level above (Level 4).

Three of the four burials in Level 3 and two of the three burials in Level 4 could not be identified from the

Fig. 54: Vault 5 (Warden family). The wooden floor boards of Level 4, from west.

Fig. 55: Vault 5 (Warden family). Burials in Level 4, from west. The collapsed coffin of Ann Maria Browett is on the left.

Level 1

Human burial	Coffin construction	Coffin shape	Wood type	Textiles	Personal items/(notes)
HB 574 Middle adult female	Lead/wood, fabric covering, shield-shaped coffin plate.	Fish-tail	-	Decorated silk edging. Silk satin covered-buttons and ornamental satin ribbons.	(Ann Maria Warden d.1842)
HB 573 Middle adult prob male	Lead/wood	Fish-tail	-	Undyed wool union coffin lining, with concertina folds and copper alloy tacks.	(Joseph Warden? d.1856)
HB 607 Old adult prob female	Lead/wood, black-painted plate with urn motif. Urn motif on grips and escutcheon.	Fish-tail	Elm	Black dyed wool coffin cover with metal coffin lace.	Two tortoise shell hair combs. (Sophia Warden? d.1860)

Level 2

Human burial	Coffin construction	Coffin shape	Wood type	Textiles	Personal items/(notes)
HB 597 *Adult male*	Lead/wood, black-painted rectangular coffin plate with urn motif. Urn motif on grips and escutcheon.	Fish-tail	-	Fabric covering with coffin lace. Frag of undyed wool union.	(Left *in situ*; Edwin Warden? d.1861)
HB 587 Young adult prob male	Lead/wood, fabric covering, rectangular brass coffin plate.	Fish-tail?	Elm	Undyed wool union from ?winding sheet, finished with silk ribbon.	(George Warden d.1863)
HB 598 Middle adult female	Lead/wood, Shield-shaped coffin plate.	Fish-tail	Elm	Wool tabby 'coffin fabric'; wool hair net.	Prob hair pin (Sarah Emma Warden d.1866)

Level 3

Human burial	Coffin construction	Coffin shape	Wood type	Textiles	Personal items/(notes)
HB 333 Not analysed	Lead/wood, fabric covered.	Single-break	-	-	(Left *in situ*; cherry leaves associated)
HB 334 Adolescent	Lead/wood, fabric covered, coffin lace, black-painted iron coffin plate. Grips and escutcheon with urn motif.	Single-break	-	Four copper alloy clothing/shroud hooks.	-
HB 335 Adult female	Lead/wood, black-painted casket-shaped iron coffin plate.	Single-break	-	-	-
HB 336 Middle adult male	Lead/wood	Single-break	-	Threads, possibly from wool union.	(Alfred Browett d.1869)

Level 4

Human burial	Coffin construction	Coffin shape	Wood type	Textiles	Personal items/(notes)
HB 304 Middle adult female	Lead/wood, covered with 'dark velvet-like material', grip plates of 'goblet/ chalice design', plain grips	Single-break	-	Frags undyed wool union; large fragment of felted garment, undyed wool tabby; satin silk ribbon.	Tortoise shell hair comb. (Juniper leaves)
HB 321 Child	Lead/wood, grip plates of 'goblet/ chalice design' – identical to HB 304.	Single-break	-	Frag of mattress cover, thick wool tabby with small rosettes; wool tabby sleeve ornaments; ribbon bows from ?bonnet; silk-covered buttons	-
HB 297 Adult prob female	Lead/wood, painted white. Rectangular brass coffin plate and grip plates with fleurs-de-lys on corners	?	Elm	Dyed black silk from garment; ribbons from ?cap; frags undyed wool tabby	Wedding ring; false teeth (Ann Maria Browett d.1894)

Table 14: Vault 5 coffin details. (Preliminary on-site assignments of age/sex are given in italics.)

coffin plates, which were too damaged and corroded. These five unidentified burials should belong to the period after 1866 (the date of the final burial in Level 2). Seven members of the Warden and Browett families are listed in the St. Martin's burial records for this period. The details are given in Table 15.

As has been noted, two of these people – Ann Maria Browett (d.1894) and Alfred Browett (d.1869), her husband – have been identified in the vault from coffin plates, so the remaining five people should correspond to the five unidentified burials in Levels 3 and 4. Given the organisation of the vault the possibilities are fairly limited, and tentative identifications are shown in both Table 13 and Table 15.

Two of those listed were children of Alfred and Ann Maria Browett who died young – their daughter, another Ann Maria, who died in 1868 aged 22 and their son Frederick, who died in 1870 aged 16. Both were still living with their parents at their home in Yew Tree Road, Edgbaston. The others are all Wardens, from a different branch of the family.

In terms of the preservation of textiles in the coffins, some of the fullest evidence came from HB 321, a child burial in Level 4, which if correctly identified as Charles Herbert Mostyn Warden dates to 1895, and was the last burial in the vault. Here were found fragments of wool tabby ornamented with ribbon bows, presumably from a shroud, ribbon bows perhaps from a bonnet, fragments of a mattress cover in a thick wool tabby ornamented with small rosettes, probable wool and silk sleeve ornaments, and a silk covered button rosette (Walton Rogers, this volume, Chapter 5, Figs 125, 128, colour, & 129, colour). It is easy to imagine the child being tucked up in the coffin as if in bed.

Although all of the coffins from Vault 5 were of composite wood and lead construction (and where wood samples were taken it was all identified as elm), a general progression can be discerned in their development. Those from Levels 1 and 2, dating to the 1840s–60s, have a

fish-tail shape, while those from Levels 3 and 4, dating from the late 1860s to the 1890s are of the simpler 'single-break' type. This issue is discussed further by Hancox in Chapter 5.

The burial of Ann Maria Browett (HB 297), who died in 1894 aged 81, deserves special mention. Her life is explored in particular detail in Chapter 6. She was buried in an unusual coffin of lead and elm, painted white and fitted with a brass coffin plate and grips with fleurs-de-lys corners (Fig. 56; Fig. 115, Chapter 5). Within the coffin, fragments of black-dyed silk trimmings seem to be from a dress worn in life, which was perhaps a little out of fashion when Ann Maria was buried in it (Walton Rogers, this volume, Chapter 5). Silk ribbons, found in association with short lengths of light brown/grey curls of hair suggest she wore a bonnet. She was wearing her wedding ring, a simple gold band with a Birmingham hallmark. She was also fitted with dentures. These were made of Vulcanite, a derivative of rubber, and the teeth themselves were made of porcelain, with a gold coil spring linking the upper and lower sets (Hancocks, this volume, Chapter 4).

Vault 5 is likely to have been built between 1812, the year of Joseph Warden's marriage, and 1842, the date of what was probably the first burial in the vault, that of Joseph's first wife Ann Maria. Perhaps it was built towards the earlier part of this range, as it was simply a matter of good fortune that none of Joseph's children appear to have died before reaching adulthood.

Vault 30: Haines family

Vault 30 was situated in the southwest corner of the churchyard, close to the west front and entrance to the church (Fig. 35). Compared to the vaults to the north of the church (traditionally the least favoured part of the churchyard, in the shadow of the church), this may perhaps be considered a privileged location. Vault 30 was abutted to the south by two brick-lined graves (V35 and V36) superimposed one above the other.

Human burial	Name	Abode	Date of death	Year	Age
HB 333 or HB 335?	Mary Elizabeth Warden	Charlotte Road, Edgbaston	17 August	1867	20 or 21
HB 333 or HB 335?	Ann Maria Browett	Yew Tree Road	5 February	1868	22
HB 336	**Alfred Browett**	Yew Tree Road	22 March	**1869**	58
HB 334	Frederick Bright Browett	Yew Tree Road	20 September	1870	16
HB 304?	Mary Hannah Warden	Balsall Heath Road	18 January	1871	50
HB 297	**Ann Maria Browett**	Edgbaston	13 April	**1894**	81
HB 321?	Charles Herbert Mostyn Browett	Edgbaston	25 October	1895	11

Table 15: Members of the Warden and Browett families buried at St. Martin's from 1867. (Information mainly from church burial records; burials identified from coffin plates in bold.)

Fig. 56: Vault 5 (Warden family). Detail of the collapsed coffin of Ann Maria Browett, from north.

Fig. 57: Vault 30 (Haines family). Brick foundation, probably for a chest tomb, surmounting the barrel roof of the vault.

The vault, measuring 2.70m × 2.80m externally, was very well built and survived in an excellent condition. The gently-sloping vaulted roof was surmounted by a rectangle of brick work, which was probably the foundation for a chest-tomb monument (Fig. 57). Photographs of Second World War bomb damage to the church show a chest tomb in this position, surrounded by iron railings. This was clearly a high-status structure.

The interior of the vault had been whitewashed. Both the east and west wall of the vault had evidence of bricked-up openings, suggesting that burials were inserted from both sides.

Level 1

Human burial	Age group assigned	Sex assigned	Identified individual	Date of death	Age
HB 831	Infant	-	James Haines or Alfred Haines	1831 1839	9 months 11 months
HB 830	Infant	-	William Haines	1831	2 yrs 5 mths
HB 840	Old adult	Male	**William Haines**	**1851**	54 years
HB 829	Young adult	Male	**Frank Haines**	**1860**	19 years
HB 841	Old adult	Prob female	**Jane Lloyd Haines**	**1864**	64 years

Level 2

Human burial	Age group assigned	Sex assigned	Identified individual	Date of death	Age
HB 794	Middle adult	Male	**William Tertius Haines**	**1869**	37 years
HB 792	Middle adult	Prob male	**Campbell Lloyd Haines**	**1878**	42 years
HB 793	Old adult	Prob female	**Eliza Haines**	**1904**	60 years

Table 16: Vault 30 burial details (names in bold indicate individuals identified from coffin plates).

Name	Age	Date of birth	Date of death
James Haines	9 months	13th July 1830	25th April 1831
William Haines	2 yrs 5 months	10th November 1828	8th July 1831
Alfred Haines	11 months	30th October 1838	1st September 1839

Table 17: Vault 30, individuals recorded as buried in the vault according to the vault record book but not identified by coffin plates.

Vault 30 contained the remains of six adults and two infants (Table 16). All the adults could be identified from surviving coffin plates. Five of the six adults comprise William Haines (d.1851), his wife Jane Lloyd Haines (d.1864), and three of their sons who died in relative youth – Frank (d.1860, age 19), William Tertius (d.1869 age 37) and Campbell Lloyd (d.1878 age 42). The sixth adult, Eliza Haines (d.1904 age 60), is a more distant relative, connected to the family by marriage (Chapter 6).

The St. Martin's vault record book provides an independent listing of those buried in the vault (see Chapter 6). From this it emerges that three further children of William and Jane Haines were apparently buried in the vault, all of whom died in infancy. The relevant details are shown in Table 17.

Strangely, only two infant burials were discovered in the vault, one of an infant (HB 830) around William's age and one of an infant (HB 831) around the age of James or Alfred. For reasons that cannot satisfactorily be explained, one of these younger infants was missing.

Nevertheless, it is clear that the vault was built for William Haines (senior) and his immediate family. William was a 'Gentleman and Solicitor' and Clerk to the Street Commissioners, a successful and wealthy man, whose career is explored in some detail in Chapter 6.

The burials in the vault were arranged on two levels (Fig. 58). The earliest burials, in the 1830s, must have been of the children who predeceased William (HB 830 and HB 831). They were placed on the floor of the vault (Level 1) in good quality lead coffins of fish-tail shape (Table 18; Fig. 59). The next burial, in 1851, was of William Haines himself (HB 840). He was placed in a coffin, next to the north wall of the vault, which was distinguished by having two coffin plates or *deposita* bearing his personal details, one fixed to the outer wooden case of the coffin and a second, a simple lead rectangle, fixed to the inner lead shell (Fig. 60, colour). A similar arrangement was noted with the coffin of Isaac Ainsworth from Vault 23 (above).

William was followed into the vault by his son Frank (HB 829), who died in 1860 at the age of 19. DNA analysis suggests that he suffered from tuberculosis (see Chapter 4), which may well have been the cause of his early death. Unusually, his coffin was orientated with his head to the east (Fig. 59). The coffin may have been put in the 'right way round' initially but was perhaps moved when space was needed to add the coffin of his mother, who died a little over three years later in 1864.

Jane Lloyd Haines (HB 841) was buried in an elaborate coffin next to her husband. The outer wooden case was fabric-covered and the lid was ornamented with four

Level 1

Human burial	Coffin construction/ textiles	Wood type	Personal items/(notes)
HB 831 Infant	Lead/wood, fish-tail, two small handles.	Elm	(James d.1831 or Alfred d.1839)
HB 830 Infant	Lead/wood, fish-tail, remains of fabric lining.	-	(William d.1831)
HB 840 Old adult male	Lead/wood, fish-tail, inner (rectangular) and ornate outer coffin plates, traces of fabric covering, fabric lining and remains of ?shroud.	Elm	(William d.1851)
HB 829 Young adult male	Lead/wood, fish-tail, rectangular lead coffin plate, lozenge pattern on lead shell, remains of fabric lining.	Elm	(Frank d.1860)
HB 841 Old adult prob female	Lead/wood, ?fish-tail, shield-shaped coffin plate, good survival of fabric covering and decorative brass studding. Silk satin ribbon with looped edges inside.	Elm	(Jane Lloyd d.1864)

Level 2

Human burial	Coffin construction/textiles	Wood type	Personal items/(notes)
HB 794 Middle adult male	Lead/wood, slight fish-tail, shield-shaped *depositum*, other decorative escutcheons, some fabric remains inside. Bone button from ?shroud on chest.	Elm and oak	(William Tertius d.1869)
HB 792 Middle adult prob male	Lead/wood, slight fish-tail, shield-shaped *depositum*, fleurs-de-lys and urn-motif escutcheons, ?plaster lining, large amounts of fabric inside. Darned woollen stockings on legs.	-	(Campbell Lloyd d.1878)
HB 793 Old adult prob female	Lead/wood, single-break, shield-shaped coffin plate, traces of two wreaths on coffin, fabric remains throughout interior.	-	Plain gold wedding ring (Eliza d.1904)

Table 18: Vault 30 coffin details.

panels picked out with brass studs (Fig. 60, colour). In the centre of one of the panels, over the chest, was a shield-shaped *depositum*. It seems that shield-shaped *deposita* were a family tradition (or perhaps a speciality of the family's undertakers) because all the other coffins in the vault where the shape of the outer plate was recorded bore a *depositum* of closely similar design. This contrasts with the Warden/Browett vault where a variety of designs were used, apparently randomly. Fragments of silk satin ribbon were recovered from within the coffin.

The remaining three burials were placed on the upper level within the vault (Level 2). Curiously, given the overall quality of the construction of the vault, the supports for the upper floor were a rather *ad hoc* affair. These comprised mortared stacks of bricks built in the four corners of the vault, together with a 'cross wall' in the middle which had the effect of separating the coffins of William and Jane Haines from the other burials in the lower level (Fig. 58). This 'cross wall' was in reality two skins of bricks which had been built rather awkwardly around the shape of the coffins. The brick stacks and 'cross wall' supported iron girders on which eight flagstones had been placed to create the floor of the upper level; the floor was not quite level and sloped towards the centre (Fig. 61). This floor was not dissimilar to the

flagstone floor observed in Vault 5 (see above) and was probably built at around the same time, to judge from the dates of the burials in the two vaults.

The first burial in the upper level was of William Tertius Haines (HB 794), who died in 1869 aged 37. He was followed nine years later by his brother, Campbell Lloyd Haines (HB 792), who died in 1878 aged 42. Both were buried in closely similar lead coffins of a slight fish-tail shape with the characteristic shield-shaped *deposita* on the outer wooden lid (Fig. 58). A peculiarity of Campbell's grave clothes was that he wore heavily darned, multicoloured woollen stockings (see Walton Rogers, this volume, Chapter 5 for full details, Figs. 133 & 134). Like that of their brother Frank, the coffins of William Tertius and Campbell Lloyd, were found in the unusual orientation of having the head end to the east.

The final burial in the vault was of Eliza Haines (HB 793), who died in 1904 aged 60. Unlike the others buried in the vault, she was not a close relative of William Haines (see Chapter 6) and was buried in the vault 26 years after the last of his close family. Her burial is the most recent dated deposition which was uncovered during the excavations, and was one of the last in St. Martin's as a whole, where the final documented funeral took place in 1915. Her coffin differs from all the others in the vault, being of single-break type, with straight sides and

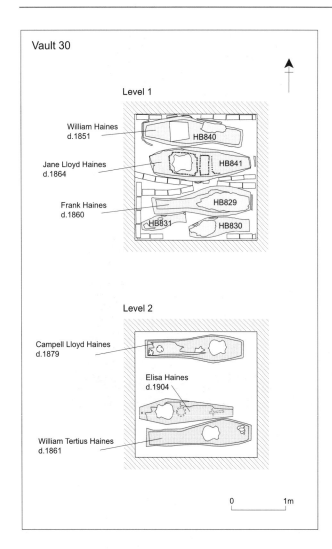

Fig. 58: Vault 30 (Haines family). Plans of burials in vault.

Fig. 59: Vault 30 (Haines family). Burials in Level 1, south end of chamber, from east. The coffin of Frank Haines (right) and the coffins of two infants (left).

lacking any suggestion of a fish-tail. It was nevertheless of composite wood and lead construction and bore the typical shield-shaped *depositum*. A point of note for this burial is that remains of two wreaths were observed on the lid of the coffin, one circular, in the centre, and one cruciform, at the foot (Fig. 58). The survival of these wreaths, even just as a trace, is unique at St. Martin's, and is in part explicable because the burial is comparatively recent. Floral tributes did not make their appearance in English burials until the late 1860s (Litten 1991, 70) and may have taken longer to catch on in Birmingham, so most of the burials at St. Martin's probably took place before the practice started. Plant remains are associated with a few other burials (Ciaraldi, this volume, Chapter 5) but seem to have been placed in the coffin, with either practical or symbolic intent.

Eliza Haines was buried wearing her wedding ring, a plain gold band. Wedding rings were very rarely found during the St. Martin's excavations, with only two other examples being noted. One was with the burial of Ann

Maria Browett (HB 297) in Vault 5 and the other with an unidentified burial (HB 666) in Vault 21. Ann Maria Browett's burial was in 1894, a similarly late date to that of Eliza Haines, and although undated HB 666 was the last burial in Vault 21 and could well also be of a comparatively late date. As many others buried in the churchyard must have worn wedding rings during life, it seems that the practice must have been to remove the ring before burial.

The Haines vault was built in the western extension to the churchyard which was created in 1810 by the purchase of land in Spiceal Street. However, it is likely to have been built between 1826, the year of William Haines' marriage, and 1831, the date of the first (probable) burials in the vault, two of William's sons. At this time William was in his early thirties and already well advanced in a successful career as an 'Attorney and Solicitor' (Chapter 6). The vault continued in use until 1904, or for more than 70 years. Not all of William Haines' children were buried in it. His daughters – Sarah, Emma and Jane –

Fig. 61: Vault 30 (Haines family). Flagstone floor to Level 2 of vault.

were all buried elsewhere, presumably with their husbands, perhaps in another family vault.

The remaining family vaults, which did not contain any identifiable burials, are described below in a more summary manner.

Vault 2

Structure type	Rectangular burial vault
Exterior dimensions	2.0m × 2.6m
Orientation	East-west
Construction	Clamped red brick, limed mortar
Roof type	Vaulted (collapsed)
Flooring	Quarry tiles, clamped red brick (mixed, dry-laid)
Internal divisions	Brick partition
Internal features	Whitewashing, iron straps
Human burials	(HB 132, HB 140, HB 151), HB 121

Table 19: Vault 2 structural summary.
(Note: in this and other structural summary tables the stratigraphic sequence of the burials is represented by the order in which the burial numbers are listed, earliest first. Burials which belong to the same stratigraphic level are bracketed together.)

The mixture of flooring materials may reflect an initial lack of materials or an episode of repair. The double-skin barrelled roof was briefly recorded prior to its collapse during machining. On the north-west corner, Vault 2 cut into V19, an earlier brick-lined grave. On inspection of V19 it was clear that elements of this grave had needed to be rebuilt to repair the damage caused by the initial excavation of the cut to receive Vault 2. In Vault 2 this episode is reflected by an example of 'making good' with mortar spread over some rough brickwork, where the two structures inter-cut. The original entrance to the vault was located at the western end; this had been sealed with a thick slab of slate (Fig. 62).

Two large piles of disarticulated human bone were located in the southwest and northwest corners of the vault. This material had been strategically placed in apparent 'blind spots', when viewed from the entrance opening. These remains may represent a reorganisation of burials within the vault, or alternatively may be the remains of earlier burials that were disturbed by the construction of Vault 2. At a later stage, all of the burials within the vault appear to have been covered or 'blinded' with a layer of clean yellow building sand. This episode may represent an attempt to sanitise the interior of the vault in readiness to receive further burials or, alternatively, an act of closure.

There were four articulated skeletons within Vault 2, all orientated east-west (Table 20). Three of the burials (HB 132, HB 140 and HB 151) lay side-by-side; the fourth (HB 121) lay over HB151. Two of the burials (HB 121 and HB 151) had been separated from the others by a low brick partition.

The associated coffins were constructed of wood with

Fig. 62: Vault 2 from west, showing slate slab used to seal the entrance.

Human burial	Age group	Sex assigned	Coffin type	Textiles
HB 132	Child	-	Wood (oak/elm)	-
HB 140	Middle adult	Male	Wood	-
HB 151	Young adult	Prob male	Wood (oak)	-
HB 121	Young adult	Male	Wood (oak)	Pinked silk ribbon and fragments

Table 20: Vault 2 burial details.

metal fittings. Samples of the wood from the coffins of HB 121, HB 132 and HB 151 were examined and identified as oak, although HB 132 also included elm (Gale, this volume, Chapter 5). The use of oak, a more durable and expensive wood than elm, may have in part been intended to compensate for the lack of a lead shell in the construction of the coffins. A pinked silk satin ribbon and other textile fragments, presumably part of funerary garments, were recovered in association with HB 121 (Walton Rogers, this volume, Chapter 5).

Vault 4

Structure type	Rectangular burial vault
Exterior dimensions	2.1m × 2.65m
Orientation	East-west
Construction	Clamped red brick, cement mortar
Roof type	Vaulted (collapsed)
Flooring	Natural sandstone
Internal features	Whitewashed, putlocks
Human burials	(HB 269, HB 270, HB 268), (HB 266, HB 267)

Table 21: Vault 4 structural summary.

Vault 4 abutted onto Vault 5, the Warden family vault, to the west and was abutted by a brick-lined grave, V03, to the east, the whole forming Vault Group V. Given the layout these three structures, it is probable that they were built in sequence. Vault 5 is the earliest, and was probably constructed in the period 1812–1842, and most likely in the earlier part of that range (see above). The earliest dated burial in the brick-lined grave V03 is of 1862 (see below), so the construction of Vault 4 should be placed somewhere between 1812 and 1862. Given that all the directly datable family vaults were built by the 1840s, it is likely that Vault 4 was built in the earlier part of this range.

Internal features of Vault 4 included a single row of putlocks that had received coffin supports. The remains of a collapsed barrelled roof were found within the vault.

Vault 4 contained five articulated adult skeletons, all orientated east-west (Table 22). The three earlier burials (HB 269, HB 270 and HB 268) lay side by side and were beneath two later burials (HB 266 and HB 267), also lying side by side.

Human burial	Age group	Sex assigned	Coffin type	Textiles/ personal items
HB 269	Adult	Prob female	Wood (pine/exotic)	Fragment of wool tabby
HB 270	Old Adult	Male	Wood	Fragments of wool tabby. Bone hair comb.
HB 268	Adult	-	Wood	-
HB 266	Old Adult	Prob male	Wood	Bone hair combs
HB 267	Old Adult	Prob male	Wood	-

Table 22: Vault 4 burial details.

Although the associated wooden coffins survived in a fragmentary state, analysis of wood samples from the coffin of HB 269 revealed both pine and an exotic wood of probable tropical origin, although it could not be identified further (Gale, this volume, Chapter 5). All five coffins had a *depositum* present but they appeared to be of the stamped variety that tend not to survive well in the vault environment, and all proved to be unreadable. A variety of other coffin furniture was recorded.

Three bone combs or hair slides were recovered, all in a poor state of preservation (Bevan, this volume, Chapter 5). Two simple combs were associated with burials HB 266 and HB 270; a more elaborate decorative bone comb (SF 53) was also associated with HB 266. Skeletal analysis suggested that both these skeletons were male; the presence of the combs must cast doubt on this identification.

All the burials within Vault 4 were overlain by a silty-sandy fill that contained gravestone fragments, coffin material, a large amount of disarticulated human bone, and the remains of two hobnailed leather shoes. This layer probably represents the re-deposition of grave clearance material. The backfilling episode appears to have contributed to the poor preservation of the remains in Vault 4. The added weight and damp nature of the backfill had compounded the problem.

Vault 21

Structure type	Rectangular composite burial vault
Exterior dimensions	2.50m × 2.86m
Orientation	East-west
Associated structures	V11, V12, V20, V24 (Vault Group IV)
Construction	Clamped red brick, limed mortar
Roof type	Vaulted
Flooring	Natural sandstone
Internal divisions	Brick partition
Internal features	Brick coffin supports; graves cut into natural sandstone
Human burials	Rock-cut graves: (HB 734, HB 721), HB 714 Vault chamber: (HB 707, HB 667), HB 666

Table 23: Vault 21 structural summary.

This vault was a curious construction, built hard up against the medieval foundations of the west tower of the church (Fig. 35). It incorporated within it, at its south end, closest to the church, two graves which had been cut into the natural sandstone (Fig. 63). One of these graves contained the remains of an infant (HB 734), while the other contained the remains of two adults superimposed one upon the another. The lower burial (HB 721) was of a middle adult woman, while the upper burial (HB 714) was of an old man (Table 24). In all three cases the wooden coffins were very degraded, although two handles and a coffin plate were recovered from the coffin for HB 714.

The brick-built vault was definitely built later than the rock-cut graves as the base of its eastern wall incorporated an arch which spanned over the soft backfill of the rock-cut grave containing the two adults (the feet of these burials protruded beyond the line of the wall).

The construction Vault 21 appears to have proceeded in the following manner. The cut for the vault was excavated through the graveyard soil down to the bedrock and a flat floor was excavated into the natural sandstone in the northern two-thirds of the vault. In the southern third of the vault the 'floor' comprised the fill of the rock-cut graves. The west and north walls of the vault were built in the normal manner. The eastern wall, as has been noted, incorporated an arch at its base spanning over the adult rock-cut burials. The arch would have served both to protect the burials from damage and to provide structural stability over the soft backfill of the grave – it is not clear which was the primary motivation. The south wall of the vault was so close to the medieval foundations of the church that these encroached into the vault interior and had to be incorporated into the build. However, these foundations were clad in brickwork to give the appearance of a continuous panel.

The vault roof was sprung from the north and south walls in the normal manner. The entrance had been at the west end of the vault, where the wall showed evidence of having been dismantled and then bricked up again, presumably to admit new burials (Fig. 64). At one stage an opening had also been knocked through part of the eastern wall and then bricked up again from the outside.

Within the vault a brick partition wall ran east to

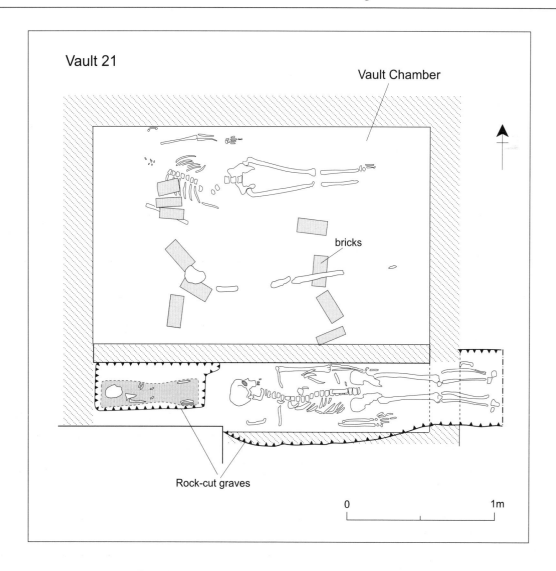

Vault 21

Vault Chamber

bricks

Rock-cut graves

0   1m

Fig. 63: Vault 21. Plan of vault chamber and associated rock-cut graves.

west, separating the main chamber, to its north, from the rock-cut graves, to its south. Three adult burials were found within the main chamber (Table 24). The coffin of what appeared to be the earliest of these, HB 707, was placed on the floor of the chamber against the north wall of the vault. The wooden coffin was in a very degraded state – mainly a stain – although a large amount of tacks were noted from around the skeleton, which may have fixed a coffin covering or lining. Next to this burial was a second, HB 667. The coffin was likewise very degraded but had been supported on brick coffin supports.

These two coffins would have filled the floor space of the main chamber. The third and final burial (HB 666) was placed above HB 707 against the northern wall of the vault. The wooden coffin, which survived only in a fragmentary state, was raised on brick coffin supports which seem to have been placed directly on the coffin below – the whole had collapsed when the coffins had

rotted. Associated with this burial, a probable male, was a plain gold wedding ring.

The curious construction of Vault 21, and particularly the incorporation of the rock-cut graves, demands explanation. Possibly those constructing the vault were constrained by a lack of space, and the incorporation of the rock-cut graves and the church foundations could not be avoided. Perhaps this was the case, but the care taken not to disturb the graves and to incorporate them into the structure seems somewhat unnecessary and unusual. This was a very densely used part of the graveyard, with many earth-cut burials, and it would have been almost impossible not to destroy several graves in the construction of the vault. Generally, not much compunction about this matter seems to have been displayed. A more interesting possibility is that the rock-cut graves were deliberately incorporated so that earlier family members could be included in the vault.

Fig. 64: Vault 21 from the west. The church foundations can be seen on the extreme right.

Burials in rock-cut graves

Human burial	Age group assigned	Sex assigned	Coffin type	Coffin details
HB 734	Infant	-	Wood	Fragmentary
HB 721	Middle adult	Female	Wood	Fragmentary
HB 714	Old adult	Male	Wood	Fragmentary, two handles and coffin plate

Burials in vault chamber

Human burial	Age group assigned	Sex assigned	Coffin type	Coffin details/personal items
HB 707	Middle adult	-	Wood	Very degraded, mainly stain
HB 667	Adult	-	Wood	Degraded, brick supports
HB 666	Adult	Prob male	Wood	Fragmentary, brick supports, wedding ring

Table 24: Vault 21 burial details.

Vault 16

Structure type	Rectangular burial vault
Exterior dimensions	2.65m × 3.45m
Orientation	East-west
Construction	Red brick, limed mortar
Roof type	Vaulted
Flooring	Concrete backfill
Internal divisions	Raised brick plinth
Internal features	Whitewashed
Human burials	None recorded

Table 25: Vault 16 structural summary.

Vault 16 had been backfilled with a layer of concrete at some point. There had been entrances at both the east and west ends of the vault. The bricked-in east-facing entrance appeared to be associated with the concrete backfilling episode, and therefore a later feature. The original entrance had been at the western end of the vault. This opening appeared to have been converted into a large air-vent by an infilling of bricks with large gaps. The chamber was sealed by a well-built barrelled roof. Only a visual inspection of this vault was possible due to the concrete backfill. The interior of the vault had been whitewashed and a raised brickwork plinth was visible to the rear of the vault. Although no human remains were recorded it is possible that a number of individuals lay sealed beneath the concrete backfill. As the vault was to be unaffected by the landscaping programme, no further excavation was carried out.

Vault 34

Structure type	Irregular-shaped burial vault
Exterior dimensions	2.84m × 2.92m
Construction	Machine-cut red brick, cement mortar
Roof type	Vaulted
Human burials	None recorded

Table 26: Vault 34 structural summary.

This vault, which can best be described as L-shaped, was situated against the western side of the church. The irregular design of the structure may be due to it being built around one of the buttresses of the church. This would suggest a construction date after the 1872 rebuild of the church, or alternatively an earlier vault may have been partially rebuilt to accommodate the foundations of the church. As the vault was severely truncated by live services the relationships were not clear. No detailed work was carried out as Vault 34 was to be preserved *in situ*.

Discussion: dating and use of the family vaults

Introduction

Five of the extramural family vaults at St. Martin's produced enough evidence, in terms of legible coffin plates, to identify the families to which they belonged. These vaults were:

    Vault 5 – the Warden family (13 burials)
    Vault 9 – the Jenkins family (11 burials)
    Vault 18 – the Home family (4 burials)
    Vault 23 – the Ainsworth family (9 burials)
    Vault 30 – the Haines family (8 burials)

Between them these vaults produced evidence of 45 burials. A further five probable family vaults were uncovered during the excavations (Vaults 2, 4, 16, 21 and 34). Vaults 16 and 34, which were not going to be affected by the landscaping works, were not investigated beyond summary recording of their fabric. The other three vaults contained a total 12 burials (or 15 if one includes the three burials from rock-cut graves which were incorporated into Vault 21). The large chambered vault (Vault 10), which contained 20 burials, was earlier than the family vaults as a group and is excluded from this discussion.

Thus those family vaults which could be assigned to a particular family represented a half of the whole and the majority of the recorded burials, so it is reasonable to assume that they are representative, although each had its own peculiarities.

When discussing the burials from these vaults, however, certain distinctions must be borne in mind. Although 45 burials were identified in these vaults, for various reasons (usually to do with the preservation of the remains) only just over half of the skeletons (24) were fully analysed scientifically. Furthermore, less than half of the burials (21) were associated with legible *deposita*. These two subsets of burials overlap but do not coincide; there were burials that were identified from *deposita* which were not analysed and there were burials which were analysed for which no identifying coffin plate was preserved. In the event, only 15 of the burials in the family vaults directly identified from *deposita* were fully analysed.

However, documentary research on the families buried in the vaults (Chapter 6), most importantly the evidence from the parish burial register listing those who were buried at St. Martin's, was used to supplement the direct evidence from *deposita* to suggest who the other burials in the family vaults – those not directly identified – might be. A first guiding principle in this analysis was that if a family member was listed as being buried at St. Martin's during the period in which a family vault was known to be in use (information provided by the *deposita*) then there was a strong possibility that this individual was buried in the appropriate family vault. For each individual, the sequence of burials in the vault, established archaeologically, often narrowed down the possibilities considerably, while (where this information was available) the age group and sex assigned to the skeletons further narrowed down the possibilities. In many cases it could be suggested, with a good degree of confidence, which burial was likely to be that of an individual identified from documentary sources as having died and been buried at the appropriate time.

The arguments are sometimes fairly complex, and were given on a vault-by-vault basis above. However, the outcome of the analysis is that it has proved possible in each case to determine who the vault 'founder' was, when the vault was likely to have been built, which type of family members were buried in the vault (wives, sons, grandchildren, in-laws, etc.), and the period over which a vault was used. When these results are taken together various interesting patterns emerge, which shed light on the phenomenon of the 'family vaults' as a whole.

Who founded the vaults?

In each case somebody – called here the 'vault founder' – must have decided to have the vault built, arranged permission, and organised and financed its construction (or, conceivably, decided to buy a vault that had been built speculatively). Who was he? The social realities of the period, the early 19th century, suggested that in all probability the vault founder was a man, although the decision to build a family vault may well have been something that a husband and wife decided together.

During the documentary research on the individuals known or suspected to have been buried in the vaults, the name of the probable 'founder' of each vault usually became quickly apparent. However, a more systematic analysis of the relationships between those buried in the vaults confirmed this impression (Table 27)

From Table 27 it will be apparent that the founder's wife (or in one case wives) was always buried in the vault and that his children (mainly sons) predominated amongst the burials in the vaults. So the names of the 'vault founders' have been firmly established. The one possible exception is Vault 23, where the documentary evidence suggests that two of the brothers of the presumed founder, Isaac Ainsworth, were also buried in the vault, and its purchase may have been a joint venture. Nevertheless, from the point of view of the family relationships (and also the organisation of the burials in the vault), Isaac emerges as the central figure.

When were the vaults used and built?

There are various strands of evidence which contribute to the dating of the family vaults at St. Martin's. The two most important and reliable are the dates of the burials provided by *deposita* and inference from burial records, and the location of the vault (i.e. whether it was located within the 1810 extension or not).

It is assumed that a vault must have been built by the date of the earliest burial within it. This is not an absolutely watertight assumption, however, as it is possible that burials were exhumed from elsewhere (for example from a brick-lined grave) to be put in the family vault when it was built. The date of such a burial would then give a misleadingly early date for the building of the vault. Nevertheless, it is reasonable to assume that in most if not all cases the date of the earliest burial in a vault provides a sound *terminus ante quem* for the

construction of the vault, and there were no examples of this assumption being contradicted by other sources of evidence.

In four out of the five family vaults at St. Martin's which have been analysed, there are two possible dates for the 'earliest burial' which may be used. The first is the date of the earliest burial definitely attested by a surviving legible *depositum*. The second is the date of the earliest burial which is attested from documentary sources and which is likely to be identified with one of the burials in the vault for which a legible *depositum* was lacking. The strength of this argument is variable (see the individual vault descriptions above) but on the whole the inferences are considered to be reliable.

Using this principle, and the corresponding principle for the date of the last burial in each vault, the 'use range' of each vault can be established. The data are shown in Table 28.

From this it can be seen that the use of the family vaults spans the period from 1811 to 1904, a period of a little over 90 years. The individual vaults were in use for shorter periods, from as little at 17 years to as much as 73 years. This difference is probably mainly explained by family fortunes – five of John Home's children (perhaps all of them, although this cannot be certain) died before the age of 12 years, while many of William Haines' sons lived on into middle adulthood. It can also be seen that, in terms of the period of use of the vaults, two slightly overlapping groups emerge, one essentially pre-Victorian (before 1837) and the other essentially Victorian (1837–1901). The Ainsworth (Vault 23) and Home (Vault 18) vaults were used in the period from 1811 to 1846, while

Vault	Probable founder	Wife	Son	Daughter	Brother	Son-in-law	Sister-in-law	Grand-child	Un-known	Total
Vault 5	J. Warden	2	2	2		1		2	3	13
Vault 9	W. Jenkins	1	6	1					2	11
Vault 18	J. Home	1		2						4
Vault 23	I. Ainsworth	1	2		2		1	2		9
Vault 30	W. Haines	1	4	1					1	8
Totals	**5 'founders'**	**6**	**14**	**6**	**2**	**1**	**1**	**4**	**6**	**45**

Table 27: Relationships of those in family vaults to the probable founder (includes all probable and possible identifications; the total includes the founder).

Vault	Family	Date of first burial (probable)	Date of first burial (definite)	Date of last burial (probable)	Date of last burial (definite)	Use range (probable)	Duration
Vault 23	Ainsworth	1811	1827	1846	1837	1811–1846	35 years
Vault 18	Home	1816	1828	-	1833	1816–1833	17 years
Vault 9	Jenkins	1816	1827	-	1882	1816–1882	66 years
Vault 5	Warden	-	1842	1895	1894	1842–1895	53 years
Vault 30	Haines	1831	1851	-	1904	1831–1904	73 years

Table 28: Use range of family vaults.

the Haines (Vault 30) and Warden (Vault 5) vaults were used in the period 1831 to 1904. The use of the Jenkins vault (Vault 9), however, straddles the two periods. Again this would appear to be largely a matter of family fortunes: Joseph Warden was fortunate, unlike William Jenkins, that none of his children appear to have died in infancy or childhood, but if they had then the 'use range' of the Warden family vault would look rather similar to that of the Jenkins family vault.

Another way of looking at the use range of the family vaults is to examine the frequency of burials through the decades in which they were used. These data are presented in Table 29.

From Table 29 it can be seen that there are two apparent peaks in the frequency of burials in the family vaults. The first is in the period 1811 to 1840. This is shortly after the vaults were probably built (see below) and is accounted for very largely by deaths in infancy or childhood of the founders' children. The second peak is in the decade 1861–70, which is the time that many of the founders' children were dying in middle adulthood. From the 1880s onwards the numbers buried in the vaults declined significantly.

Examining the use range of the vaults does not establish when they were built, other than that they were

presumably built before the date of the first burial in them. However, it is reasonable to suppose that a man would not set about founding a family vault prior to getting married, so the date of the marriage of the vault founder may be used as one means to establish the earliest likely date for the construction of each vault. This information is shown in Table 30.

A number of interesting inferences may be drawn from Table 30. One is that, for four of the five vaults, the date of construction can be pinned down to within a decade. A second is that for three of vaults the decade in question is 1810–1820, and that all three were built in the northern extension to the churchyard. The Warden vault could be later and the Haines vault almost certainly is so; both were built in other parts of the churchyard.

Taking account of the date of the Haines vault, and of the likelihood that the fact that the Warden vault was not used for burial until 1842 was simply a matter of good luck (none of Joseph Warden's children appear to have died in childhood), a date range of 1810 to 1830 can be proposed for the construction of the family vaults at St. Martin's.

An historical context for this may be suggested. Firstly, following the demolition of the houses and shops that had surrounded the churchyard in the 18th century and

Decade	Infant	Child	Adolescent	Young adult	Middle adult	Old adult	Total
1811–20	2	3		1			6
1821–30	1			1		2	4
1831–40	4					3	7
1841–50				1		2	3
1851–60			1			3	4
1861–70			1	3	4	3	11
1871–80					2	2	4
1881–90						1	1
1891–1900		1				1	2
1901–10						1	1
Totals	**7**	**4**	**2**	**6**	**6**	**18**	**44**

Table 29: The frequency of burials in the family vaults.

Vault	Name of probable founder	Year of marriage of founder	Age of founder when married	Date of first burial	Age of founder at time of first burial	Inferred date range for building of vault
23*	I. Ainsworth	1782	25	1811	54	1810 – 1811
18*	J. Home	before 1804	<26	1816	38	1810 – 1818
9*	W. Jenkins	1809	25	1816	32	1810 – 1816
5	J. Warden	1812	25	1842	55	1812 – 1842
30*	W. Haines	1826	29	1831	34	1826 – 1831

Table 30: Inferred date ranges for construction of family vaults (an asterisk indicates that the vault was built within the 1810 extension to the churchyard).

the consequent extension of the churchyard in 1810, the northern part of the churchyard in particular suddenly became a much more attractive and prestigious place to be buried and establish a family monument. The extent of the transformation of the churchyard and its setting that took place in the years around 1810 has been emphasised in Chapter 2 and need not be repeated here. Secondly, the extension to the churchyard provided a 'one-off' opportunity to build a vault in virgin ground, without disturbing earlier burials. This opportunity may have been seized not only by Isaac Ainsworth (Vault 23), John Home (Vault 18) and William Jenkins (Vault 9), but also by the anonymous builders of Vault 2 and Vault 17 (although in the former case a brick-lined grave had been built earlier and was disturbed by the vault). Thirdly, the period 1810 to 1830 was that in which several men who had made their fortunes as part of Birmingham's central role in the 'Industrial Revolution' may have wanted to build family vaults (and the monuments above them) in the churchyard in order to demonstrate their 'arrival'. Some, like Joseph Warden, were immigrants from relatively humble origins. Most of these men, as members of the same class and church community, are likely to have known each other. Isaac Ainsworth and John Home, the saddler and chemist, were rather older than Joseph Warden and William Jenkins, the iron merchant and brassfounder; both the latter were very wealthy men by the time of their deaths (Chapter 6).

Some construction of vaults, as well as their use, may have continued at St. Martin's as late as the 1870s, although the rebuilding and extension of the church in 1872 involved the destruction of both graves and vaults (Chapter 2). Vault 23 (which was not investigated in detail) was a curious construction built up against one of the buttresses of the western end of the church, and therefore apparently later than 1872 in date. To accommodate its awkward position it was of an irregular L-shape, and it may be speculated whether it was really a 'new build' or whether it was a reconstruction of an older vault necessitated by the rebuilding of the church.

Who was buried in the family vaults?

This question has a short answer – both the direct evidence of the coffin plates and the indirect evidence from documentary research points to them having been used for the families of the vault builders, mainly their wives and children. Burials of a third generation – the grandchildren of the founder – are comparatively rare (see Table 27 above). However, closer examination of the data suggests that there are some interesting patterns in who was, and who was not, buried in the family vaults. The basic data for the five vaults which provide information on this matter are presented in Table 31.

The table includes all the identified individuals in the family vaults, including those directly identified from legible coffin plates (indicated 'Y' in the third column) and those inferred, with greater or lesser confidence, from

documentary sources. The patterns discussed below hold up if only those directly identified from coffin plates are included in the analysis (a much smaller sample of 21), although some patterns are not so marked.

The first point to note is that there is an imbalance between male and female burials, with males predominating and accounting for 59% of the whole. A similar bias was noted in the skeletal analysis of all the adult burials from St. Martin's (earth-cut graves and vaults), with 58% of the adults who could be sexed classified as males (see Chapter 4). The data presented here differ in that juveniles (individuals under the age 20) form part of the analysis and account for a lot of the variation. However, if the juveniles are removed from the calculation there is still a bias towards males, there being 17 adult males (57%) in comparison with 13 adult females (43%). Interestingly, the variation is all accounted for by young and middle adult males, with the numbers of old (over 50) adult males and females being equal (see Table 32).

An analysis of the burial records from St. Martin's for a total period of two and a half years, sampling burials in the early and mid 19th century, has been carried out (see Chapter 4). This revealed that 55% of the adults buried in this period were male. It is interesting that three independent lines of evidence should all point in the same direction, and some of the possible reasons for a general bias towards male burials are explored in Chapter 4. In the case of the family vaults, however, there appears to be some very specific reasons for the bias. It is apparent from Table 31 that much of the variation is accounted for by two of the families, Jenkins (Vault 9) and Haines (Vault 30). This becomes particularly clear if the data relating to these two families are presented separately from the rest (Table 33).

The bias towards males in these two vaults is very striking, with nearly three quarters of the burials being male. When the age groups of the burials are examined, the source of the bias becomes clear. While the number of old adult males and females is the same (4 each), there are no young and middle adult females represented, no female children or adolescents and only one female juvenile (the infant Frances Jenkins who died in 1834 at the age of 11 months). The absence of young and middle adult females may be explained by the fact that many of these will have married and would normally be buried with their husbands elsewhere. We know that William Haines had three daughters – Sarah, Emma and Jane – who were not buried in his vault (see Chapter 6). The near absence of juvenile females is more puzzling. It may simply be the case that these two wealthy families were particularly 'blessed' with sons.

Although a bias towards males is apparent in the family vaults, and particularly in the vaults of the wealthy and influential Jenkins and Haines families, the bias towards adults is still more striking. Table 34 compares the proportions of burials in the various age groups derived from the parish burial register, from the anthro-

V	HB	C	First name	Family Name	M	F	I	C	A	YA	MA	OA	UK	Year
5	574	Y	Ann Maria	Warden		1						1		1842
5	573	N	Joseph	Warden	1							1		1856
5	607	N	Sophia	Warden		1						1		1860
5	597	N	Edwin	Warden	1						1			1861
5	587	Y	George	Warden	1					1				1863
5	598	Y	Sarah Emma	Warden		1					1			1866
5	333	N	Mary Elizabeth	Warden		1					1			1867
5	334	N	Frederick	Browett	1				1					1870
5	335	N	Ann Maria	Browett		1					1			1868
5	336	Y	Alfred	Browett	1							1		1869
5	304	N	Mary Hannah	Warden		1					1			1871
5	321	N	Charles H M	Warden	1			1						1895
5	297	Y	Ann Maria	Browett		1						1		1894
9	-	N	Samuel	Jenkins	1		1							1816
9	861	Y	Vernon	Jenkins	1		1							1827
9	-	N	Frances	Jenkins		1	1							1834
9	-	N	William	Jenkins	1							1		1846
9	-	Y	Edmund	Jenkins	1					1				1848
9	-	Y	Mary	Jenkins		1						1		1861
9	-	Y	Leoline	Jenkins	1						1			1862
9	-	N	Thomas	Jenkins	1							1		1871
9	-	Y	Leonard	Jenkins	1							1		1877
9	-	Y	Helen	Jenkins		1						1		1882
18	552	N	Sophia Frances	Home		1		1						1816
18	901	N	Amelia	Home		1		1						1819
18	575	Y	John	Home	1							1		1828
18	576	Y	Frances	Home		1						1		1833
23	697	N	Isaac	Ainsworth	1			1						1811
23	698	N	Emma	Ainsworth		1	1							1814
23	-	N	John	Ainsworth	1					1				1815
23	-	N	Isaac	Ainsworth	1					1				1821
23	691	Y	Hannah	Ainsworth		1						1		1827
23	702	Y	Isaac	Ainsworth	1							1		1837
23	-	N	Benjamin	Ainsworth	1							1		1833
23	-	N	John M	Ainsworth	1								1	1846
23	-	N	Mary Ann	Ainsworth		1							1	1845
30	-	N	James	Haines	1		1							1831
30	830	N	William	Haines	1		1							1831
30	840	Y	William	Haines	1							1		1851
30	829	Y	Frank	Haines	1				1					1860
30	841	Y	Jane Lloyd	Haines		1						1		1864
30	794	Y	William Tertius	Haines	1						1			1869
30	792	Y	Campbell Lloyd	Haines	1						1			1878
30	793	Y	Eliza	Haines		1						1		1904
			44 People	**Totals**	**26**	**18**	**6**	**4**	**2**	**6**	**6**	**18**	**2**	
				Totals %	59 %	41 %	14 %	9 %	5 %	14 %	14 %	41 %	5 %	

Table 31: Analysis of burials in family vaults.

(V-Vault number, HB-Human Burial number, C-coffin plate [Y-legible coffin plate present, N-not present], M-Male, F-Female, I-Infant, C-Child, A-Adolescent, YA-Young Adult, MA-Middle Adult, OA-Old Adult, UK-Unknown. The age groups are defined in Chapter 4.)

	St. Martin's		Spitalfields	
Male infants	4	**10%**	39	**10%**
Female infants	2	**5%**	29	**8%**
Male children and adolescents	4	**10%**	13	**3%**
Female children and adolescents	2	**5%**	10	**3%**
Young and middle adult males	8	**20%**	46	**12%**
Young and middle adult females	4	**10%**	45	**12%**
Old adult males (more than 50 years)	9	**20%**	101	**26%**
Old adult females	9	**20%**	100	**26%**
Total	42	100%	383	100%

Table 32: Sex and age group of burials in the family vaults, with comparative figures for Christ Church, Spitalfields, London.

All males	13
All females	5
Total	**18**
Male infants	4
Female infants	1
Male children and adolescents	1
Female children and adolescents	0
Young and middle adult males	4
Young and middle adult females	0
Old adult males (more than 50 years)	4
Old adult females	4
Total	**18**

Table 33: Sex and age group of burials in the Jenkins and Haines vaults.

pological analysis of the skeletons (both vaults and earth-cut graves) and from the identified burials in the vaults. The data are derived from Table 92 and Table 93 in Chapter 4, and from Table 31 opposite.

Evidently, infant burials are grossly under represented amongst both the anthropological sample and the identified burials in the vaults. There would appear little doubt that the figures derived from the burial register provide a fair reflection of infant mortality in Birmingham during the earlier part of the 19th century, as is apparent, for example, from a government report of 1842:

> In the parish of Birmingham, in the year registered from July 1, 1838, to June 30, 1839, the total number of deaths of all ages was 3,305; of which number 1,658 were under five years of age. Of this last number, more than one-half died in their first year (Report on the State of the Public Health in the Borough of Birmingham 1842, 207).

Put in percentage terms, the proportion of those dying under the age of five years in 1838–9 was 50%. This differs from the figure derived from the St. Martin's burial register (42%) but we are not quite comparing like with like (under 5 years in the first case, under 4 years in the second) and of course there were fluctuations from year

to year. In broad terms a figure of 40% to 50% may be taken to represent the norm for deaths in infancy for the period as a whole. Clearly, at 15% and 14% respectively, the figures derived from the anthropological analysis and from the identified individuals in the vaults do not accurately reflect the level of infant mortality. Interestingly, the proportion child burials (4–12 years) is the same (10%) for each of the three sources and, compared to the gross mismatch for infant burials, the figures for adolescent burials (13–19 years) are not wildly discrepant (and the absolute numbers are low). It is therefore infants in particular, rather than juveniles in general (those under 20 years), that are under represented. This situation may be seen in microcosm in the Home family vault (Vault 18), where, as has been seen, three infants (two boys and a girl) were apparently not buried in the vault, while two children (both girls) were.

Table 34 also shows comparative figures for the 'named sample' of burials in the crypt at Christ Church, Spitalfields, London (a sample spanning the date range 1729 to 1859). The same age groups are used, with the figures derived from the list of the named sample published in Cox 1996, 119–125. The pattern is broadly similar, with infants again grossly under represented (the London Bills of Mortality show that actual death rates of infants in London did not differ greatly from those in Birmingham). At Spitalfields, the discrepancy was explained by the suggestion that "children were often buried in the most convenient place" (Cox 1996, 20), for example in the parish where the family lived or in the churchyard. If this was so, then at St. Martin's one would expect to find a much higher proportion of infants buried in the earth-cut graves, but this is not the case (the churchyard was not investigated at Christ Church, Spitalfields). Infants are under represented 'across the board', although the phenomenon is slightly more marked in the vaults than in the earth-cut graves (Chapter 4). Two possible explanations may be suggested. First, the remains of infants (many of whom may have been buried simply in a winding sheet, without a coffin) could have been missed by the excavators. While this may explain

Age group	Register	Register	Skeletal analysis	Skeletal analysis	Identified individuals from vaults	Identified individuals from vaults	Spitalfields named sample	Spitalfields named sample
	Number	%	Number	%	Number	%	Number	%
Infant	575	42%	*73	15%	6	14%	*68	18%
Child	135	10%	52	10%	4	10%	12	3%
Adol.	33	2%	19	4%	2	5%	11	3%
Adult	638	46%	352	71%	30	71%	292	76%
Total	1381	100%	496	100%	42	100%	383	100%

*Excluding foetal remains

Table 34: Age at death from three independent sources (parish burial register, skeletal analysis and identified individuals in vaults), with comparative figures from the 'named sample' at Christ Church, Spitalfields.

part of the pattern it is very unlikely to be the whole answer, given the methods of recovery employed at St. Martin's (see Chapter 4). Second, the remains of infants were perhaps buried in a special area of the churchyard – or perhaps in the detached burial ground on Park Street – which was not encompassed by the excavations.

The very marked under representation of infants at St. Martin's is an important finding, with obvious wider implications for the interpretation human remains from cemeteries in general, especially in situations where documented mortality rates do not provide a control.

With particular respect to the interpretation of burials in vaults, it is clear that those buried in the family vaults do not represent the family group in any straightforward sense but are a subset of that group determined largely by social and cultural factors. To summarise what may be concluded from the analysis of the vault burials at St. Martin's:

– Infant burials (birth–3 years) are grossly under represented.
– Child burials more closely reflect overall mortality levels.
– There is an overall bias towards male burials in all age groups except 'old adult'.
– The bias towards males is more marked in some vaults than others.

Greater understanding of these patterns could be obtained if it were known exactly how many children were born into each family and who they all were. Unfortunately, the time and financial limitations on the research undertaken at St. Martin's precluded undertaking the research which would be necessary to attempt to establish this. Thus family members not buried at St. Martin's (and therefore not recorded in the parish burial register) may well have escaped attention. Nevertheless, the patterns are clear enough and, interestingly, some but not all of these patterns are also to be found at Christ Church, Spitalfields, as the comparative figures in Table 32 and Table 34 show.

Vaults had a significance which went beyond a function as simply a 'repository for the dead' but had social and symbolic functions which are further explored in Chapter 8.

Brick-lined graves

Introduction

This was the largest group of burial structures, with 24 examples identified. The essential difference between a brick-lined grave and a family vault is that the former is only wide enough to accommodate a single coffin (or several coffins one above the other). Otherwise, there are many constructional similarities between the two types of burial structure. Although designs vary, the most typical form of brick-lined grave consisted of a rectangular chamber cut through the earth down to the natural sandstone (Fig. 65). The chamber was then lined with courses of bricks that were one or two skins thick, laid in stretcher and header courses and bonded with mortar. The finished examples measured approximately 2.1–2.5m in length, 0.9–1.4m in width, and up to 2.5m in depth. Interior effects include whitewashing of the walls. The interior brickwork features often included built-in putlocks to receive coffin supports and serve as air-vents; alternatively putlocks were sometimes cut out of the existing brickwork. Iron fixtures associated with coffin supports were also identified. Flooring was usually formed by incorporating the natural sandstone into the design. In other cases, courses of dry-laid or mortared bricks laid flat formed the flooring.

The roofing of the brick-lined graves was variable. Ten had a surviving barrel-vaulted roof (Fig. 66), and in a further two cases although the roof had collapsed a former barrel vault was inferred (Table 35). The remainder appear to have been roofed with a single ledger-stone or with several slabs (Fig. 67), although these was usually missing when the graves were excavated and had to be inferred from the construction. It is possible that some of these graves were originally vaulted, but that the vaulted roof was removed to insert later burials and replaced with a ledger-stone. This possibility is discussed further in the section on the dating and use of the brick-lined graves below.

Fig. 65: Typical construction of a brick-lined grave.

Vault No.	Roof type	No. of burials	Identified individuals/notes
1	Gravestones	0	Cleared
3	Vaulted (collapsed)	3	Helen Mary Walker d.1862 John Sansom d.1873
6	Ledger-stone, gravestones	1	-
7	Ledger-stone	2	Very poor quality build
8	Ledger-stone (missing)	4	-
11	Vaulted, slate slabbed	2	Sarah Parker d.?1825. Shouldered, lower and upper chambers. Lead coffin.
12	Vaulted	1	-
13	Ledger-stone (missing)	2	Lead coffin
14	Ledger-stone (missing)	4	Lead coffins × 3
15	Vaulted (collapsed)	2	Lead coffins × 2
17	Slabbed	2	Truncated
19	Vaulted	1	Cut by V02, family vault
20	Vaulted	2	Shouldered, upper and lower chambers
22	Ledger-stone (missing)	3	Orientated north-south
24	?	0	Extremely truncated
25	Ledger-stone (missing)	0	Composite rock-cut and brick-built construction
26	Vaulted, unknown	1	Upper and lower chambers. Lead coffin
27	Ledger-stone (missing)	2	-
28	Ledger-stone (missing)	2	-
31	Vaulted	3	High barrel vault
32	Vaulted	1	High barrel vault
33	Vaulted	2	Elizabeth Robinson d.1831 Benjamin Robinson d.1834 High barrel vault
35	Vaulted	2	Shouldered, upper and lower chambers
36	Vaulted	1	Below V35. Lead coffin

Table 35: Summary of brick-lined graves.

Fig. 66: Brick-lined grave V19 from north, showing barrel-vaulted roof.

Fig. 67: Brick-lined grave V06, showing slab roof.

Although most of the graves were of rectangular shape, there were three examples of shouldered or 'coffin-shaped' graves (Figs. 68 & 69). There were four examples of brick-lined graves that consisted of an upper and lower chamber. In these cases, rather than inserting new burials into the existing chamber, a new chamber was built on top using the vaulted roof (generally fairly flat) of the lower chamber as the floor for the upper chamber (Fig. 73). All three of the shouldered graves were of this dual-chamber type. There was also one grave (V25) which

combined a rock-cut lower part with a brick-built upper part (Figs. 74 & 75). With one exception (V22) the brick-lined graves were orientated east-west.

In three of the graves no burial was found, although one of these (V01) had evidently been cleared out and another (V24) was severely truncated. A total of 43 burials was uncovered in the other graves, varying in number from one to four in each grave. The coffins were usually stacked one above the other, although in many cases they may originally have been separated from each other by timber supports lodged in putlocks; such timber supports had usually rotted. The dual-chamber type of graves had a maximum of one burial per chamber.

The burials were mostly in wooden coffins, although the coffins had usually decomposed badly and the fittings were highly corroded. There were only nine definite examples of burials in composite lead and wood coffins.

Only four individuals were identified from legible coffin plates, and a fifth individual from other documentary evidence. This evidence indicates a minimum use range for the brick-lined graves from 1825 to 1873. However, a variety of other evidence, discussed later, can be used to further investigate the date range of the brick-lined graves.

A brief summary description of each brick-lined grave is provided below, followed by a discussion of the use and date of the graves. The three brick-lined graves which contained burials with legible, or partially legible, *deposita* are described first in chronological order, followed by those for which no such evidence was available.

V11

This grave formed part of a cluster of burial structures (Vault Group IV) located immediately to the north of the west tower of the church. The burial chamber has been identified as a shouldered brick-lined grave. The term 'shouldered' relates to the coffin-like shape of the burial

chamber (Figs. 68 & 69). The structure exhibited two phases of construction, a lower and an upper chamber, both formed of a single skin of clamped red bricks, laid in stretcher courses and bonded with a weak greyish-brown limed mortar. The lower chamber was built to receive a single burial. The natural sandstone formed the floor of the chamber. The chamber was sealed by a narrow barrelled roof, which had settled to a virtually flat level. This roof formed the floor of the upper chamber, again built to receive a single burial, and sealed by three slate slabs mortared into position (Fig. 69). The quality of brickwork in this build was inferior to that of the lower chamber.

This grave contained the remains of two individuals (Table 37). HB 625 was located in the lower chamber and comprised the very poorly preserved remains of an adult or possibly an older adolescent. The associated

Structure type	Shouldered brick-lined grave
Exterior dimensions	0.95m × 2.30m
Associated structures	V12, V20, Vault 21, V24 (Group IV)
Construction	Clamped red brick, limed mortar
Roof type	Vaulted (lower), slate slabbed (upper)
Flooring	Natural sandstone (lower), clamped red brick (upper)
Internal divisions	Lower and upper chambers
Human burials	HB 625, HB 584

Table 36: V11 structural summary. (Note: in this and the other structural summary tables the stratigraphic sequence of the burials is represented by the order in which the burial numbers are listed, earliest first. Burials which belong to the same stratigraphic level are bracketed together.)

Fig. 68: Shouldered brick-lined grave V11 before excavation, from east.

Human burial	Age group	Sex assigned	Coffin type	Coffin details
HB 625	Adult	-	Lead/wood	Fabric covered, oval *depositum* plate, handles
HB 584	Adult	Prob male	Wood	Fragmentary, rectangular *depositum*, six handles

Table 37: V11 burial details.

Fig. 69: Shouldered brick-lined grave V11, showing the upper burial HB 584 with rectangular depositum.

coffin survived as fragments of a fabric-covered lead and wooden coffin, with coffin grips and an oval *depositum*. The *depositum* was badly corroded but elements of the script were readable: '*Sarah Parker...Died November...*'. The National Burial Index lists three Sarah Parkers buried at St. Martin's during November, in 1777, 1790 and 1825 (see Chapter 6). The last of these dates provides a *terminus ante quem* for the construction of the grave.

HB 584 was located in the upper chamber and comprised the remains of a probable adult male (Fig. 69). The associated coffin survived as fragments of wood, coffin grips and a rectangular *depositum*.

V33

Structure type	Rectangular brick-lined grave
Exterior dimensions	1.27m × 2.46m
Associated structures	V31, V32 (Group I)
Construction	Clamped red bricks
Roof type	Vaulted
Flooring	Natural sandstone
Internal features	Putlocks
Human burials	HB 789, HB 779

Table 38: V33 structural summary.

This grave formed part of a cluster of three brick-lined graves (Vault Group I), of similar design, located just outside the southwest corner of the church. The grave butted against grave V32 to the east. The construction of V33 comprised a single skin of clamped red bricks laid in stretcher courses. It was roofed with a high barrel vault. The floor of the burial chamber was formed by the natural sandstone covered with a layer of clean sand.

The burial chamber contained two adult burials, one above the other (Tables 39 and 40). The later burial (HB 779) has been identified from a *depositum* that reads '*Captain Adjutant Benjamin Robinson Died June 5th 1834 Aged 60 Years*' (see Chapter 6). The associated coffin, which survived in a collapsed state, was constructed of wood and fabric and decorated with metal

Burial	Name	Age	Date of death
HB 789	Elizabeth Robinson	55	14th March 1831
HB 779	Capt Adj Benjamin Robinson	60	5th June 1834

Table 40: V33 identified burials.

Human burial	Age group	Sex assigned	Coffin type	Coffin details
HB 789	Adult	-	Wood	Fragmentary wood and metal fittings
HB 779	Adult	Prob male	Wood	Fabric covered with decorative studding, flaming urn lid motif, legible *depositum*

Table 39: V33 burial details.

studs. The coffin bore an elaborate lid motif in the form of a flaming urn (Fig. 114, Chapter 5). The coffin for the earlier burial (HB 789) survived only as fragmentary wood and metal fittings. The earlier burial is very probably that of Captain Robinson's wife Elizabeth, who died three years earlier than her husband, in 1831, aged 55. In his will Captain Robinson instructed that he should be "interred in the same grave with my dear wife" (see Chapter 6).

V03

Structure type	Rectangular brick-lined grave
Exterior dimensions	1.2m × 2.25m
Associated structures	Vault 4, Vault 5 (Group V)
Construction	Clamped red brick, cement mortar
Roof type	Vaulted (collapsed)
Flooring	Natural sandstone
Internal features	Whitewashed, putlocks
Human burials	(HB 185, HB 190), HB 189

Table 41: V03 structural summary.

This burial chamber was situated to the north of the church and formed part of Vault Group V, abutting Vault 4 to the west, which is likely to be earlier. The north and south elevations of the structure were formed with a double skin of bricks, while the east and west elevations were formed by a single skin. Internal features included three rows of four putlocks that had received timber coffin supports, one of which had survived. No *in situ* roof was present at the time of excavation and V03 appeared to have been backfilled at some point. However, evidence from the brickwork suggests that a barrelled roof had sealed the grave (Table 42). Although of a relatively simple design, V03 comprised a high-status solid construction in overall good condition.

There were three burials within this grave (Table 42). The two earlier burials, an infant (HB 185) and a child (HB 190), lay side by side. Lying with the remains of the child was a complete necklace (SF 5) incorporating some 300 pink glass beads attached to a copper alloy pendant inlaid with a cut-glass rose (Fig. 135, colour, Chapter 5). HB 189, an old adult male, overlay the two earlier burials

Fig. 70: Brick-lined grave V03 showing the burial of John Sansom (HB 189) with shield-shaped depositum.

Human burial	Age group	Sex assigned	Coffin type	Coffin details	Personal items
HB 185	Infant	-	Wood	Stain only, legible shield-shaped *depositum*	-
HB 190	Child	-	Wood	-	Beads
HB 189	Old adult	Male	Wood	Legible brass shield-shaped *depositum*; brass handles and fittings.	-

Table 42: V03 burial details.

Burial	Name	Age	Date of death
HB 185	Helen Mary Walker	18 mths	23rd December 1862
HB 189	John Sansom	65	3rd March 1873

Table 43: V03 identified burials (from deposita*).*

(Fig. 70). The adult male (HB 189) has been identified from his shield-shaped coffin plate as John Sansom, a retail brewer who died in 1873 aged 65, and the infant (HB 185) lying beneath him as Helen Mary Walker, his granddaughter, who died in 1862 aged 18 months (Table 43) (see Chapter 6). The child (HB 190) has not been identified, but judging from the beads was presumably a girl and may have been another of John Sansom's granddaughters.

The associated coffins appear to have been of a wooden construction with metal fittings, although they survived only as dark stains in the surrounding fills. The back-filling episode appears to have contributed to the poor preservation of the coffins.

V01

Structure type	Rectangular brick-lined grave
Exterior dimensions	1.22m × 2.24m
Construction	Clamped red brick, limed mortar
Roof type	Slabbed
Flooring	Natural sandstone
Internal features	Whitewashing, pointed
Human burials	None

Table 44: V01 structural summary.

This was a typical example of a brick-lined grave, sealed with inverted gravestones, which were inscribed with a late-17th-century date, although they had evidently been re-used. When uncovered, V01 was situated directly under the stump of a large mature tree that may date from the landscaping episodes of the 1870s. The absence of burials within this burial chamber suggests that V01 was cleared ahead of a tree-planting programme.

V06

Structure type	Rectangular brick-lined grave
Exterior dimensions	1.18m × 2.38m
Construction	Red brick, limed mortar
Roof type	Ledger-stone, slabbed
Flooring	Natural sandstone
Internal features	Whitewashed
Human burials	HB 152

Table 45: V06 structural summary.

Human burial	Age group	Sex assigned	Coffin type
HB 152	Adolescent	-	Wood

Table 46: V06 burial details.

V06 was a fairly well built burial structure. The burial chamber was sealed by a limestone ledger-stone and a smaller upturned gravestone (Fig. 65). The ledger-stone was chamfered and inscribed; unfortunately the inscrip-

tion was unreadable due to weathering.

The brick-lined grave contained a single inhumation of an adolescent (HB 152; Table 46). The associated coffin survived as fragmentary wood and metal fittings, with corroded coffin grips and *depositum*. A layer of light yellow sand covered the burial. As in the case of Vault 2 (above), this may represent an attempt to sanitise the area to receive further burials or, alternatively, may be an act of closure.

V07

Structure type	Rectangular brick-lined grave
Exterior dimensions	0.97m × 2.05m
Construction	Red brick, limed mortar
Roof type	Ledger-stone
Flooring	Natural sandstone
Internal features	Whitewashed, putlocks
Human burials	HB 144, HB 141

Table 47: V07 structural summary.

Human burial	Age group	Sex assigned	Coffin type
HB 144	Child	-	Wood
HB 141	Middle adult	Male	Wood

Table 48: V07 burial details.

V07 was a fairly poorly built, or at least badly planned, burial chamber. The exterior brickwork was not pointed. The south elevation had been particularly poorly constructed; subsequently a double-skin brick buttress had been placed against it (Fig. 71). The buttress appears to have had the opposite effect to that intended, as both the south and north elevations had begun to collapse inwards. The internal features exhibit a similar lack of planning to the exterior. A single row of integral putlocks to receive coffin supports existed on the north and south elevations, but were at different heights and would therefore not have been level. A section of a timber coffin support survived, the species of which has been identified as Scots pine (Gale, this volume, Chapter 5). At the base of the chamber were four blue Victorian gully bricks standing on end; these appear to have been used as makeshift rests for wooden coffin supports. The same type of gully bricks were used around the church to channel water away from the roof down-pipes, and probably date to the church re-build of 1872. The chamber was sealed by a chamfered ledger-stone that had partially collapsed into it. Two vertical joints in the brickwork of the west elevation appeared to indicate the former entrance to the chamber. The general brickwork was of such poor quality that when the heavy ledger-stone was laid down it caused two vertical cracks to form down the east-facing elevation.

Fig. 71: Brick-lined grave V07 from south, showing buttress added to the south wall.

V07 contained the remains of two individuals (HB 144 and HB 141), one above the other (Table 43). The earlier burial (HB 144), of a child, was found in a coffin which survived as fragmentary wood and metal fittings, with coffin grips and nails. The later burial (HB 141) was of a middle adult male, found within the fragmentary remains of a wooden coffin.

V08

Structure type	Rectangular brick-lined grave
Exterior dimensions	1.02m × 2.25m
Construction	Clamped red brick, limed mortar
Roof type	Ledger-stone (missing)
Flooring	Natural sandstone
Internal features	Whitewashed
Human burials	HB 233, HB 226, HB 224, HB 221

Table 49: V08 structural summary.

V08 was a fairly poorly built burial chamber which survived in a correspondingly poor condition. Initially the chamber was constructed of a single skin of clamped red bricks laid in header and stretcher courses and bonded with a weak sand-rich limed mortar. However, the south and north elevations had been poorly constructed, and subsequently two single-skin brick buttresses had been placed against the exterior of each elevation. The burial chamber was probably originally sealed by a ledger-stone,

but was found backfilled with a brown sandy-silt and general building rubble.

V08 contained the remains of four individuals, three adults and a child, stacked one above the other (Table 50). With the exception of the uppermost coffin, which survived in relatively good condition, the wooden coffins were in a fragmentary, partially decomposed state, with associated fragmentary and corroded coffin furniture. Analysis of samples of the coffin wood showed that all the coffins were of elm (Gale, this volume, Chapter 5). With the two lower burials, both of middle adult females, were found the remains of box, a sprig in the case of HB 226 but just leaves in the case of HB 233 (Ciaraldi, this volume, Chapter 5).

Human burial	Age group	Sex assigned	Coffin type	Plant remains
HB 233	Middle adult	Female	Wood (elm)	Box leaves
HB 226	Middle adult	Female	Wood (elm)	Sprig of box
HB 224	Child	-	Wood (elm)	-
HB 221	Old adult	Male	Wood (elm)	-

Table 50: V08 burial details.

V12

Structure type	Rectangular brick-lined grave
Exterior dimensions	1.20m × 2.15m
Associated structures	V11, V20, Vault 21, V24 (Group IV)
Construction	Red bricks; hard grey limed mortar
Roof type	Vaulted
Flooring	Dry-laid bricks
Internal features	Whitewashed
Human burials	HB 703

Table 51: V12 structural summary.

This grave formed part of Vault Group IV and abutted Vault 21 and grave V11. It was built with a double skin of bricks on the north and south elevations, and a single skin on the east and west elevations. All the bricks were laid in irregular header and stretcher courses and bonded with a hard grey limed mortar.

The single burial at the base of the grave (HB 703) lay within the decayed remains of a coffin (Table 52). The grave appeared to have been cleared out at some point, and backfilled with a sandy earth containing fragments of brick, stone and slate.

Human burial	Age group	Sex assigned	Coffin type	Coffin details
HB 703	Adult	Male	Wood	Very decayed, 8 coffin grips, fabric lining

Table 52: V12 burial details.

V13

Structure type	Rectangular brick-lined grave
Exterior dimensions	1.28m × 2.20m
Associated structures	V25, V26 (Group III)
Construction	Clamped red brick, limed mortar
Roof type	Ledger-stone (missing)
Flooring	Natural sandstone
Internal features	Brick coffin supports, sandstone slab
Human burials	HB 449, HB 440

Table 53: V13 structural summary.

Internal features of this brick-lined grave included four stacks of two bricks that served as makeshift rests for wooden coffin supports. At the east end of the chamber was a grey sandstone slab leaning against the brickwork; this may have served as a chute of some description. The chamber was probably originally sealed with a ledger-stone.

V13 contained two burials (HB 449 and HB 440), one above the other (Table 54). The coffin associated with the earliest burial (HB 449) survived as staining and

Human burial	Age group	Sex assigned	Coffin type
HB 449	Old adult	Female	Wood
HB 440	Young adult	Prob female	Lead/wood

Table 54: V13 burial details.

fragmentary wood with corroded coffin grips and iron nails. The coffin associated with the later burial survived as staining and fragmentary wood with some lead lining and iron nails.

V14

Structure type	Rectangular brick-lined grave (truncated)
Exterior dimensions	1.05m × 1.25m (surviving)
Construction	Clamped red brick
Roof type	Ledger-stone (missing)
Flooring	Natural sandstone
Internal features	Whitewashed
Human burials	HB 342, HB 330, HB 312, HB 264

Table 55: V14 structural summary.

V14 comprised a fairly poorly built burial chamber, which had been heavily truncated by modern groundwork.

The chamber contained four adult burials laid one on top of another (Table 56). The coffin for the earliest burial (HB 342) survived as fragmentary wood, which has been identified as elm (Gale, this volume, Chapter 5), with metal fittings. The other three coffins were of composite wood and lead construction. Wood samples from two of these coffins were analysed. The coffin for HB 330 employed oak in the construction and that for HB 312 employed oak, elm and pine for the covering and

Human burial	Age group	Sex assigned	Coffin type	Coffin details
HB 342	Middle adult	Prob female	Wood (elm)	Very fragmentary
HB 330	Adult	-	Lead/ wood (oak)	-
HB 312	Old adult	Female	Lead/ wood (oak, elm and pine)	-
HB 264	Old adult	-	Lead/ wood	Incised lozenge pattern on lead shell, traces of fabric lining

Table 56: V14 burial details.

lining of the lead shell. The lead shells of all three coffins were in a degraded state; the shell of the coffin for the uppermost burial (HB 264) had been decorated with an incised lozenge pattern on its sides.

V15

Structure type	Rectangular brick-lined grave
Exterior dimensions	1.30m × 2.50m
Roof type	Vaulted (collapsed)
Flooring	Natural sandstone
Internal features	Whitewashed
Human burials	HB 255, HB 256

Table 57: V15 structural summary.

Fig. 72: Brick-lined grave V15 showing the two burials (HB 255 and HB 256) in lead/wood coffins.

V15 was a fairly well-built burial chamber in average condition. The chamber had been sealed with a barrelled roof that had collapsed inwards.

This burial chamber contained two individuals (HB 255 and HB 256) both interred in lead coffins (Fig. 72; Table 58). The earlier burial (HB 255) comprised the remains of an adult with good survival of head hair. The associated coffin consisted of a lead shell with the remains of elm wood, fabric lining and a silk ribbon, possibly from a shroud.

The later burial (HB 256) comprised the remains of a well-preserved adult with a good amount of head hair surviving. The associated coffin consisted of a lead shell with the remains of wood and fabric lining. This burial was not removed from the site for analysis.

V17

Structure type	Rectangular brick-lined grave
Exterior dimensions	0.80m × 2.30m
Associated structures	V16, V18 (Group VI)
Construction	Red bricks, limed mortar
Roof type	Slabbed
Flooring	Natural sandstone
Internal features	Whitewashed
Human burials	HB 225, HB 186

Table 59: V17 structural summary.

This brick-lined grave had been truncated. The chamber was sealed with four limestone slabs mortared into place.

The burial chamber contained the remains of two adults buried one above the other (Table 60). The associated coffins survived as fragmentary wood with the remains of black wool coffin covers, in one case with the remains of white metal lace on one face (Walton Rogers, this volume, Chapter 5), coffin grips, nails and coffin plates.

Human burial	Age group	Sex assigned	Coffin type	Coffin details
HB 225	Adult	-	Wood	Black wool coffin cover with metal coffin lace
HB 186	Adult	-	Wood	Black wool coffin cover

Table 60: V17 burial details.

Human burial	Age group	Sex assigned	Coffin type	Coffin details
HB 255	Adult	Prob male	Lead/wood (elm)	Fabric (wool) lining, silk ribbon from ?shroud.
HB 256	-	-	Lead/wood	Fabric lining

Table 58: V15 burial details.

V19

Structure type	Rectangular brick-lined grave
Exterior dimensions	1.07m × 2.51m
Associated structures	Vault 2
Construction	Clamped red brick, limed mortar
Roof type	Vaulted
Flooring	Natural sandstone, dry-laid bricks
Human burials	HB 262

Table 61: V19 structural summary.

This burial chamber lay immediately north of, and was cut by, the larger 'family vault', Vault 2. The western end of V19 was built onto a slight outcrop of natural sandstone, which formed the floor at the western end of the chamber. Flooring at the eastern end of the chamber comprised dry-laid bricks placed flat. The barrelled roof that sealed the chamber was in an overall good condition, although some damage had occurred during the later construction of Vault 2. This damage was evident on the eastern half of the roof, where a partial re-build was clearly visible.

V19 contained a single adult burial (HB 262; Table 62). The associated wooden coffin was reasonably well preserved, with elaborate oval grip plates in the form of winged cherubs, coffin grips and *depositum*. Analysis of wood samples (Gale, this volume, Chapter 5) showed that it was constructed of elm and pine, while study of textile samples (Walton Rogers, this volume, Chapter 5) showed that it had a black wool coffin cover with white metal coffin lace, and the remains of wool union and silk ribbon coffin lining.

Human burial	Age group	Sex assigned	Coffin type	Coffin details
HB 262	Adult	-	Elm/pine	Comparatively well preserved, eight coffin grip plates and *depositum* with winged cherub design, grip handles, black wool cover with coffin lace, wool union and silk ribbon coffin lining.

Table 62: V19 burial details.

V20

This shouldered (i.e. coffin-shaped) brick-lined grave, close to the north side of the church, survived in a good state of preservation. It comprised two chambers, one above the other, which had clearly been built at different times. The lower chamber was built of a single

Structure type	Shouldered brick-lined grave (2 chambers)
Exterior dimensions	1.06m × 2.51m
Associated structures	V11, V12, V21, V24 (Group IV)
Construction	Red brick; limed mortar
Roof type	Vaulted
Flooring	Natural sandstone (lower), brick (upper)
Internal divisions	Upper and lower chambers
Human burials	HB 768, HB 746

Table 63: V20 structural summary.

skin of clamped red bricks on the east, south and west elevations and a double skin on the north elevation; natural sandstone was incorporated into the build of the south wall and floor. All the brickwork was laid in stretcher courses and bonded with a light brown limed mortar.

Fig. 73: Shouldered brick-lined grave V20 showing upper chamber. The remains of a child (HB 746) in the upper chamber can be seen resting on the vaulted roof to the lower chamber.

Human burial	Age group	Sex assigned	Coffin type	Coffin details
HB 768	-	-	Wood	Good condition with fabric covering and handles
HB 746	Child	-	Wood (elm)	Very fragmentary with highly corroded fittings

Table 64: V20 burial details.

The vaulted roof of the lower chamber formed the flooring for the upper chamber (Fig. 73). The upper chamber was built of more regular bricks, but was of noticeably inferior construction to the lower chamber. It too was sealed with a barrelled roof.

Each chamber contained a single burial (Table 64). Although the coffin in the lower chamber was in a good condition, with associated coffin furniture, the burial itself (HB 768) was in a poor state of preservation and was not removed from the site. Analysis of wood fragments from the coffin in the upper chamber, which had contained a child (HB 746; Fig. 73), revealed it to have been made of elm (Gale, this volume, Chapter 5).

V22

Structure type	Rectangular brick-lined grave
Exterior dimensions	2.42m × 1.07m
Construction	Clamped red brick, limed mortar
Roof type	Ledger-stone (missing)
Flooring	Natural sandstone
Internal features	Whitewashed, putlocks
Human burials	HB 677, HB 669, HB 661

Table 65: V22 structural summary.

This grave was built adjacent to the north boundary wall of the churchyard. Interestingly, it was orientated north-south, a peculiarity it shared with a nearby family vault, Vault 23, in a similar position. Both structures may have been orientated in this way to maximise the number of graves that could be lined along the wall.

Human burial	Age group	Sex assigned	Coffin type
HB 677	Child	-	Wood
HB 669	Middle adult	Male	Wood
HB 661	Old adult	-	Wood

Table 66: V22 burial details.

The chamber contained three burials, a child and two adults, stacked one above the other (Table 66). The grave had been backfilled at some time, which had contributed to the poor preservation of the coffins. In all three cases the coffins survived only as stains, fragmentary wood and corroded metal fittings.

V24

Structure type	Possible burial structure (truncated)
Exterior dimensions	0.90m × 1.40m (surviving)
Associated structures	V11, V12, V20, V21 (Group IV)
Construction	Clamped red brick, limed mortar
Human burials	None recorded

Table 67: V24 structural summary.

This structure comprised the extremely truncated remains of a possible burial structure. After a record of the brickwork was made, no further work was carried out.

V25

Structure type	Rectangular composite brick-lined grave
Exterior dimensions	1.40m × 2.60m
Associated structures	V13, V26 (Group III)
Construction	Rock cut; clamped red brick, limed mortar
Roof type	Ledger-stone (missing)
Flooring	Natural sandstone
Internal features	Putlocks cut into natural sandstone and brickwork
Human burials	None

Table 68: V25 structural summary.

This burial chamber was the only example of what has been termed a 'composite brick-lined grave'. V25 forms part of a group of three brick-lined graves (V13, V25 and V26). The earliest phase of this structure comprised a deep rectangular chamber cut into the natural sandstone (Fig. 74). Three rows of putlocks to receive timber coffin supports were cut into the sandstone. The latest phase of construction comprised a double skin of clamped red bricks, laid in irregular header and stretcher courses and bonded with a limed mortar (Fig. 75). The quality of construction was particularly poor. One row of putlocks had been cut into this brickwork. The chamber had been backfilled with general graveyard fill and no burials were found. The chamber was probably sealed with a ledger-stone, but none was present.

Fig. 74: Composite rock-cut and brick-lined grave V25. The rock-cut lower part and brick-built upper part of the grave, with putlocks for coffin supports, can be seen.

Fig. 75: Composite rock-cut and brick-lined grave V25 showing construction of upper brick-built chamber.

V26

Structure type	Sub-rectangular brick-lined grave
Exterior dimensions	1.09m × 2.09m
Associated structures	V13, V25 (Group III)
Construction	Clamped red brick, limed mortar, corbelled design
Roof type	Vaulted (lower); ledger-stone (missing, upper)
Internal divisions	Upper and lower chambers
Human burials	HB 489

Table 69: V26 structural summary.

V26 was wider at the west end (1.09m) than at the east end (1.02m), giving it a slight coffin-shape. The grave had two chambers. The lower chamber had a vaulted roof which formed the floor for the upper chamber. The build of the upper chamber was corbelled and comprised a single skin of clamped red bricks on the east and west elevations, and a double skin on the north and south elevations. No roof to the upper chamber survived but it is assumed that it was sealed with a ledger-stone.

This grave contained a single adult burial (HB 489) in the lower chamber, in coffin, shell and case (Fig. 76; Table 70). Analysis has identified the wood as elm (Gale, this volume, Chapter 5). A *depositum* was recorded, but no inscription was identified. Fragments of silk ribbons were also recovered from the coffin (Walton Rogers, this volume, Chapter 5).

Fig. 76: Brick-lined grave V26, from west. The lower chamber, containing a burial (HB 489) in a lead/wood coffin.

Human burial	Age group	Sex assigned	Coffin type	Coffin details
HB 489	Old adult	Male	Lead/ wood (elm)	Illegible *depositum*, silk ribbons from interior

Table 70: V26 burial details.

V27

Structure type	Rectangular brick-lined grave
Exterior dimensions	*c.*1m × 2.30m
Construction	Clamped red brick, limed mortar
Roof type	Ledger-stone (missing)
Flooring	Natural sandstone
Human burials	HB 570, HB 522

Table 71: V27 structural summary.

V27 was situated outside the west entrance to the church. The chamber had been backfilled with broken, fire-blackened roofing tiles and fragments of dressed grey sandstone. This material may well be associated with air-raid damage to the church during the Second World War.

V27 contained two adult inhumations (HB 570 and HB 522) stacked one above the other (Table 72). The

Human burial	Age group	Sex assigned	Coffin type	Coffin details
HB 570	Adult	-	Wood	Stain and fragmentary wood, fish-tail shape, iron handles
HB 522	Adult	-	?Lead/ wood	Decomposed wood, slight trace of possible lead shell. Handles.

Table 72: V27 burial details.

associated coffins survived as fragmentary wood, metal fittings and coffin handles. One coffin was of a recognisable fish-tail shape and the other preserved slight traces of a possible lead shell.

V28

Structure type	Rectangular brick-lined grave
Exterior dimensions	1.16m × 2.39m
Construction	Clamped red brick, limed mortar
Roof type	Ledger-stone (missing)
Flooring	Natural sandstone
Human burials	HB 663, HB 652

Table 73: V28 structural summary.

V28 was also situated outside the west entrance to the church, but close to the west boundary wall of the churchyard. The burial chamber was probably originally sealed by a ledger-stone but this did not survive.

V28 contained two adult inhumations (Table 74). The earliest burial (HB 663) was quite disturbed and the associated coffin survived only as a dark stain in the surrounding fill. Two corroded coffin handles were also present. The coffin for the later burial (HB 652) survived as fragmentary wood, metal fittings and coffin handles.

Human burial	Age group	Sex assigned	Coffin type	Coffin details
HB 663	Adult	Male	Wood	Decomposed, 2 corroded handles
HB 652	Adult	Prob female	Wood	Fragmentary wood, 4 corroded handles

Table 74: V28 burial details.

V31

Structure type	Rectangular brick-lined grave
Exterior dimensions	1.20m × 2.35m
Associated structures	V32, V33 (Group I)
Construction	Clamped red brick (particularly thin), limed mortar
Roof type	Vaulted
Flooring	Dry-laid bricks
Internal features	Putlocks, partially whitewashed
Human burials	HB 777, HB 761, HB 756

Table 75: V31 structural summary.

This grave formed part of a group of three brick-lined graves (Group I) at the south-west corner of the church. V31 has been truncated by the 1872 foundations of the church. It was sealed by a vaulted roof which had collapsed into the interior along with an earthy fill containing disarticulated human bone.

V31 contained three adult burials (HB 777, HB 761 and HB 756) stacked one above the other (Fig. 77; Table 76). The associated coffins were of a wooden construction and only survived as fragmentary wood or stains in the

Human burial	Age group	Sex assigned	Coffin type
HB 777	Middle adult	-	Wood
HB 761	Middle adult	Prob male	Wood
HB 756	Middle adult	Prob male	Wood

Table 76: V31 burial details.

surrounding fills. Some coffin furniture survived in a highly corroded state.

V32

Structure type	Rectangular brick-lined grave
Exterior dimensions	1.35m × 2.29m
Associated structures	V31, V33 (Group I)
Construction	Clamped red bricks
Roof type	Vaulted
Flooring	Natural sandstone
Internal features	Putlocks, brick coffin supports
Human burials	HB 724

Table 77: V32 structural summary.

This grave was butted against V31 to the north and V33 to the west. The construction of V32 comprised a single skin of clamped red bricks laid in stretcher courses. It was roofed with a high barrel vault.

V32 contained one adult burial (HB 724; Table 78). The associated coffin survived partially, with metal fittings. Coffin supports were formed by two lines of mortared bricks running across the width of the chamber.

Human burial	Age group	Sex assigned	Coffin type	Coffin details
HB 724	Middle adult	-	Wood	Sides and base definable, associated handles and nails.

Table 78: V32 burial details.

V35

Structure type	Shouldered brick-lined grave (2 chambers)
Exterior dimensions	0.60m × 2.30m
Associated structures	Vault 30, V36 (Group II)
Construction	Clamped red bricks, limed mortar
Roof type	Vaulted
Flooring	Dry-laid brick (lower); barrel vault (upper)
Internal divisions	Upper and lower chambers
Human burials	HB 866, HB 865

Table 79: V35 structural summary.

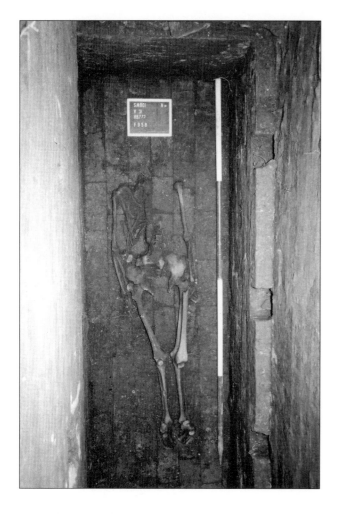

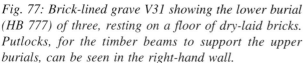

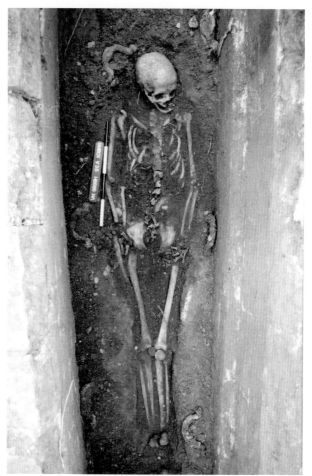

Fig. 77: Brick-lined grave V31 showing the lower burial (HB 777) of three, resting on a floor of dry-laid bricks. Putlocks, for the timber beams to support the upper burials, can be seen in the right-hand wall.

Fig. 78: Brick-lined grave V35 showing the burial in the upper chamber (HB 865) surrounded by six grip handles from the decayed coffin.

V35 is a further example of a shouldered brick-lined grave, a departure from the more usual rectangular form. It was constructed above an earlier brick-lined grave, V36, and immediately south of family vault Vault 30 (Haines family). The construction of V35 comprised two chambers, one above the other. The lower chamber, floored with dry-laid bricks placed flat, was built of a single skin of bricks and sealed with a shallow barrelled roof, which also provided the floor for the upper chamber. The upper chamber was likewise built of a single skin of bricks and sealed with a vaulted roof.

The lower chamber contained the remains of an adult male (HB 866) and the upper chamber an adult female (HB 865; Fig. 78). The coffins and coffin furniture associated with both burials were in a poor state of preservation.

V36

Human burial	Age group	Sex assigned	Coffin type	Coffin details
HB 866	Adult	Male	Wood	Fragmentary, corroded remains of six handles and *depositum*
HB 865	Middle adult	Female	Wood	Fragmentary, corroded fittings, six handles

Table 80: V35 burial details.

Structure type	Rectangular brick-lined grave
Exterior dimensions	1.02m × 2.14m
Associated structures	Vault 30, V35 (Group II)
Construction	Clamped red brick, limed mortar
Roof type	Vaulted
Flooring	Dry-laid brick
Human burials	HB 868

Table 81: V36 structural summary.

Human burial	Age group	Sex assigned	Coffin type	Coffin details
HB 868	Middle adult	Female	Lead/ wood (elm)	Fish-tail shape, fabric covering, oval *depositum* (illegible). Hair comb with burial.

Table 82: V36 burial details.

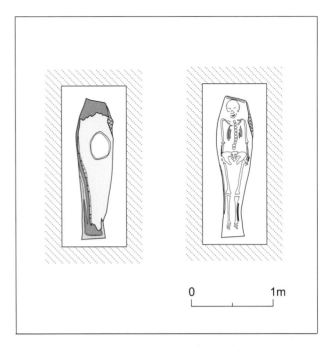

Fig. 79: Plan of burial HB 868 in brick-lined grave V36.

This simple, typical brick-lined grave was uncovered below the double-chambered grave V35 and immediately south of Vault 30 (Haines family vault). It was roofed with a low barrel roof.

The grave contained a single burial (HB 868) that had been interred in a fabric- and wood-covered lead fish-tail coffin (Fig. 79; Table 82). Analysis of a sample of the coffin wood (Gale, this volume, Chapter 5) has identified the wood as elm. Breaches in the wood case revealed an incised lozenge pattern on the lead shell. A tortoise shell hair comb (SF 49; Bevan, this volume, Chapter 5) found in the coffin supports the identification of the occupant as a female.

Discussion: the use and date of the brick-lined graves

Twenty-one of the brick-lined graves which were investigated contained burials. While the number of burials in each grave varied from one to four, graves with two burials in them were the most common, accounting for nearly half of the total (Table 83). Graves with a single burial were the next most frequent.

It may be supposed that brick-lined graves were built mainly for husband and wife couples or individual (unmarried?) adults. An analysis of the combinations of burials in each vault supports this supposition (Table 83). Using the age/sex assignments from the anthropological analysis, supplemented by evidence from *deposita* and documentary sources, it can be seen that four of the ten graves with two burials contained a male/ female adult pair. Three of the other graves with two burials were adult pairs that could be a male/female combination. It seems that the instruction of Captain Robinson (V33, HB 779) in his will that he should be "interred in the same grave with my dear wife", was a sentiment commonly shared (and is, of course, evident from a casual survey of any churchyard or cemetery). Two graves contained an adult with a child. An anomaly is one grave of two burials (V13) that contained a female and a probable female. However as one was classified as an 'old adult' (over 50) and the other a 'young adult' (20–35), this could easily be, say, a mother and daughter combination (the old adult was the earlier of the two burials).

The theme of what is taken to be husband/wife or parent/child combinations is broadly followed in the graves with three or four burials. In one case with three burials (V03) it is known that John Sansom, 65 years old when he died, was buried with his infant granddaughter and another, unidentified, child who may be another granddaughter. A further example (V22) comprises two adults and a child.

With one exception, the graves with a single burial all contained an adult, either male or female, the exception being an adolescent. It would appear, based on this admittedly small sample, that a brick-lined grave was not used for the burial of a child or an infant alone.

Of the 19 adult burials where an assessment of the age of the burial was possible, seven were old adults (over 50), eleven were middle adults (35–50) and one was a young adult (20–35). The question of age group distributions is discussed in Chapter 4.

The question of the significance of the different construction techniques (single-chamber/dual-chamber, vaulted roof/slab roof) used in the building of the brick-lined graves is problematical. No simple correlation between construction technique and the number and combination of burials in a grave was evident. It may be observed, however, that building a brick-lined grave with a vaulted roof involves a considerable degree of brick-laying skill, while building one roofed with simply a ledger-stone or slabs is much more straightforward. In the former case, wooden shuttering needs to be erected to support the vaulted roof while it is being constructed, while building a brick-lined grave with a slab roof is a task that unskilled men – gravediggers, for example –

could readily accomplish. It might be concluded from this that graves with a vaulted roof were more expensive and high status.

It is worth observing in this context that a brick-lined grave with a vaulted roof was essentially a smaller version of the family vaults described above. The constructional techniques were basically the same, except that the span of the vault between the two load-bearing walls (the north and south walls) was greater in the case of the family vaults. Furthermore, in both cases, if new burials were to be inserted without demolishing the roof, it would be necessary to dig down beside one of the non-load-bearing walls (the east or west wall), dismantle much of the wall in order to admit the new burial and then rebuild it again afterwards. This was a considerable undertaking, although it was evidently done on at least a few occasions. It was done, for example, in the case of Captain Benjamin Robinson (V33), whose coffin was put into a vaulted grave above that of his wife, Elizabeth, who had died three years before him. And it was done in the case of the nearby V31, which contained three burials in a brick-lined grave with a vaulted roof.

To insert a new burial into a brick-lined grave in this manner would require that a substantial area of ground was kept clear of recent burials at one or other end (east or west) of the grave. The space would not only need to be big enough to dismantle and rebuild the wall, but to get a heavy coffin in and do this with decorum, mourners onlooking. Examination of the plan of the earth-cut burials in relation to the vaults (Fig. 28) shows that such areas clear of burials were maintained at one end of many of the brick-lined graves and family vaults (the clear space is particularly evident in the case of Vault 5, one of the family vaults, which was located in a very densely used part of the churchyard). Obviously, it would often have been necessary to clear not-so-recent burials to create this space, as well as to make space to build the grave itself.

All this would have required forward planning by both the family and the sexton. But while death is predictable, the date of death and family relationships at the time are not, and graveyards are not on the whole very well-planned places. To add a new burial to a brick-lined grave *ad hoc* solutions would often have been necessary, especially after the passage of many years when new burials may have 'blocked' access to a brick-lined grave except from above. One solution might have been to demolish the vaulted roof and rebuild it. This would be problematic, as pre-existing burials in the grave would make erecting the necessary timber shuttering very difficult. Another solution, evidently adopted in at least four cases, would be to build a new grave above the old one, using the roof of the earlier grave as the floor of the later one. This is perhaps the origin of the 'dual-chamber' graves noted above (V11, V20, V26 and V35). A third solution – by far the simplest – would be to demolish the vaulted roof to admit the new burial and replace it with a ledger-stone or stone slabs (even recycled gravestones). With one exception (V06, where the single burial had been sealed with sand as if to prepare it for a new burial), all the brick-lined graves roofed with ledger-stones or slabs (or considered to have been once so roofed) contained two or more burials. Thus, while the evidence is not compelling, it may be that the use of a ledger-stone or slabs to roof a brick-lined grave was not a cheap alternative to a grave with a vaulted roof but a practical solution to adding a new burial in difficult circumstances (whatever solution was adopted, it would need to take account of the nature of the memorial above the grave).

When these problems are taken into consideration it is perhaps not surprising that the church's fee for a 'fresh interment' in a brick grave at St. Martin's in 1848 (see Chapter 8) was £1 15s 6d, exactly the same as the charge for a new brick grave. By way of contrast, the charge for an earth-cut grave was a mere 6s 4d. Whether those paying the fee always got their money's worth is another question. Conveniently for those involved, the evidence was quickly buried.

The date of the brick-lined graves can be established from a number of sources of evidence. Only three *deposita* provided direct evidence of date. These were the *deposita* of Benjamin Robinson (V33, HB 779), who died in 1834, and the *deposita* of John Sansom and his granddaughter

Number of burials	Frequency	Combinations M-Male adult; F-Female Adult; ?-Adult, sex unknown; A-Adolescent; C-Child, I-Infant. The order of the burials in the grave is followed.						
4	2	F/F/C/M	F/?/F/?					
3	3	I/C/M	C/M/?	?/M/M				
2	10	C/M	F/M x2	F/F	M/?	?/? x 2	?/C	M/F x2
1	6	A	M	?	M	?	F	
Total	**21**							

Table 83: Frequency and combinations of burials in brick-lined graves. (Note: for this analysis, 'probable' sex assignments are merged with the more secure assignments.)

Helen Walker (V03, HB 189 and HB 185), who died in 1873 and 1862 respectively. The range of 1834–1873 can be expanded slightly by taking account of Benjamin Robinson's wife Elizabeth (see above). She died, according to the burial records, in 1831. An earlier date yet is suggested by the burial of Sarah Parker (HB 625) who was buried in the lower chamber of the dual-chamber grave V11. On the *depositum* only the name and month of death, November, could be read. Burial records list three Sarah Parkers who were buried in St. Martin's in November, in 1777, 1790 and 1825. Whichever date refers to the Sarah Parker in question, the use range of the brick-lined graves in the churchyard is pushed back to at least 1825. Thus, taking the coffin plate and documentary evidence together, a use range of at least 1825–1873 can be established.

Other lines of evidence bear on the dates during which the brick-lined graves were used. First, there is the location of the graves within the churchyard. Nine (V01, V07, V08, V15, V17, V19, V22, V26 and V28) of the 24 brick-lined graves are located in the extension of the churchyard to the west and north which took place in 1810. Second, the vault groupings provide an indication of probable date in five further cases. Vault Group I comprises three tightly clustered graves, V31, V32 and V33, tucked into a space at the south-west corner of the church. The graves were constructionally very similar, two of them sharing a high barrel vault (this had collapsed in the case of the third) which is very distinctive and contrasts with the generally flatter roofs found elsewhere. The whole is suggestive of a family group. V33, is dated to the 1830s by the dated burials within (Benjamin and Elizabeth Robinson) and the other two graves are unlikely to be greatly dissimilar in date. As V31 was slightly truncated by the foundations of the 1872 rebuild of the church, a range from about 1830-1870 can be suggested for this group. In Vault Group II, two graves (V36 and V35, the latter built on top of the former) were butted up against the Haines family vault (Vault 30), which had been built by at least 1831 and was used for burial through to 1904 (see above). Graves V36 and V35 are therefore likely to be later than 1830. Finally, in grave V07, Victorian gully bricks of the same type used in the 1872 rebuilding of the church were used as makeshift coffin supports, suggesting a date similar to or not much later than the date of the church.

By the various means described above some indication of dating was obtained for 16 of the 24 brick-lined graves investigated. Taken together, there was nothing to definitely suggest the use of any of the graves before 1825, and most of the evidence pointed towards use during the middle fifty years of the 19th century, from 1825 to 1875. The general evidence of the character of the brickwork and building materials employed, and the character of the coffins and coffin furniture, together with occasional personal items such as hair combs, are all consistent with a similar period of use.

The date of the use of a brick-lined grave is not, however, the same as the date of its construction. It was argued above, in the context of the discussion of the date of construction of the family vaults, that many of these family vaults may have been built in the period *c.*1810–1830, shortly after the marriage of the vault founder and at the time when he was in the early stages of establishing a family. They were built as a provision for the future rather than for immediate use and in at least one case – the Warden family vault (Vault 5) – may have stood empty for decades before a burial took place in them. Were brick-lined graves similarly sometimes built well in advance of their use?

An important practical consideration here is that while it was conceivably possible to have a brick-lined grave built in the period between the death of an individual and their funeral, usually a space of about one week, this would not be possible for a family vault. The latter had to be planned well in advance. Reserving a plot in a chosen churchyard or cemetery is a common phenomenon, however, often done at a relatively early stage in life. It would have been particularly important to do so in a churchyard as crowded as St. Martin's, with hundreds of new burials taking place each year (Chapter 2). The construction of a brick-lined grave for future use would be the most secure method of reserving a burial place for one's self, one's spouse and perhaps one or two other members of close family. This might suggest that some of the brick-lined graves, at least, were built a significant time before the first burial was laid in them.

In terms of their function and social status, there may not have been a major difference between brick-lined graves and family vaults. The difference may reflect little more than one's aspirations for one's family, or the realities of family size. The brick-lined grave or family vault was hidden from view. The part on view was the monument erected above, whether a gravestone or a more elaborate chest-tomb, for example. Unfortunately, in St. Martin's churchyard none of the monuments associated with brick-lined graves or family vaults survived, so it was not possible to compare the above-ground monuments with the below-ground structures. Some illustrations and photographs showing the monuments in the churchyard do exist, but the information is too imprecise to suggest correlations with the excavated vaults, except very tentatively in one or two cases. Nevertheless, it is clear that monuments in churchyards and cemeteries can be very imposing, especially those of the Victorian period, and that in terms of the materials used and the skilled craftsmanship employed most such monuments were probably more expensive – often considerably so – than the comparatively simple structures below ground. This is reflected in the 1848 scale of charges at St. Martin's. The total fee for a 'Brick Grave' was £1 15s 6d while the fee for a 'Tomb without railings, without vault' was £4 5s.

Although the focus of the excavations at St. Martin's

was on the below-ground structures, it is important to bear in mind that this was probably not the most important part of any tomb. It was the above-ground monuments that displayed status and were the focus for mourning and remembrance, and it cannot be assumed that there was any simple correspondence, in terms of ostentation and cost, between what was below ground and what was above ground.

4   The People: Physical Anthropology

Megan Brickley, with Helena Berry and Gaynor Western
and with contributions by Annete Hancocks and Michael Richards

Overview

It is reported that "extreme hardship hit the urban and rural poor in the mid-nineteenth century with the lowest real-wages for over a century" (Black 1985, cited in Roberts and Cox 2003, 307). The analysis of the human bone from St. Martin's churchyard indicates that for many of the inhabitants of Birmingham this was indeed the case. Although it is recognised that there may in fact be some overlap between the socio-economic status of individuals buried in vaults and earth-cut graves, there were a number of features that emerged from the skeletal analyses which almost certainly reflect differences between the two groups. As discussed in the 'Approach' section, in this chapter the word vault is used to refer to all individuals buried in any type of structure, and so also includes individuals buried in brick-lined graves.

The recently published survey on developments in health in Britain from prehistoric times to the present day (Roberts and Cox 2003) suggests that there are a number of significant trends in patterns of health through time. In a number of important respects, the individuals analysed from St. Martin's have started to display a more modern pattern of health. For example, some of the patterns found from investigations of dental health and arthropathies (joint diseases) mirror the types of patterns observed in the modern British population, probably reflective of changes in diet and some aspects of lifestyle. However, there were still noteworthy differences in the patterns of health found. In particular the pattern and prevalence of some of the metabolic conditions investigated (diseases that result in a disruption to bone formation, mineralization remodelling, or a combination of these) were very different to those that would be expected in a developed country like Britain today. The distribution of metabolic diseases found provides a stark reminder of just how difficult and hard life would have been for many of the individuals buried at St. Martin's. The prevalence of scurvy (vitamin C deficiency), for

example amongst the juveniles buried in earth-cut graves, is by today's standards quite shocking. Although no cases of scurvy were found amongst the children of the more affluent individuals buried in the vaults, the better off were not entirely protected form conditions such as rickets (juvenile vitamin D deficiency), which were found in individuals from both the vaults and earth-cut graves.

The period covered by the investigation is one in which infant mortality was high and in a number of cases there was some evidence that the 'osteological paradox' may be influencing the pattern of health recorded for the skeletal remains of juveniles. The osteological paradox is the suggestion that individuals that display evidence of skeletal pathology are paradoxically more healthy than those that do not, as they were able to live with a condition for sufficiently long for changes in the bones to occur (Wood *et al.* 1992). Overall, the juveniles from earth-cut graves seem to have lived with a higher burden of general chronic deficiency diseases and this appears to have made them less able to withstand some of the infectious conditions that would have been prevalent at this time. There are a number of indications that the more urban and industrialised lives led by these individuals had an effect on their health, most notably through the vitamin D deficiency diseases.

Overall, the results of investigations into the various pathological conditions reveal that there were very real links between prevalence of diseases and the socio-economic status of the individuals under investigation. There were also very clear sex differences in the pattern of pathology. Probably the area in which this is most strikingly illustrated is in the investigations of various types of trauma. When all trauma, not just fractures, are considered there are clear differences between the more affluent individuals buried in vaults and those from earth-cut graves. Those from earth-cut graves were more likely to have experienced all forms of trauma that were investigated. The trauma data also provided the clearest sex-related differences, and the effect that the socio-economic status of women had on their likelihood of having suffered from trauma was particularly marked. These differences were found to be statistically significant. The women from vaults were the least likely to have suffered from trauma and this is almost certainly linked to the fact that women of this social class would not have undertaken work, certainly outside the home. In contrast women from earth-cut graves had relatively high levels of trauma and this is almost certainly linked to them undertaking work outside the home, in particular in places like workshops where accidents were relatively common.

Skeletal analyses also gave an indication that those buried in vaults were part of a new middle class. The backgrounds, certainly of older individuals from these families, would have been similar to that of many of the individuals buried in earth-cut graves. Many of the men from the vaults would have come from relatively humble backgrounds, and would have had to work hard to establish their business and the place of their families in a rapidly changing society. A good example of such an individual is Joseph Warden, from Vault 5. Although Joseph Warden was not one of the individuals included in skeletal analysis, his background, outlined in Chapter 6, would have mirrored that of a number of men from the emerging middle classes who were buried in the vaults. Many of the families that owned vaults were engaged in trades rather than professions. The crude prevalence rate (CPR) for fractures was very similar for men from both the vaults and earth-cut graves, although there was a difference in the types of fracture sustained.

The range and type of pathological lesions recorded in this investigation were far greater than those found in a number of previous investigations from elsewhere in Britain. However, it not clear to what extent this difference may be related to developments in the field of palaeopathology in recent years. Over the last ten years there have been very significant advances in the development of diagnostic criteria for pathological conditions in human skeletal material. There is also more attention being paid to the way in which material is recorded, as indicated by recent publications (e.g. Brickley and McKinley 2004). The results contained in this report certainly indicate that the application of new ideas on diagnosis and recording of skeletal material has considerable potential.

Much of the growth of Birmingham during the 18th and 19th centuries would have come from migration into the city. High population levels and migration would have made the spread of disease a problem and evidence for a number of conditions such as tuberculosis and brucellosis (a chronic disease of animals, which can be passed to humans) was found. Although a wide range of infectious conditions were recorded there were some notable exceptions, for example syphilis. Future work on infectious disease may shed more light on the development of these conditions and possible changes in skeletal responses to the conditions.

Results obtained from investigations of a number of pathological conditions do indeed seem to back up the potential value of using some diseases as indicators of past status. For example, the levels of joint diseases such as gout and diffuse idiopathic skeletal hyperostosis (DISH), which as discussed in the following sections have been linked to diet and lifestyle, were higher in individuals buried in the vaults. However, the interpretation of such conditions is not completely straightforward as both gout and DISH were also present in some of the individuals buried in earth-cut graves. It is important to also note that the differences between levels of these conditions in the two groups were not statistically significant.

One factor that helped the investigation of health in 18th- and 19th-century Birmingham was the availability of contemporary written material. Used in combination with the evidence derived from the study of the skeleton, this material has a significant potential to enable more to be learned about health in past communities. Written sources are useful as they often provide additional information that cannot be determined from only undertaking skeletal analysis. Wherever possible, written sources have been used to provide additional information throughout this report. An overview of living and working conditions is provided in Chapter 7.

The following report contains a great deal of valuable information on the lives of individuals in the past and helps to give an idea of what it might have been like to live in Birmingham in the 19th century. With the application of newer diagnostic techniques for palaeopathology, and the use of techniques like aDNA (the analysis of DNA from archaeological bone) and stable isotope analyses, far more information has been gained than was previously possible. However, there is still much to be learned about the health of people who lived through this important period in Britain's history. It would be extremely valuable, if the opportunity arose, to be able to carry out a study of a rural community from this time period, and also to look at individuals who lived during the period immediately preceding this one, from approximately 1600 onwards.

Introduction

During the excavations, 857 human burials, mainly from the late 18th and 19th centuries, were recovered in addition to a significant amount of disarticulated human bone. The time and resources available were such that it was not possible to analyse all the human bone following recommended guidelines for recording archaeological bone (Brickley and McKinley 2004). In order to obtain the maximum information from the site a strategy had to be adopted in which resources were targeted at areas that would produce the greatest returns in terms of information obtained and data generated.

In the case of the disarticulated human bone it was felt

that very little information would be obtained from undertaking detailed analyses of this material, which was largely recovered from the churchyard soil and had no discrete context. It was decided that a 'rapid scan' of this bone to identify any items that might potentially yield higher levels of information should be undertaken. A number of skulls with intact facial regions were present and the possibility of individuals having non-Caucasoid ancestry was considered as Birmingham was known to have some early non-European immigrants, but all skulls examined appeared typically Caucasoid ('white'). The rapid scan also identified bones that displayed evidence of pathological lesions or trauma, most commonly healed fractures, non-specific evidence of infection, such as periosteal new bone formation, and areas of bone that may have been affected by osteomyelitis. There were also significant numbers of juvenile bones with evidence of vitamin D deficiency (bowing typical of changes caused by rickets). Amongst the adult bones there were numerous examples of joint surfaces affected by eburnation and/or pitting, often surrounded by osteophyte formation indicating osteoarthritis.

All of these changes are frequently found in archaeological human bone and represent a range of pathological conditions commonly manifest in such material (Roberts and Manchester 1995). However, one adult skull demonstrated evidence of surgical intervention during the life of the individual. On the left parietal bone there was a circular trephination, shown in Figure 80. The edges of the skull were well healed, demonstrating that the individual had lived after the procedure was undertaken. However, there is no indication as to why this operation was performed. The procedure is very ancient and was performed by previous populations across the world. Often the procedure is used following injury to the skull,

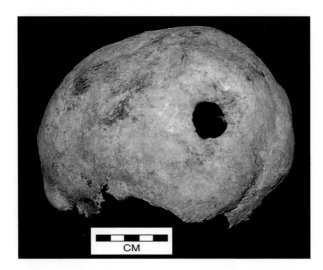

Fig. 80: Well healed trephination on the left parietal of a cranial vault recovered during excavation of disarticulated human bone.

particularly fracture (Brothwell 1981, 121), but there was no evidence of such injury having occurred in the case found. As this skull was incomplete and there was no associated skeleton it was not possible to say anything about the individual, apart from the fact that they were an adult at the time of death.

In order to suggest differential diagnoses for many of the conditions which occur less commonly in archaeological bone, the complete skeleton is often required. Having a complete skeleton enables the distribution of changes across the bones to be assessed and factors such as the age and sex of the affected individual can be taken into consideration. It is not surprising, therefore, that from the rapid scan of the disarticulated human bone carried out no firm evidence for a wider range of pathological conditions, as discussed later in this report, was found. The assemblage did however provide an indication of the likely findings from analysis of complete individuals. The quantity of disarticulated human bone recovered and examined was large, but as no formal recording to allow the minimum number of individuals to be estimated was undertaken it is not possible to put a figure on the number of individuals represented. What is clear from the bone recovered was that the churchyard had been intensively used for a considerable period of time with burials routinely disturbing earlier interments. In some cases disturbed human bone had been gathered up and placed in discrete deposits, but the majority of the bone came from the general churchyard soil. It was also clear that individuals of all ages and both males and females had been buried and disturbed by later burials.

Recovery and cleaning methods

Individuals from earth-cut graves were excavated according to the recommendations in McKinley and Roberts (1993). Once located, adult individuals were fully uncovered before being photographed and lifted. The various skeletal elements were bagged separately, labelled and boxed before being removed from site to the human bone laboratory at the University of Birmingham. For an untrained excavator, identification of all skeletal elements in an infant or small child can be difficult, especially in a busy site situation, and due to time available it was decided that for these individuals bones would not be lifted and bagged by element as for the older individuals. In order to proceed at a reasonable speed and ensure maximum recovery, it was decided that such individuals would be lifted as a block of soil (bulk soil sample).

Thus, when individuals of this age were encountered they were uncovered sufficiently for a photograph to be obtained. All soil and loose material removed during cleaning was placed in a sealable sample container, and once the photograph had been taken and the on-site recording form completed, a bulk soil sample containing all the bones was removed using a shovel and placed in the sample container. The complete block of soil and associated loose material were then taken back to the human bone laboratory at the University of Birmingham. In the laboratory, bones were then carefully removed from the soil before the loose soil was wet sieved and the residue carefully sorted to retrieve any pieces of bone or tooth. As a result of this retrieval strategy, recovery of small elements such as tooth buds and epiphyses from infants was excellent. This procedure allowed both rapid work on site and excellent retrieval of human bone.

The adult human bone was cleaned at the University of Birmingham human bone laboratory using cold water and soft brushes. The soil type present on site did not permit cleaning simply by dry brushing, and bone had to be washed. Skulls were placed on a mesh or sieve to prevent the loss of teeth during the cleaning process. Soft tooth brushes were occasionally used during cleaning, but for all delicate bone and areas such as the teeth soft-bristled artists' brushes were used. The human bone was allowed to dry thoroughly at normal room temperature, out of direct sunlight, before being re-bagged and boxed. Where delicate areas of bone or pathological features that might be damaged were noted, these bones were wrapped in acid-free tissue paper to prevent them from being knocked or damaged prior to analysis.

It is recommended in McKinley and Roberts (1993) that all bone should be marked with a unique ID number. However, due to restrictions of time and resources and the scheduled re-burial of the skeletal material, it was decided that it would not be an economical use of the resources available to mark the bones in this instance. The lack of marking did impose a number of restrictions, however. As this internationally important collection was to be out of the ground for such a limited period of time, the team were keen that other researchers should, if at all possible, be given access to the material for research purposes. However, the lack of marking meant that the small number of researchers who were able to obtain access to the collection were only able to examine material that had already been recorded for the report, as the risk of unmarked bones becoming mislaid or mixed-up was too great. Only a small number of bones were marked and these were those examined in a NERC-funded project to investigate vitamin D deficiency diseases. Marking ensured that the bones could all be returned to the correct box when the investigations were complete.

After cleaning and drying, bones were re-packed in plastic bags in which holes had been punched, to allow the contents to 'breathe'. Bags were labelled using indelible markers and each individual was packed in separate box. Younger juveniles were placed in polythene storage boxes, which allowed the contents to be seen and occupied less space that the cardboard skeleton boxes, while adults were placed in standard acid-free cardboard boxes. Some individuals had very long femora, and longer boxes were ordered to accommodate these individuals without squashing bones or placing undue pressure on them. More complete individuals were placed in two boxes to ensure that over-packing did not damage bones. Separate

skull boxes were not used, but the system described above was considered adequate for the very short-term storage prior to recording and re-burial. Humidity and other environmental conditions of the storage areas were not measured, as the storage was only short-term.

Approach

Before work on recording started, a brief assessment was made of all the articulated individuals recovered during the excavation. The phasing of the burials, where this was available was considered along with the type of burial (vault, earth-cut) the completeness of the individual and the quality of the preservation of the bone. All individuals were then assigned to one of the following groups:

– Group 1, individuals from vaults (including brick-lined graves).
– Group 2, individuals >75% complete from securely dated contexts.
– Group 3, individuals 25–75% complete from securely dated contexts.
– Group 4, individuals >75% complete from contexts not securely dated.
– Group 5, individuals 25–75% complete from contexts not securely dated.
– Group 6, individuals < 25% complete from securely dated contexts.
– Group 7, individuals < 25% complete from contexts not securely dated.

The various groups were ranked in order of importance and work on analysis started at Group 1 and moved down the list. By the end of the period of recording, all individuals in Groups 1–4 had been completed and approximately half of the individuals from Group 5 had been recorded. In total, 505 of the excavated individuals were recorded during the analyses undertaken.

As the description of the vaults and brick-lined graves in Chapter 3 indicates, the various structures differed greatly in terms of their construction and probable cost. Some of the brick–lined graves were relatively simple structures and the individuals buried here may not have been amongst the wealthiest inhabitants of Birmingham. It is also possible that for various reasons some more wealthy individuals were buried in an earth-cut grave. The very real social and economic differences between unskilled labourers and skilled craftsmen and their families, both of whom would have been buried in earth-cut graves, are discussed more fully in Chapter 7. However, due to a lack of detailed information regarding the potential social and economic status of each individual, throughout the rest of this report, individuals were divided into one of two groups: those buried in an earth cut-grave or those buried in any type of structure (all referred to as vault burials). Overall, it would be safe to say that those buried in vaults are from the middle classes and those from earth-cut graves are from a working class background.

The importance of the collection from St. Martin's was such that it was possible to obtain extra funding and support from a number of sources to undertake additional research on the collection. The period during which those buried at St. Martin's lived was known to have been typical of the conditions required to produce a high prevalence of diseases linked to vitamin D deficiency (most frequently caused by low light levels). Therefore, in collaboration with Dr Simon Mays of English Heritage, a NERC grant was obtained to investigate skeletal indicators of the condition. As part of the NERC project, a research assistant undertook very detailed analyses of a wide range of skeletal features that may be linked to vitamin D deficiency in all the individuals excavated. The results obtained on the prevalence of rickets and osteomalacia (conditions linked to vitamin D deficiency) were different to those obtained during the 'standard' recording undertaken to produce this report. This disparity is not surprising, and serves to illustrate the differences between what can be learned from basic skeletal reporting and detailed research. However, in order to provide the most accurate information possible it was decided to use the results generated by the NERC project in the section of this report dealing with metabolic diseases.

Osteomalacia can greatly weaken the skeleton, and one of the individuals in which the condition was definitely present and all the individuals with possible cases of the condition had a large number of bones missing and were poorly preserved. Because of the very poor condition of the bone, these individuals were only examined as part of a NERC funded project as they had been excluded from full analysis during the initial assessment of material (most were placed in Groups 5 – 7). This example demonstrates that if possible, all individuals excavated during archaeological projects should be recorded during skeletal analysis.

Tuberculosis was also known to be an important condition in the 18th and 19th centuries, but there are problems with identifying individuals who may have had the condition from skeletal remains (discussed more fully in the section on infectious conditions). In order to gain a better understanding of the condition DNA tests were undertaken on some of the excavated individuals. The work on the identification of aDNA from *M. tuberculosis*

was undertaken by Helen Donoghue and Mark Spigelman of University College London.

Quantity and nature of the material

In total 123 individuals were uncovered in the vaults during the excavations at St. Martin's. A number of these burials were not taken to the University of Birmingham for full analysis. This was either because they were in 'uncompromised' coffins (see Chapter 3) or because the bone was in such a poor condition that lifting was not practical. For some of these 25 burials some on-site recording was possible and some age/sex determination was attempted. This information is listed in Appendix 4. However, the data were very incomplete and are not used in the analysis of the human bone presented in the main report. These burials were left *in situ* or were reburied in an alternative vault.

The rest of the individuals from vault burials were taken to the University of Birmingham for full analysis. Throughout this chapter it is stated that there were 99 individuals from vaults that were fully analysed, but at a late stage in the production of the report it became clear that there may in fact only have been 98. It seems likely that HB 119, may have been buried in an earth-cut grave close to Vault 7, rather than buried within the vault.

Surface preservation

The surface preservation was recorded using the various stages of weathering described and illustrated by Behrensmayer (1978) as the system developed specifically for human bone, published in Brickley and McKinley (2004), was not available at the time the work was undertaken. Although the Behrensmayer system of 'scoring' the surface condition of bone was developed using animal bone, which weathers slightly differently to human bone, the broad categories adopted during the analysis using these stages allowed a clear indication of the condition of the bone to be obtained. During the recording of human bone from St. Martin's scores were awarded based on the condition of the majority of bone in a skeleton, rather than separate scores being awarded for individual bones. Where the bones of a skeleton had varied levels of preservation (greater than two stages) the

	Excellent (Stage 0)		Good (Stage 0-1)		Fair (Stage 2-3)		Poor (Stage 3-5)		Varied (greater than 2 stages)		**Grand Total**
	No.	%	No.	%	No.	%	No.	%	No.	%	
Vault	14	1.67	25	2.98	27	3.22	22	2.62	11	1.31	99
Earth-cut	117	13.95	332	39.57	172	20.50	80	9.54	39	4.65	740
Total	131	15.61	357	42.55	199	23.72	102	12.16	50	5.96	839

Table 84: Number and percentage of individuals from both vaults and earth-cut graves recorded from each of the preservation categories.

skeleton was recorded as being 'varied'.

All of the individuals removed from the site during the excavation were evaluated and the bone surface preservation scored, not just individuals later selected for detailed analysis. Table 84 shows that the majority of the skeletal material excavated had good levels of bone surface preservation, with just under 60% of all individuals being scored as excellent or good. The data presented in Table 85 show the percentage of individuals from the two types of burial scored at each level of preservation.

These data demonstrate that the levels of surface preservation of the bone were in fact better in the earth-cut graves than in the vaults. Just under 60% of the individuals from earth-cut graves were scored as excellent or good, compared to 40% of those from the vaults. There was also a higher proportion of individuals from the vaults in which there was variable preservation across the skeleton.

The quality of bone surface preservation in individuals from the vaults may in part be related to fluids being present within the coffins in the past. However, the range of preservation recorded from individuals from the vaults was not as great as that recorded during the analysis of individuals from the vaults of Christ Church, Spitalfields, London (Molleson and Cox 1993). At St. Martin's there were considerably fewer cases of soft tissue preservation (information on cases of tissue preservation can be found in Appendix 4), but the number of individuals buried in vaults at St. Martin's was far smaller than at Christ

Church, Spitalfields (99 compared to 968). No evidence of adipocere formation was found during the analysis of the bones recovered from the vaults at St. Martin's. However, like Christ Church, Spitalfields (Molleson and Cox 1993, 10–11) there was evidence of chemical degradation of some of the bones recovered. Minerals present in the coffin liquor, possibly leached from the coffin metal, had entered bones. Lead is a soft metal and the fabric of many of the coffins would soon have been perforated, allowing the escape of coffin liquor. Once the skeletal material had dried out following escape of the coffin liquor the minerals seem to have re-crystallised 'bursting' apart bones and causing bones below the 'tidemark' of the coffin liquor to become friable and powdery. It is likely that the poor preservation seen was caused by brushite as at Christ Church (Molleson and Cox 1993, 15), but no tests were undertaken to confirm this. This type of degradation is probably one of the main reasons why overall levels of bone surface preservation were lower in the vaults than in the earth-cut graves. Differential effects of varying degrees of immersion in coffin liquor was probably also the reason why there was a higher percentage of individuals from the vaults in which there was variable preservation of bone across the skeleton. Another difference in the preservation of the bone from St. Martin's to that found at Christ Church, Spitalfields was that there were no cases of fungal remains found on the bones analysed in the present study. Some of these differences may be because burials at Christ

	Excellent (Stage 0)	Good (Stage 0-1)	Fair (Stage 2-3)	Poor (Stage 3-5)	Varied (greater than 2 stages)	**Grand Total**
Vault	15%	25%	27%	22%	11%	100%
Earth-cut	14%	45%	24%	11%	6%	100%
Total	15.5%	42.5%	24%	12%	6%	100%

Table 85: Percentage of individuals from each type of burial with different levels of surface preservation.

		ECG	Vault	Total
Excellent	Count	117	14	131
	Expected count	115.5	15.5	131.0
Good	Count	332	25	357
	Expected count	314.9	42.1	357.0
Fair	Count	172	27	199
	Expected count	175.5	23.5	199.0
Poor	Count	80	22	120
	Expected count	90.0	12.0	120.0
Varied	Count	39	11	50
	Expected count	44.1	5.9	50.0
Total	Count	740	99	839
	Expected count	740.0	99.0	839.0

Table 86: Crosstabulation of surface preservation levels in individuals from vaults and earth-cut graves (ECG).

Church, Spitalfields were 'intramural' and those from St. Martin's were from an 'extramural' context.

When the data on bone preservation were analysed statistically, it was found that the individuals from the vaults showed significantly more surfaces assessed as poor and fewer assessed as good compared to expected figures, although the numbers assessed as excellent were as expected. Full figures on surface preservation levels are provided in Table 86.

During recovery of bones from the coffins in the vaults it was noted that, as at Christ Church, Spitalfields, there were also considerable quantities of dipterid fly puparia cases present in coffins. However, in the present study detailed examination of all the insect remains was not undertaken, as an assessment of this material indicated that full analysis would yield relatively little information.

Tables detailing the relationship between estimated age and sex and bone preservation are provided in Appendix 6 (Tables 1–2). In summary, it was found that adults and juveniles did not differ significantly in the preservation group to which they were assigned. However, this could be because less well-preserved individuals were not fully recorded and so were not included in the analysis. When the data was analysed statistically there was found to be no relationship between the age of individuals and the percentage present ($X^2 = 2.56$, df = 3, p = 0.465). There was also no statistically significant difference between the preservation (percentage present) of males and females ($X^2 = 5.62$, df = 3, p = 0.131).

One interesting trend that was observed is that the juveniles had more 'excellent' surface preservation than would be expected. This may be an artefact created by the fact that the earth-cut grave sample is biased towards individuals with 75%+ preservation, and this is known to increase the chance that surface preservation will be excellent. Adults had fewer 'excellent' surfaces than expected and more 'fair' surfaces than would have been expected statistically.

Completeness of individuals

Another measure of the preservation of individuals can be gained from an assessment of the completeness of each skeleton. All individuals excavated, not just those selected for analysis, were assessed and assigned to one of four categories of completeness shown in Tables 87 and 88 below. A full inventory of the bones and teeth present in each individual, along with summary information on things such as pathological conditions recorded, is available in Appendix 5.

Statistical analysis of the data generated on the completeness of individuals from the different types of burial demonstrated that there was no significant difference in the degree of completeness between those buried in vaults and those from earth-cut graves.

However, the two measures of preservation discussed, surface preservation and completeness, were found to be related. Statistical analysis of the data gathered demonstrated that there was a statistically significant relationship between surface preservation and percentage completeness ($X^2 = 151.36$, df = 12, p <0.000). The analyses indicated that skeletons with excellent preservation of bone surfaces were much more likely to have a high percentage completeness and less likely to be <50% complete (using crosstabulation generated during chi square calculations).

The assessment of sex is discussed in the section on demography, but Table 5 in Appendix 6 shows the number and percentage of all individuals analysed in

	>75%		~75%		~50%		<25%		Grand Total
	No.	%	No.	%	No.	%	No.	%	
Vault	47	5.60%	18	2.15%	11	1.31%	23	2.74%	99
Earth-cut	288	34.32%	132	15.73%	144	17.16%	176	20.99%	740
Total (vault & earth-cut)	335	39.92%	150	17.88%	155	18.47%	199	23.73%	839

Table 87: Number and percentage of individuals from both vaults and earth-cut graves recorded from each of the completeness categories. Percentages are of the total number of individuals assessed. These data represent the results of the assessment of the majority of excavated burials.

	>75%	~75%	~50%	<25%	Grand Total
Vault	47.47%	18.18%	11.11%	23.23%	100%
Earth-cut	38.92%	17.84%	19.46%	23.78%	100%
Total	39.93%	17.88%	18.47%	23.72%	100%

Table 88: Percentage of individuals from each type of burial with different degrees of completeness. These data represent the results of the assessment of the majority of excavated burials.

each age sex category and the percentage present. The data on completeness in each sex category are summarised in Table 89 below. The data presented in this table strongly reflect the policy adopted in selecting individuals for analysis, with 66% of all those selected falling into the most complete preservation category. Statistical analysis indicated that there was no relationship between the age and the percentage present.

Another measure of preservation is the degree of fragmentation or completeness of a bone. Even if the bone surfaces are well preserved the amount of information that it will be possible to obtain from bones that have become fragmented will be reduced. The degree of fragmentation that had taken place in the bones from St. Martin's was investigated through analysis of the femur. The total number of measurements taken on the femora were divided by the total number of measurements that it was theoretically possible to take, given the number of individuals in which the bone was present (only adults were included in the analysis).

The pattern appears to indicate that femurs in the vaults were more fragmented and less complete than those in earth-cut graves. However, were a relationship to exist between the percentage completeness of an individual and the degree of fragmentation, as implied by Von Endt and Ortner (1984), then this finding (detailed in Table 90) may be an artefact created by the nature of the vault/earth-cut assemblages used in this analysis. The greater degree of fragmentation recorded from vault burials is likely to be a result of the fact that all individuals from vaults were fully analysed. However, only the more complete individuals from earth-cut graves were fully analysed. Therefore a greater proportion of less complete individuals were recorded from the vaults.

To demonstrate that the degree of fragmentation is related to percentage completeness, the fragmentation in the different percentage completeness categories was analysed for vault and earth-cut burials separately. The results are presented in Table 91; they clearly indicate that percentage completeness decreases as the degree of fragmentation increases. The higher degree of fragmentation calculated for individuals buried in vaults is probably a result of all these individuals being analysed, whereas individuals <25% complete from earth-cut graves were not analysed. However, while the results do not clearly distinguish the vaults from the earth-cut graves on the basis of degree of fragmentation, a possible tendency for less complete individuals from vaults to be more heavily fragmented than similarly preserved earth-cut interments is perhaps suggested.

Demography (age and sex)

For adults, age at death was determined using degenerative changes at the pubic symphysis, auricular surface and sternal rib end, following guidance given in Buikstra and Ubelaker (1994) and Bass (1995) together with the appropriate casts produced to accompany these techniques. For younger adults epiphyseal bone union was also assessed. Although dental wear was assessed and recorded following the system set out in Buikstra and Ubelaker (1994), this information was not used to assist in the determination of age at death. In the experience of the author and other researchers (for example, Walker *et al.* 1991) this method has been found to be unreliable in skeletal material of this date, probably as a result of changes in diet compared to earlier periods.

Because some of the individuals in the assemblage

	>75%	~75%	~50%	<25%	**Grand Total**
Sex assigned					
Male	81.56%	14.89%	2.84%	0.71%	100%
Probably male	60%	25%	12.5%	2.5%	100%
Ambiguous	50%	50%	0%	0%	100%
Probably female	55.88%	32.35%	8.82%	2.94%	100%
Female	68.42%	26.32%	4.21%	1.05%	100%
Undetermined	57.22%	20.32%	9.63%	12.83%	100%
Grand Total	66.14%	21.58%	6.73%	5.54%	100%

Table 89: Percentage completeness by sex as a percentage of row total.

Adults only	Right femur measurements taken as a % of the theoretical total.	Left femur measurements taken as a % of the theoretical total.	Left and right combined measurements taken as a % of the theoretical total.
Vaults	64.80%	66.60%	65.70%
Earth-cut graves	76.70%	80.90%	78.80%

Table 90: Fragmentation pattern recorded from the femur in individuals from vaults and earth-cut graves.

were of known age it was possible to gain an idea of the way in which age-related changes affected individuals from this group. In particular, features of the auricular surface relating to age were carefully noted to allow a revised system of scoring age-related changes of the auricular surface to be used. It is hoped that this additional information on the ages of some individuals helped to improve the accuracy of age determination in the individuals analysed. However, the considerable problems associated with age determination in archaeological skeletal material are recognised (Cox 2000; Jackes 2000) and as in previous investigations some problems were encountered. Data on the ages recorded from coffin plates and other sources compared to the ages assigned during skeletal analysis are given in the tables of data for each vault presented in Chapter 3. Individuals of known age and/or sex are marked with a '*' symbol in the individual catalogue (Appendix 5). Due to the difficulties of determining age at death in adult individuals the broad age-categories suggested by Buikstra and Ubelaker (1994) were used: young adults (20–35 years), middle adults (35–50 years) and old adults (50+ years). Although in some instances, particularly in younger adults, sufficient information may have been recorded during analysis to give a slightly narrower age at death estimate, for the purposes of analysing the data gathered, all adult individuals were considered within the age categories above. The Buikstra and Ubelaker (1994, 9) categories were also used for the juvenile individuals (Foetal

[<birth], Infant [b–3 years], Children [3–12 years], and Adolescent [12–20 years]).

The sex of the adults recorded was determined based on the dimorphic aspects of the pelvis and skull (Buikstra and Ubelaker 1994; Bass 1995; Brothwell 1981). Individuals were placed in one of six categories: male, probably male, ambiguous (individuals in who the skeletal areas required were present, but which did not display strongly male or female characteristics), probably female, female and undetermined (individuals who were missing the skeletal areas required for sex determination). No attempt was made to determine the sex of the juvenile individuals recorded. The number and proportion of individuals placed in each age/sex category is shown in Table 92 below.

Tables 3–4 in Appendix 6 give a further breakdown of the data gathered on age and sex for individuals from the vaults and earth-cut graves presented separately. When these figures are considered it can be seen that the proportion of individuals buried as juveniles was higher in the earth-cut graves than the vaults. In earth-cut graves juveniles accounted for 32.80% of all individuals buried, but in the vaults the figure was lower at 20.20%. When tested there was found to be a significant difference in the number of juveniles buried from each group ($X^2 = 5.94$, df = 1, p≤ 0.025). What is not clear is the extent to which these figures reflect a real difference in the mortality of children from the two groups, as it is possible that juveniles, especially young infants, were less likely to be

Fragmentation measure for left and right femora combined	75-100% complete	50-75% complete	25-50% complete	1-25% complete
Vault	84% (n = 213)	77.40% (n = 93)	48.30% (n = 60)	10.20% (n = 78)
Earth-cut	82.80% (n = 1185)	63.40% (n = 246)	58% (n = 24)	-

Table 91: The relationship between fragmentation of bones and the percentage completeness of individuals.

	Male		Probably Male		Ambiguous		Probably female		Female		Undetermined		**Grand total**	
Age Group	No.	%	No.	%	No.	%	No.	%	No.	%	No.	%	No.	%
Foetus	-	-	-	-	-	-	-	-	-	-	9	1.78	9	1.78
Infant	-	-	-	-	-	-	-	-	-	-	73	14.46	73	14.46
Child	-	-	-	-	-	-	-	-	-	-	52	10.30	52	10.30
Adol.	0	0	0	0	0	0	0	0	0	0	19	3.76	19	3.76
Yng adult	19	3.76	11	2.18	2	0.40	4	0.79	22	4.36	4	0.79	62	12.28
Mid adult	68	13.47	15	2.97	3	0.59	14	2.77	29	5.74	6	1.19	135	26.73
Old adult	40	7.92	9	1.78	2	0.40	10	1.98	42	8.32	7	1.39	110	21.78
Adult	13	2.57	5	0.99	1	0.20	6	1.19	3	0.59	17	3.37	45	8.91
Grand total	140	27.72	40	7.92	8	1.58	34	6.73	96	19	187	37.03	505	100

Table 92: A breakdown of the number and percentage of all individuals assessed assigned to each age and sex category. A dash denotes information that was not recorded.

given a vault burial. Fuller information and discussion of social biases in the burial of juveniles is provided in Chapter 3. The proportion of juveniles buried in the vaults at St. Martin's was similar to that from Christ Church, Spitalfields, London, where 22.20% of those from the crypt were juveniles (Molleson and Cox 1993, 26).

Infant mortality is known to have been very high during this period and approximately 50% of individuals died before the age of 20 (Roberts and Cox 2003, 303–4). The percentage of individuals recorded as juvenile from St. Martin's is lower than would be expected. Although, as discussed by Roberts and Cox (2003), there are a number of problems with age at death reported in sources of this period, data from sources such as burial registers still provide useful information. Data on age at death in the St. Martin's burial registers were investigated for a two-and-a-half-year period. The years investigated were 1813, part of 1814, and 1836. Data on 1381 burials from these years were recorded from the burial registers. It is impossible to be certain that the burials recorded during this two-and-a-half-year period are entirely representative of the entire period during which the individuals examined were buried, but these data do provide an interesting additional source of data. The data recorded from the burial registers shows that 53.80% of individuals buried in St. Martin's churchyard and Park Street were juveniles (below the age of 20). Table 93 below shows the number and percentage of individuals from the burial registers who would have been placed in each of the age categories used during skeletal recording.

The possible reasons for the higher percentage of individuals recorded as juvenile in the burial registers than during the skeletal investigations are discussed in Chapter 3.

Analysis of the data on the sex of the individuals buried indicated that a higher proportion of the individuals examined appeared to be male than female. From the whole site those assessed as male accounted for 35.64% of the total, whereas the figure for females was lower at 25.74% (195 [38.61%] were indeterminate, ambiguous or not assessed). However, when tested using chi square there was found to be no significant difference between the numbers of males and females buried at the site.

Although the proportion of males was buried at Christ Church, Spitalfields was also higher; there was in fact very little difference between the numbers of each sex, with males accounting for 37% of the total and females for 36% (15.50% had no pelvis or were ambiguous) (Molleson and Cox 1993, 26). The findings from Christ Church, Spitalfields were very different to those obtained from St. Martin's, where males were more likely to be buried in a vault than females. Further information on the differential burial of males and females in vaults at St. Martin's is given in Chapter 3.

The slight gap between the numbers of males and females being buried at St. Martin's is maintained when the vaults and earth-cut graves are considered separately (as in Tables 3 and 4 Appendix 6). In order to gain an idea of any possible differences in burial pattern between males and females, data obtained on 638 adults (those aged 20 years or over) from the parish burial registers were considered. From the burial register data it could be seen that a slightly higher proportion of men than women were buried at St. Martin's, with 55% of the adult individuals listed being male. However, no significant difference was found between the numbers of males and females in the burial registers when a chi square test was used. If it is real, the slightly higher proportion of males being buried than females could be related to socio-economic factors operating during this period. It is possible that there were a large number of males who moved into Birmingham with its rapid expansion, to work in the established industries there and also the construction industry. As is demonstrated later in this chapter, for example in the consideration of trauma, the types of work that many of the males were engaged in, particularly those from the lower socio-economic groups, were hazardous. Accidents, often resulting in fatalities, were relatively common.

When only the adult individuals recorded during skeletal analysis (for whom sex could be determined) are considered 58% (180) were male and 42% (130) were female. The figure of 58% obtained for males from the skeletal analysis is higher than the 55% found for male burials from the burial records. When examined statistically, no significant difference was found between the numbers of males and females recorded during skeletal analysis and in the burial records examined. However, given the importance of demographic assessment in anthropological analyses it is worth considering the slight differences found between the records and skeletal investigations further.

This difference between the two sources could, in part, be related to the relatively high (compared to Spitalfields) percentage of those examined for which a sex could not be determined, 11.90%. In a number of cases, incompleteness of the skeleton due to disturbance by later burials or poor preservation meant that areas required for sex determination were absent. It is possible that a high proportion of these less completely preserved individuals

	N	%
Infant (birth – 3 years)	575	41.64
Child (4–12 years)	135	9.76
Adolescent (13–19 years)	33	2.39
Adult	638	46.20
Total	1381	100

Table 93: Number of individuals from the burial registers who would have been placed in each of the age categories used during skeletal recording. Age categories have been modified slightly, as chronological rather than physiological age is recorded in the burial registers.

may have been female. For example, in the case of two individuals from vaults (HB 625 and HB 789) who were known to be female from written sources, either directly or from a process of elimination (described in Chapter 3) it was not possible to determine the sex from skeletal analysis.

In addition to the factors listed above, mis-assignment of sex during skeletal analysis almost certainly contributed to the differences between results from skeletal and documentary analysis. In two instances, HB 270 and HB 266, individuals that had been classified as a male and probable male from skeletal analysis were associated with female items. Both HB 270 and HB 266 were buried in vaults and had hair combs of the type worn by ladies of the period (see Bevan, Chapter 5). From notes made independently during skeletal analysis by Berry, Brickley and Western, it is clear that there were some discrepancies regarding the age and sex categories that HB 270 and HB 266 should be assigned to. One reason for mis-assignment of sex that should be considered is the possibility raised by Walker (1995) that 'male' cranial features may develop in post-menopausal women. Both HB 270 and HB 266 were placed in the old adult age category. Some additional work, funded by the Nuffield Foundation, was undertaken on the problem of mis-assignment of sex in older women, and further information on this work will be published in the future.

The burial register contains a record of all those buried in the parish, although the exact place of burial is not listed. In the mid 19th century many individuals were buried in the 'overflow' burial ground in Park Street. Park Street was a lower status site (see Chapter 2) and it could have been that more women were buried there than in the churchyard. The slight difference between the burial register data and skeletal analysis may be because skeletal analysis was only undertaken on individuals from St. Martin's.

The research on the burial registers also indicated that, as in previous investigations, some of the older adults may have been aged too young. Of the adult individuals recorded in burial registers, 24% would be classified as young adults, 24% as middle adults and 52% as older adults. The data derived from skeletal analyses does not match this pattern. Only 20% of adults were classified as young adults, 44% as middle adults and 36% as old adults. It is likely that some of the young adults and quite a few of the older adults were erroneously placed in the middle adult category. Some evidence that this was happening is apparent from the results obtained from some of the known-age individuals. In the case of HB 336, HB 574 and HB 576, written sources indicated that they were 58, 52 and 53 years old respectively. There were some differences in notes made during recording by Berry, Brickley and Western. However, the differences in the notes made were not related to the scoring of features assessed, which were fairly consistently scored, but more to the way in which the changes recorded at different skeletal sites should be interpreted and the age category

		Males	Females	Total
20–35 years	Count	78	73	151
	Expected	83.07	67.93	151.0
36–50 years	Count	91	60	151
	Expected	83.07	67.93	151.0
51+ years	Count	182	154	336
	Expected	184.85	151	335.85

Table 94: Crosstabulation of numbers of males and females from the burial registers that would be placed in each age category.

that should be selected. When information was entered into the database, HB 336, HB 574 and HB 576 were placed in the 'middle adult' category.

The number of individuals of each sex from the burial registers that would be placed in each age category is shown in Table 94 above, with information on expected values from chi-square test. There was no significant difference between the number of men and women in each age category ($X^2 = 2.47$, df = 2, p≤ 1).

Although not statistically significant, there were higher numbers of females placed in the young adult category than would be expected and less males in this category than would be expected. In the older adult category there were fewer males than would be expected, but more females.

As certain medical conditions discussed in the following sections are strongly age-related, it is important to know if there was a significant difference between the age of death of males and females from the burial registers. To determine if there was any difference in the age at death between males and females a Mann-Witney U test was calculated. No significant difference between ages at death was found between males and females (z = 0.211, p = <0.833, two tailed test).

It is clear that due to individual differences in rates of physiological aging, correctly placing individuals who fall close to the rather arbitrary age divisions used in chronological age categories will be difficult. However, further work on the data gathered during analysis will hopefully lead to the publication of additional information on features that may prove useful in this difficult task.

Throughout this report it should be remembered that there are real differences in physiological, chronological and social ages. Chronological age bands of the type used here are just a convenient way of categorising individuals recorded during skeletal analysis. In addition to considering the possibility of different rates of physiological change in the individuals discussed, it should also be considered that ideas on social age have changed considerably since the period when these individuals lived. Many of the juveniles would in fact have been in employment and have been economically active. The majority of those in the adolescent category from working class families would have been in employment and, depending on the type of work they did, may not have lived in the family home. A high proportion of working class individuals in the 'child' age category would also have undertaken some work. Fuller discussion of the proportion of juveniles engaged in paid employment, and the types of work they undertook, can be found in Chapter 7.

The differences found during osteological analysis in the proportion of men and women of different age categories compared to the evidence from written records, are probably related to all of the problems briefly mentioned above. However, with the large sample size available from this collection, although there may be individual errors, it should be possible to gain some idea of broad patterns of differences in pathological conditions between individuals in the different age and sex categories.

Normal variation

Stature

Stature was estimated using the formula for white males and females published by Trotter (1970). Where possible the femur and tibia were used in combination to calculate stature, but if one or other of the bones was not measurable then just the measurable leg bone was used. Only when it was not possible to use the bones of the legs were bones from the arms used.

There was a significant difference between the height of males and females in both the individuals from the vaults and the individuals from the earth-cut graves (p = 0.000). However, there was no significant difference in the height of either sex between those buried in the vaults and those in the earth-cut graves (p = 0.56).

As shown in Table 95 below, the estimated stature of individuals from St. Martin's was similar to that calculated for males and females from Christ Church, Spitalfields (Molleson and Cox 1993, 24). At Spitalfields stature was calculated for each individual using a range of bones and the results varied between 154.04cm and 158.52cm for females and 167.91cm and 170.27cm for males. If anything, individuals from St. Martin's are slightly taller, but not significantly so. The range of statures calculated for individuals at St. Martin's was broader than those calculated for Christ Church, Spitalfields. At St. Martin's the stature of females ranged from 139–170.5cm and in males it varied between 156cm and 185cm. The figures obtained for St. Martin's are certainly very close to the mean stature calculated by Roberts and Cox (2003) combining data from 11 British sites from the period. In the survey by Roberts and Cox

(2003, 308) the mean for males was 171cm and 160cm for females. Stature estimates for each individual are given in the Individuals Catalogue, Appendix 5.

The study undertaken by Roberts and Cox (2003) examined data from all periods in British prehistory and history, and as a result it was possible to see that average stature had changed very little since the medieval period. Stature is related to a wide range of factors, including nutrition genetics and other secular trends (Roberts and Cox 2003, 308). Data gathered from a range of sites of this period demonstrated that mean stature was not necessarily greater at sites that might be considered of higher status. This will be due to the wide range of factors affecting stature and will also probably be influenced by factors such as sample size available. Full sets of descriptive statistics for each measurement taken from males and females from St. Martin's are available in Tables 6 and 7 in Appendix 6.

A range of frequently recorded non-metric traits was recorded for adult individuals from St. Martin's. The traits recorded and there prevalence are presented in Table 8 in Appendix 6.

Abnormal variation

The following section of the report deals with the range of pathological and traumatic conditions recorded during the analysis of the human skeletal remains from St. Martin's. The data recorded reveal a number of interesting trends, but the limitations of this type of research should be borne in mind. Few of the many diseases and traumatic injuries that can affect humans will leave any trace upon the skeleton. In particular, acute infectious conditions, which would have been common during the period in which the individuals buried at St. Martin's lived, may well kill an individual before any diagnostic changes are manifest in the skeleton. With a large urban population such as that in Birmingham, this is a serious drawback. It is known from documentary sources that acute infectious conditions would have caused significant mortality (Roberts and Cox 2003, 328).

The diseases that tend to leave characteristic changes on the skeleton are frequently chronic, long-term conditions, which an individual can live with for some time. Although the diseases that fit into this category are limited, there are a range of conditions that it may be possible to diagnose from the examination of human skeletal remains, which provide interesting and useful information on various aspects of past human health, living and working conditions, diet and activity.

Another point that should be considered in the examination of pathological conditions from human skeletal remains is that bone can only react to degenerative disease, stress or pathogens in a limited number of ways. Additional new bone can be formed, bone can be resorbed, or a combination of both these processes may occur. Not surprisingly, with such a limited

Males			Females		
N.	Mean	SD	N.	Mean	SD
173	171.8	5.59	124	159.1	5.65

Table 95: Summary statistics for adult stature (cm).

repertoire of change many pathological conditions can, at least superficially, resemble one another. Often in order to suggest a diagnosis for pathological changes observed in a skeleton the exact distribution of changes across the skeleton needs to be considered. Therefore, for accurate diagnosis of some pathological conditions a well-preserved, complete skeleton is required. The difficulties that this requirement imposes when dealing with archaeological skeletal material will be apparent from the previous sections dealing with the quantity and nature of the material. There are frequently missing elements in archaeological skeletons and some areas of the bone surfaces may be poorly preserved, due to conditions in the ground, decomposition and factors affecting the skeleton since burial, including excavation.

Obtaining information on traumatic injuries suffered by individuals in the past from the analysis of skeletal material also has limitations. Again, there are many types of trauma that will leave no evidence on the skeleton. In particular, trauma that only affects the soft tissues is unlikely to leave any evidence. In such cases, the only change likely to be seen on the bone are those related to non-specific infections that may have arisen with pathogens entering at the site of a wound. However, such non-specific change is likely to be difficult to accurately attribute to soft tissue trauma. The most commonly recorded changes related to trauma recorded in human skeletal material are fractures and, as discussed at the start of the section where this evidence is dealt with, there are limitations involved with the diagnosis and interpretation of fractures in archaeological bone.

The data presented in the following sections are broadly grouped by different categories of disease, for example, infectious disease, congenital conditions, trauma, etc. However, as can be seen from the example given above involving an infection as a result of trauma, not all conditions can be neatly classified in this manner and there will be some inevitable overlap. There are a number of conditions discussed that could have been place under a number of the headings selected to present these findings under, and to some extent their placement in the following sections is arbitrary.

Diagnosis of pathological conditions is often difficult, even in clinical medicine, where there are the benefits of an individual's case history, the opportunity of questioning the patient and the presence of soft tissue, which may be used to undertake biochemical analyses. All these diagnostic tools are missing in the study of disease from archaeological skeletal material (palaeopathology) and often a firm diagnosis cannot be provided, but only a range of possible diagnoses suggested. These limitations should be borne in mind when considering the information contained in this report. Most of the conditions discussed were identified with a reasonable degree of confidence, but where this was not the case and the diagnosis suggested was just a strong possibility this is made clear. There were many skeletal changes recorded

during the analysis of the human bone from St. Martin's where the range of possible diagnoses for the abnormality observed was large. Due to the limitations on the study undertaken, it was not possible to obtain multiple radiographs or to undertake histological analysis in all cases. In addition, the space available for this report is insufficient to provide detailed descriptions and pictures of pathological changes for which it was not possible to suggest a reasonably firm diagnosis, and therefore only the most obvious cases are detailed.

Another consideration, with all the data provided in this section of the report, is that for each pathology the figures given can only be taken as a minimum possible prevalence for the condition being discussed. Problems such as missing bones and areas of bone with poor levels of preservation inevitably mean that there would have been more pathology present than it was possible to record. However, the large sample number at St. Martin's (505 individuals were recorded) and the relatively good levels of preservation (more complete, well preserved individuals were selected for analysis) mean that it should be possible to gain a good idea about the types of pathology from which individuals suffered. The relative prevalence of the various conditions recorded is discussed in the next section. In most instances true prevalence figures are provided (number of cases and number of bones that were present and could possibly have been affected) for each condition; if there is any variation from this method of presenting the data then a full explanation is provided. The most frequent deviation from this method of providing information is to give the crude prevalence rate, referred to as the CPR throughout the report. This is the number of individuals recorded as having a condition (for example a hypoplastic defect of tooth enamel) out of the total number of individuals who had one or more teeth and so could be assessed for the condition. There are clearly some problems with reporting the CPR of pathologies, but there are a number of reasons why this figure was calculated for some conditions. In some cases it was done because the disease/condition being considered can affect such a wide range of skeletal areas (e.g. it is not specific to a particular joint or teeth) and in other cases it was done to allow direct comparison between the data obtained from St. Martin's and other published studies. The data on numbers of bones present from which prevalence data was calculated are available in Appendix 7. This Appendix includes data on each area of all the bones recorded (e.g., for a long bone, proximal joint surface, proximal 1/3, middle 1/3, distal 1/3, and distal joint surface), each side (if applicable) and the burial type (earth-cut or vault) for adults and juveniles.

As recommended in Mays *et al.* (2002) basic statistical analyses were undertaken to determine if the findings relating to the various pathological conditions discussed were significant. Due to the nature of the data available, in all cases the test used was Chi-square. The number of degrees of freedom was '1' and the significance level selected was 0.05.

All Individuals analysed are listed in the Individual Skeleton Catalogue under their HB number, and the information contained in this catalogue includes summary descriptions of the pathological conditions recorded in each skeleton. This information forms Appendix 5 of this report. Individuals are also referred to by HB number in the following section, making it possible to identify individuals in the catalogue, and obtain some further information on those discussed.

Congenital disease

Congenital diseases are conditions that an individual is born with, i.e. the condition originated during prenatal growth and development. Therefore, such conditions can either be caused by an inherent genetic defect or by factors affecting the foetus during its development. Contributory factors could include infection or environmental conditions, for example malnutrition. Many congenital diseases affect the soft tissues, but it has been estimated that around 40% of these conditions affect the skeleton (Aufderheide and Rodríguez-Martín 1998, 51). The full range of diseases that could be placed under this heading is very large, ranging from very slight skeletal changes that are not detrimental and may not be noticed by the affected individual, to serious defects that are incompatible with life.

At the less serious end of the spectrum, it is difficult to draw a clear distinction between conditions that might be classified as a non-metric trait (listed in Table 8, Appendix 6) and those that might be considered a congenital disease or condition. In this report all conditions recorded that were not on the list of non-metric traits selected for systematic recording are considered here.

Developmental defects of the vertebral column, ribs and associated areas of the skull are relatively common and a range of such conditions recorded in the material from St. Martin's is given in Table 96 below, with their prevalence.

In Klippel-Feil syndrome a number of cervical vertebrae are congenitally fused, leading to a "short neck, low posterior hair line, and limited movement of the neck" (Barnes 1994, 67). Examples of the condition have been reported from archaeological contexts from many different time periods around the world (Aufderheide and Rodríguez-Martín 1998, 60).

Atlas occipitalisation results when the first cervical vertebrae (atlas) is partially or completely fused to the occipital bone of the skull. This is a relatively common condition and it has been reported to affect approximately 1% of the population (Aufderheide and Rodríguez-Martín 1998, 59). The condition can lead to a shortened neck, and may also be linked with other developmental defects of the skeleton, such as vertebral fusion and soft tissue defects, for example abnormal development of the urinary tract (*ibid.*). However, it is likely that this condition would not have been very debilitating for the individual concerned.

There is strong evidence of a genetic origin for the irregular segmentation of ribs, and this produces a wide range of abnormal variation (Barnes 1994, 71–2). However, the majority of rib defects, such as those recorded at St. Martin's, have little impact on the affected individual. The prevalence of rib defects recorded was relatively low at 1.76%, but it is difficult to obtain comparative data on these conditions so it is not clear how this compares to other sites.

A range of different numerical errors in segmentation of the spine was recorded. The normal number of presacral segments is seven cervical vertebrae, twelve thoracic vertebrae and five lumbar vertebrae. As can be seen from Table 96 below, there were a number of individuals in whom deviations from the normal number were recorded, for example the presence of six lumbar vertebrae. Such minor segmental shifts are relatively common and would have little impact on the affected individual.

Cleft defects in the posterior arch of vertebrae were recorded in both the thoracic and lumbar spinal regions. The prevalence of these defects was low and it is unlikely that they would have caused any adverse effects to the affected individuals. Clefts in the sacral arch were more common. These are caused by a minor delay in the development of the neural arch and frequencies as high as 25% have been reported (Barnes 1994, 117–119). These conditions are very different to the more serious problem associated with defects of the neural tube, spina biffida cystica. No cases of spina bifida cystica were recorded in the skeletal material from St. Martin's. The types of defects recorded would not have had any serious consequences for the affected individuals.

During recording, the spine of each individual was laid out in articulation. Viewing the spine in articulation, along with consultation of photographs taken on site, was used to assess spinal defects and abnormal curvature. Scoliosis refers to a lateral curvature of the spine with rotation of the vertebrae towards the concavity (Aufderheide and Rodríguez-Martín 1998, 66). Scoliosis can be related to a number of pathological conditions as well as congenital defects. In total 27 individuals were recorded as having some evidence of scoliosis but not all appeared to be caused by a congenital defect. Eleven of the 27 cases were considered to have a congenital cause; in seven of these individuals the condition was mild, but in three of the individuals the changes were more severe, in particular HB 183, a young adult of undetermined sex, shown in Figure 81. The skeletal changes present in this individual would have had a significant impact on this person. Mild unilateral multiple hemimetamere hypoplasia was present in the thoracic vertebrae (T3–T5) of HB 420, a young adult male. In this condition only one half of the vertebral body develops and the vertebral

Condition	Prevalence calculation method	No cases	No observable elements/individuals	Prevalence
7th cervical rib	As % of individuals with C7	4	264	1.52%
Cleft sacral arch	As % of individuals with a sacrum (adults)	20	293	6.83%
Spina bifida occulta	As % of individuals with a sacrum (adults)	0	293	0%
L6 present	As % of individuals with either L5 or S1	17	303	5.61%
T13 present	As % of individuals with T12 (adults)	6	294	2%
Atlas occipitalisation	As % of all individuals with an occipital (adult)	1	304	0.33%
Cleft thoracic arch	As % of all thoracic arches (adult)	1	3286	0.03%
Cleft lumbar arch	As % of all lumbar arches (adult)	1	1479	0.06%
Klippel-Feil syndrome	As % of all adult individuals with 1 or more cervical vertebrae	2	297	0.67%
Sacralisation of L5 to L6	As % of all L5 or 6 in adults	23	311	7.40%
Lumbarisation of S1	As % of S1 body or arches (adults)	5	277	1.81%
Lumbarisation of T12	As % of T12s	4	294	1.36%
Rib segmentation errors including: wide rib, rib spur, bifurcated rib, conjoined rib	As % of individuals (adult & subadult) with 1 or more ribs	8	452	1.76%
Congenital scoliosis	As % of individuals with 1 or more vertebrae	11	331	3.32%
Congenital kyphosis	As % of individuals with 1 or more vertebrae	4	331	1.21%

Table 96: Congenital defects of the vertebral column, ribs and associated areas of the skull. C = cervical vertebra, T = thoracic vertebra, L = lumbar vertebra, S = sacral segment.

segments present are laterally wedged resulting in scoliosis (Barnes 1994, 62). The condition was not severe and there was no fusion of the affected vertebrae, which can lead to severe scoliosis (Barnes 1994, 62).

Kyphosis is another type of abnormal curvature of the spine, but with this condition there is anterior curvature, so the affected individual bends forward (Ortner 2003, 463). Four individuals from St. Martin's were recorded as having kyphosis. Assessment of these individuals demonstrated that in each case the defect occurred in the thoracic region of the spine, typically below the level of the eighth thoracic vertebra. In two of the cases (HB 319 and HB 755) the deformities recorded fitted closely with those expected from Scheuermann's Disease, a deformity that develops in adolescents (*ibid.*). In the case of HB

170 the deformity was probably as a result of a developmental delay defect of the centrum. The final case, HB 198, had defects that resulted in a combination of kyphosis and scoliosis of the spine. In the modern population juvenile kyphosis occurs far more frequently in males, and all of the affected individuals identified in the present study were male.

Some comparative data on the prevalence of scoliosis and kyphosis in post medieval Britain is provided by Roberts and Cox (2003, 354). Their survey produced a CPR of 1.6% for kyphosis/scoliosis and 0.3% for scoliosis, slightly lower than the 3.3% prevalence for congenital scoliosis (the TPR for all types of scoliosis was 8.2% 27/ 331 individuals with 1 or more vertebrae) and 1.2% prevalence for kyphosis recorded at St. Martin's. The

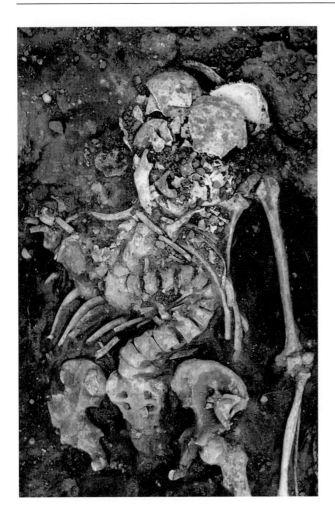

prevalence at St. Martin's may be a little higher because of the approach taken to recording these conditions, rather than any real difference between sites.

The prevalence of the skull and appendicular skeleton are listed in Table 97 below. Calcaneo-navicular bar defect is one of the most frequent coalition defects of the foot and can cause rigid flat foot (Resnick and Niwayama 1988, 3563–4). Although in some cases the condition can be associated with severe pain, symptoms associated with this defect are often less severe than other coalition defects of the feet (*ibid.*).

In a young child the mendosa suture separates the interparietal and supraoccipital areas of the occipital bone of the skull. If the suture fails to unite during normal development, and is retained, then the interparietal remains as a separate bone (Barnes 1994, 142). Retention of the suture has been noted in individuals from a range of archaeological contexts (*ibid.*). Individuals from a number of past cultures (e.g. South American individuals) have been reported to have a much higher prevalence than the 0.65% prevalence recorded at St. Martin's.

Cleft palate and lip was one of the more serious conditions recorded during analysis of the human bone from St. Martin's and would have had a significant impact upon the affected individual, HB 669 (a middle adult male from a vault burial) shown in Figure 82. The

Fig. 81: Site photograph of HB 183 showing the position of the bones in the ground prior to excavation.

Condition	Prevalence calculation method	No cases	No observable elements/individuals	Prevalence
Calcaneo-navicular bar defect	As % of individuals with either a calcaneus or navicular	3	265	1.13%
Mendosa suture retained	As % of individuals with an occipital (adult)	2	304	0.65%
Genu valgum (knock knees)	As % of individuals with a tibia (adult)	1	305	0.33%
Non fusion of navicular epiphysis	As % of all naviculars	2	405	0.49%
	As % of all adult individuals with a navicular	2	242	0.83%
Cleft lip/palate	As % individuals with 1 or more maxilla (adult & juveniles)	1	391	0.26%

Table 97: Defects of the skull and appendicular skeleton.

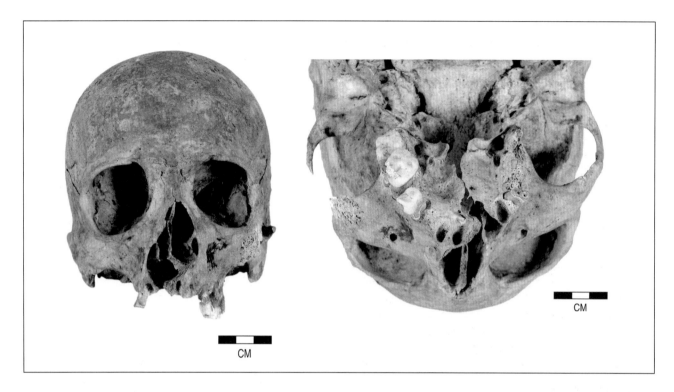

Fig. 82: Skull of HB669. (a) frontal view showing the cleft in the right side of the maxilla; (b) viewed from below the cleft in the palate is apparent.

two halves of the palate normally unite along a central suture, which runs along the roof of the mouth, but failure of the two halves to fuse results in a cleft palate, allowing access to the nasal cavity from the mouth. The condition is serious because the cleft between the mouth and nasal cavity makes it hard for an infant with this condition to suck and therefore obtain adequate nutrition (Roberts and Manchester 1995, 39).

It is apparent from the medical literature that, certainly from the 1820s, attempts were being made to correct the soft tissue defects of the lip associated with a cleft lip. In *The Lancet* a procedure for undertaking an operation to correct the outward appearance of the lip and bring about union without a cleft is described (Cooper 1824a). It is clear from the description provided that such operations had been carried out for a number of years previously and were being undertaken by surgeons across the country, not just in London. It is suggested that such operations could be very successful and produce good visual results. However, the author cautions against undertaking the operation in young infants, and advocates waiting until "completion of the dentition" (Cooper 1824a, 108). A number of instances of performing the operation upon young infants are discussed, all of which resulted in the death of the child. The risk of infection, shock and possible blood loss attendant upon such a procedure were clearly too much for most young children to survive.

The operation described would only have corrected the outward appearance of the defect and would not have remedied the cleft in the palate. However, another report in *The Lancet* of the same year details a series of operations undertaken in 1821 to correct the cleft in the palate of a young man (Cooper 1824b, 365). The procedures described are far more complex and difficult than those undertaken to unite a cleft in the lip and it is clear that such operations were still being developed and were not routinely undertaken.

In the description of these operations, it was stated that the patient elected to undergo this treatment as his voice had been extremely nasal, and conversing with strangers, which his job had come to require, was difficult. It is reported that the treatment, which managed to almost completely bridge the cleft, led to a great improvement in the patient's communication confidence (Cooper 1824b, 369). As only soft tissue is involved it is not possible to determine if such an operation has been undertaken from the examination of skeletal material.

Comparative data on the prevalence of the various congenital conditions reported is hard to come by, and so it is difficult to assess whether the number and frequency of the conditions reported for St. Martin's is similar to other sites. It was possible to obtain some prevalence information for neural arch defects for Christ Church, Spitalfields, where it is reported that there was a prevalence of 2.3%, a lower figure than the 6.83% recorded at St. Martin's.

However, of the conditions recorded, the cleft palate and lip in HB 669 and severe scoliosis in HB 183 are the only conditions that are likely to have had a serious impact on the affected individual, making the crude prevalence of such conditions low (0.40%, 2/505 of all individuals assessed). This is mirrored by the very low incidence of such conditions recorded in adult individuals for all the sites of this period reviewed by Roberts and Cox (2003, 357). There have been a small number of individuals reported from British sites with a cleft palate and/or lip, and these are detailed in the survey by Roberts and Cox (2003, 179), but none are from the period covered by the present study.

Joint disease

Diseases affecting the joints and their surrounding structures are often the most frequently recorded conditions in both archaeological bone and the modern population (Rogers 2000, 163). The results obtained from the analysis of the human bone from St. Martin's were no exception. A wide range of different conditions which could come under the heading of joint disease were recorded and these are considered in the following section.

Osteoarthritis (OA)

Of the joint diseases recorded in archaeological bone OA is probably the most frequently observed. The condition, which affects synovial joints, is primarily a disease of the cartilage. However, once the cartilage has disintegrated the underlying bone at the joint surface can come into contact and joint movement will eventually result in a polishing of the bone surface (eburnation). During analysis of human bone from St. Martin's OA was diagnosed using the criteria set out in Rogers and Waldron (1995, 43–44).

The condition is strongly age related, but there are many contributory factors including genetic predisposition, activity patterns and trauma; the latter can include disruption of a joint surface due to a fracture or dislocation (as noted later in the discussion on trauma) or injury involving just the soft tissues and cartilaginous plates.

The spine is a frequent site of changes related to OA and a CPR of 19.59% was recorded at St. Martin's (58/296, 296 individuals had one or more vertebra available for analysis and 58 of the individuals examined had one or more vertebra affected by OA). This is slightly higher than the 13.49% CPR for spinal OA reported by Roberts and Cox (2003, 352) for other post medieval British sites. Table 98 above gives more detailed information on the prevalence of changes in different areas of the spine recorded during analysis of the individuals from St. Martin's. Changes were present in all areas of the spine, but the most frequently affected regions were T3–T5 and the lower lumbar vertebrae (L3–L5). Information on working conditions and the health of the inhabitants of Birmingham, drawn from a range of sources, is provided in Chapter 7. One of the sources consulted mentions the

Vertebra	Total vertebrae present	No. observable	No. of vertebrae with OA	% prevalence
C1	272	266	1	0.37%
C2	275	267	16	5.99%
C3	259	251	21	8.36%
C4	263	255	17	6.66%
C5	262	252	13	5.15%
C6	266	255	7	2.74%
C7	264	261	9	3.44%
T1	280	269	20	7.40%
T2	281	270	27	10.00%
T3	285	270	56	20.70%
T4	290	269	58	21.50%
T5	290	267	55	20.59%
T6	293	266	26	9.77%
T7	297	273	12	4.30%
T8	292	269	7	2.60%
T9	298	273	7	2.50%
T10	297	276	15	5.40%
T11	298	287	17	5.90%
T12	294	281	10	3.50%
L1	308	290	9	3.10%
L2	305	290	9	3.10%
L3	303	292	19	6.50%
L4	301	296	29	9.79%
L5	295	290	35	12.00%
S1	278	254	21	8.26%

Table 98: The prevalence of osteoarthritis in the different regions of the spine. No. observable = the number of vertebrae with 1 or more apophyseal joint observable. Percentage is calculated as a percentage of vertebrae with observable apophyseal joints.

poor posture adopted by many individuals employed in workshops. The prevalence of OA in the spine recorded from St. Martin's could in part reflect the conditions under which many individuals worked.

Tables 9–12 in Appendix 6 give information on the distribution of OA across the skeleton for each individual in which the condition was present. These data demonstrate that many individuals had multiple joints affected, especially those in the older age categories. Table 99 below summarises this information, and gives the prevalence of OA at joints where it was observed during the skeletal analysis. Changes associated with OA, including eburnation, pitting of the joint surface and bone growth marginal to the joint are shown in Figure 83.

Table 99 demonstrates that in addition to the spine, some of the most commonly affected skeletal areas in the individuals analysed from St. Martin's were the clavicle, the joints of the hands and also the femur at the knee. These joints were also found to be commonly affected during the analysis of individuals from Christ Church, Spitalfields, and here in many instances a combination of these joints were affected. However, too little was known about the occupation of the affected individuals from

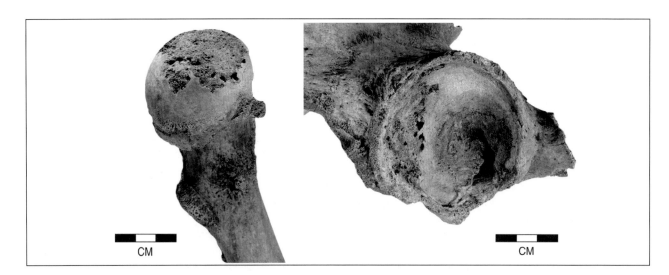

Fig. 83: Changes related to osteoarthritis at the hip joint of HB 157.

	No. of cases	A (number of bones)	B (number of individuals)	Total % Prevalence
Right clavicle	16	291	-	5.50%
Left clavicle	15	288	-	5.20%
Right scapula	12	294	-	4.10%
Left scapula	9	300	-	3.30%
Right humerus	Prox. = 2 Dist. = 5	Prox. = 265 Dist. = 282	-	Prox. = 0.75% Dist. = 1.80%
Left humerus	Prox. = 1 Dist. = 5	Prox. = 280 Dist. = 282	-	Prox. = 0.40% Dist. = 1.80%
Right ulna	Prox. = 0 Dist. = 1	Prox. = 281 Dist. = 233	-	Prox. = 0% Dist. = 0.40%
Left ulna	Prox. = 4 Dist. = 1	Prox. = 292 Dist. = 245	-	Prox. = 1.40% Dist. = 0.40%
Right radius	Prox. = 5 Dist. = 1	Prox. = 273 Dist. = 258	-	Prox. = 1.80% Dist. = 0.30%
Left radius	Prox. = 2 Dist. = 1	Prox. = 281 Dist. = 273	-	Prox. = 0.70% Dist. = 0.30%
Right carpal	13	-	265	4.90%
Left carpal	13	-	269	4.80%
Right metacarpal	15	-	285	5.30%
Left metacarpal	10	-	294	3.40%
Hand phalanx	14	-	303	4.60%
Right innominate	12	294	-	4.10%
Left innominate	10	297	-	3.40%
Right femur	Prox. = 8 Dist. = 15	Prox. = 293 Dist. = 288	-	Prox. = 2.70% Dist. = 5.20%
Left femur	Prox. = 5 Dist. = 12	Prox. = 303 Dist. = 303		Prox. = 1.70% Dist. = 4%
Right Patella	6	210	-	2.90%
Left Patella	6	205	-	2.90%
Right tibia	Prox. = 7	Prox. = 276	-	2.50%
Left tibia	Prox. = 4	Prox. = 275	-	1.40%
Right tarsal	2	-	260	0.80%
Right metatarsal	7	-	238	2.90%
Left metatarsal	4	-	232	1.70%
Foot phalanx	1	-	214	0.50%

Table 99: Prevalence of all OA (primary and secondary to trauma) at the joints at which it was observed. A = Total of adult bone element where applicable. B= Total number of adult individuals with bone element where applicable. Prox. = proximal joint surface, Dist. = distal joint surface.

Spitalfields to form any firm conclusions about the possible occupational causes of these changes to be determined, but they were strongly linked to increasing age (Waldron 1993, 69–72). Waldron reported that the joints of the knee were not commonly affected, but without prevalence data for Spitalfields it is difficult to tell if the levels documented at St. Martin's really are different, and the bones of the knee more frequently involved.

When males and females from all burial types were compared, females appeared to have slightly higher levels of OA than men, with 24.62% (32/130) and 21.67% (39/180) respectively. However, when tested statistically there was no significant difference between the sexes. Table 13, Appendix 6, gives data on the prevalence in males and females in the various age categories. The results show a different pattern to that recorded at Christ Church, Spitalfields. At St. Martin's the only age group in which females had a lower prevalence than males was the middle adult group, and there the difference in prevalences was small. However, at Christ Church, Spitalfields the only age group in which women had a higher prevalence than males was the young adult category; in all other groups men were more commonly affected (Waldron 1993, 67–8). The pattern recorded at St. Martin's is closer to that observed in people living today, as in the modern population there is a tendency for females rather than males to display a higher prevalence of OA (Waldron 1993, 67). In Table 100 below the prevalence of the condition in individuals from vaults and earth-cut graves is presented. Overall, levels of OA are slightly higher in individuals from the earth-cut graves than from the vaults, but this difference is not statistically significant. However, as the figures in Table 100 show, prevalence is sex dependent, and in fact females from vaults have the highest prevalence of OA (30.77%). As mentioned previously there was no significant difference in the pattern of OA between males and females.

As has been noted already, precise comparisons between sites are difficult, as detailed information is rarely provided in reports. Another factor to be considered when making comparisons is the strongly age-related nature of the condition; therefore, sites with more older individuals might be expected to have a higher prevalence of OA. However, the information given is often too limited to allow comparisons between individuals from different age categories and far more rudimentary comparisons of crude prevalence rates have to be made. The CPR gathered by Roberts and Cox (2003, 352) for non-spinal OA in post medieval British sites was 11.02%. The figure recorded for St. Martin's was twice as high at 22.16% (78/352 adults) although, as mentioned, this may be reflect a different age profile at the site. However, modern investigations of the prevalence of OA reported by Waldron (1993, 68) have produced results that are significantly higher than those obtained from previous analyses of archaeological bone. It is therefore possible that the results obtained from St. Martin's are more similar to levels found in the modern population. In their survey of human bone from British sites of all periods Roberts and Cox certainly found that there was a general increase in joint diseases such as OA with time, and the prevalence of these conditions for post medieval sites was higher than from medieval sites (Roberts and Cox 2003, 353).

Other arthropathies

Pyogenic arthritis (PyA)
Pyogenic arthritis is caused by infection of a joint. A range of bacteria have been linked to PyA (Studley 2003), but infections tend to be quite severe and often lead to joint destruction. Prior to the introduction of antibiotics many individuals with this condition would have died, with those that were able to survive left with complete fusion of a joint (Studley 2003).

One middle adult female, HB 668, had bony changes that appeared typical of those caused by pyogenic arthritis, giving a CPR of 0.28% (1/352) for this condition. The right femur and tibia were ankylosed in a flexed position with a 50-degree angle at the knee joint. Pyogenic organisms can affect a joint through a number of mechanisms: blood borne infection, directly from adjacent infected tissue or from a penetrating wound at the site. The condition can therefore be the result of an injury (Rogers and Waldron 1995, 88). In the affected individual from St. Martin's the condition had progressed to its final stage, with the occurrence of bony fusion, so it was not possible to determine the initial cause. Although this individual was recorded as having pyogenic arthritis, it is possible that the changes recorded were due to another

Vaults		Earth-cut graves	
All adults			
16/79	20.25%	62/273	22.71%
Males			
5/34	14.71%	34/146	23.29%
Females			
8/26	30.77%	24/104	23.08%

Table 100: Comparison of CPR of non-spinal OA in males and females from vault and earth-cut burials.

condition, such as neuropathic arthropathy (Charcot's joint). The knee is the most commonly involved joint in this condition, but parts of the spine and joints of the upper body are also often involved (Ortner 2003, 585–587), which was not the case in HB 668.

Whilst the infection was active this individual probably had symptoms associated with systemic infection. At the time these would almost certainly described as fever and the joint would have been painful. However, the fusion of one of her knee joints would have had a much greater impact on this individual and would have had a significant impact on her mobility.

Rheumatoid arthritis (RA)
Rheumatoid arthritis is a chronic joint disease that is frequently classed as an autoimmune condition (Aufderheide and Rodríguez-Martín 1998, 99). In modern individuals RA is a relatively common condition affecting about 1% of the population. RA mainly affects older people and is more common in women than men (Rogers and Waldron 1995, 55). One possible case of RA was recorded during the analysis of material from St. Martin's, in HB 658, an older adult female. In this individual, in addition to extensive eburnation, a smooth-walled, non-proliferative erosion was present at the articulation of the capitate and trapezoid of the left hand. The hands were not complete so it was not possible to assess the full extent of possible changes. With only one characteristic erosive lesion being recorded, this case must remain a possible, rather than a definite, instance of RA. However, if this were a case of RA it would have caused stiffness of the joints, particularly in the mornings, swelling and pain around affected joints (Gupta 2004).

Rheumatism is frequently mentioned in medical literature of this period (for example Abernethy 1826), although it is often employed as a 'catch all' term and was applied to a wide range of joint diseases. It is therefore difficult to obtain any information on the conditions discussed in the sections above from such sources. What is clear is that joint diseases of various types were common during this period and that the figures obtained from the analysis of the human bone only give an indication of the minimum prevalence of these conditions in the individuals buried at St. Martin's.

Schmorl's nodes
Schmorl's nodes are depressions observed in the end plates of vertebrae. The exact cause of these lesions is unclear and there is some debate as to whether they are caused by a herniation of material from the intervertebral disk (Rogers and Waldron 1995, 27) or whether the herniation of material is secondary to necrosis beneath the endplate (Peng *et al.* 2003, 879). However, whatever the exact pattern of events in disruption of the vertebral end plates and herniation of disk material, such nodes have been linked to physical activities, such as contact sports (Resnick and Niwayama 1988, 1530), and to acute trauma (Fahey *et al.* 1998).

The distribution of Schmorl's nodes in the spine recorded from individuals from St. Martin's mirrors the distribution commonly recorded in archaeological bone, with the lower thoracic and upper lumbar vertebrae being most commonly affected (Rogers and Waldron 1995, 27).

The prevalence of Schmorl's nodes recorded at St. Martin's (Table 101) was broadly similar to that recorded during analysis of the human bone from the Cross Bones burial ground, a pauper cemetery in London (Brickley *et al.* 1999, 38). These crude data suggest that there were no notable differences in overall levels of activity and trauma which may have led to the formation of nodes between these two sites.

Gout

Gout is caused by an inflammatory response to the deposition of uric acid crystals within joints and associated soft tissues, resulting from high levels of uric acid (hyperuricaemia) being present in the blood (Rogers and Waldron 1995, 78). Affected joints can be very painful during attacks, which occur during the 'acute gouty arthritis' stage of the disease, and in the final stages large amounts of urate crystals may be deposited within tissues around joints (tophi) (Aufderheide and Rodríguez-Martín 1998, 108–9). Idiopathic gout, the most commonly found form of the disease, has a much higher prevalence in males than females in the modern population. Although it can occur in all age groups, it most commonly develops in older adults, from around the 5th decade of life onwards (Resnick and Niwayama 1988, 1619).

Gout is frequently referred to in the medical literature dating to the period of the present investigation. At the time gout was considered to be a "constitutional disorder" arising from a failure to eliminate "morbid products" from the blood (*Periscopic Review* 1855, 515). Although it was thought that in some cases heredity played a role, more space was devoted to consideration of habits of indulgence and excess that could lead to the development of the disease. It is clear from the range of literature on the subject that medical opinion was divided on the exact cause, nature and effects of the condition. However, a number of characteristics of the condition were recognised. For example, it was noted that it rarely appeared in young individuals, almost never prior to puberty (because they drank less at this age), that men were more often affected than women, and that "more rich persons than poor have the gout" due to differences in diet (Armstrong 1825, 33–34). The main causes were considered to be "1. Intemperance, 2. Indolence, and, 3. Vexation" (Armstrong 1825, 34 referring to work by Cadogen [no date]).

It is no unusual thing for a man to eat of five or six different dishes at dinner, and afterwards to drink five or six different wines, and a continuance of such habits, combined with indolence, is almost sure to bring on an attack of gout (Armstrong 1825, 34–35).

However, to date there has been no evidence of the

Vertebral body	No. Present	No. with nodes		Upper surface		Lower surface		Both surfaces	
		No.	As % of present	No.	As %	No.	%	No.	%
C3	273	0	0%	0/265	0%	0/264	0%	0/261	0%
C4	277	0	0%	0/269	0%	0/269	0%	0/267	0%
C5	275	0	0%	0/269	0%	0/272	0%	0/269	0%
C6	276	2	0.72%	2/271	0.7%	1/269	0.37%	1/269	0.37%
C7	274	0	0%	0/270	0%	0/272	0%	0/270	0%
T1	282	1	0.35%	0/273	0%	1/269	0.37%	0/269	0%
T2	282	0	0%	0/265	0%	0/266	0%	0/263	0%
T3	285	3	1%	0/265	0%	3/271	1.11%	0/264	0%
T4	296	7	2.36%	3/281	1%	7/275	2.55%	3/273	1%
T5	296	38	12.84%	6/279	2.15%	36/278	12.95%	4/274	1.46%
T6	300	70	23.33%	17/285	5.96%	65/277	23.46%	12/274	4.38%
T7	303	93	30.69%	36/284	12.67%	87/239	36.40%	30/281	10.68%
T8	304	96	31.58%	53/292	18.15%	90/292	30.82%	47/286	16.43%
T9	304	119	39.14%	63/289	21.79%	109/292	37.33%	53/286	18.53%
T10	306	110	35.95%	64/289	22.14%	97/294	32.99%	51/286	17.83%
T11	307	109	35.50%	71/285	24.91%	92/287	32%	54/278	19.42%
T12	304	77	25.33%	61/282	21.63%	49/285	17.19%	33/278	11.87%
L1	307	51	16.61%	40/287	13.93%	32/290	11%	21/285	7.37%
L2	307	42	13.68%	32/287	11.14%	24/289	8.30%	14/285	4.91%
L3	309	29	9.39%	22/293	7.51%	15/295	5%	8/292	2.74%
L4	308	19	6.17%	10/297	3.36%	13/298	4.36%	4/294	1.36%
L5	303	9	2.97%	6/291	2%	3/284	1%	0/282	0%
S1	289	2	0.69%	2/279	0.72%	-	-	-	-

Table 101: Prevalence of Schmorl's nodes. The No. present refers to the number of vertebrae with either upper, lower or both surfaces present

condition from post medieval skeletons, and this has led to doubt being cast upon the ability of workers to recognise the condition in skeletal material (Roberts and Cox 2003, 311). Certainly, it is only in the later stages of the condition that changes that could be used to suggest a diagnosis in archaeological bone are present. Urate crystals or chalky masses are unlikely to be present in skeletal material, particularly when buried in earth-cut graves. Indirect evidence for the condition was found during investigations at Christ Church, Spitalfields, where one of the adult males was found wearing a 'gout boot' (Molleson and Cox 1993).

Analysis of the skeletal material excavated from St. Martin's identified four possible cases of gout. The CPR for gout in all individuals analysed from St. Martin's was 1.14% (4/352 adult individuals). However, a difference in the CPR was found when individuals from vaults and earth-cut graves were considered separately. The prevalence of gout appeared to be slightly higher in individuals from vaults (1.27%, 1/79 adults) than earth-cut graves (1.10%, 3/273 adults) but these differences were not statistically significant.

The first case, HB 740, an old adult female, had lytic erosions of the peri-articular area of the distal articulation of one of the proximal hand phalanges, shown in Figure 84. The lytic defects are surrounded by a sclerotic response. Limited lytic lesions are present on the adjoining surface of the intermediate phalanx. The changes are unlikely to be due to RA as this was the only joint from the hands that was affected.

Two of the other cases were in adult males, HB 58 and 792, and the third, HB 67, was a female. Two of these individuals were classified as older adults and one (HB 792) as a middle adult, Campbell Lloyd Haines, from Vault 30. In each of these cases metatarsals were affected, in particular the first metatarsal phalangeal joint. In addition, in HB 792 a hand phalanx also displayed typical erosive lesions.

Diffuse idiopathic skeletal hyperostosis (DISH)

DISH (or Forestier's disease) is a condition that affects the anterior longitudinal ligament of the spine, as well as other areas of the skeleton, often resulting in joint fusion through ligamentous ossification (Resnick and Niwayama 1988, 1563). In the spine, DISH has often been described as having the appearance of flowing candle wax (Rogers and Waldron 1995, 49) and this is illustrated in Figure 85. Clinical investigations have demonstrated that the condition is often painless and frequently no symptoms are apparent during the life of an affected individual (Aufderheide and Rodríguez-Martín 1998, 97). In the modern population the condition is widely reported to

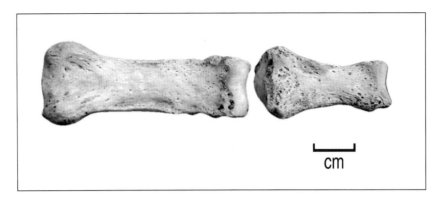

Fig. 84: Some of the erosions around the margins of one of the finger joints, possibly linked to gout, in HB 740.

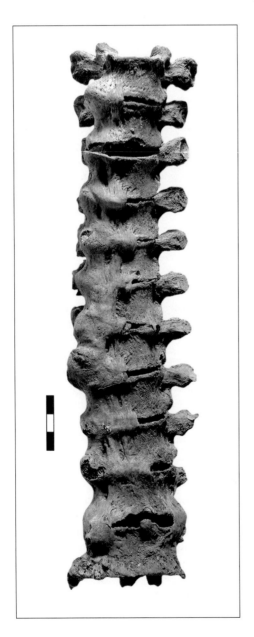

Fig. 85: Part of the spine of one of the individuals affected by DISH, showing new bone formation on the right side of the thoracic and lumbar region, in HB 369.

have an incidence of between 6 and 12% although many studies are based on individuals in hospitals; it is normally found in individuals over the age of fifty years and men are more frequently affected than women (Rogers and Waldron 1995, 48). The presence of this condition in individuals from St. Martin's is in itself unlikely to have had a significant impact on morbidity.

DISH was diagnosed using the criteria set out in Aufderheide and Rodríguez-Martín (1998, 97–98). In total, eight definite cases of DISH were recorded during the analysis of individuals from St. Martin's, giving a prevalence of 2.42% (8/331 adult individuals with one or more vertebra). The prevalence of the condition in those buried in vaults and earth-cut graves was slightly different with 3.22% for vault individuals (2/62) and 2.23% for earth-cut individuals (6/269). However, when tested this difference was not found to be statistically significant. All of the affected individuals were older adult males. In addition, there were another six individuals who may have had early cases of DISH, but the changes did not meet the diagnostic criteria of Aufderheide and Rodríguez-Martín, and four of these individuals were female.

The survey by Roberts and Cox (2003) found that there was a rise through time in the prevalence of DISH, and in earlier periods the sites at which it was found were often of higher status, for example monasteries. DISH has been associated with obesity and Type II diabetes (Roberts and Cox 2003, 311), both of which can be associated with over consumption of food. The prevalence of DISH at post medieval British sites varies considerably from 0% at the Cross Bones burial ground, a pauper site (Brickley *et al.* 1999), to 5.79% at Christ Church, Spitalfields, used by individuals of relatively high social status (Molleson and Cox, 1993). When compared to the results from other studies the prevalence of DISH recorded at St. Martin's is in line with what might be expected. The individuals from vaults do appear to have slightly higher levels of DISH than those from earth-cut graves, and prevalence is higher than all other sites reported for this period apart from Christ Church, Spitalfields, which was probably of slightly higher status.

Ankylosing spondylitis (AS)

AS is an inflammatory disorder, not linked to infection, which leads to progressive fusion of sacro-iliac joints and the spine. The exact causes are unknown, but the data available suggest that it has a strong genetic component (Aufderheide and Rodríguez-Martín 1998, 102). Just one possible case was recorded during the analysis of the material from St. Martin's, HB 433, an older adult female. The sacro-iliac joints were affected, but the rest of the vertebral column was not involved. The lack of involvement of the spine or any areas of the appendicular skeleton make the suggested diagnosis far from certain and a number of other conditions could have produced the changes recorded. However, the sacro-iliac joint has been noted to be the joint at which changes connected with AS are first manifest (Peh 2002). The CPR for the possible case of AS was low, 0.30% (1/331 adults with 1 or more vertebra/sacral segment).

In the modern population the frequency of AS has been estimated to be between 0.10–0.20%. Although morbidity associated with the condition can be considerable, most affected individuals experience few problems and many mild cases (similar to the possible case from St. Martin's) go unreported (Peh 2002).

Conclusions

Apart from DISH, where higher levels were recorded at Christ Church, Spitalfields, a higher prevalence of many joint diseases was recorded at St. Martin's than at many of the other sites of this period in Britain. However, it is difficult to be sure if this is real or related to a different age profile or the recording techniques employed at St. Martin's. One area where these results may indicate a real shift is the higher levels of OA. It is possible that with this condition we are beginning to see trends emerging in the data from St. Martin's that are far more reflective of the modern pattern of the condition. Changes in 'lifeways' experience by early inhabitants of industrialised Birmingham may have been responsible for producing some of the first patterns of disease that reflect those seen in the modern population. Although not very marked, there were slight differences observed between adults from vaults and from earth-cut graves, and these support a link between socio-economic factors and the prevalence of these conditions.

Infectious diseases

During the period covered by the present study, infectious diseases would have played an important role in the morbidity and mortality of the population. Prior to the introduction of antibiotics, such conditions would have accounted for many deaths (Roberts and Manchester 1995, 124). As discussed in the introduction many infections will leave no skeletal evidence, but it is known from documentary sources that they had an important role in the health of individuals living in the past. For example, data derived from sources such as the Report on the Sanitary Condition of the Labouring Population of Great Britain (1842) and reports of the Commissioners on the State of Large Towns and Populous Districts (1839; 1845) demonstrate that epidemics of infectious diseases were an important cause of mortality during the post medieval period (Fig. 86). Many of these conditions would have had a serious impact on a population living in industrialised urban areas such as Birmingham. Important infectious conditions listed include smallpox, scarlet fever, measles, diarrhoea, tuberculosis, pneumonia, and gastroenteritis. Although vaccinations were available for conditions such as smallpox, it was stated that many individuals, particularly those of Irish descent, were reluctant to have their children vaccinated and many died in outbreaks of the condition.

One of the most common changes linked to infection recorded on archaeological bone is periosteal new bone formation, or periostitis as it is often called. This is a non-specific reaction to inflammation/infection at the bone surface. A thin layer of woven bone is formed over the bone surface beneath the periosteum, but with time the newly formed bone will be remodelled and eventually completely resorbed. Therefore, the cases recorded from archaeological bone are just a snapshot in time; if healing is complete before an individual dies then no changes will be recorded. The other limitation of this type of change is that it is rarely possible to determine the causative agents responsible for the lesions and, as discussed below, there are a wide range of infective organisms that could cause periosteal new bone formation.

The prevalence of periosteal new bone formation on a number of different bones (femur, tibia, fibula, humerus and ulna) for males and females from different age groups, as well as the juveniles, are set out in Tables 14–18, Appendix 6. Analysis of the data recorded demonstrated that the tibia was the most commonly affected bone, and figures as high as 30% prevalence were recorded in the case of adult males in whom a more specific age could not be determined. Only a few age/sex categories had no cases of new bone formation recorded. Overall, the prevalence rates of periosteal new bone formation in the bones of the legs were much higher than in the bones of the arm. There are a number of possible reasons for this, which are discussed by Roberts and Manchester (1995, 130). For example, closeness of the tibia to the skin and varicose ulceration could cause high prevalence rates of bone changes in these regions. Comparative data on juveniles is not available and so it is not possible to assess if the pattern recorded from St. Martin's is seen at other sites. Involvement of the arms was far more common in juveniles than adults. The age/sex category in which the prevalence of periosteal new bone formation was consistently the highest was the young adult males, and for every bone the prevalence recorded for the young adult males was higher than that

BIRMINGHAM.

ABSTRACT of the CAUSES of DEATH registered from July 1st to December 31st, 1837, both inclusive.

Area in Acres.	Population according to Census of 1831.	Families in 1831.			
		Employed chiefly in Agriculture.	Chiefly in Trade, Manufactures, and Handicraft.	Other Families.	Total.
2,660	110,914	301	20,763	2,870	23,934

Sporadic Diseases.

Diseases.	Males.	Fem.	Total.
Epidemic, Endemic, and Contagious Diseases			
Cholera	3	3	6
Influenza	2	5	7
Small-pox	44	45	89
Measles	4	8	12
Scarlatina	..	2	2
Hooping Cough	2	4	6
Croup	5	10	15
Thrush	1	1	2
Diarrhœa	12	13	25
Dysentery	2	2	4
Ague	..	1	1
Typhus	33	42	75
Erysipelas	4	2	6
Syphilis	1	1	2
Hydrophobia	..	..	..
Total	**113**	**139**	**252**
Of the Nervous System.			
Cephalitis	5	3	8
Hydrocephalus	18	17	35
Apoplexy	14	11	25
Paralysis	8	13	21
Convulsions	45	27	72
Tetanus	..	..	..
Chorea	..	..	..
Epilepsy	4	2	6
Insanity	5	5	10
Delirium Tremens	1	..	1
Disease	5	5	10
Total	**105**	**83**	**188**
Of the Respiratory Organs.			
Laryngitis	..	..	4
Quinsey	1	3	4
Bronchitis	10	1	11
Pleurisy	..	..	..
Pneumonia	43	25	68
Hydrothorax	1	3	4
Asthma	19	8	27
Consumption	185	163	348
Decline	5	1	6
Disease	9	3	12
Total	**273**	**207**	**480**
Of the Organs of Circulation.			
Pericarditis	..	1	1
Aneurism	1	..	1
Disease	13	17	30
Total	**14**	**18**	**32**
Of the Digestive Organs.			
Intestinal Canal.			
Teething	15	5	20
Gastro-Enteritis	55	45	100
Peritonitis	1	1	2
Tabes Mesenterica	3	2	5
Ascites	..	..	..
Ulceration	6	3	9
Hernia	..	..	..
Colic	..	..	..
Constipation	1	1	2
Worms	..	1	1
Disease	6	2	8
Pancreas. Disease	..	..	..
Liver. Hepatitis	..	2	2
Jaundice	2	3	5
Disease	10	6	16
Spleen. Disease	..	..	..
Total	**99**	**71**	**170**

Diseases.	Males.	Fem.	Total.
Of the Urinary Organs.			
Nephritis	..	..	..
Ischuria	2	..	2
Diabetes	1	..	1
Granular Disease	..	..	..
Cystitis	..	..	..
Stone	1	..	1
Stricture	1	..	1
Disease	4	..	4
Total	**9**	**..**	**9**
Of the Organs of Generation.			
Orchitis	..	..	..
Childbed	..	11	11
Paramenia	..	..	..
Ovarian Dropsy	..	3	3
Disease	..	3	3
Total	**..**	**17**	**17**
Of the Organs of Locomotion.			
Arthritis	..	..	..
Rheumatism	1	2	3
Disease	2	2	4
Total	**3**	**4**	**7**
Of the Integumentary System.			
Carbuncle	..	..	..
Phlegmon	..	..	..
Ulcer	..	..	..
Fistula	2	..	2
Disease	..	..	..
Total	**2**	**..**	**2**
Of Uncertain Seat.			
Inflammation	5	5	10
Hæmorrhage	2	..	2
Dropsy	28	26	54
Abscess	5	11	16
Mortification	5	5	10
Scrofula	6	7	13
Carcinoma	3	11	14
Tumor	2	1	3
Gout	1	..	1
Intemperance	1	..	1
Atrophy	3	3	6
Debility	9	5	14
Starvation	1	..	1
Malformations	..	..	..
Sudden Deaths	..	2	2
Total	**71**	**76**	**147**
Old Age	28	52	80
Violent Deaths	30	15	45
Causes not specified	14	16	30
Total	**761**	**698**	**1,459**

Fig. 86: Causes of death in Birmingham in 1837 according to the Report of the Commissioners on the State of Large Towns and Populous Districts 1839.

recorded for the females. This pattern was noted in a review of literature on the condition (Roberts and Manchester 1995, 129), and it may be linked to levels of stress and trauma experienced by young males due to a range of socio-economic factors.

Where, in addition to the bone immediately below the periosteum, the compact bone of skeletal elements had clearly been involved in the infection, the term osteitis was used during recording. In the absence of soft tissues the full extent of infection present is difficult to assess, and as pointed out by Roberts and Manchester (1995, 126) the application of such terms is in many ways arbitrary. However, in recording of the bone from St. Martin's the different terms used denote differences in severity of involvement of the bones assessed through visual analysis. Prevalence of osteitis in the femur, tibia and fibula in each age and sex category is presented in Tables 19–21, Appendix 6.

There are a number of possible causes or contributory factors that can be linked to non-specific indicators of infection, for example direct infection of the affected area, trauma leading to infection, or changes caused by blood-borne bacteria from infections in other areas of the body.

The survey by Roberts and Cox (2003, 344) demonstrated that the CPR of periosteal new bone formation at post medieval British sites was 26.26%. The figure for 'non-specific infection' was 3.32%; it was 1.40% for osteitis, and 0.53% for osteomyelitis. In order to compare data obtained from St. Martin's a CPR was calculated for individuals with one or more bones affected by periosteal new bone formation. The CPR for all individuals from the site is 22.58%. Results for individuals of different ages from vaults and earth-cut graves are presented in Table 102 below.

The CPR of 22.58% is lower than that calculated by Roberts and Cox for a range of sites of this date. However, the figures obtained for different age and sex groups at St. Martin's varied markedly. For example, the prevalence for adolescents and young adults was much higher than the overall CPR. There were also differences noted between individuals buried in vaults and earth-cut graves at St.

Martin's. When tested it was found that there were significant differences in the CPR of periosteal new bone formation in individuals from vaults and earth-cut graves ($Xc^2 = 7.74$, df = 1, $p \leq 0.01$). The older adults were fairly similar in both groups, but the patterns in the other age groups were different. The CPR for young and middle adults was much higher in individuals from earth-cut graves than those from vaults. The pattern is reversed in children and adolescents, and it is possible that the osteological paradox (Wood *et al.* 1992) has played a role in producing the pattern found. The slightly higher prevalence of periosteal new bone formation in children and adolescents from the vaults (21.43% compared to 17.54%) may in fact indicate better levels of health. Infections may have been far more likely to cause the death of less healthy individuals buried in earth-cut graves. The results of the analyses of other disease categories, for example the metabolic diseases, indicate that children from earth-cut graves may have been living with much higher levels of chronic deficiency diseases, indicative of poorer levels of health. The numbers of infants from both types of burial were so small that it is difficult to interpret the results obtained for these individuals.

Tuberculosis (TB)

Tuberculosis is a chronic infection caused by *Mycobacterium tuberculosis* or *M. bovis* (the animal form of the disease), both of which can affect soft tissues as well as the skeleton (Aufderheide and Rodríguez-Martín 1998, 118). Infection can occur either as a result of consumption of infected food, for example milk or meat, or by means of droplet infection from infected individuals (e.g. coughing). As a result, tuberculosis is more prevalent in areas with high population densities (Roberts and Manchester 1995, 137). The living conditions for many people in Birmingham during the period of this study would have been ideal for high levels of infection with tuberculosis. An investigation in Birmingham a little later than the period covered by the present study found that around 10% of milk brought into the city was infected with tuberculosis (B. M. J. 1908, 48).

Vaults													
Infant		Child		Adolescent		Young Ad.		Middle Ad.		Old Ad.		Adult	
0/6	0%	2/12	16.67%	1/2	50%	0/8	0%	4/27	14%	4/19	21.05%	1/25	4%
Earth-cut grave													
Infant		Child		Adolescent		Young Ad.		Middle Ad.		Old Ad.		Adult	
7/67	10.45%	4/40	10%	6/17	35.29%	25/54	46.29%	28/108	25.93%	25/91	27.47%	5/20	25%
All individuals													
Infant		Child		Adolescent		Young Ad.		Middle Ad.		Old Ad.		Adult	
7/73	9.58%	6/52	11.54%	7/19	36.84%	25/62	40.32%	32/135	23.70%	29/110	26.36%	6/45	13.33%

Table 102: CPR of periosteal new bone formation. Number of individuals in each age category with periosteal new bone formation present on one or more bones. All individuals = combined data from individuals buried in vaults and earth-cut graves.

No 'classic' cases of TB-related skeletal changes in the spine, of the type described by Ortner and Putschar (1981), were recorded during the analysis of the bone from St. Martin's. However, a range of other changes, which may be linked to TB, were identified during the skeletal analysis.

There were 43 cases (individuals with one or more affected ribs recorded) of periosteal new bone formation on the pleural surfaces of ribs. It is possible that such changes were related to TB, but other possibilities should also be considered. For example, new bone formation on ribs could be the result of a range of chronic lung or respiratory infections. Twelve of the individuals with such rib changes from St. Martin's were female, 23 were male and the sex could not be determined in eight cases. In many cases where this type of bone change was recorded, the changes were present on more than one rib. Cases of periosteal new bone formation on ribs broken down by age/sex category are presented in Table 22, Appendix 6.

There were three possible cases of tuberculosis from St. Martin's in which spinal lesions were present. In the first example, HB 904 (adolescent from an earth-cut grave), there were lytic lesions with destructive foci in the lower thoracic and upper lumbar vertebral bodies. No osteoblastic activity could be detected and only the vertebral bodies were involved. Unfortunately the skeleton of this individual was very fragmentary, as can be seen from the vertebra shown in Figure 87, and it was not possible to examine other common locations of skeletal changes linked to tuberculosis. Two tests were carried out for MTB DNA (i.e. the DNA of the organism responsible for the infection), discussed more fully later in this section, but neither test produced a positive result. The lack of positive result does not however mean that this individual did not have TB. Unfortunately negative results do little to clarify the situation, so it still remains

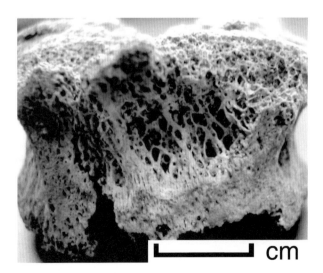

Fig. 87: Lytic lesion on a vertebra from HB 904, possibly linked to tuberculosis.

uncertain if this individual suffered from TB or not. In the second individual, HB 220 (young adult, earth-cut grave), a lytic lesion was present in the ninth thoracic vertebra, but other large lesions in T7 and T8 had the appearance of Schmorl's nodes and there were no other skeletal changes associated with the condition. Although destructive lesions in the spine are frequently used as a diagnostic feature of tuberculosis in archaeological skeletons, caution should be exercised as there are wide ranges of infective organisms that can also cause destructive lesions of the spine (Ortner 1999, 256–7). In the third case, HB 193 (child, earth-cut grave), in addition to widespread lesions on the spine, changes consistent with tuberculous osteomyelitis were present in the innominates, left scapula, ribs and skull. It has been reported that multiple tuberculous lesions are more common in children than adults (Aufderheide and Rodríguez-Martín 1998, 133) and the changes recorded in this individual are consistent with a diagnosis of tuberculosis. If these lesions were taken as an indication of TB this would give a CPR of 0.71% (3/423 individuals categorised as a child or older).

Another skeletal change observed that may be linked to tuberculosis was endocranial change in the skull. In one individual (HB 467, an adolescent from an earth-cut grave) extensive patches of new bone formation were noted on the endocranial surface of the skull. The appearance of the new bone formation matched that of Serpens Endocrania Symmetrica (SES), described and named by Hershkovitz *et al.* (2002). In their study of the Hamann-Todd collection, Hershkovitz *et al.* found a link between SES and TB. It is possible that the young adult from St. Martin's suffered from intra-thoracic disease and this possible diagnosis is supported by the presence of rib lesions in this individual. However, the changes observed could also be linked to a chronic meningeal infection. Reports of tubercular meningitis exist in the medical literature from towards the end of the period of this study (Robinson Hill 1860).

It was also noted at Christ Church, Spitalfields that although tuberculosis would have been prevalent in London at that time, very few individuals manifested the 'classic' changes associated with the condition (just two, CPR 0.21%) (Waldron 1993; Roberts and Cox 2003, 339). As concluded in the report on the human bone from Spitalfields, for some reason during this period it seems relatively rare for tuberculosis to have spread to the bones and joints (Molleson and Cox 1993, 83).

A review of prevalence rates of skeletal changes associated with tuberculosis undertaken by Roberts and Cox (2003, 339) produced a low CPR from sites of this date across Britain. The total CPR for definite cases was 0.47%, and the CPR for rib lesions was 4.76% at the Newcastle Infirmary (Boulter *et al.* 1998, cited in Roberts and Cox 2003, 339), where these changes were considered separately.

It is known from documentary sources dating to this

period that tuberculosis was a common condition and constituted a serious health problem, being a significant cause of morbidity and mortality. Data gathered as part of the *Chadwick Report* demonstrated that deaths from such conditions were extremely common:

> The numbers affected with pulmonary diseases *[the category in which TB would have been placed]* are much greater than those affected with any of the other classes of disease...the deaths from this class of diseases, 678, form one-third of the whole number of deaths (Report on the Sanitary Condition of the Labouring Population of Great Britain 1842, 200).

Although there was probably a lumping together of a range of conditions under headings such as scrofula and consumption it is clear that the problem was widespread. Research on some of the individuals from the vaults meant that death certificates were obtained and in one case the cause of death given was phthisis. The term was widely used and not all deaths attributed to the condition may actually have been related to tuberculosis. However, in the case of Alfred Browett (HB 336) the presence of TB was backed up by DNA investigations. DNA analysis also proved positive in another 11/17 samples analysed. For positive results to be obtained it is likely that the individual died of the condition. Individuals who were tested for TB and the number of positive or negative test results are given in Appendix 5. The majority of samples were taken from individuals who were suspected of having tuberculosis from skeletal analysis. However, in five of the 11 positive cases of TB identified there were no skeletal changes present that would give a firm indication that the individuals had suffered from the condition. Absence of skeletal changes is a common finding in investigations of TB in archaeological skeletal material (Roberts and Buikstra 2003). However, four of the six individuals who produced negative test results did have rib lesions, which could be linked to TB. As discussed earlier, negative test results give very little information and do not mean that an individual did not have the condition tested for.

Research on the London Bills of Mortality by Roberts and Cox (2003) for the period demonstrated that here a cause of consumption was attributed to 25% of deaths at the end of the eighteenth century (2003, 338). Figures for Birmingham provided in the Report of the Commissioners on the State of Large Towns and Populous Districts (1839) give a very similar figure, 24.79%. The figures produced in the Report on cause of death are given in Figure 86 and from this information it can be seen that 'consumption' is the largest single cause of death listed for the period investigated. Malnutrition, overcrowded living conditions, poorly ventilated houses, and the establishment of urban dairies (in the 1851 census for Birmingham there were 258 'cowkeepers and milk sellers') would all have contributed to pulmonary tuberculosis being a major cause of death during this period (see Chapter 7). For tuberculosis, cases of the condition recorded during

visual analysis of archaeological bone only gives a small insight into the full prevalence of the condition in the past. Only a small percentage of affected individuals would have any skeletal involvement.

Brucellosis

This is a condition that can be passed from a wide range of animals to humans, either through infected meat or milk, and it is possible that the infection was present in the community from which the individuals buried at St. Martin's came. Changes in the vertebrae that may be linked to infection with brucellosis were recorded in three male individuals (HB 287, 553 and 580). Changes to a vertebral body from HB 553 are shown in Figure 88. One of the individuals concerned was an older adult, the second a middle adult and the third was an adolescent. In each case, a number of vertebrae were involved and bone formation as well as lytic destruction was noted. However, no changes in other bones of the skeleton that could be linked to brucellosis were recorded. The CPR of possible cases of brucellosis was 0.81% (3/371 adolescent and older individuals). Males have been noted to be affected more frequently than females (Ortner 2003, 216), and all three of the possible cases from St. Martin's were in males. All the lesions recorded had sclerotic bone present, and two of the individuals also had evidence of destructive lesions – noted to be a feature of earlier stages of the condition (*ibid.*). Vectors of brucellosis include goats, sheep, dogs, pigs, horses and cattle, all of which would have been present in Birmingham at the time of this study, and meat and milk from some of these animals would have been common dietary components for individuals living in the area. No possible cases of the condition were reported from Christ Church, Spitalfields (Molleson and Cox 1993), Cross Bones burial ground (Brickley *et al.* 1999) or the burial ground at Kingston-upon-Thames (Start and Kirk 1998). However, the

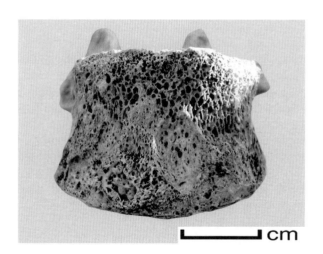

Fig. 88: New bone formation and lytic areas, possibly linked to brucellosis on a vertebra from HB 553.

possibility that the lesions recorded in individuals from St. Martin's may have been due to tuberculosis or another infectious disease cannot be ruled out.

Syphilis

Syphilis is known to be a common condition during the period of study and has been noted in a number of skeletal collections of this date from London, for example Christ Church, Spitalfields (Molleson and Cox 1993) and the Cross Bones burial ground (Brickley *et al.* 1999) St. Bride's Lower Churchyard (Conheeney and Waldron in press, cited by Roberts and Cox 2003). The condition is also reported from the contemporary Quaker burial ground at Kingston-upon-Thames (Start and Kirk 1998) and the Newcastle Infirmary (Boulter *et al.* 1998, cited in Roberts and Cox 2003). The total CPR for syphilis from sites of this period calculated by Roberts and Cox (2003, 341) was 0.77%. However, no evidence was found of skeletal changes associated with either acquired or congenital syphilis during the analysis of the human bone from St. Martin's. Although skeletal changes are not produced with the condition until the tertiary stage in acquired syphilis (which can occur up to ten years after the initial infection), it is still slightly surprising that no cases were recorded.

Contemporary documentary accounts show that the condition was considered a problem in Birmingham at this time. A report by Parker (1855, 557) details the treatment given to patients with the secondary stage of the disease in the Queen's Hospital Birmingham. Slightly later case reports detail the condition in a married woman of 32 years of age, who was admitted to Birmingham General Hospital in 1859. The woman was suffering from syphilis and it was noted as part of her case history that she had given birth to seven children "of which five died young; two when four months old" (Russell 1860, 166). Congenital syphilis could have been a contributory factor in the deaths of some of these children. A number of details in some of the cases reported by Russell indicate that changes had occurred in these individuals, which would be manifest on the bone.

Although not as virulent as in earlier years of the post medieval period, by the late eighteenth century the condition was still widespread and a moralistic view of infected individuals became stronger and more pervasive (Roberts and Cox 2003, 341). No cases were recorded in the analysis of the limited numbers of individuals of this period from St. Philip's Cathedral (Brickley 2001), and it would be interesting to see if absence of skeletal evidence of this condition was maintained if future individuals of this period from the Midlands region became available for analysis.

Sinusitis

In all 14 individuals from St. Martin's had evidence for nasal or sinus infections. The true prevalence of such infections is difficult to calculate as the nasal sinuses are almost completely enclosed by the bones of the skull. Unless techniques such as endoscopy or radiography are used, it is only when damage and breaking of the skull has occurred that these areas can be inspected and changes recorded. Neither endoscopy nor radiography were applied to the study of changes in the sinuses of the individuals from St. Martin's. A study by Roberts and Lewis (1994, cited in Roberts and Manchester 1995) found that individuals from an urban site had much higher levels of infection than those from a contemporary rural site (the prevalences were 38% and 55% respectively) (Roberts and Manchester 1995, 131). However, the study by Roberts and Lewis used endoscopy to examine the skeletal material, and so the prevalences recorded will be much higher than those from St. Martin's.

Factors that can lead to the development of sinusitis include things such as smoke, environmental pollution and dust. All of these would have been common in Birmingham during the period covered by this study. Of the 14 individuals identified as having evidence for infection, the majority (9) were women, three were men and the sex of two individuals could not be determined. The affected individuals fell into all adult age categories.

The prevalence of sinusitis at St. Martin's was 5% (14/279 adults with maxilla), higher than the CPR reported for both the Cross Bones burial ground (Brickley *et al.* 1999), and St. Bride's Lower Churchyard in London (Conheeney and Waldron in press, cited by Roberts and Cox 2003). However, a recent study undertaken by Roberts on individuals from Christ Church, Spitalfields produced a CPR of 18.02% (Roberts in prep., cited by Roberts and Cox 2003). In this study an endoscopic technique was used to undertake the examination, so these results are almost certainly more accurate than the present study, or previous reports mentioned above. All of the affected individuals from St. Martin's came from earth-cut graves, but it is not possible to be sure if this difference between individuals from vaults and earth-cut graves is real, possibly related to jobs undertaken, or if it is due to different taphonomic effects operating on skulls. It has been noted that sinusitis can be related to abscesses in the upper jaw (Roberts and Manchester 1995, 131) and five of the affected individuals in the present study had such an abscess, but it is not possible to be certain if infection in the sinuses was linked to the presence of an abscess.

Although there are many problems with the way in which sinusitis was investigated, the prevalence recorded may reflect real patterns of the condition. In a report on public health in Birmingham dusty conditions associated with some forms of employment were noted:

Also the dusty employments of pearl button making,...appear to produce detrimental effects on the air-passages...The process of lackering metals we believe to be very unhealthy; this proceeding is carried on in hot rooms, the atmosphere of which is extremely impure, generally by young females (Report on the Sanitary Condition of the Labouring Population of Great Britain 1842, 216).

If these reports are accurate it is possible that the high level of sinusitis seen in females from St. Martin's may reflect the conditions in which many of these women would have worked.

Poliomyelitis

Today, disability due to this condition is rare, but it is likely to have been far more significant before the introduction of vaccinations. This viral infection can cause paralysis of muscle groups, often resulting in wasting of the muscle and possible arrested growth of associated bones (Roberts and Manchester 1995, 134). Not all individuals affected by the condition will exhibit related skeletal changes, so it is impossible to gain a complete picture from the archaeological record, but data from archaeological bone does give an additional insight into past health. One individual from St. Martin's exhibited skeletal changes that could indicate that they had suffered from poliomyelitis (HB 675, a middle adult probable female from an earth-cut grave). There was atrophy and reduction in size of the left os coax, femur, tibia (the fibula was damaged post mortem and could not be measured), patella and tarsals. There was a discrepancy of 44mm between measurements of the left and right tibia and femur. Although the changes are consistent with those caused by poliomyelitis, it is possible that the atrophy and reduction in size of some of the bones in this individual had an alternative cause, for example trauma.

Meningeal reactions

New bone formation was recorded on the endocranial (internal) surfaces of bones from three juvenile individuals, all from earth-cut graves. In HB 766, a foetus from an earth-cut grave, new bone formation was recorded in the frontal bone. The endocranial surface of the sphenoid and temporal were affected in HB 583. Figure 89 illustrates the types of changes seen on the temporal of HB 583. Finally, in HB 814 the endocranial surface of the frontal and fontanelle were affected. The prevalence of this type of change was 2.65% (3/113 juveniles with one or more areas of skull that could be affected present). Various diseases can produce this type of new bone formation in the skull, for example "epidural hematoma, meningitis and meningoencephalitis" as well as conditions such as scurvy and trauma (Schultz 2003, 93). No histological work was undertaken, and so accurate diagnosis of the causes of the changes observed cannot be made.

Other non-specific bone changes

A range of other non-specific bone changes, probably linked to infections, were recorded during the analysis of the human bone and brief descriptions of the changes documented are included in the Individuals Catalogue, Appendix 5. Due to the limitations of the study of palaeopathological conditions outlined in the intro-duction, in many cases it was not possible to offer a firm diagnosis for the changes recorded.

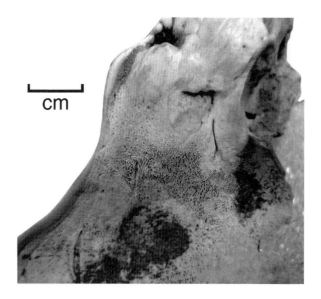

Fig. 89: New bone formation on the petrous portion of the temporal bone of HB 583.

Conclusions

A number of studies have suggested that the prevalence of lesions related to infectious disease increases with population density (Roberts and Manchester 1995, 129). Given the nature of infectious conditions, finding higher levels of these conditions associated with denser pop-ulations is not surprising. At St. Martin's, as at other urban sites of this period, there were certainly relatively high levels of indicators of infectious disease. Overall, the data recorded indicates a fairly high level of infectious disease with possible differences between the way in which individuals from vaults and earth-cut graves are affected. The range of possible infections recorded in individuals from St. Martin's was far wider than that for some of the other sites of this period. However, there are also some interesting differences between the findings of this and previous studies. The lack of individuals with evidence for syphilis or osteomyelitis possibly indicates that affected individuals were not as robust as those from other sites, as we know these conditions were present in the population at this period. It is probable that many affected individuals succumbed to these or other con-ditions before skeletal changes became manifest.

Trauma

The term trauma covers a wide range of injuries and conditions, and as mentioned in the introductory section only a small proportion of these will be evident in archaeological human bone. However, these conditions are important in the study of past populations as the types of trauma suffered will not only be related to lifestyle and occupation, but also to the underlying health of individuals, as fractures can have a pathological cause.

	No. of cases (no. of individuals affected follows in brackets)	Prevalence as % of individuals in each age/sex group	
Foetus	0	0/9	0%
Infant	1 (1)	1/73	1.37%
Child	0	0/52	0%
Adolescent	0	0/19	0%
Young adult male	5 (3)	3/30	10%
Young adult female	2 (2)	2/26	7.69%
Young adult unsexed	2 (2)	2/6	33.33%
Middle adult male	57 (33)	33/83	39.76%
Middle adult female	7 (6)	6/43	13.95%
Middle adult unsexed	0	0/9	0%
Old adult male	59 (32)	32/49	65.31%
Old adult female	16 (15)	15/52	28.85%
Old adult unsexed	12 (7)	7/9	77.78%
Adult male	11 (7)	7/18	38.89%
Adult female	0	0/9	0%
Adult unsexed	0	0/18	0%

Table 103: The CPR of fractures of any type by individual as a percentage of the age/sex group.

One of the most commonly recorded conditions that could be placed under the heading trauma is fracture. Careful examination of fractures, often aided by radiological images, can give some indication of the possible causes and clinical severity of the injury (Roberts and Manchester 1995, 65).

The very crude data on fractures presented in Table 103 above gives an idea of the overall prevalence of fractures and their distribution in the different age/sex categories. The overall CPR for fractures from St. Martin's was 21.39% (108/505), but when only the adults are considered, as at most archaeological sites, the prevalence rises to 30.40% (107/352). The CPR for individuals buried in vaults was lower than those from earth-cut graves, 14.14% (14/99) and 23.15% (94/406) respectively, a significant difference (Xc^2=3.84, df = 1, $p \leq 0.05$). These results indicate that a range of factors in the lives of individuals from earth-cut graves made sustaining a fracture more likely. The difference between the two groups was particularly marked in the females. The CPR of fractures in females from vaults was just 3.85% (1/26) compared to 21.36% (22/103) in those from earth-cut graves (Xc^2=4.34, df = 1, $p \leq 0.05$). The number of women in each age category is different for vaults and earth-cut graves, and although there are far more older adult females buried in earth-cut graves than vaults the prevalence of women with a fracture is very different when each age group is examined separately. For example, 16.67% (1/6) of older adult women from a vault had a fracture compared to 30.43% (14/46) of older adult women from an earth-cut grave. The pattern in adult males from the two groups was far more similar with those from vaults having a CPR of 38.23% (13/34) compared to 42.18% (62/147) in individuals from earth-cut graves. There was no significant difference between

the two groups of males (Xc^2=0.77, df = 1, $p \leq 1$). These differences in the prevalence of fractures recorded are almost certainly related to the types of work and activities undertaken by many of the women in earth-cut graves. As at many other archaeological sites there was a significant difference in the prevalence of fractures between males and females (Xc^2=20.068, df = 1, $p \leq 0.001$).

The figures obtained from St. Martin's are much higher than the CPR from Kingston-Upon-Thames, a burial ground used by middle class individuals, where just 3.61% (13/360) of individuals recorded were affected by fractures (Start and Kirk 1998). However, few other site reports present data in this format so it was not possible to compare the crude prevalence of fractures at St. Martin's to other British sites of the period.

Like many other investigations of archaeological bone, the number of fractures recorded in the juveniles is very low (often there are no cases reported). The left clavicle of HB 563, an infant from an earth-cut grave, was fractured towards the medial end of the shaft, and this is shown in Figure 90 along with the radiograph of the bone. The fracture had occurred relatively recently and was still healing at the time of death. Fractures of the clavicle shaft are a common injury in infancy and early childhood in the modern population (Glencross and Stuart-Macadem 2000, 200).

It is likely that children in the past did sustain fractures fairly frequently, as they do today, and historical evidence dating from the period in which some of those buried at St. Martin's lived, discussed later, suggests this to be the case. However, there are a number of possible reasons why fractures in juveniles are so rarely recorded in archaeological bone. Many fractures occurring in juveniles may be 'green stick' fractures, i.e. not complete,

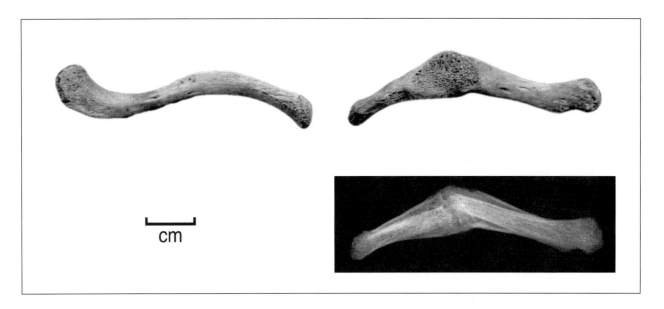

Fig. 90: Fractured left clavicle of infant HB 563. The difference between the right and left (fractured) clavicle can be seen at a gross level, and the radiograph of the left clavicle shows the location of the fracture beneath the callus.

and secondly healing and general bone growth may be so rapid as to soon obliterate the evidence or make it far less obvious than in adults. In juveniles a fracture would probably have had to occur relatively close to the time of death for changes to be apparent in archaeological bone. Time was not available to undertake the kind of synthetic approach to the analysis of possible childhood trauma advocated by Glencross and Stuart-Macadam (2000). However, the likelihood of trauma in childhood, possibly leading to fractures, was considered during the recording of the adult human bone.

Evidence for the occurrence of trauma, and possibly a fracture in childhood, came from HB 338, an old adult male from an earth-cut grave. In this individual there had been disruption of the distal epiphyseal growth plate of the right humerus. The most likely cause of such a deformity is an intra-articular fracture through the lateral condyle of the humerus up into the distal metaphysis (Salter 1999, 307). The highest incidence of fractures to the distal humerus occurs in toddlers and children below the age of ten (Glencross and Stuart-Macadam 2000, 201). However, as the individual lived for a considerable time after the event that caused the changes recorded it is difficult to be certain. HB 118, discussed under work-related fractures, may also have sustained his fracture during childhood.

Table 103 on the previous page illustrates that in all age categories the prevalence of fractures is higher in men than women. This probably reflects social and cultural factors operating at the time, the various types of work undertaken by men and women, and various social/ sporting activities, as well as different levels of exposure to violence. The other feature of fractures in archaeological bone that is well demonstrated in Table

103 is the cumulative nature of fractures: the older an individual gets the greater is their chance of having sustained one or more fractures (Roberts 2000, 345).

Table 23 in Appendix 6 gives fracture prevalence data by bone and by side of the body. In summary, the thoracic vertebrae, metacarpals and ribs were the most commonly affected areas of the skeleton with prevalence rates of 2.9%, 2.8% and 2.3% respectively. Ribs were also found to be amongst the most frequently affected bones in other post-medieval British sites, in the survey undertaken by Roberts and Cox (2003), but the prevalence produced by this survey was higher than at St. Martin's at 4.23% (Roberts and Cox 2003, 302). For most bones, the prevalence of fractures recorded at St. Martin's was higher than that reported by Roberts and Cox (2003). The only other bones in which a higher prevalence of fractures were reported by Roberts and Cox were the femur (0.2% compared to 1.25% [produced by Roberts and Cox 2003]) humerus (0.1% compared to 1.09%) and ulna (0.6% compared to 0.64%).

Most of the fractures recorded in the bones from St. Martin's would have been simple, closed fractures, such as the fractured fibula shown in Figure 91. The majority of these fractures were well healed, with no evidence of infection or malalignment. However, it is possible that some fractures of a more serious nature, involving open wounds and infection, were not recognised as the individual died shortly after the accident. Many bones from archaeological sites are damaged or broken and prior to the development of changes related to healing, which are visible with the naked eye, fractures may not be identified. Although in theory they should be iden-tifiable, it is possible that fractures occurring around the time of death might be mistaken for breaks caused during

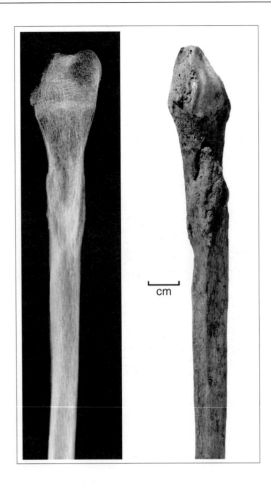
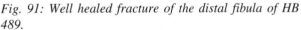

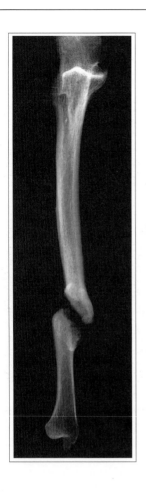

Fig. 91: Well healed fracture of the distal fibula of HB 489.

Fig. 92: Radiograph of an un-united fracture of the ulna from HB 733.

the period of burial or excavation of the individual.

It is noted by Roberts (2000, 339) that more complex comminuted fractures are today associated with road traffic accidents where there was considerable force in the impact. The lack of motorised vehicles on the streets during the period under study may be one reason why most of the fractures seen from St. Martin's were simple fractures. Only one of the fractures discussed in the case notes of Mr Hunt, a Birmingham surgeon (Hunt 1855d), was linked to a road traffic accident and, possibly because the vehicle involved was not motorised, the fracture that occurred was simple. However, widespread use of horses for transportation and leisure activities probably resulted in fractures linked to falls and kicks. The wide range of fractures that can result from such accidents and changes in accidents linked to changes in riding practice through time (due to the style of riding for ladies, and the types of protective clothing now worn) make it difficult to be sure which fractures could have been linked to such activities.

Non-union of fractures

There were a couple of cases in which non-union of

fractures had occurred, although the fractured ends of bones had healed. This could have been because of trapped soft tissues at the fracture site, or because of movement of the affected area, preventing proper healing. The first case was in the left scaphoid of HB 207, a middle adult male. The fracture had occurred across the 'waist' of the bone, separating the proximal and distal halves. The proximal pole of the scaphoid has undergone avascular necrosis to some extent, which may have resulted in non-union of the two halves. Non-union is a relatively common complication due to the particularly precarious blood supply to the scaphoid (Salter 1999, 568). A more serious case of non-union was present in HB 733, a middle adult female, where there was a non-united fracture of the right ulna that had occurred two thirds of the way down from the proximal end. The non-union of the fracture resulted in the development of a pseudoarthrosis. Figure 92, a radiograph of the ulna of HB 733, clearly shows the changes that occurred. The distal end has moved posteriorly in relation to the proximal end and would have been angled at about 40 degrees medially, and there was an overlap of approximately 2cm. This had allowed the radius to remain in articulation with the ulna and

Fig. 93: Callus formation around an unhealed rib fracture from HB 270.

despite the medial distortion of the whole forearm it appears to have been used. In one of the old adult females, HB 322, an un-united fracture of the left clavicle was recorded. Such a fracture is usually caused by a fall on the hand, with forces being transmitted through the forearm and arm to the shoulder. Delayed union may complicate a fractured clavicle that has been inadequately treated during the first few weeks.

An un-united rib fracture was present in HB 270, an older adult male from a vault. Figure 93 shows that a healing callus consisting of porous woven bone was present, and it is likely that had this person lived longer the fracture would have healed completely. A healing rib fracture of this nature was also present in another older adult male from a vault, HB 267.

Multiple trauma and fractures in the process of healing at the time of death

In HB 578, an older adult female from an earth-cut grave, there was a number of rib fractures in various states of healing; these are shown in Figure 94. There were four well-healed fractures and a further two where spiculated bone was present around the fracture site. There must have been at least two separate incidents in which the injuries recorded occurred. Investigations undertaken as part of the NERC-funded vitamin D deficiency project, demonstrated that at the time of death this woman was suffering from vitamin D deficiency (osteomalacia) and this is why the most recent rib fractures had failed to heal

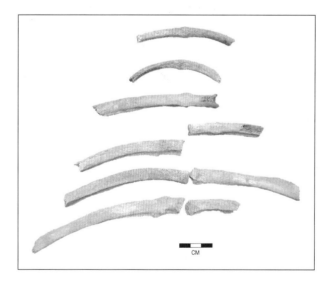

Fig. 94: Six ribs with evidence for fractures from HB 578. The top two fractures are well healed, but speculated bone is present around the fractured ends of the lower four ribs.

properly. The good state of healing in four of the fractures suggested that the woman had not suffered from osteomalacia when these injuries were sustained.

The very small amounts of newly laid down woven bone around one of the rib fractures recorded in HB 589 an old adult male from an earth-cut grave indicated that the injury occurred very close to the time of death. However, a second well-healed fracture present on the same rib in this individual indicated that they had been involved in more than one incident leading to injury. HB 340, a middle adult male, also had a number of rib fractures in various stages of healing. The state of healing of rib fractures in HB 755, 647, 497, 292, 267, 170 and 118 indicates that the fracture had occurred close to the time of death in these individuals, as recently formed new bone was present. Therefore complications arising from trauma are a likely cause of death in these individuals.

The number of individuals who appeared to have undergone more than one incident in which they sustained injuries, and/or to have died while some of these injuries were still healing, seems very high. Of the 11 individuals who died with healing rib fractures, nine were men, one was a woman and one undetermined. Two of the individuals affected, HB 270 and HB 267, were from vaults and the rest were from earth-cut graves. In most cases of well-healed fractures it is impossible to determine when during the life of the individual the incidents occurred. However, with healing fractures, such as those discussed above, the fracture probably occurred within the last couple of months of life and so the age at death of the individual becomes more important. Most of the individuals who had died while rib fractures were still in the process of healing were placed in the older adult category (7), three were classified as middle adults and just one as a young adult. One of the individuals with fractures still healing was simply classified as an adult, as a more precise age could not be determined. In most cases of fracture the injury would not have been serious enough to kill the individual and they would have survived to suffer more trauma in the future. Six of the individuals with healing rib fractures had undergone more than one incident in which a fracture was sustained.

It has been demonstrated that the risk of morbidity associated with rib fractures increases significantly from the age of 45 onwards (Holcomb *et al.* 2003, 553). In individuals over the age of 65 morbidity and mortality has been shown to be significant, with much higher levels of associated complications and mortality resulting from the initial injury and later complications (Bulger *et al.* 2000). Individuals in older age categories are also more likely to already be suffering from an existing medical condition (comorbidity) (Holcomb *et al.* 2003), which may weaken them. The young male who died with healing rib fractures (HB 170), had suffered from an earlier fracture affecting his foot, but this was well healed. Buhr and Cook (1959, cited in Glencross and Stuart-Macadam 2000, 200) report that injuries to the bones of the hands and feet are more likely to be sustained by males of wage-earning age. However, as discussed in Chapter 7 the 'wage-earning age' would have begun much lower during this time period. This individual (HB 170) was also affected by slight kyphosis during life, but this may have

gone un-noticed. After his death a cranial autopsy had been performed, but there was no evidence from the skeletal analysis as to what the cause of death may have been. Pulmonary complications following fractured ribs are a significant cause of morbidity and mortality (Sirmali *et al.* 2003). It may have been that this young man was admitted to hospital for treatment of his injuries, and his death in hospital may have made the performing of an autopsy more likely.

Although rib fractures are relatively common, both in the present population and in studies of archaeological skeletal material, they are not given a great deal of consideration, particularly in studies of archaeological material. However, such fractures are a significant cause of pain and disability (Kerr-Valentic *et al.* 2003). Particularly in cases of multiple rib fractures, pain can be very significant and can be debilitating (Karmakar *et al.* 2003). The use of rib fractures in investigations of archaeological skeletal material and further interpretations of the data from St. Martin's are discussed more fully in Brickley (in press).

There are a number of causes of fractured ribs. Today the most common causes are road traffic accidents, followed by falls, assault and work-related accidents (Sirmali *et al.* 2003; Linman *et al.* 2003). Road traffic accidents would not have been as common in the period under study as they are today, and prior to the advent of motorised vehicles injuries many not have been as severe. However, accidents involving road traffic did occur and cases of dangerous driving were reported in the press of the time. For example, the *Birmingham Daily Post* reported a case of 'Furious driving' in New Street on the 9th of March 1858. In this case the young carter admitted being tipsy at the time due to drinking gin and whisky because of the cold.

Multiple fractures were recorded in a large number of individuals, and more than four fractures (excluding multiple rib fractures) were recorded in six individuals, all males. However, in these cases, as none of the fractures were still healing, it is impossible to determine if the injuries were sustained in more than one incident, although this is likely.

Many of these individuals had more than one fracture and those with rib fractures that were still healing fit the pattern of injury recidivists, first described in archaeological skeletal material by Judd (2002). Investigations by Judd of the profile of these individuals in the clinical literature demonstrated that in all studies undertaken the characteristics of these individuals was similar. They were generally young, certainly when the first injuries occurred, male, often of low socio-economic status and/ or unemployed and often involved in illegal activities (Judd 2002, 90). Judd noticed that injuries to the hands and feet were highest in young males, and this was generally linked to work-related accidents (Judd 2002, 91). It is possible that a number of the males from St. Martin's with multiple injuries also fit this profile.

Work-related fractures

As mentioned above, injuries to the hands and feet have been linked to work-related accidents (Judd 2002). The frequency of injuries to the hand occurring in workers in Birmingham was noted in a report to the Children's Employment Commission in 1842 and summarised by Hopkins (1998):

> Accidents at the workplace were not uncommon, the principal categories of injuries being sprains and contusions, wounds, fractures, burns and scalds. Injuries to the fingers, as might be expected, were commonplace, given the widespread use of stamps and presses (Hopkins 1998, 112).

Six of the individuals analysed had a fracture of a hand phalanx, 5.56% (6/108) of individuals with one or more fractures. Five of the individuals were older adult males from earth-cut graves (HB 57, 118, 589, 780, and 857) and the sixth was HB 793, Eliza Haines, an older adult female from a vault.

In three of the males the fracture was located in the first proximal phalanx of the right hand. In the case of HB 118, the head of the 1st metacarpal was also fractured. The changes seen in this individual suggest that the injury may have occurred while they were relatively young (before the age of 16) prior to the fusion of the epiphysis. In HB 589 the injury had also occurred in the first proximal phalanx, but in this individual it was the left hand that was affected. In the fifth male, HB 780, the fracture had occurred in one of the right intermediate and distal hand phalanges. The changes recorded for this individual were consistent with a crush fracture. The fracture to the fingers of Eliza Haines had occurred in the fourth or fifth left proximal hand phalanx. There was some mal-alignment, but the fracture was well healed.

The similarity in location of four of the five fractures of hand phalanges in the males would indicate that these fractures were probably the result of a similar type of accident. It is possible that an accident of the type described in the report of the Children's Employment Commission caused these fractures. It is also likely that the crush fracture seen in HB 780 resulted from working with stamps or presses. It is unlikely that Eliza Haines sustained her injury in a work-related accident of the type suggested for the other individuals. However, fractures of the phalanges are relatively common and can also be caused by falls and finger jams (e.g. trapping fingers in a door) (Divelbiss 2004).

Evidence of violence

It is difficult to be certain, as accidents can produce similar features to those that would be sustained in inter-personal violence, but there are a number of cases of fractures recorded at St. Martin's for which violence should certainly be considered as a possible cause of the injuries recorded. One example is HB 270, an old adult male buried in a vault, who had evidence of a possible healed blade injury, shown in Figure 95 (colour). The lesion was located on the superior aspect of the right parietal bone. The linear indentation is almost 4.2cm long, running approximately 3cm from the sagittal suture laterally in the coronal plane, and if this defect was caused by a blade injury it was well healed. Most cut marks on the cranium linked to inter-personal violence are on the left-hand side, because they are the result of face-to-face combat by right-handed individuals (Boylston 2000, 361). However, it is possible for such injuries to be inflicted on the right hand side of the skull, either because of the position of the attacker relative to their victim or because the attacker was left handed.

There were four possible cases of depressed skull fractures. The first was in HB 153, an old adult male buried in an earth-cut grave. A large depressed oval skull fracture was present on the left side of the frontal bone. As can be seen from Figure 96, some healing had taken place prior to death, although the depression of the outer table of the skull was not yet fully remodelled. In the same individual the right gonion of the mandible has an abnormal deviation, and it is possible that there was a

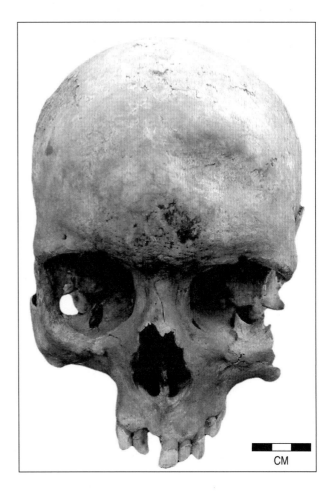

Fig. 96: Depressed skull fracture on the frontal bone of HB 153.

well-healed fracture of the mandible. Another example of a depressed skull fracture, also to the frontal bone, was HB 140, a middle adult male buried in a vault. However, in this case the fracture, which was located on the right hand side above the orbit, was well healed. HB 824, an old adult male from an earth-cut grave, had two partially healed depressed fractures to the posterior aspect of the left parietal bone. For much of the period during which many of the individuals buried at St. Martin's lived, England was at war. It is possible that some of the individuals buried at St. Martin's may have been war veterans, such as Benjamin Robinson (HB 779) discussed in Chapter 6. Therefore, some of the injuries that could be linked to violence may not have been sustained in Birmingham, but during military campaigns.

Finally, HB 290, a middle adult male from an earth-cut grave, had a possible peri-mortem depressed skull fracture. On the left side of the skull in the region where the parietal and occipital meet there is a depression. However, the depression is not clearly defined, but there is a concentric, sharp edged crack in the bone surface. It is not clear if a blow in life or pressure on the skull soon after burial caused this.

Nasal fractures are another injury that in many cases may be linked to inter-personal violence, although this is not the only cause. During analysis of the skeletal material from St. Martin's five cases of fractured nasal bones were recorded giving a prevalence of 1.98% (5/253 individuals with left or right nasal bone). The overall figures for nasal fractures are lower than the 7% prevalence reported in a study by Walker (1997 cited in Jurmain 1999). All of the cases of fractured nasal bones, such as that in HB 792 shown in Figure 97, were in males, and when the prevalence in the different groups was considered an interesting finding was made: males in vaults had a much higher prevalence of such fractures than those from earth-cut graves, 11.11% (3/27) compared to 2.11% (2/95), a significant difference ($Xc^2 = 4.34$, df = 1, $p = \leq 0.05$). As suggested by Jurmain (1999, 199) the pattern observed here almost certainly represents culturally patterned inter-personal aggression.

Domestic violence was frequently reported in the Police Courts of the period and this type of assault could result in rib and other fractures in women. For example in a case headlined 'A brutal husband' in the *Birmingham Daily Post* on 25th February 1858 it was reported that a certificate from the doctor who had examined the woman expressed the opinion that she "would not be able to leave her bed for at least a week." It was also stated that "at least two of her ribs were broken." A case in March of the same year gave more details of the circumstances of the assault, in which the woman was beaten with a chair leg. In this instance the defence of the accused was that the woman "was in the habit of taking from his pockets the money he had worked hard for, and going out and spending it in drink, and that she was out till three o'clock over-night". In this case the reasons given in defence of the assault were not considered acceptable and the man was sent to the house of correction for six weeks.

The woman noted in the section above as having some rib fractures that were still healing at the time of death had four unhealed rib fractures and six healed fractures. However, it is not possible to be sure if any of the fractures recorded in women from St. Martin's were linked to domestic violence. Victims of domestic violence today frequently have maxillofacial injuries (Le *et al.* 2001) but no injuries of this nature were recorded during the analysis of the females from St. Martin's. Nevertheless, the possibility that some of the individuals included in this study may have been victims of domestic violence should be considered.

Also possibly linked to violence are a number of fractures in bones of the hand. Bennett's fractures of the first metacarpals have been linked to boxing (Burrows 1908), although a range of other activities that cause trauma in the hand should also be considered, for example such fractures may be linked to some occupational activity involving reciprocating machinery, or certain types of riding accidents (S. Mays pers. com.). Seventeen Bennett's fractures were identified in the individuals from St. Martin's. The prevalence recorded in the left and right hands were similar, with 3.23% (8/248) for the left hand and a slightly higher figure for the right, 3.83% (9/235). The presence of the fracture was strongly linked to sex with a prevalence of 5.9% in men for both hands compared to just 0.6% in women. Only one of the affected

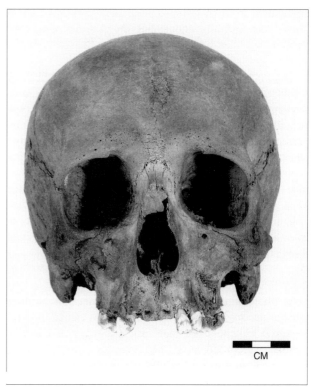

Fig. 97: Fracture of the nasal bones of HB 792.

individuals came from a vault, the rest were from earth-cut graves. Although Bennett's fractures have been linked to fighting, some other fractures of the hand commonly caused by the types of fighting engaged in by modern individuals were absent. However, the methods employed during fights have changed through time and further research is being undertaken on the high prevalence of these fractures at St. Martin's. Although there were probably a number of causes of this type of fracture, the predominant cause was clearly linked to an activity or occupation that the males from earth-cut graves were engaged in.

Aris's Gazette, published from 1741, contains information on casualties in Birmingham and most weeks there were several casualties due to 'excessive drinking'. Excessive drinking was probably involved in a number of the incidents that led to trauma occurring, particularly those that might be linked to inter-personal violence. *The Birmingham Daily Post,* published from the mid 1800s, has accounts of proceedings at Birmingham Police Court, and there are numerous accounts of violent incidents occurring after excessive drinking. One example was printed on the 14th April 1858, under the headline 'Brutal assault'. The following details were given:

> The complainant and his brother, with the prisoner *[previously described as "a rough looking young fellow"]* and several others, were on the day named, drinking at the Half Moon, in Dudley Street, when a dispute arose between the prisoner and the complainants brother as to which was the 'best man'. They went into the street to fight, and the prisoner got his opponent down, and savagely ill used him, severely spraining his leg and otherwise injuring him. Complainant seeing his brother so severely handled, went to his assistance and was received by the prisoner with a tremendous blow in the mouth with a large stone, which knocked out 3 of his teeth and a piece of jaw bone…

Brawling in the streets of Birmingham was a frequent occurrence and many of the cases that came before the Birmingham Police Court involved young men. Often multiple injuries were inflicted on those involved and in many of the reports injuries to the head are specifically mentioned.

Fractures linked to pathological conditions

In many of the older individuals with fractures, osteoarthritis had developed in associated joints, and the trauma that caused the fracture was almost certainly a contributory factor in the development of the condition. One possible example is the well-healed fracture of the fibula in HB 718 and associated evidence of trauma (e.g. large exostoses to the calcaneus) is almost certainly linked to osteoarthritic changes around the navicular. There were at least three other cases of such changes associated with fractures.

There are a number of pathological conditions that can lead to fractures. One of the most common conditions in the present population is age-related bone loss leading to osteoporosis and fractures. Research has demonstrated that individuals in the past were also at risk of sustaining such fractures (Brickley 2002a; 2002b). Fractures related to osteoporosis commonly occur in the hip (proximal femur), wrist (distal radius) and spine (commonly crush fractures to thoracic and lumbar vertebrae). Vertebral compression fractures that might be linked to age-related osteoporosis were recorded in eight individuals. Six of the eight were recorded as older adults, one was placed in the middle adult category and for one individual it was not possible to determine an age at death. Unusually, given the profile of individuals affected today (discussed in the section on metabolic disease), seven of these individuals were recorded as male and the sex of the eighth individual was ambiguous. Colles' fractures, discussed later, may also be linked to age-related osteoporosis.

Treatment of trauma

Fractures are one of the few areas of palaeopathology where it is possible to infer something about the treatment of the individual from the skeletal evidence available. Treatment for those who could not afford to employ a doctor privately was available from a number of sources (J. Reinarz pers. comm.). From 1733 there was a workhouse in Birmingham, which would probably have given assistance to individuals with chronic illnesses, and in 1766 it opened its own infirmary. In 1799 the General Hospital opened with 40 beds and this took in the 'deserving poor'. A dispensary with no beds, but facilities to provide treatment to outpatients was opened in 1792, and a number of specialist hospitals were opened in the 1800s. The Orthopaedic Hospital opened in 1817 and in 1823 the Eye Hospital opened, but in the early years of this institution it mainly treated outpatients. In 1841 the Queen's Hospital opened, which also catered for the working poor and had 70 beds; by this time the number of beds available at the General Hospital had almost doubled (*ibid.*).

Although it has been demonstrated that it is possible to make inferences on the treatment of fractures from archaeological bone (Roberts and Manchester 1995, 94–8), due to time factors the fractures recorded from St. Martin's were not studied systematically to determine if there had been any therapeutic intervention. However, a number of cases for which some information on treatment could be deduced were noted. There were many well-healed and well-aligned fractures, for example the fracture that had occurred close to the midshaft of the femur of HB 140. In this instance, illustrated in Figure 98, the fracture was well healed and the lack of rotation and angulation probably indicates that the fracture had been set. Information on setting of fractures in casts is discussed later in this section when Mr Hunt's published case reports on the treatment of fractures with new techniques are considered. However, a certain amount of caution is needed as studies of wild apes have demon-

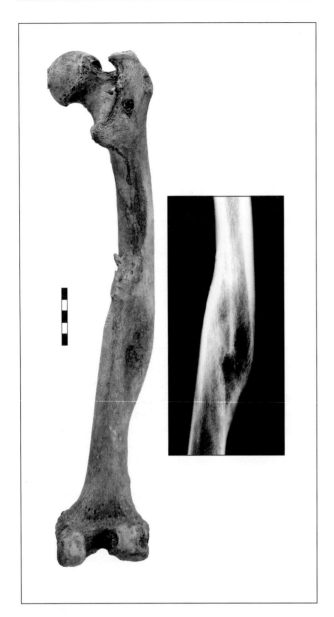

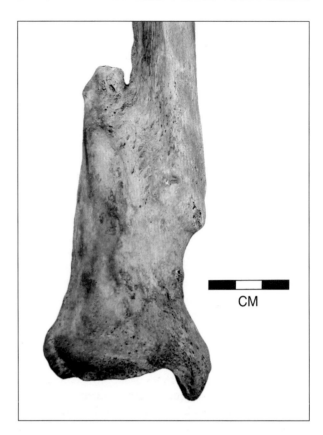

Fig. 99: Slight malalignment and overlap of the fractured bone ends in a fracture of the distal tibia from HB 258.

Fig. 98: Gross and radiological view of a fractured femur in HB 140.

strated that fractures can heal in a satisfactory manner with no medical intervention (Jurmain 1989; Jurmain and Kilgore 1998). In addition, in the forearm or lower leg where two bones occur adjacent to one another, if only one is fractured the complete bone may provide a certain amount of support during healing.

Analysis of the human bone demonstrated that there were other examples where although the bone was well healed, rotation shortening and lack of alignment or some other deformity were present. An example is the right lower leg of HB 258, which had almost certainly not been reduced, shown in Figure 99. In HB 733 there was a very poorly aligned fracture of the right radius, which was situated at an angle of 45 degrees in relation to the proximal part. However, from the cases noted above it is

not really possible to draw any firm conclusions about medical treatment in Birmingham at this period. All that can be said is that, although treatment was available, some individuals did not receive comprehensive treatment for the fractures they had sustained.

Some information on fractures occurring in Birmingham during the later part of the period in which individuals buried at St. Martin's would have lived was found in reports written by Benjamin Hunt for the *British Medical Journal*. Benjamin Hunt had worked at the Queen's Hospital, Birmingham as a surgeon, and in 1855 he wrote a series of reports on 'The Modern Treatment of Fractures' (Hunt 1855a; b; c; d). The treatment he described was the setting of fractures in moulds made of various substances (for example plaster of Paris and starch). The cases he presents therefore all relate to fractures that would have benefited for this type of cast rather than more traditional splints, and where the affected individual was admitted to hospital. The examples given therefore tend to be fractures of the tibia/fibula and the femur. However, it is interesting to see the types of individuals who sustained fractures and the circumstances surrounding their accident; quite a lot of information is given in some of the 30 cases he discusses (Hunt 1855a–d).

Of the 30 cases discussed, six concerned juveniles and it is clear that, as suggested earlier, accidents involving fractured bones in juveniles were relatively common. In each of these cases it is reported that recovery was good and fairly rapid and that there was no deformity of the affected limbs. Hunt states that "in childhood, the fragments unite much sooner" (1855d, 838). Few details are given of the accidents involving juveniles, but where some information is given it appears that the accidents occurred in the domestic setting and while children were playing, for example tripping while running.

Of the cases involving adults, the majority (21) relate to males, and just three fractures involving females are reported. Fractures in males seem to have occurred relatively evenly across all age categories (if the same categories are applied that are used to describe age in archaeological human bone). However, all of the cases of fractures in females reported occurred in individuals who would be described as older adults, and age-related bone loss may have played some role in their occurrence.

In many cases some information on the circumstances of the fracture is provided and from this it can be seen that the most common place for these types of fractures to occur was in the work place. Eleven of the fractures in males occurred at work. A number of the men included as a case study worked in the construction industry, and accidents on building sites seem to have been relatively common. Outside the work place the most frequently given cause of accidents was slipping on frozen pavements. In two of the cases in females it is reported that the lady concerned was intoxicated at the time of the accident, one falling down stairs and the other slipping on some orange peel (Hunt 1855b and c).

Most of the fractures reported by Mr Hunt were not of a very serious nature, but it is known that more serious accidents did occur in the workplace. For example, in a report of the Birmingham Pathological Society in 1853, details are given of an accident involving a 17-year-old girl. The accident involved machinery in a factory and the girl suffered "great contusion of the chest and compound fracture of the thigh, with laceration of the soft parts and considerable haemorrhage" (Pemberton 1853, 443). In this case the injuries were so serious that the leg had to be amputated, and unfortunately the girl died 18 days later.

Clearly there are gender and status differences in the prevalence of trauma observed. Economic factors, for example relating to the types of work undertaken and lifestyle of the individuals buried at St. Martin's, had an important impact on the type and prevalence of traumas recorded.

Other trauma

Fractures are the most obvious form of trauma recorded in archaeological skeletal material, but there is a range of other indicators of trauma that it is possible to record during skeletal analysis.

Dislocation

It is often difficult to be sure from the study of archaeological bone if a dislocation occurred. It will only be possible to detect cases of dislocation where the bones are mis-aligned for sufficiently long for a new joint surface to start developing. Many dislocations are comparatively easy to treat and many may reduce themselves without medical intervention (Roberts 2000, 342). Therefore, any information gathered is simply a minimum prevalence of possible cases that occurred.

In HB 842, an old adult female from an earth-cut grave, the right ulna appears to have been dislocated, probably during the same accident that caused the fracture of her radius. The styloid process of the right ulna is displaced superiorly and the superior border of the articular surface has a lip of new bone measuring 7.4mm in height. The ulna no longer sits in the ulna notch and a new articulation has been created. There was also possible evidence for dislocation in HB 531, a middle adult male from an earth-cut grave. The right ulna was affected by an enthesophyte at its proximal end and it is possible that this and other changes at the elbow joint were secondary to dislocation. Eburnation of joint surfaces and osteophyte formation had also occurred at the joint. A third possible case of dislocation was recorded in HB 211, an old adult male from an earth-cut grave. In this case the joint involved was the right elbow. Extensive osteophyte formation was present around the distal humerus and proximal radius and ulna, and an enthesophyte is present on the olecranon process. However, the changes present in this individual are not clear enough for it to be certain that this joint was dislocated.

Dislocations of the type described above may result in pain and limited joint movement, and even with modern medical treatment a number of these types of injuries have a poor functional outcome (Azmi *et al.* 1998). All of the individuals in whom there was possible evidence of dislocations were buried in earth-cut graves. There were treatments available at the time for dealing with dislocations (Cooper 1824c), but it is possible that the individuals discussed above did not seek medical help or could not afford to do so.

Traumatic myositis ossificans

Skeletal changes described as myositis ossificans can be caused by injuries that result in avulsion of tendon or muscle attachments to bone. Mineralization of the haematoma or other soft tissues at the site of the injury can result in the formation of an irregular mineralised lesion known as myositis ossificans traumatica (Aufderheide and Rodríguez-Martín 1998, 26). Three possible cases of the condition were recorded during the analysis of the human bone from St. Martin's, giving a CPR of 0.85% (3/352 adults). Two of the affected individuals were males (HB 198 and HB 847) and one was female (HB 83). All of those affected were buried in earth-cut graves.

In each case, the area involved was the bones of the leg; two of the cases involved the femur and the third the fibula. The region of the femur near to the thigh is one of the most commonly affected skeletal sites (Ortner 2003). In the case of the affected fibula the condition was probably linked to the event that also caused the tibia to fracture in this individual (HB 847). The prevalence by individual bone was left fibula 0.39% (1/256), left femur 0.32% (1/316) and right femur 0.32% (1/317).

Spondylolysis

Spondylolysis is the separation of the neural arch from a vertebral body, most frequently in the lower lumbar spine (Roberts and Manchester 1995, 78). The exact causes of the condition are not known, but there is probably an element of genetic susceptibility to stress fractures occurring at this site in affected individuals. Stress fractures could be caused by bending and lifting (*ibid.*) or other activities which place low-grade stress on this region of the spine (Ortner 2003, 148). During the analysis of the human bone from St. Martin's seven cases of spondylolysis were recorded, giving a prevalence of 2.11% (7/331 individuals with one or more area of spine). There was no sex difference in affected individuals (three males and females, and one undetermined) but all affected individuals were buried in earth-cut graves. The prevalence of the condition recorded for St. Martin's is lower than that for the modern population, where it is estimated to have a prevalence of 4%–6% (McTimoney and Micheli 2003).

Osteochondritis dissecans

Trauma to a joint that results in damage to the cartilage and the underlying bone, producing a characteristic lesion at a joint surface, is referred to as osteochondritis dissecans. Reviews of the literature on the condition have found that in the modern population it commonly occurs in adolescents or young adults and is far more frequent in males than females (Ortner 2003, 351). Fourteen lesions were recorded from ten individuals during the analysis of the human bone from St. Martin's, giving a CPR of 2.7% (10/371 adolescents and adults). As in the modern population, males were far more frequently affected than females; in this case eight of the affected individuals were males, one was female and one undetermined.

It has been reported that the most frequently affected site is the knee (Ortner 2003, 352). However, as Table 104 below indicates, at St. Martin's the most frequently affected joint was the elbow, and the right elbow was far more commonly affected than the left. The side difference indicates that the occurrence of the condition is linked to some type of activity or occupation carried out by these individuals, and that mechanical stress was experienced from quite a young age.

Little attention is paid to osteochondritis dissecans in the modern clinical literature, indicating that the condition has no serious consequences for affected individuals. However, the pattern found in individuals buried at St. Martin's does give an indication of the

Affected bone	Observations	% Prevalence
Left humerus	2/292	0.68%
Right humerus	7/320	2.19%
Left femur	1/318	0.31%
Right femur	1/302	0.33%
Left tibia	1/290	0.34%
Right scapula	1/317	0.32%
Right 1st metatarsal	1/206	0.49%

Table 104: Prevalence of osteochondritis dissecans on different bones. The prevalence was calculated using the number of each joint surface present for adolescents and adults.

factors affecting the different sexes and socio-economic groups buried here.

Conclusions

Of all of the medical conditions considered in this report, trauma has probably provided some of the clearest evidence of definite socio-economic differences in the patterns found. The sex-related differences were also striking. In particular, the differences between fractures and other trauma suffered by women from the vaults and earth-cut graves were very marked. These differences are almost certainly linked to they types of work and other activities undertaken by these groups. Evidence that work-related activities could have an impact on the type of injuries sustained was also shown when phalangeal fractures were considered. Many of these fractures were almost certainly linked to these men working with stamps and presses. There were also a number of males with multiple traumas, who may fit the pattern today termed 'injury recidivists'. Although detailed work on possible age-related bone loss is still being undertaken, males did seem more likely to have sustained a fracture that could be linked to age-related bone loss. Today such fractures are a serious social and economic burden upon society, but the fractures occur more frequently in females. Full information on measures of possible age-related bone loss using techniques such as metacarpal radiogrammetry are required before the possible pattern of fractures linked to age-related bone loss can be commented upon. All the fractures examined are ante mortem, and were well healed. It could be that women were more liable to suffer more serious fractures (such as hip fractures) and did not survive for the fracture to heal. Perimortem fractures of this nature would be very difficult to identify during rapid skeletal recording of the type undertaken at St. Martin's. Alternatively, it could be because the skeletons of women that had undergone age-related bone loss were less likely to survive and so were not fully recorded.

Metabolic disease

The term metabolic bone disease is used to describe all

those conditions caused by a disruption of bone formation, mineralization or remodelling, or a combination of these processes (Albright and Riefenstein 1948). This group of conditions comprises a wide range of diseases, a number of which are linked to deficiencies and therefore provide valuable information on socio-economic aspects of life in the past.

Scurvy

The development of scurvy is linked to a deficiency of vitamin C (ascorbic acid). Vitamin C can be obtained from a wide range of foods, in particular fruit and vegetables. Potatoes were an important source of vitamin C, especially for poorer members of society (Roberts and Cox 2003, 307). During the 1840s the potato blight had a dramatic impact on this source of the vitamin, as potato crops failed across Britain (Brickley and Ives in press). Cases of scurvy have rarely been recorded in archaeological skeletal material (Brickley 2000), probably partly due to the ephemeral nature of many of the associated skeletal changes, but also because in the past it has rarely been considered as a differential diagnosis during the study of human bone. Certainly there were no cases described in the reports from British sites of the post medieval period reviewed by Roberts and Cox (2003, 306). However, there was at least one possible case of scurvy from the Cross Bones burial ground (Brickley *et al.* 1999), but analysis of this skeletal collection was undertaken prior to the publication of a paper dealing with dry bone manifestations of scurvy (Ortner and Erickson 1997) and so a firm diagnosis was not suggested (Brickley *et al.* 1999, 38).

Scurvy was certainly known during this period, and a number of deaths listed in the London Bills of Mortality are recorded as being due to the condition (Roberts and Cox 2003, 306). Evidence indicating that scurvy was not uncommon in the population of Birmingham at this time comes from some of the early newspapers published in the town. For example, in editions of *Aris's Gazette* published in January and February 1742 advertisements appear for 'Dr Ratcliff's Only True Specific Tincture for the tooth-ache and all disorders and defects of the gums and teeth'. Amongst the many claims made for this wondrous substance (which purported to cure tooth ache without drawing) was the statement that 'it perfectly cures the scurvy in the gums, and causeth them to grow up to the teeth again in a very short time'. Problems of the gums and loosening of the teeth are commonly found symptoms of scurvy, and chronic bleeding of the gums has been considered an important clinical sign of the condition (Ortner 2003, 387).

Recent research on the diagnostic criteria for scurvy in skeletal material (Ortner and Ericksen 1997), and increasing awareness of the importance of these conditions (Brickley 2000), has resulted in greater attention to changes associated with scurvy during the recording of human bone. The most common period for infants to be affected by scurvy is between eight and ten months of age, but it can occur at other ages (Ortner 2003, 384). During analysis of the assemblage from St. Martin's six possible cases of infantile scurvy were identified (HB 762, 854, 316, 612, 767 and 802), all individuals classified as infants or foetus' from earth-cut graves. No possible cases were identified from juveniles buried in vaults. A full description and discussion of these cases is given in Brickley and Ives (in press). In all these cases a number of bones was affected across the skeleton, most notably the skull and scapulae, but there were none of the characteristic changes of the long bones described in Ortner (2003, 386–7). Scurvy would have resulted in affected infants failing to thrive, and as a result of the deficiency they would have been prone to contracting infections secondary to the condition (Resnick and Niwayama 1988, 3095). The prevalence of scurvy in infants was found to be 10.53% (6/57 infants that had either a frontal bone or scapula).

In adult scurvy the number of characteristic skeletal lesions that will be present are far fewer (Ortner 2003, 387) and are subtler. No plausible cases were identified during skeletal analysis, although the condition almost certainly existed in the adult population of Birmingham at this time.

Vitamin D deficiency

Vitamin D deficiency was widespread during the period in which the individuals buried at St. Martin's were living. Vitamin D (a prohormone rather than a 'true' vitamin) is essential for proper mineralization of newly formed bone (Steinbock 1993, 978). Failure of bone mineralization can result in skeletal changes indicative of a state of deficiency, termed rickets in juveniles and osteomalacia in adults. Although some vitamin D can be obtained from dietary sources, the primary source of this prohormone is production within the body as a result of exposure of the skin to sunshine (Brickley 2000, 188). In many respects vitamin D deficiency is linked to air pollution and factors that lead to a reduction in the amount of sunlight available (Steinbock 1993, 979). As a result vitamin D deficiency was probably at its most prevalent in urban areas with high concentrations of industry, particularly those that produced high levels of particulates and material that blocked out sunlight. An account of a legal case brought because of pollution caused by a steam engine, on which Mr Haines (buried in Vault 30) worked, is given in Chapter 6.

Some of the urban conditions that would have resulted in the development of rickets are described in Chapter 7. Writing in 1824, Cooper noted that affected children lived "in the low alleys of this town who are deprived of healthy proper nourishment, and get scarcely anything, perhaps a little gin, which their mothers give them by way of comfort" (1824d, 138). It was noted that with the condition the bones became "spongy at the extremities" and joints "exceedingly enlarged" (*ibid.*). Things improved little as the century progressed and in 1889 it was reported by Owens that there was a high prevalence of rickets to be found "in large towns and thickly peopled districts, especially where industrial pursuits are carried on" (Owens 1889, 114). It was further noted in the report by Owens that there was a concentration of cases in the region of the Black Country (part of the Midlands region of Britain close to Birmingham). In summary, it was stated that rickets "though not unknown in rural districts, is mainly a disease of towns and industrial regions, and especially of large industrial towns" (*ibid.*, 116). A year later Palm wrote, "It is in the narrow alleys, the haunts and playgrounds of the children of the poor, that this exclusion of sunlight is at its worst, and it is there that victims of rickets are to be found in abundance" (Palm 1890, cited in Steinbock 1993, 979). However, it was not until the early twentieth century that the specific role that vitamin D and exposure to sunlight played in the prevention of rickets was fully appreciated (Steinbock 1993).

As outlined at the start of this chapter, the research undertaken on conditions linked to vitamin D deficiency involved all the articulated individuals excavated, not just the 505 individuals fully analysed for the production of this report.

Rickets

Skeletal changes indicative of rickets in infants and children were identified and recorded using the criteria set out in Ortner and Mays (1998). Changes typical of those recorded are shown in Figure 100. In addition to the manifestations described in Ortner and Mays' paper, four additional features of rickets were found (raised medial flaring at the distal tibia epiphysis, changes in femoral neck angle, superior flattening of the proximal femoral epiphysis, and compensatory porosity/new bone formation at concave surface of deformed bones). A publication detailing all the additional diagnostic criteria identified from the work on the bone from St. Martin's has been submitted for publication (Mays *et al.* in press). At present no criteria exist for the identification of residual deformities associated with rickets in adult individuals. The range and quality of preservation of individuals with vitamin D deficiency related changes meant that it was possible to get a good idea of the way in which deformities persisted into adulthood, particularly those of the long bones. Figure 101 shows deformities in the femur typical of those caused by rickets and how these can persist into adulthood. However, the range of such deformities is very wide as is illustrated by those seen in Figure 102.

Table 24 in Appendix 6 gives the CPR of rickets in individuals from vaults the and earth-cut graves in the different age and sex categories. The CPR for rickets for all individuals from St. Martin's was 7.5% (38/505). Although the pattern of the condition in those buried in vaults and earth-cut graves is slightly different, no significant differences were found in the prevalence of rickets between individuals with different burial types,

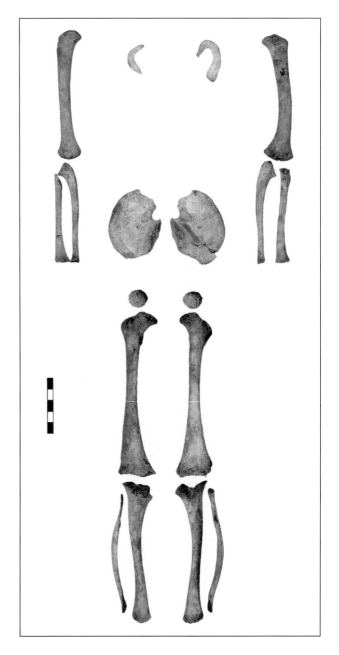

Fig. 100: Changes related to rickets were apparent in many of the long bones of the skeleton as well as the ribs (abnormally acute angle) and ilium concavity in HB 100.

even when the data for adults and juveniles was analysed separately.

At 3.65% the CPR for rickets calculated from a range of British sites of this period surveyed by Roberts and Cox (2003, 310) was much lower than the figure produced for St. Martin's. Although it is known that Birmingham was very polluted during this period, the higher figures produced by this study are almost certainly partly due to the very detailed approach taken to the recording of the condition.

In addition to the CPR, the prevalence for a range of long bones was calculated, and this information is

Fig. 101: Comparison of femora from an adult with residual changes related to rickets and a juvenile with an active condition. Femoral bending is apparent in both bones, which came from the disarticulated bone recovered from the site.

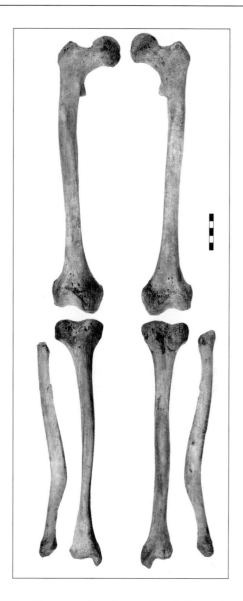

Fig. 102: Changes related to residual rickets in the leg bones of one of the individuals examined, HB 72.

	Vaults		Earth-cut graves	
	Number	% prev.	Number	% prev.
Juveniles	2/20	10%	18/133	13.53%
Adults	7/79	8.86%	11/273	4%

Table 105: The CPR of rickets (healed and active) in adults and juveniles from vaults and earth-cut graves.

presented in Tables 25–30 in Appendix 6. In summary, these calculations demonstrate that the femur was the most frequently changed element, with a prevalence of 6.27% (55/877 left and right femora) and the ulna the least frequently affected, with a prevalence of just under 0.92% (8/871 left and right ulnae).

Osteomalacia
Osteomalacia is the adult form of vitamin D deficiency. At present, no systematic diagnostic criteria for identifying osteomalacia in archaeological bone have been published, but work undertaken during this project has resulted in the production of a set of guidelines (Brickley *et al.* in press).

Seven definite cases and a number of possible cases of osteomalacia were recorded during the analysis of the individuals from St. Martin's. The diagnosis of osteomalacia was made following analysis of bone fractures characteristic of those produced by the condition. In all cases bone sections were examined using scanning electron microscopy (SEM) to confirm the diagnosis.

Osteomalacia is associated with significant levels of morbidity and individuals with the condition frequently experience bone pain (Plehwe 2003, 23). Other consequences include muscle weakness and pain (Holick 2003, 300). Osteomalacia is often present in individuals who have suffered from age-related bone loss and the combination of these two conditions makes these individuals particularly prone to osteoporosis-related fractures (Steinbock 1993, 980).

Due to poor bone preservation as a result of osteomalacia it was not possible to accurately determine the age and sex of many of the affected individuals, but today osteomalacia has been noted to be more common in elderly individuals in whom there may be impaired vitamin D synthesis (Plehwe 2003, 22). However, all the affected individuals were from earth-cut graves. The prevalence of osteomalacia at other sites is not known because it is rarely reported, but hopefully this will change in future. Although the NERC-funded project involved study of the whole human bone assemblage from St. Martin's, in order to make the prevalence of this condition comparable to others investigated at the site only the four individuals who were identified during the analysis of the 505 individuals elsewhere used to produce this report are used in the calculation of the CPR. Following these criteria the CPR for osteomalacia was 1.14% (4/352 adult individuals).

The levels of vitamin D deficiency recorded in adults and juveniles from St. Martin's were high. This finding is almost certainly indicative of high levels of pollution and poor housing conditions, possibly compounded by an inadequate diet, amongst certain sections of society. Although due to the complex aetiological factors involved with these conditions interpretation is not straightforward, there do appear to be socio-economic factors involved in the prevalence of these conditions.

Cribra orbitalia

Recently there has considerable debate on the causes of cribra orbitalia, which is summarised by Roberts and Manchester (1995, 166–9). The porosity of the bone in the orbital roof (without new bone formation) referred to as cribra orbitalia is related to stress suffered by an individual, but linking the stress to specific causes is difficult. Of the various possible causes of cribra orbitalia, anaemia is probably one of the most frequently suggested. The term anaemia is used to describe a range of conditions involving a reduction or defect in the production of red blood cells (Ortner 2003, 363), and may be linked to a range of deficiencies or genetic abnormalities, not all of which affect the bone. However, when discussed in relation to archaeological bone the most commonly considered and accepted factor in the skeletal changes observed is iron deficiency (Roberts and Manchester 1995, 166).

In the present study cribra orbitalia was graded according to the system set out by Stuart-Macadam (1991). Information on the grades recorded for different individuals is available in the site archive. The data presented here are based on the presence or absence of

the changes in one or more orbits. Table 106 below gives the prevalence of cribra orbitalia observed in individuals of different age categories. It can be seen from these data that the most commonly affected individuals are the juveniles, in whom there was a prevalence of 20.79% (21/101) compared to 5.80% (17/293) for the adults. This fits with the findings of a number of previous studies in which it is noted that the condition was most common in individuals below the age of twelve and decreased with advancing age (Roberts and Manchester 1995, 169). In some studies, particularly in the Americas, associated vault lesions have been recorded, but no associated vault lesions were recorded from St. Martin's. The data presented below also indicates that amongst adults women were affected slightly more frequently than males, with TPR of 6.19% (7/113) and 5.59% (9/161) respectively.

The review of British sites of this period by Roberts and Cox (2003, 307) found that the CPR for cribra orbitalia at post medieval sites in Britain varied considerably, from low levels at sites such as Kingston-upon-Thames (0.28%) to high levels at sites such as the Newcastle Infirmary (24.87%) and Christ Church, Spitalfields (14.57%). Roberts and Cox suggest that the high levels of cribra orbitalia seen at Christ Church, Spitalfields may be due to the fashionable infant feeding practices adopted by the more affluent individuals buried there. It is known that during this period it was

Age Group	Individuals affected	Prevalence	
Foetus	0	0/5	0%
Infant	8	8/45	17.78%
Child	8	8/36	22.22%
Adolescent	5	5/15	33.33%
Young adult male	1	1/29	3.45%
Young adult female	3	3/21	14.28%
Young adult unsexed	1	1/5	20%
Middle adult male	6	6/76	7.89%
Middle adult female	0	0/38	0%
Middle adult unsexed	0	0/5	0%
Old adult male	1	1/39	2.56%
Old adult female	2	2/46	4.35%
Old adult unsexed	0	0/6	0%
Adult male	1	1/17	5.88%
Adult female	2	2/8	25%
Adult unsexed	0	0/3	0%
Total	38	38/394	9.64%

Table 106: The number and prevalence of individuals in each age/sex category affected by Cribra orbitalia. Individuals affected = individuals with cribra orbitalia in either orbit. Prevalence is calculated as a percentage of individuals with a piece of either orbit.

fashionable to feed infants substances known as 'pap' or 'panada'; these were mixtures of flour or breadcrumbs with water, often of dubious cleanliness. Weight is possibly added to this suggestion by the pattern of cribra orbitalia observed in juveniles from earth-cut burials and vaults at St. Martin's. The prevalence of cribra orbitalia was high in both groups of juveniles, but it was slightly higher in those from the vaults, 27.27% (3/11 individuals with one or more orbit) compared to 20% (18/90 individuals with one or more orbit), from earth-cut graves. However, this difference was not statistically significant, and it is not known how long lesions would persist following the event/ illness that caused them (many individuals with cribra orbitalia were well past the age of weaning). It should also be remembered that, as discussed in Chapter 3, not all juveniles from families with a vault would have been given a vault burial, and so some individuals from these families will have been excluded from this investigation.

Overall the prevalence of cribra orbitalia for all sites of this period examined was found to be 8.95% (Roberts and Cox 2003, 307), fairly close to that found from all individuals from St. Martin's (9.64%). This figure indicates that anaemia and related deficiencies were quite common. The living conditions and food availability that are responsible for producing any of the deficiency diseases discussed above will almost certainly pre-dispose an individual to other deficiency diseases. It would not have been uncommon for an individual to suffer from more than one condition.

Osteoporosis

Osteoporosis is the term used to describe bone that has undergone levels of bone loss and architectural changes that have left the bone liable to fracture. There are a number of possible causes of osteoporosis, and in addition to being linked to increasing age and hormonal changes (particularly in women after the menopause) the condition can also be brought about by another disease process or as a reaction to drugs (Brickley 2000, 191). During the time period covered by the present study, the primary effect of osteoporosis would have been fractures related to the condition (Brickley 2002a). Unlike today, people would not have worried about the condition, as they were unaware that it existed. At the time fractures in older individuals, particularly women, would have been put down to their feebleness. For example, writing in 1824 about femoral neck fractures, a type typically associated with osteoporosis, Sir Astley Cooper opined,

Women are much more liable to this species of fracture than men; we rarely in hospitals observe it in the latter, but our wards are seldom without an example of it in the aged female. The more horizontal position of the neck of the bone and the comparative feebleness of the female constitution are the probable reason for this peculiarity (Cooper 1824c, 106).

A number of fractures linked to age-related bone loss

were discussed in the section on trauma, where eight individuals were recorded as having vertebral compression fractures. The prevalence of compression fractures in the spine was 2.42% (8/331 adults with 1 or more vertebrae). Of these individuals, two were from vaults and the rest were from earth-cut graves, giving a slightly higher CPR for individuals from vaults (2.53% [2/79] compared to 2.19% [6/273]). In addition, a number of codfish-shaped vertebrae, a feature associated with osteoporosis, were noted in HB 601, an adult male from an earth-cut grave. Lateral wedging of thoracic vertebrae 11 and 12 in HB 264, an older adult of unknown sex from a vault, may be linked to osteoporosis. All the affected individuals were male, and this is slightly surprising as in the modern population females are more frequently affected by age-related bone loss and associated fractures than males (Brickley 2000).

Colles' fractures, fractures to the distal radius, have also been linked to osteoporosis, and toady are the most common fracture in Caucasian (white) women below the age of seventy (Stevenson 1991). Most Colles' fractures are sustained when a falling individual puts out a hand for protection, and the pattern of fractures in the lower arm at St. Martin's may reflect this behaviour. In total, six Colles' fractures were recorded, four in the right arm (prevalence 1.44%, 4/278 distal right radius in adults) and two in the left (prevalence 0.69%, 2/289 distal left radius in adults). The overall CPR was 1.70% (6/352), but was slightly higher for individuals buried in vaults (2.5%) than those from earth-cut graves (1.5%). Three of the Colles' fractures recorded were in males, two in females and one in an undetermined individual; half were in individuals recorded as old adults and half in those recorded as middle adults.

As mentioned in the concluding section on trauma, the pattern observed here may reflect the fact that males sustained less serious fractures linked to age-related bone loss than females. Alternatively, they may have had better access to health care ensuring greater levels of survival. Research on documentary sources from this period has demonstrated that fractures related to age-related bone loss were a significant problem (Brickley 2002b), and it is likely that many of the cases described above are linked to the condition.

A systematic study of age-related bone loss in the individuals from St. Martin's, using metacarpal radio-grammetry (Ives and Brickley 2004), is being undertaken by Rachel Ives, and the results will be published in the next couple of years. This work will probably give a more accurate picture of the patterns of age-related bone loss experienced by the community. Other fractures recorded may, as a result, be linked to osteoporosis in individuals identified as having low levels of cortical bone.

The initial results produced by the present study suggest that osteoporosis related fractures and deformities have a CPR of approximately 2.84% (10/352 adult individuals). This is a higher figure than that reported for Christ Church, Spitalfields or St. Bride's Lower Churchyard, London (Molleson and Cox 1993; Conheeny and Waldron in press [cited in Roberts and Cox 2003, 355]). The total CPR reported for both these London sites was 1.20%, a much lower figure than that recorded at St. Martin's, but this difference may reflect the research interests of the authors, rather than a real difference.

Paget's disease

There was one possible example of Paget's disease (osteitis deformans) recorded during the analysis of the human bone from St. Martin's. Paget's disease is relatively common in the modern population, but rarely recorded in archaeological bone (Roberts and Manchester 1995, 184). The exact cause of the condition is unknown, but it may be linked to viral infection, although genetic factors may also play a role. In this condition excessive and abnormal remodelling of bone is present, leading to deformity of affected skeletal areas in time and the affected individual may experience pain and reduced joint mobility (Resnick and Niwayama 1988, 2127–8). The possible case recorded from St. Martin's was in HB 330, and adult of unknown age or sex buried in a vault. The bone of this individual was poorly preserved and very fragmentary. However, bowing of the right femora and a disorganisation of the usual bone structure observed at the broken end of the bone suggest that this individual had a pathological condition and one likely diagnosis is Paget's disease. This case has to remain just a 'possible' case as no histological or radiological investigations were undertaken.

Conclusions

Study of the pathological conditions considered under the heading of 'metabolic diseases' has produced particularly interesting results. The conditions reviewed here reflect socio-economic and environmental conditions. Different prevalences of the conditions were found for adults and juveniles and those buried in vaults and earth-cut graves. The findings on a range of deficiency diseases really do give an indication of the high levels of pollution and low levels of health and nutrition. Whereas other themes investigated as part of this study have produced patterns similar to the modern population, this is one area where the results are very different. High levels of fractures often associated with age-related bone loss were recorded in males and this is also very different to the pattern seen in the modern population. However, further work is required before the reasons for this pattern can be established.

Neoplastic disease

The term neoplastic disease covers conditions in which there has been unusual or new cell growth. Such a disease can result in benign or malignant growths or tumours. This type of disease can affect all the tissues of the body.

However, only those that affect bone, either through primary involvement, or where malignant cells have spread from the affected tissue and formed secondary deposits or metastases on bone tissue, will be recognisable in archaeological bone. In many cases, due to partial preservation and only having dry bone to analyse, it was not possible to provide a firm diagnosis and a range of differential diagnoses are suggested.

Benign conditions

For reasons discussed in the introductory section, the finding of benign neoplastic conditions in archaeological skeletons is relatively common. Benign tumours do not kill the affected individual, and so can develop, often over a significant period of time.

Osteoma (ivory/button)

This benign type of tumour is one of the most commonly recorded neoplastic conditions in archaeological skeletons. During the analysis of the human bone from St. Martin's three individuals affected by osteomas were recorded. In each case the affected area was the frontal bone of the skull. HB 32, an older adult female, had two osteomas; HB 297, a probable adult female, had one osteoma, as did HB 663, a probable male adult. The prevalence rate for this condition was 1% (3/298 adult frontal bones). In the modern population the most common location for these lesions is the external surface of cranial and facial bones. Osteomas may be related to the presence of Gardner's syndrome, an autosomal condition, but this is uncommon (Aufderheide and Rodríguez-Martín 1998, 375). In the majority of cases, including those discussed above, the presence of an osteoma would be asymptomatic and clinically insignificant.

Osteochondroma

In the modern population osteochondroma is one of the most commonly diagnosed benign neoplasms (Roberts and Manchester 1995, 187). Four cases of the condition were recorded during analysis of the human bone from St. Martin's. The condition, also referred to as cartilaginous exostosis, starts to develop during growth and although it can develop on any bone it is most commonly located near the growth plate of long bones (Ortner 2003, 508). The condition only really has an adverse effect on the affected individual if the swelling is very large or inconveniently located (Roberts and Manchester 1995, 187).

In two of the affected individuals the bone involved was the femur: HB 874, an older adult female, and HB 85, a middle adult probable male. The other two possible cases were both in the humerus, the first in HB 503, an adolescent, and the second in HB 616, a middle adult male. In all cases the tumour was relatively small and would have had a limited impact on the affected individual. The crude prevalence rate of this condition was 1.08% (4/371 adults and adolescents) and the prevalence by bone element was 0.63% for the left femur (2/316) and 0.32% for the humerus (1/304, left and 1/306, right).

Osteoid osteoma

Osteoid osteoma is relatively common condition in the modern population, today accounting for around 10% of benign tumours reported (Aufderheide and Rodríguez-Martín 1998, 376). The condition develops in young individuals, usually between 10 and 25 years of age (*ibid.*), and the most frequent location for this type of tumour is the long bones (Ortner 2003, 506). Two cases of this condition were recorded from the human bone analysed from St. Martins, both in middle adult females, HB 737 and HB 226. Neither of the recorded cases occurred on long bones, however. The first was located on the left mandibular ramus next to the joint and the second was on the frontal bone of the skull. Although not fatal, these tumours are known to cause considerable pain, and so would probably have had a significant effect on the affected individuals. The prevalence of this condition in individuals was 0.54% (2/371 individuals in the categories of adolescent or older who were assessed).

Giant cell tumour

One possible case of giant cell tumour was identified, in HB 107, an older adult female. It is reported that this type of tumour accounts for between 5% and 10% of benign tumours in the modern population, although there are geographical differences in the prevalence reported (Aufderheide and Rodríguez-Martín 1998, 386). The region affected in the individual from St. Martin's was the neck of the left femur, illustrated in Figure 103. The CPR was 0.26% (1/371) and the prevalence by bone element was 0.31% (1/316).

Malignant conditions

Malignant neoplastic conditions are often referred to as cancers. During the time period in which the individuals buried at St. Martins lived, all such conditions would have been incurable and many malignant conditions if not directly responsible for death would almost certainly have contributed to the death of the affected individual. A small number of possible malignant conditions was recorded during the analysis of the human bone from St. Martin's.

Chondrosarcoma

There was one possible case of chondrosarcoma, a relatively common primary bone malignant tumour; today this is the second most frequent tumour of this type. However, it is possible that chondrosarcomas are the result of malignant degeneration of a previously benign cartilaginous tumour, such as an osteochondroma (Aufderheide and Rodríguez-Martín 1998, 381–2). The changes recorded were present in the sphenoid and the areas bordering the sutures of HB 408, an older adult female. The other possible diagnosis of the pathological

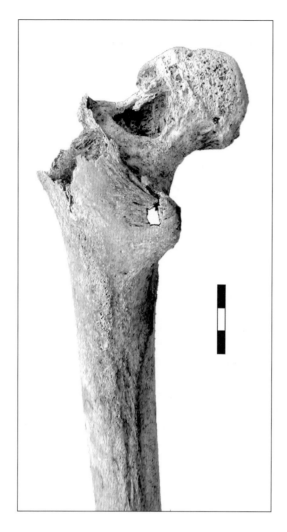

Fig. 103: Left femur of HB 107 showing a lytic lesion in the neck of the femur. The lesion has perforated the cortex and there is evidence of remodelling around the edge, but no sclerosis.

changes in this individual is chondroma, a slow growing tumour of the cartilage and meningeal structures. The CPR was 0.26% (1/371) the prevalence by bone element was 0.34% (1/295 sphenoid bones).

Metastatic carcinoma

There was one possible case of metastatic carcinoma recorded in HB 843, an older adult female. The right scapula and clavicle were affected with new bone formation and the pattern and distribution of the changes make it possible that they may be linked to metatasis from one of the soft tissue organs, in this case possibly the breast. However, there were no lytic lesions present so it is not possible be completely certain of the suggested diagnosis.

There were at least another five individuals with pathological changes present that may be linked to neoplastic conditions. However, a neoplastic condition was just one of a wide range of differential diagnoses that

Fig. 104: Lytic lesions on the anterior surface sternum of HB 281. No sclerotic response was present.

could be suggested in each case. These cases included a lytic lesion on the sternum of HB 281, a middle adult male, shown in Figure 104, and a well defined blastic lesion on the inside of the pelvic inlet of HB 107, an older adult female.

The crude prevalence rate of the various neoplastic conditions recorded at St. Martin's was slightly higher than that reported from other sites of the period: 0.54% for malignant neoplasms (2/371), 2.70% for non-malignant conditions (10/371), and 3.23% for both combined (12/371). Roberts and Cox (2003, 352) found a CPR of 0.30% for sites of this period where such conditions were reported. It was recognised at the time that cancer affecting the bone tended to affect older individuals and was rare (Quain 1855). The figure for such condition reported in the London Bills of Mortality rarely exceeded 0.50% (Roberts and Cox 2003, 352), but such deaths may have been more frequent in Birmingham. The abstract of the register of causes of death from 1837 (Fig. 86) gives a CPR of 1.17% (17/1,459) for deaths from carcinoma and tumours. The abstract only covers a six-month period, but it is possible that such conditions were more common in Birmingham, due to the high number of carcinogenic factors that would have been present.

However, it is difficult to make comparisons. To date, with the exception of osteomas, tumours have rarely been detailed in skeletal reports (Anderson 2000, 205). As a result, exact comparisons with data from other sites are not possible, and even where conditions are reported there is rarely any information on prevalence. When using written sources, such as the London Bills of Mortality or abstracts from death registers, as above, it should be remembered that accuracy of diagnosis in the past would have been different to that available today.

Although the results from St. Martin's appear broadly in line with those obtained from other archaeological sites and historical texts of the period, as more detailed data become available in the future it would be interesting to investigate the possible impact environmental factors on the prevalence rates recorded for this site. A recent review of clinical literature on neoplastic disease demonstrated that there is a link between the development of these conditions and socio-economic status, environment (rural or urban) and exposure to carcinogenic substances (Anderson 2000, 209). It is likely that a number of factors related to the urban and industrialised environment in 18th/19th century Birmingham will have contributed to the development of such conditions. For example, inhalation of soot and lead dust have both been linked to carcinoma (*ibid.*), and many other substances that would have been used in, or been a by-product of, industries in Birmingham would also have contributed to the development of neoplasms.

As early as the 1850s, a number of individuals in the medical profession wrote that malignant conditions should no longer be considered incurable and gave advice for their effective treatment (Pope 1855). However, with the remedies proposed, such conditions would still almost certainly have remained fatal. Malignant conditions were poorly understood. For example, it was thought that they were related to "vitiated secretion of bile" (Pope 1855, 859) and could therefore be cured by a healthy diet, lack of constipation and temperance to ensure a healthy liver and bilary secretion. The diagnosis of tumours with the aid of microscopic examination, and the possibility of treating cancer using surgery, developments that would lead to some success in cancer care, were only just starting to be investigated (*Periscopic Review* March 9th 1855). These diagnostic methods were still in the very early stages of development and, leaving aside the problems of ensuring the removal of all malignant tissue, treatment involving surgery was still risky due to the possibility of infection, loss of blood and shock.

Dental disease

The study of the dentitions of individuals from archaeological contexts has a huge potential to reveal information on life in the past. For example, disruptions to the formation of dental enamel during growth (known as hypoplastic defects) give an indication of childhood stress that was survived by the individual affected. The diet of individuals will also have a significant impact on the dentition, both through the amount of attrition foods consumed cause and the number of dental caries that develop. Oral hygiene practices have a role to play in dental health and poor oral hygiene may be reflected in periodontal disease. It may also be possible to see evidence for dental treatment, and in collections of this period evidence of restorative dentistry is often found. In addition to wear from foodstuffs, social and cultural practices may also wear teeth in a distinctive pattern, for example pipe smoking or habitually using the teeth while working. In total 438 of the 505 individuals examined from St. Martin's had some area of the jaw and dentition that could be recorded and included in an analysis of the dental health of those buried at the site.

Approximately 13% of teeth had been lost post mortem, a higher number than the 9% reported by Whittaker (1993, 51) for Christ Church, Spitalfields. However, recovery of teeth during excavation at St. Martin's was good, as the figure for Spitalfields is derived only from well-preserved skulls from vault burials, whereas that for St. Martins comes from all individuals analysed from all contexts. Ante and post morten tooth loss in each of the age categories considered are summarised in Table 107 below.

Overall, levels of ante-mortem tooth loss in individuals from St. Martin's classified as a child or older was 26.68%, compared to a figure of 12.50% for the sample examined at Christ Church, Spitalfields (Whittaker 1993, 51). In particular, loss of teeth during life at St. Martin's was far higher in middle and older adults than in these age groups at Spitalfields. One factor which may have influenced these results was the selection practice employed for the 96 individuals examined from Spitalfields, where only individuals with 12 or more teeth were included in the analysis (*ibid.*, 50). In the recent study by Roberts and Cox (2003), data on ante-mortem tooth loss was gathered from five British sites of this period producing a total prevalence of 24.4% (*ibid.*, 327).

This is similar to the figure obtained at St. Martin's, but this average figure conceals a wide variation in totals obtained from different sites.

It is not possible to be sure why teeth were lost. There are a number of possible causes of ante-mortem tooth loss which include severe alveolar resorption, deliberate extraction and trauma. However, it is known that during this period the extraction of teeth was a common practice and a range of instruments for tooth extraction were in widespread use (Whittaker 1993, 53). Formal training in dentistry was not available in Britain until 1856 (Roberts and Cox 2003, 323), so any treatment received by most of the people examined as part of the present study would have come from individuals with variable levels of training and expertise. Certainly poorer individuals would have had little access to treatment, possibly only extraction services provided by individuals who set themselves up as dentists. Reports from the period indicate that the quality of treatment given by these individuals who worked as dentists was very variable (Whittaker 1993, 49).

Two of the individuals examined from the vaults at St. Martin's had fillings but no evidence of this type of work was found in individuals from the earth-cut graves. The first filling was of gold foil, pushed into the cavity at the distal interproximal region of the right maxillary first premolar of HB 587, a young adult probable male. The second filling was made of a dark metal amalgam (probably mercury based) and was located in the right first mandibular molar of HB 829, a young adult male. This filling is shown in Figure 105 (colour). A number of fillings dating from this period have been reported, for example at Christ Church, Spitalfields (Whittaker 1993) and St. Nicholas's Church, Sevenoaks in Kent (Boyle and Keevil 1998). As at St. Martin's, the fillings found were all associated with more affluent members of society. In addition to fillings, two sets of dentures were also discovered at St. Martin's.

Age Group	No. individuals with maxilla or mandible	No. permanent teeth	No. deciduous teeth	No. of teeth lost AM	Number of teeth lost AM as % of teeth	No. of teeth lost PM	Number of teeth lost PM as % of teeth
Foetus	5	0	13	-	-	-	-
Infant	62	12	807	0/12	0%	0/12	0%
Child	46	358	492	1/395	0.25%	36/394	9.14%
Adolescent	17	383	0	6/435	1.40%	46/429	10.72%
Young adult	57	1457	0	133/1699	7.83%	109/1566	7%
Middle adult	123	2298	0	879/3522	25%	345/2643	13%
Old adult	96	1,010	0	1273/2511	50.70%	228/1238	18.42%
Adult	32	455	0	196/763	25.70%	112/567	19.75%
Total	438	5973	1312	2488/9337	26.65%	876/6849	12.79%

Table 107: Ante and post mortem tooth loss. AM = ante mortem, PM = post mortem. Number of teeth lost ante mortem is calculated using only number of erupted permanent teeth.

Dentures by Annette Hancocks

A single complete set of vulcanite dentures were recovered from Vault 5, HB 297 (SF 16) and a partial copper alloy denture plate from HB211, an earth-cut burial. The vulcanite dentures are typical of the mid-19th century (R. Fea pers. comm.) and belonged to Ann Maria Browett (nee Warden), who died in 1894. The dentures were in an excellent state of preservation (Fig. 106, colour). The second set of dentures, recovered from an earth-cut grave (HB 211), were much less sophisticated in design and comprised a partial copper-alloy denture, which acted as a banding around the remaining teeth. This type of denture was not designed to be removable and so was very difficult to maintain, posing oral hygiene problems.

The majority of 19th-century dentures were constructed with a mixture of natural 'Waterloo' teeth and ceramic teeth sprung with gold spiral springs. The complete set of dentures recovered comprise a complete upper and lower set of 'tubeless' tube teeth, using platinum pins to hold the teeth in place. The gold coil springs were a long-standing holding-in device and were attached to each denture by a rotary pin. The dentures from St. Martin's are comparable to some examples from Christ Church, Spitalfields (Molleson and Cox 1993, 53–60.)

The vulcanite dentures involved a complex process of manufacture. Initially a beeswax cast would be taken of the profile of the individual's mouth and this would form the basis for a mould for casting the dentures, which would have been formed from a vulcanite casting solution. Porcelain teeth of the size and shape best suited to the patient's needs were mounted in pink wax as trial dentures that could be checked in the mouth for appearance and function.

The wax trial dentures were embedded in plaster in a metal flask (i.e. box) and the wax washed away with boiling water. The tinted rubber/sulphur mix, brown for the base, pink for the gum, was packed between and around the porcelain teeth. The flask, when filled, was clamped and subjected to 100lbs steam pressure, at about 160°C, for approximately two hours. After the flask had cooled, the denture was separated from the plaster, trimmed with files and scrapers and polished.

Both sets of dentures would have been expensive items, but the vulcanite set associated with Ann Maria Browett, would have been more costly than the copper-alloy denture associated with the old adult male in an earth-cut grave (HB 211). The value placed on dentures is illustrated by a report in the *British Medical Journal* of 1854, in which a set of artificial teeth were clearly retrieved and re-used following an accident in which they were swallowed by their owner (Thursfield 1854).

Periodontal disease

Periodontal disease has been linked to infection of the gingival tissues by a number of types of bacteria. "Much of the damage in periodontal disease is actually caused

Age Group	% with alveolar resorption	
Infant	0/3	0%
Child	0/292	0%
Adolescent	17/331	5.14%
Young adult	355/1388	25.58%
Middle adult	1384/2023	68.41%
Old adult	698/857	81.45%
Total	2454/4894	50.14%

Table 108: The prevalence of alveolar resorption. Prevalence is calculated from individuals who had one or more tooth in a socket that could be scored using the system for recording alveolar bone resorption set out in Brothwell (1981).

by inappropriate triggering of the immune response by such factors" (Hillson 1996, 262). The damage linked to periodontal disease is bone loss, which as mentioned previously can proceed to the extent that teeth are no longer supported in the jaw and are lost. Assessing the amount of bone loss linked to periodontal disease is difficult, as the processes involved are complex and it is likely that teeth continue to slowly erupt throughout life, resulting in possible exposure of the roots of teeth above the alveolar bone (Hillson 1996, 263). There are a number of suggested techniques for obtaining more accurate estimates of bone loss involving the use of radiographs (*ibid.*), but due to time and resources available it was not possible to employ such techniques in the present study.

During the recording of material from St. Martin's, bone loss associated with periodontal disease was recorded using the simple scoring system illustrated by Brothwell (1981, 155). Although there are problems associated with this type of simple scoring system, it does enable an indication of the possible extent of periodontal disease to be gained. Information on the presence of alveolar resorption around each tooth for individuals in each age and sex category is set out in Table 31, Appendix 6; summary information is presented in Table 108 above.

More detailed information on the scores awarded for the severity of bone loss is available from the site archive. However, even from the basic information presented above it can be seen that the number of teeth with areas of bone loss around them increases with age. Clinical investigations have demonstrated a strong link between periodontal disease and increasing age (Hillson 1996, 266). When the prevalence of periodontal bone loss around individual teeth was examined (Table 31, Appendix 6), it was observed that there were no definite patterns to the way in which teeth were affected, and the presence of bone loss in different areas of the mouth was fairly uniform.

Caries

Caries is the destruction of dental tissues through exposure to acids present in the mouth, which are produced by

Age Group	% with carious teeth	
Infant	1/42	2.4%
Child	14/45	31.11%
Adolescent	7/16	43.75%
Young adult	34/54	62.96%
Middle adult	83/123	67.48%
Old adult	43/77	55.84%
Adult	15/27	55.56%
Total	197/384	51.30%

Caries Location	% of total lesions
Crown	9.9
Gross crown	21.1
Approximal	12.7
Cement enamel junction	28.2
Buccal & lingual	9.8
Root	18.3

Table 109: The prevalence of caries in individuals in each age category. Individual prevalence (CPR) is calculated from individuals who had one or more teeth present that could be assessed for the presence of caries.

Table 111: Proportion of carious lesions recorded at each location in adult individuals.

Juveniles		Young adults		Middle adults		Old adults		Total	
20/713	2.81%	116/1290	8.99%	239/2042	11.70%	113/895	12.63%	488/4940	9.88%

Table 110: Summary data on caries prevalence (TPR, calculated using numbers of teeth recorded) in the different age categories.

bacteria present in dental plaque (Hillson 1996, 269). Prior to the appearance of a clear cavity there are a number of possible indicators of caries, discussed by Hillson (1996, 229). However, in the present study only cases where a cavity was clearly visible were recorded as caries due to limitations on the time and resources available. For each individual the area of the tooth affected by caries was recorded, but the severity of cavities observed was not scored, just recorded as present or absent.

The individual prevalence of caries (CPR) is given in Table 109 above. These figures are calculated for individuals with one or more teeth present that could be recorded for caries presence.

The data on the percentage of individuals affected by caries presented in Table 109 shows that the prevalence of caries increases with age, until the older adult age category. The slightly lower prevalence of caries in this category is almost certainly due to high levels of ante-mortem tooth loss. The figures obtained for St. Martin's were lower than those recorded in individuals from Christ Church, Spitalfields, where the total prevalence of caries was 87%, and the middle adult age category had 100% prevalence (Whittaker 1993, 51). Caries prevalence is clearly not directly linked to social status as a prevalence of 92.20% was recorded at the Cross Bones burial ground (Brickley *et al.* 1999), a burial ground used by paupers. At St. Martin's no significant difference was found between the prevalence of caries between individuals from vaults or earth-cut graves. Figures provided by the survey of post medieval skeletal collections by Roberts and Cox (2003, 326) give a CPR of 53.88% for individuals affected by caries during this period, slightly higher than the figure obtained for St. Martin's.

The prevalence of caries was different between the sexes at St. Martin's, with women having a higher prevalence of caries than men, 71.3% (72/101) compared to 60.3% (94/156). However, when the very crude CPR data were analysed, the differences were not found to be significant (Xc^2=3.26, df = 1, $p \leq 0.1$). This sex difference is also apparent when prevalence of total teeth present affected by caries is considered, 14% in females compared to 10.50% in males. More detailed information on prevalence and the differences between vault and earth-cut individuals can be found in Table 32, Appendix 6. However, the sex difference in rates of caries found at St. Martin's mirrors that found in clinical studies, where in almost all studies females have been found to have higher rates than males (Hillson 2000, 261). Females were also observed to have higher rates of caries than males at St. Thomas' cemetery, Belleville, Ontario, Canada, but although various factors, such as dietary and age-related differences, were considered no clear reason for the sex-related differences emerged (Saunders *et al.* 1997).

Tables 33 and 34 in Appendix 6 give detailed information on the prevalence of caries in each tooth in every age and sex category. The information for the permanent dentition is summarised in Table 110 above.

For the St. Martin's teeth, 9.88% had a carious lesion; this is lower than the figure of 17.99% recorded for Christ Church, Spitalfields (Whittaker 1993, 51). In the study by Roberts and Cox (2003, 326) in which data was gathered from post medieval sites across Britain, the percentage of teeth affected varied considerably. The lowest figure recorded was 5.38% for Ennis Friary, Co. Clare and the highest 26.92% for Rivenhall. However, the total percentage of teeth affected by caries from all sites was 11.22%, only slightly higher than the figure of 9.88% produced for St. Martin's.

The more detailed information presented in Table 33, Appendix 6 demonstrates that the percentage of teeth affected by caries is age related and the prevalence of caries shows a consistent rise with age, but for women there is a peak in the middle adult years. The other feature that emerges from this table is that the distribution of caries within the dentition varies considerably, with the first permanent molars, the first of the permanent teeth to erupt, having the highest prevalence of caries at almost 20%. The incisors, which erupt slightly later and importantly have no fissures on the crown, were the least frequently affected teeth at around 7%.

Table 111 above summarises information obtained on the type of caries recorded and its location. Further information on the distribution of the various types of caries recorded in the teeth of the permanent dentition is available in Table 35, Appendix 6. The most frequently recorded type of caries was lesions that had progressed to the large caries stage. In the first molar this type of lesion accounted for around 27% of all lesions recorded. In the maxilla, mesial (approximal) caries was also very common, particularly in the first molar. The distribution of caries in different teeth was very similar in deciduous teeth, with molars being the most frequently affected and incisors least affected.

Refined carbohydrates, and in particular sugars, have been linked to the development of dental caries and the high levels of caries recorded at St. Martin's and other sites of this period probably reflects increased sugar consumption. The pattern of caries recorded at St. Martin's is far more modern in pattern than earlier British collections examined by Roberts and Cox (2003) and reflects the start of urban industrialised living. At the end of the period of the present study import duties were lifted on refined sugars (Hillson 1996, 283) making sweetened foods far more affordable by a wider section of society.

Abscesses

Infection of dental pulp by bacteria can in some cases lead to the development of an acute periapical abscess. Bacteria can enter the dental pulp as a result of dental caries, or less usually when teeth are broken and the pulp exposed. Abscesses develop when pus gathers and then starts to drain from the infected area, often through the bone (Hillson 1996, 284–85). During the recording of

the dentition of individuals from St. Martin's the direction of any drainage of abscesses was recorded. This information is available from the site archive, but the data presented below is simply on the presence or absence of an abscess. X-rays were not routinely taken and so the data gathered only give an approximate indication of the prevalence of this type of lesion.

Table 36 in Appendix 6 gives detailed information on the prevalence of abscesses associated with each tooth, in every age and sex category. From these data it could be seen that the maxilla was more frequently affected than the mandible, 3.30% and 1.90% respectively. However, in both the upper and lower jaw the cheek teeth were far more commonly involved than the anterior teeth, with the second molar being the most frequent site for an abscess. There was very little difference between the sexes. This information is summarised in Table 112 below.

The percentage of teeth with evidence of an abscess from St. Martin's (2.63%) was close to the figure of 2.20% found in a survey of British sites of this period (Roberts and Cox 2003, 327).

An abscess would have been extremely painful for the affected individual and some evidence of this was found in two of the individuals with an abscess. In HB 755 and HB 808 there was evidence that the person had been chewing using just one side of their mouth, almost certainly due to the pain caused by an abscess on the opposite side. Both these individuals, HB 755 (an adult male) and HB 808 (a middle adult male), were from earth-cut graves. In each case it was the left hand side of the mouth that they avoided chewing with (indicated by less dental wear). There was a third possible case, HB 672 (a middle adult male), but in this case the area of the dentition in which the abscess, if present, would have been located was missing. However, there was clear evidence from the dentition present that this individual had only been chewing on the right hand side of their mouth for some time.

Calculus

Dental calculus is plaque that has become mineralised and during life is firmly attached to the teeth. The build up of plaque is often greatest in areas of the mouth close to salivary glands, as saliva is a source of minerals (Hillson 1996, 255). Although during life plaque is difficult to remove, after death the attachment to the teeth is considerably weakened and it is easily dislodged during careless handling or cleaning. Considerable care was

Juveniles		Young adults		Middle adults		Old adults		Total	
9/988	0.91%	32/1713	1.86%	120/3363	3.57%	61/2369	2.57%	222/8433	2.63%

Table 112: Summary data on abscess prevalence in the different age categories. Prevalence is calculated from the number of abscesses observed out of the total number of tooth sockets and surrounding areas of bone that could be observed.

Juveniles		Young adults		Middle adults		Old adults		Adults (unknown age)		Total	
195/ 814	24%	886/ 1457	61%	1585/ 2197	72%	740/ 957	77%	278/ 468	59%	3684/ 5893	63%

Table 113: Summary data on calculus prevalence (TPR, calculated using numbers of teeth recorded) in the different age categories.

taken during the cleaning of the dentitions of individuals buried at St. Martin's, and no tooth brushes were used in the cleaning of the teeth. However, although great care was taken some calculus will almost certainly have been lost and so the figures reported below should be taken as a minimum prevalence.

During the analysis of the dentitions of individuals from St. Martin's calculus was recorded using the scoring system set out by Brothwell (1981, 155), but in addition the affected tooth surface was also recorded. This detailed information on the severity of calculus recorded and the tooth surfaces affected is available from the site archive, but the information presented here is based just on the presence or absence of calculus of any severity. Table 37 in Appendix 6 gives detailed information on the prevalence of calculus in each tooth in every age and sex category and this information is summarised in Table 113 above.

From Table 113 it can be seen that the prevalence of calculus increases with age and that the levels recorded were quite high for all age categories. An age-related increase in the prevalence and extent of calculus formation has been recorded in the modern population (Hillson 1996, 260) and so the pattern found at St. Martin's is not surprising. The more detailed information in Table 37, Appendix 6, reveals that in all age groups the prevalence of teeth affected by calculus is higher in men than women, 72% (2222/3105) and 63% (979/1566) respectively, mirroring the pattern found in living populations (Hillson 1996, 260). All areas of the dentition were affected but the prevalence of calculus on the teeth of the mandible was higher than in the maxilla, 54% and 68% respectively. In the maxilla the most commonly affected teeth were the molars, with the anterior teeth having a much lower prevalence. However, in the mandible the calculus was more evenly distributed and there was a high prevalence of calculus on the incisors. Although the location of salivary glands behind the anterior teeth of the mandible can lead to a build up of plaque in this area, the pattern recorded may be related to the fact that the anterior teeth of the maxilla are more visible than the mandible and so people may have taken more care with cleaning these teeth.

In many site reports calculus prevalence is reported on an individual basis (number of individuals with one or more teeth affected compared to the total number of individuals with one or more teeth). To enable comparisons to be made with St. Martin's this information

Age Group	% with calculus on teeth	
Infant	4/33	12.12%
Child	18/45	40%
Adolescent	15/17	88.24%
Young adult	46/57	80.70%
Middle adult	112/117	95.73%
Old adult	72/78	92.31%
Adult	19/25	76%
Total	286/372	76.88%

Table 114: Summary data on calculus prevalence in the different age categories by individual. The prevalence (CPR) is calculated from individuals who had one or more teeth present that could be assessed for the presence of calculus.

was also calculated for St. Martin's. Summary data on individual prevalence are presented in Table 114 above.

When the CPR for calculus was examined it was found that individuals from earth-cut graves had a higher prevalence of calculus than those from vaults 81.37% (249/306) and 69.70 (46/66) respectively. However it is not clear if this difference is due to differences in diet or oral hygiene practices between the two groups. Full information on the CPR in each age/sex category from vault and earth-cut individuals is available in Table 38, Appendix 6.

In their review of British sites of this period, Roberts and Cox (2003, 327) found that the prevalence of calculus varied considerably, from 5.23% (Upper Penn, Wolverhampton) to 68.97% (Ennis Friary, Co. Clare). The total CPR for the period was calculated at 21.43%. The total obtained for St. Martin's is much higher than this figure, but it is not clear if this is due to the way the prevalence is calculated or if there is a real difference.

The consumption of foods rich in carbohydrates and poor oral hygiene are both linked to the formation of plaque (Hillson 1996, 258), but the processes involved in the formation of calculus are complex and poorly understood, making it difficult to make clear deductions from the prevalence of the condition (Hillson 2000, 259).

Hypoplastic defects

Hypoplastic defects are defects of the enamel, which can take the form of pits or bands. Defects occur when the formation of dental enamel is disrupted for a period during growth. In the present study, visual examination of the teeth was used to determine the presence and number of any defects. The number and type of defect was recorded together with the location of imperfections on each tooth, indicated using the schematic representation of teeth in the dental recording forms provided by Buikstra and Ubelaker (1994).

Defects in the enamel only develop during enamel formation, and so reflect disturbances up to around the age of 12 years. Once formed, enamel is not remodelled and so any imperfections that have developed will be present throughout the life of an individual. However, defects may be removed due to attrition, or deposits of calculus may conceal them. The range of factors that may lead to the development of hypoplastic defects are reviewed by Hillson (1996, 166), but in summary childhood diseases such as rickets, diarrhoea and infectious diseases may be responsible. Poor levels of nutrition may also cause defects and possibly even stress experienced by the child may contribute (Hillson 1996, 166).

Many enamel defects are not observable during visual recording and so the figures reported for St. Martin's should simply be taken as a rough estimate of the prevalence of hypoplastic defects in the individuals buried at the site.

Table 115 below illustrates that the number of teeth present affected by hypoplastic defects decreases with age. This could be due to several factors. One possibility is that individuals who have suffered stress in the past do not live as long. The other is that with age the number of hypoplastic defects visible is likely to decrease with attrition, increasing deposition of calculus and loss of teeth, either through pulling or periodontal disease. The more detailed information presented in Table 39, Appendix 6, demonstrates that women are more commonly affected than men, with a 33.73% (476/1411) prevalence compared to 26.88% (733/2727) for men. When analysed the differences between men and women were found to be statistically significant (Xc^2=21.13, df =

1, $p \leq 0.001$). A higher prevalence of hypolastic defects in women than men was also found at the Cross Bones burial ground (Brickley *et al.* 1999). Table 39 in Appendix 6 also allows the different levels of prevalence in different teeth to be observed. The most commonly affected permanent teeth were the canines, in which there was a 57% (489/857) prevalence. These teeth are developing approximately between the ages of 1 and 5 years and so this high prevalence reflects stress experienced by children during this stage of their lives.

Table 116 below gives summary information regarding hypoplastic defects recorded in the deciduous dentition. More detailed information on the prevalence of defects at each tooth is presented in Tables 39–40 in Appendix 6. From these data it can be seen that the most commonly affected deciduous tooth type are the canines, which were affected in 17% of observable cases (33/193). The second most commonly affected type of tooth was the second molar, affected in 14% (43/241) cases. The development of the canine is initiated by approximately five months in utero and the crown is usually complete by nine months after birth. The second molar takes a little longer to develop, usually being complete at just under one year old. Canines were also the most frequently affected teeth in the permanent dentition being affected in 57.11% (489/857) of teeth observed. Permanent canines develop between approximately six months and seven years of age.

The CPR for hypoplastic defects was also calculated to allow comparisons with data from other sites. In calculating this prevalence any individuals with any type (linear or pit) or size of hypoplastic defect were included in the calculations as having hypoplasia.

More detailed information on the CPR calculated for individuals in each age/sex category from each burial type is presented in Table 41, Appendix 6. There was a difference noted in the individual prevalence of hypoplastic defects between individuals from vaults and those from earth-cut graves. Those from vaults had a lower number of hypoplastic defects than the individuals from

Juveniles		Young adults		Middle adults		Old adults		Adult (unknown age)		Total	
361/ 903	40%	487/ 1381	35%	563/ 1936	29%	219/ 834	26%	84/ 397	21%	1705/ 5450	31%

Table 115: Summary data on the prevalence (TPR, calculated using numbers of teeth recorded) of hypoplasic defects in the permanent dentition in different age categories.

Foetus		Infant		Child		Adol.		Total	
0/8	0%	63/604	10.43%	47/448	10.49%	0/0	0%	110/1060	10.37%

Table 116: Summary data on the prevalence (calculated using individuals who had one or more recordable teeth) of hypoplastic defects in the deciduous dentition different age categories.

Age Group	% with hypoplastic defects	
Infant	9/33	27.27%
Child	29/45	64.44%
Adolescent	15/17	88.24%
Young adult	48/57	84.21%
Middle adult	86/117	73.50%
Old adult	53/78	67.95%
Adult	16/25	64%
Total	256/372	68.82%

Table 117: Summary data on the prevalence of hypoplastic defects in the different age categories. The prevalence (CPR) is calculated from individuals who had one or more teeth present that could be assessed for the presence of hypoplastic defects.

earth-cut graves, 47% (31/66) and 73.5% (256/327) respectively, a significant difference (Xc^2=27.35, df = 1, $p \leq 0.001$).

The figures obtained from St. Martin's were very different to those reported for other sites of this period by Roberts and Cox (2003, 327). The overall prevalence reported for sites of the period was just 0.57%. This very large difference is almost certainly due to the method of recording employed.

Dental wear

Occlusal wear was recorded using the system set out in Buikstra and Ubelaker (1994), and this information is available in the site archive. One feature which has frequently been noticed on teeth from archaeological assemblages, particularly of the 18th and 19th centuries, are grooves on the teeth caused by habitual smoking of a clay pipe. Such pipe grooves have been reported from a wide range of archaeological contexts, including the Cross Bones burial ground (Brickley *et al.* 1999). At the Cross Bones burial ground facets made by clay pipes were recorded in four individuals, one female and three males, giving a CPR of 6.67% (3/45 adults). During the recording of individuals from St. Martin's pipe grooves were recorded from 11 individuals, giving a prevalence of 3.64% (11/302 adults with part of a maxilla or mandible). One of the individuals, HB 714 (an old adult male), was classified as a vault burial, but this is the individual who may have been from an earth-cut grave who mistakenly included with individuals from vaults. The other ten individuals definitely came from earth-cut graves. Unlike the Cross Bones burial ground all of the individuals with pipe grooves were males, five older adults, five middle adults and one of unknown age. No mention is made of pipe facets in the report on the dentition from Christ Church, Spitalfields (Whittaker 1993) and it is likely that smoking clay pipes was a lower status activity.

In addition to abrasion caused through pipe smoking, there was a small number of individuals who exhibited unusual abrasion patterns, possibly linked to occupational/habitual use of their teeth: HB 258, 340, 376, 580 and 752. Only one of these individuals (HB 376) was from a vault and this individual was also the only female with abrasion caused by a habitual activity. It is likely that passing a thread between the canine and second incisor of the right maxilla caused the abrasion in this individual. The changes seen may well be linked to needlework and sewing, possibly a frequent pastime of this lady.

Non-normal morphology

During the recording of the dentition from St. Martin's a number of developmental anomalies were recorded and these are described briefly below. In HB 588, the second premolars of the mandible display a pinching at the neck which runs round the entire circumference of the teeth. In HB 275, the second maxillary incisor is abnormal in morphology, and rotated distally through 100 degrees. A supernumerary tooth was recorded in the maxilla of HB 183; between the second incisor and the canine there is an extra tooth, almost identical to the second incisor in morphology but rotated laterally through approximately 65 degrees. A peg tooth was recorded in the mandible of HB 829, which would probably have been visible above the gum; the tooth had its own roots and socket. Another congenital abnormality, enamel pearls, was recorded on the lingual surface of the root of the second right maxillary molar of HB 15, and also in HB 615.

All of the congenital abnormalities described above would have had little impact on the affected individuals. Such abnormalities are rarely recorded in archaeological reports and so it is difficult to know if the numbers recorded from St. Martin's are unusual.

Conclusions

Overall, the levels of dental health observed in the individuals buried at St. Martin's were poor. This is probably related to a change in the diet at this period with more refined carbohydrates and sugar being widely available, but little knowledge or practice of oral hygiene. Some of the patterns recorded are starting to mirror those found in the present population, with women more frequently affected by caries than men and the reverse with calculus, but there are still significant differences. As indicated above, there were clear differences recorded between the sexes, but there were also differences between those buried in vaults and earth-cut graves. The most obvious difference is that those buried in the vaults had more and better fillings and dentures. However, there were other differences indicating that those in earth-cut graves were in general worse off, for example they had more calculus (probably an indication of poorer dental hygiene) and higher levels of enamel defects. Although individuals did have to live through the period of stress for a defect to form, the results indicate that the surviving people from earth-cut graves had to live through more periods of stress than those from the vaults. There was also a general sex-related difference in the prevalence of these defects, with women exhibiting more hypoplasia than men.

Medical intervention – autopsy investigations

The period covered by the burials at St. Martin's was one in which there were important medical advances and the understanding of the medical profession increased significantly (Roberts and Cox 2003, 313). At some sites of this period it is possible to see evidence of medical intervention, for example through amputations. A number of amputated limbs have been reported from British archaeological skeletal material; in some (but by no means all) cases the procedure had clearly been successful and the wound healed (Waldron and Rogers 1988, cited in Roberts and Cox 2003, 313). No examples of amputation were recorded during the analysis of the human bone from St. Martin's, although it is known that amputations were undertaken in Birmingham's hospitals at this time (Fletcher 1853; Hunt 1855d, 837; Dolman 1860). Evidence of an amputation was however found in a skeleton of this date from the Park Street burial ground, a detached burial ground for St. Martin's used from 1810 (see Chapter 2). In this individual, an older adult male, the left leg was amputated at the level of the upper third of the femur. This individual had died soon after the amputation (Brickley, Appendix in Krakowicz and Rudge 2004).

One of the ways in which medical knowledge was furthered during this period was through undertaking autopsies, and it became increasingly common for those in the medical profession to undertake autopsies on patients who died (Roberts and Cox 2003, 315). There are reports in the early editions of the *British Medical Journal* in which investigative autopsy following the death of a patient under treatment is described (for example, Pemberton 1853). It is likely that this is what happened to the young man with healing rib fractures who had a cranial autopsy, discussed in the section on trauma.

During the analysis of the human bone from St. Martin's, evidence of autopsy was identified in seven individuals, giving a CPR of 1.39% (7/505) for this procedure. However, it is possible that some kind of post-mortem investigation or autopsy was carried out on a far larger number of individuals, but unless the bone was cut it will not be possible to confirm this. In the survey by Roberts and Cox the CPR for individuals with skeletal evidence of autopsy from this period was found to be slightly higher than that for St. Martin's, at 1.62% (Roberts and Cox 2003, 315). Most autopsies were cranial, but there was some evidence of autopsies at other skeletal locations (*ibid.*).

Examination of the skeletal material from St. Martin's revealed a similar pattern to that found in the survey of British material of this date, with evidence of cranial autopsy being present in all seven cases (HB 86, HB 116, HB 170, HB 351, HB 497, HB 558, and HB 587).

However, in the case of HB 351 investigations had been more extensive and there were saw marks on the manubrium, and the sacrum had been dissected. Of the individuals from St. Martin's with evidence for an autopsy, three were females and four were males. None of the individuals were in the older adult category, four were young adults and four middle adults. It is possible that there was more interest in the possible cause of death for younger individuals than there would have been for older adults. Information on individuals who had undergone an autopsy at Christ Church, Spitalfields is incomplete, but here all four of the seven individuals about whom information is given were young adults or juveniles. Some information on the possible reasons behind the autopsy on one of the individuals in this study is available. Documentary information relating to the death of George Warden (HB 587), and the autopsy that was performed, was discovered during research into the families buried in the vaults at St. Martin's and is described in Chapter 6. This research points to the autopsy in this case being undertaken because the young man suffered from neuralgia pain, for which he took opium. An overdose of opium was believed to be the cause of death.

The skull of HB 86 is shown in Figure 107, and HB

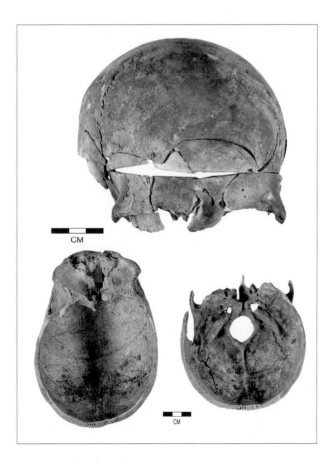

Fig. 107: Cuts made in the cranium during the autopsy of HB 86.

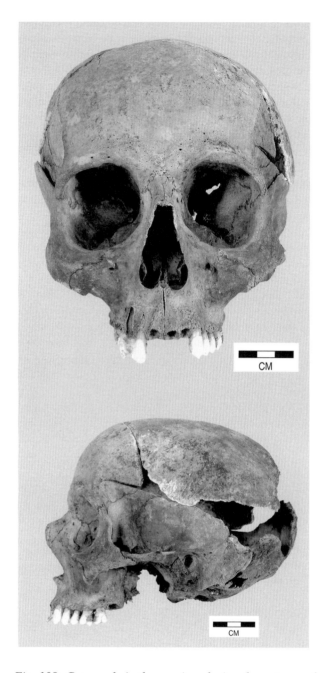

Fig. 108: Cuts made in the cranium during the autopsy of HB 587.

587 in Figure 108. In HB 86, two separate cuts had been made. The first cut appears to have been made to remove a quasi roundel of bone from the frontal bone, in the forehead region. This may have been done in order to allow observation of the frontal lobes of the brain *in situ*. The second saw cut runs circumferentially around the calvarium, which would have allowed its full removal and observation of the rest of the brain. This cut transacted the roundel, and it seems likely that this was the first cut made. In the second individual pictured, HB 587, a linear cut was made in the coronal plane across the frontal bone and sectioned horizontally from the very

posterior portion of the parietals to meet with the coronal cut at the frontal. On the right hand side of the frontal there was a series of 27 small incisive cut marks (2–6mm long, spaced about 1mm apart). It is possible that these relate to the removal of scalp prior to cutting the skull.

Analysis of the various cranial autopsies found at St. Martin's revealed a wide range of different practices, which may have been particular to different surgeons, or may have been practiced to allow different structures to be investigated. Detailed analysis of autopsy practices from archaeological bone would enable more to be said about this subject in the future.

Palaeodietary reconstruction
by Michael Richards

Summary

Eighteen bone collagen and thirty hair carbon and nitrogen stable isotope values were measured from individuals from St. Martin's churchyard. The hair and bone $\delta^{13}C$ values indicate that the protein in the diet was mainly from terrestrial sources, while the $\delta^{15}N$ values are unusually high, compared to prehistoric populations. The high $\delta^{15}N$ values are most likely due to the consumption of freshwater foods or omnivores such as pigs. Most individuals had similar hair and bone isotope values, indicating that the diet in the last few months of life, as indicated by the hair isotope values, were similar to the average lifetime diets as reflected in the bone isotope values. There were a few individuals who had different hair and bone isotope values, which may have indicated a change in diet just before death, or movement to Birmingham from elsewhere.

Introduction

Palaeodietary reconstruction using human tissue (e.g. bone collagen and hair) stable isotope analysis is a well established technique that has been widely applied in archaeology since the late 1970s. In contrast to traditional, indirect, methods of dietary reconstruction, such as analysis of faunal and plant remains, stable isotope analysis is a direct measure of past human diet. This is because as 'you are what you eat', our body tissues have been formed using components from the food we have consumed over our lifetimes. These foods each have specific 'stable isotope ratios'. If we measure the 'stable isotope ratio' of a human bone, we can determine what foods were used to create the bone, and therefore, what foods the humans consumed over their lifetime.

The resolution of the technique is such that we can only determine, generally, what protein the human consumed over the last ten or so years of their life for bone collagen protein, while hair records the last few months of diet. We can tell whether an individual derived the protein in their diet from either plants or animals, or a combination of the two. It is also possible to determine whether that protein came from marine or terrestrial sources. In areas of the world where C_4 pathway plants (e.g. maize and millet) were consumed, isotope analysis can tell us about the importance of these plants in the diet.

The first step in stable isotope analysis is to clean the samples, and in the case of bone, to extract the protein component of the bone, called collagen, as this is the best preserved bone component (it is the same fraction extracted for radiocarbon dating). The next step is to measure, in a mass spectrometer, the ratios of the isotopes of nitrogen, ^{15}N to ^{14}N, called the $\delta^{15}N$ value, and the isotopes of

carbon, ^{13}C to ^{12}C, the $\delta^{13}C$ value, of the extracted collagen. The nitrogen and carbon isotope ratios are measured relative to a standard, the AIR standard for nitrogen, and Pee Dee Belemnite for carbon. The isotope ratios are expressed as 'delta' values, measured as 'per mil' (‰).

For temperate Europe where there are no C_4 plants that were consumed by people, at least in the prehistoric period, human bone collagen and hair keratin $\delta^{13}C$ values of -20 ‰ ± 1 ‰ indicate that the protein that the individual has consumed has come from terrestrial C_3-pathway plants, or from the flesh (or milk) of animals that also subsisted on only C_3 plants. A human bone

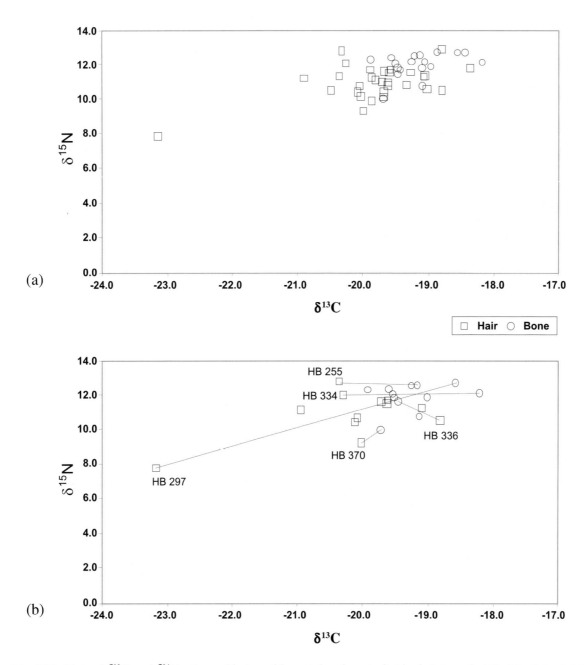

Fig. 109: Plots of $\delta^{13}C$ and $\delta^{14}N$ values of hair and bone taken from individuals interred at St. Martin's: (a) Plot of all samples; (b) plot of hair and bone pairs taken from the same individuals – in a few cases the paired bone and hair values are indicated by a solid line.

collagen or hair keratin $\delta^{13}C$ value of -12 ‰ ± 1 ‰ indicates that the protein came from marine sources, either plants or animals.

The collagen $\delta^{15}N$ values can indicate the trophic level of an organism in a food web, as there is an increase in the $\delta^{15}N$ of about 3 ‰ each step up the food chain. Therefore, if soil plant nitrogen isotope values are about 3 ‰, herbivores that consume those plants have $\delta^{15}N$ values of 6 ‰, and carnivores who consume those herbivores will have $\delta^{15}N$ values of about 9–10 ‰. Humans, as omnivores, can have values that are between these two extremes, and therefore the $\delta^{15}N$ value can be used to tell us whether the people of interest had diets more like herbivores (e.g. vegetarians) or carnivores. These hypothetical values are close to the published values for western European fauna. However, these values can vary throughout the world, and it is important to establish the local faunal $\delta^{15}N$ values before drawing conclusions about the human $\delta^{15}N$ values.

Sample preparation

Hair samples were cleaned prior to analysis in multiple washes of de-ionized water, to remove visible contaminants. Following this the hair samples were soaked for 3–4 hours in 2:1 methanol:chloroform to remove lipids. The samples were then rinsed in de-ionized water and then dried at approximately 50°C. Bone was first cleaned with a shot-blaster, then demineralised in 0.5 M HCl at 4°C for 3–5 days. The resultant solid was then rinsed three times with de-ionised water and then gelatinised in a sealed tube in pH3 HCl solution at 70°C for 48 hours. The resultant solution was then filtered through a 5–8 micron filter, and then ultrafiltered and the >30 kD was retained and lyophilised. The carbon and nitrogen stable isotope measurements of the samples were undertaken at the stable isotope laboratory, University of Bradford. $\delta^{13}C$ measurements were made relative to the vPDB standard and $\delta^{15}N$ measurements were made relative to the AIR standard. Measurement errors on both the $\delta^{13}C$ and $\delta^{15}N$ values are better than ± 0.2 ‰.

Results

The data are presented below in Table 118 and Figure 109. Hair isotope data (n=12) from a previous assessment (Richards 2002) are included. C:N ratios and %C and %N in the measured samples are good general indicators of the preservation of the samples. The hair C:N ratios and %C and %N values are within acceptable ranges, compared to the expected values for modern hair, which has a calculated expected C:N ratio of 3.4 (O'Connell and Hedges 1999a). It should be noted that as hair isotope measurements are rarely reported, agreed ranges for acceptable hair C:N values have not yet been determined. For bone the C:N ratio should be between 2.9 and 3.6, and all of these samples are within that range. Many of the samples were measured twice and the reported value is the average of the two measurements.

Discussion of the results

The new data presented here are comparable to the data from the pilot study/assessment, and for this discussion the data are grouped together. The average (1σ, n = 18) of the bone isotope data is $\delta^{13}C$ = -19.2 ± 0.4 ‰, and $\delta^{15}N$ = 12.0 ± 0.7 ‰, while the average (1σ, n = 29) of the hair data (excluding the data from HB 297 – discussed below) is $\delta^{13}C$ = -19.7 ± 0.6 ‰, and $\delta^{15}N$ = 11.1 ± 0.8 ‰.

There has been some discussion that hair and bone isotope values are not directly comparable, as the amino acid composition of bone collagen and hair keratin differs, so it is likely that the isotope values do as well. Hair isotope values have been predicted to be offset in $\delta^{13}C$ by about 1 ‰, but identical in $\delta^{15}N$ values. However this expected difference in $\delta^{13}C$ has not been observed in archaeological samples (O'Connell and Hedges 1999b). If we compare the eleven individuals with both hair and bone samples (excluding individual HB 297) the average (1σ) bone collagen isotope values are $\delta^{13}C$ = -19.3 ± 0.5 ‰, $\delta^{15}N$ = 11.9 ± 0.8 ‰, while the average hair isotope values are $\delta^{13}C$ = -19.8± 0.6 ‰, $\delta^{15}N$ = 11.2 ± 0.9 ‰. There is no statistically significant difference between the two datasets, therefore this data supports the findings of O'Connell and Hedges (1999b).

There are very few published hair isotope values from archaeological samples while there is a large body of data on bone collagen isotope values. Therefore, here no effort is made to apply any correction to the hair data and general conclusions about the diets of the individuals will be made on the bone collagen data.

Overall diet

The St. Martin's bone collagen stable isotope values are very different to published isotope values from humans from prehistoric sites in the UK. Particularly, the average $\delta^{15}N$ value is much higher than the often observed values of between 7 and 10 ‰. The St. Martin's $\delta^{15}N$ values are similar to bone collagen isotope values of humans from later medieval and post-medieval urban contexts in the UK (Müldner and Richards 2005). The relatively high $\delta^{15}N$ values could either indicate the consumption of freshwater fish in some quantity, or the consumption of pigs, which in turn have high isotopic values. Work is currently underway to explain these high $\delta^{15}N$ values often observed in later medieval and post-medieval individuals, which are not observed in any other time period in Britain.

The $\delta^{13}C$ values are similar to most of the bone collagen results produced for the UK, indicating that the diet was mainly terrestrial-based, and there was very little, if any, contribution from marine foods.

Life histories; hair vs. bone isotope values

Bone collagen stable isotope values reflect long-term diet, on the order of 10–30 years (depending on the bone sampled), while hair reflects short-term diet. Specifically, hair grows at a rate of about 1cm per month and does not

HB No	Tissue	δ ¹³C	δ ¹⁵N	%C	%N	C:N	N
HB 22	Hair	-19.7	10.1	41.8	14.4	3.4	2
HB 121	Hair	-19.0	10.6	42.7	14.7	3.4	2
HB 186	Bone	-19.5	11.4	43.7	16.3	3.1	2
HB 255	Bone	-19.1	12.6	43.8	16.0	3.2	2
HB 255	Hair	-20.3	12.8	40.9	14.2	3.4	1
HB 297	Hair	-23.1	7.8	51.0	20.2	3.0	1
HB 297	Bone	-18.5	12.8	43.8	15.8	3.2	1
HB 304	Hair	-19.6	11.7	66.8	23.3	3.3	1
HB 304	Bone	-19.5	12.1	44.6	17.4	3.0	2
HB 321	Hair	-19.7	11.6	44.9	16.6	3.2	1
HB 321	Bone	-19.1	10.8	43.4	16.5	3.1	2
HB 329	Hair	-19.7	11.0	51.1	18.1	3.3	1
HB 333	Hair	-19.9	11.7	49.1	17.1	3.3	1
HB 334	Hair	-20.3	12.1	48.3	15.9	3.5	1
HB 334	Bone	-18.2	12.2	44.1	16.2	3.2	2
HB 336	Hair	-18.8	10.6	52.9	17.2	3.6	1
HB 336	Bone	-19.4	11.7	44.0	15.6	3.3	2
HB 341	Bone	-19.9	12.3	42.9	15.4	3.2	2
HB 341	Hair	-20.9	11.2	43.5	14.9	3.4	2
HB 370	Bone	-19.7	10.0	42.7	16.1	3.1	2
HB 370	Hair	-20.0	9.3	43.2	14.7	3.4	2
HB 382	Hair	-20.0	10.2	43.0	14.8	3.4	2
HB 383	Hair	-20.4	11.4	42.7	14.1	3.5	2
HB 390	Bone	-19.5	11.9	44.4	15.9	3.2	2
HB 390	Hair	-20.1	10.5	42.2	14.0	3.5	1
HB 397	Bone	-18.4	12.8	44.4	16.0	3.2	1
HB 439	Hair	-19.7	10.5	42.5	14.9	3.3	2
HB 453	Hair	-19.9	9.9	42.7	14.9	3.3	2
HB 544	Bone	-19.0	11.9	45.4	17.1	3.1	2
HB 544	Hair	-20.0	10.7	41.1	14.0	3.4	2
HB 547	Bone	-19.0	12.2	42.8	15.3	3.3	1
HB 573	Hair	-19.6	10.8	54.1	17.5	3.6	1
HB 574	Hair	-19.1	11.4	44.7	14.5	3.6	1
HB 576	Hair	-19.9	11.3	43.3	15.6	3.2	2
HB 587	Bone	-19.2	12.6	43.7	16.7	3.1	2
HB 587	Hair	-19.6	11.5	42.4	14.3	3.5	2
HB 597	Hair	-19.3	11.6	54.3	18.8	3.4	1
HB 598	Hair	-19.1	11.3	53.5	17.9	3.5	1
HB 598	Bone	-19.6	12.4	44.5	15.9	3.3	2
HB 607	Hair	-20.5	10.5	52.1	18.2	3.3	1
HB 691	Hair	-19.6	11.0	42.8	14.8	3.4	1
HB 792	Hair	-18.4	11.9	40.4	13.6	3.5	1
HB 793	Hair	-19.3	10.8	43.3	15.2	3.3	1
HB 794	Bone	-18.9	12.7	44.1	16.3	3.2	2
HB 829	Bone	-19.3	12.2	37.6	14.1	3.1	2
HB 829	Hair	-19.8	11.1	37.0	12.7	3.4	1
HB 840	Hair	-18.8	13.0	38.0	12.7	3.5	1
HB 868	Bone	-19.1	11.8	43.7	17.0	3.0	2

Table 118: Stable isotope values and various indicators of preservation of hair samples taken from individuals interred at St. Martins.

remodel, so each centimetre of hair reflects approximately one month of diet. The hair sampled in this study is an indicator of the last few months of diet of the individual sampled.

In Figure 109(b) data from eleven samples where it was possible to get hair and bone isotope values from the same individual are plotted. For most of the individuals there is very little difference between the bone and hair values, indicating that they had a similar diet in the last few months of life as they did throughout the last years of life (e.g. HB 304 and HB 370). There are some notable exceptions to this.

For individuals HB 255 and HB 334, the hair $\delta^{13}C$ values are very different from the bone $\delta^{13}C$ values, but the $\delta^{15}N$ values are virtually identical. This may be due to a change in diet in the months before death, with the carbon isotope values showing this change but with a longer turn-over time in the nitrogen. Or, it could be due to these individuals moving to Birmingham from elsewhere. This may be supported by the $\delta^{13}C$ value of HB 334, which is the most positive $\delta^{13}C$ of all the individuals, which could indicate that this person spent most of their life elsewhere.

One individual (HB 297) has significantly different isotope values in their hair and bone, and the hair value is significantly different from all of the other hair values, with a $\delta^{13}C$ of -23.1 ‰ and a $\delta^{15}N$ of 7.8 ‰. The bone value of this individual ($\delta^{13}C = -18.5$ ‰, $\delta^{15}N = 12.8$ ‰) is similar to many of the other individuals (although with a slightly more enriched $\delta^{13}C$). There are three possible explanations for this remarkable result. Firstly, the hair sample could be contaminated or degraded and is giving an incorrect results. The C:N ratio and the %C and %N are similar to other hair values (although the C:N ratio is the lowest of all hair samples), and therefore this is unlikely. Secondly, the hair could be from a wig made form some other human hair, or based on the more negative $\delta^{13}C$ value, from an animal like a horse. Thirdly, the data represent a significant change in diet and perhaps in physiology in the last few months of life, and this change is reflected in these hair values. The lower $\delta^{15}N$ value indicates a diet of a lower trophic level, perhaps with a large contribution from plant foods. The $\delta^{13}C$ value is very unusual for humans, and could indicate a physiological change, rather than a dietary one, where quantities of certain amino acids were reduced in the hair as those amino acids were used in more important body functions, such as for internal tissue turn-over or perhaps for energy.

Individual HB 297 is Ann Maria Browett, who died in 1894, aged 81. From the textual evidence (Chapter 6) this woman never lived outside of Birmingham so the very different isotope values between the hair and bone are not due to her moving to Birmingham just before she died. As she was elderly, the other two possibilities for the isotope data are more likely – that the hair isotope value is from a wig, or else it reflects a changed diet and physiology, likely related to poor health, in the few months before she died. Her husband, Alfred Browett, HB 336 (who died in 1869 at the age of 58) has similar hair and bone isotope values indicating that his diet did not change significantly during the last few months of life.

Conclusions

The investigation of the human bone excavated from St. Martin's has provided an excellent opportunity to learn more about the lives and deaths of a cross-section of the people of Birmingham during this important period in its development. In particular, the possibility of examining individuals from different backgrounds afforded by the excavation of both earth-cut graves and vaults has enabled the impact of socio-economic factors on health to be considered.

Although written sources provide valuable information on life in the past, and have been widely used throughout this volume, the investigation of the human bone has enabled a far fuller picture of health in this community to be obtained. For example, no information is available from documentary sources on vitamin D deficiency in adults, but skeletal analysis demonstrated its presence. There is also very little information available from written sources on scurvy in Birmingham. However, skeletal analyses demonstrated the condition to have been relatively common amongst infants and children of the poorer sections of the community. Contemporary written sources say little about the comparative health of females from different socio-economic groups. Data from the human bone gave some information on differences between these two groups. In particular, differences in the levels of fractures recorded between the two groups of women were very marked. Consideration of the data produced by the wide range of specialists that worked on the St. Martin's project alongside the information from the human skeletal remains enabled important information on life and health in the past to be obtained.

As stated in the introductory sections of this chapter, it would be extremely valuable to be able to investigate a cemetery of this date from a rural population, so that the full range of differences between those that lived their lives in a rural setting and those who were born in or moved to a city could be observed. However, it would also be interesting to be able to investigate a contemporary collection of human bone from an industrial city such as Manchester. Cities such as Manchester used very different types of heavy technology to those used in Birmingham. Work was often undertaken on a much larger scale and many people worked in factories.

The collection of human bone from St. Martin's has provided a fascinating insight into the lives of individuals from this period. It has also given an indication of the full range of information that can be obtained on the lives of individuals from the past, even with basic skeletal investigations.

5   The Impedimenta of Death: Specialist Reports

Coffins and coffin furniture
by Emma Hancox

Introduction

A total of 57 boxes of coffin furniture was recovered from the excavations. This mostly consisted of grips, grip plates, *depositum* plates and nails from the coffins. The vast majority of the assemblage came from the earth-cut graves, 46 boxes, with the rest coming from the vaults and brick-lined graves. The preservation of the assemblage varied immensely. From the earth-cut graves the grips and plates were very corroded. The grips were all made of iron, and nearly all of them were too corroded to assess even the shape or decoration. There were generally only small fragments of plate surviving, none of which had any legible writing, and in most cases wood from the coffins only survived as a dark stain. In the vaults and brick-lined graves the preservation of the coffins varied greatly from structure to structure and within the structures themselves. A few coffins were in excellent condition, most were in poor to mixed condition, whilst others had rotted away almost to nothing. The coffin furniture from the earth-cut graves was assessed, but was considered too corroded and contaminated to be worthy of further study. The furniture from the vaults and brick-lined graves was worthy of further study, although the poor survival of most of the material and the fact that much of it was not recovered represented a severe limitation.

Given the limited time and resources available for the excavations and the research priorities of the work, most attention was paid to the recovery of the human remains for anthropological analysis. All the coffins (mostly very decayed) were re-buried on site and only a sample of the coffin furniture was recovered for assessment and analysis. Selected samples were also taken of the coffin wood for analysis (Gale, this chapter). Much reliance was therefore placed on on-site recording of coffins and coffin furniture, mainly through photography and written description. Ordinary context recording sheets were used to record the coffins, which led to considerable variation in the quality and comprehensiveness of recording. With hindsight, a specifically-designed coffin recording form would probably have produced a more consistent result, although most of the limitations of the evidence derive from the poor state of survival of the material itself.

Table 119 provides a quantification of the assemblage of coffin furniture which was recovered. From this table some indication of both the degree of fragmentation of the material and the levels of recovery can be gained. For example, on average about one coffin grip was recovered for each coffin from an earth-cut grave and about two for each coffin from a vault or brick-lined grave, whereas the actual number of these would have been six to eight per coffin. The degree of fragmentation of coffin plates can be judged from the similar average number of fragments (14 or 13) recovered from coffins in the earth-cut graves and brick-lined graves/vaults respectively. With most of the coffin plates in such a fragmentary state it is not surprising that it was mainly those high-quality *deposita* made of copper alloy (probably mostly brass) from the vaults that were legible. Although the recovery levels were clearly very low, it is apparent from Table 119 that decorative coffin studs (probably mainly brass), generally used to fix the fabric cover to the outer wooden case of the coffin, were much more extensively used for the coffins in the vaults than for those in the earth-cut graves.

Coffins

From the beginning of the 18th century the usual style of coffin was single-break, single-case and wooden, with a stamped iron *depositum* and six or eight stamped iron grip plates with wrought iron grips (handles). 'Single-break' denotes the familiar coffin shape, expanding from the head end to the shoulders and then, with a single break, tapering towards the feet. 'Single-case' means that the coffin was only one skin of wood thick; 'double-case'

	Quantity	Total No. of burials	Average No. per burial
Earth-cut graves			
Coffin grips	870	734	1.2
Coffin plate fragments	10,496	734	14.3
Coffin nails	3,102	734	4.2
Coffin studs	39	734	0.05
Vaults and brick-lined graves			
Coffin grips	234	123	1.9
Coffin plate fragments	1,603	123	13.0
Coffin nails	437	123	0.28
Coffin studs	55	123	2.2

Table 119: Quantification of recovered coffin furniture.

coffins had two skins of wood, sometimes of different types. All the coffins from the earth-cut graves at St. Martin's were made of wood with iron grips and grip plates. There was not enough wood left in most cases to tell if they had been single- or double-case, but they all appear to have been single-break, becoming very narrow around the feet. Some had evidence of a *depositum* but in all cases these were too fragmentary and corroded to read. All the *deposita* from the earth-cut graves were made of stamped iron, painted black, with the information about the deceased painted on in white rather than engraved. The only exception to this was HB 408. The coffin of this individual had had large copper-alloy letters attached to the lid, most of which had survived intact (Fig. 31, colour, Chapter 3). This was the earliest dated burial recorded at St. Martin's, bearing a date of 172? (the last numeral of the date was missing). The letters formed the initials of the deceased, the age at death (83) and the date. Other than this single example, due to the poor preservation, the collection bias and the problems of contamination, the material from the earth-cut graves was not of significant archaeological importance and was not recorded in detail.

The coffins from the vaults and brick-lined graves could be divided into two groups on the basis of whether they included a lead shell in their construction or were constructed only of wood. Those that included lead in their construction were probably mainly of triple-shell type, that is they comprised an outer wooden 'case', then a lead 'shell', then an inner wooden 'coffin'. The construction of coffins of this type is described in detail by Litten (1991, 101–3). However, at St. Martin's the survival of the wooden elements of the coffins was often too poor for the precise details of construction to be clear.

Litten (1991, 101) describes the triple shell as "the traditional coffin for the burial vault and brick-lined grave". The purpose of the lead shell was to arrest the decay of the body and the release of unpleasant fluids and odours. As such, they were most appropriate to the vault context, where re-opening of the vault to add new burials was anticipated. For intramural burials in crypts there

	Wood	Lead/ wood	Total	Use range
Chambered Vault				
Vault 10	10	9	19	1801 – 1833
Family Vaults with identified individuals				
Vault 23	5	4	9	1811 – 1846
Vault 18	2	2	4	1816 – 1833
Vault 9	0	11	11	1816 – 1882
Vault 5	0	13	13	1842 – 1895
Vault 30	0	8	8	1831 – 1904
Sub-totals	7	38	45	
Family Vaults with no identified individuals				
Vault 2	4	0	4	-
Vault 4	5	0	5	-
Vault 21	6	0	6	-
Sub-totals	15	0	15	
Totals: vaults	32	47	79	
Brick-lined graves				
All graves	33	10	43	1825 – 1873
Totals: all structures	65	57	122	

Table 120: Numbers of wood and lead/wood coffins in the vaults and brick-lined graves.

was also the problem of the escape of unpleasant odours into the church above, and at Christ Church, Spitalfields an order of the Vestry of 1813 stated that for hygienic reasons henceforth all further burials should be encased in lead (Reeve and Adams 1993, 78). This particular problem did not apply to the extramural vaults and brick-lined graves at St. Martin's, where odours could escape into the open air (and, as noted in Chapter 3, some of the vaults and graves were provided with ventilation, presumably to facilitate this).

Table 120 shows the numbers of coffins from the vaults and brick-lined graves which were constructed either solely of wood or of composite wood and lead construction.

The table shows that overall more than half of the coffins in the vaults and brick-lined graves were of wood construction (65 out of 122 recorded). However, the overall proportions mask significant patterns. For example, in the vaults more coffins (47 out of 79) were of lead/wood construction, whereas in the brick-lined graves wood coffins greatly outnumbered lead/wood coffins (33 out of 43). Table 120 also suggests that there may be a chronological trend, with the use of lead coffins becoming increasingly common for later burials (the use ranges given in the table generally represent only a minimum – see Chapter 3). It should be noted in this respect that an order issued by the Secretary of State in 1873 stated that all burials in the town, including St. Martin's, should henceforth be discontinued except in vaults and walled graves with an air-tight coffin (see Chapter 2); 'air-tight' implies a metal shell. Cross-cutting any chronological trend, however, is the issue of cost and status; lead coffins would have been considerably more expensive than those constructed only of wood. It is apparent from Table 120 that all the burials in Vaults 9, 5 and 30 were in lead/ wood coffins. These vaults belonged to the wealthy Jenkins, Warden/Browett and Haines families respectively (see Chapter 6), and in them even infants and children were buried in lead coffins. This contrasts with the situation in Vaults 18 and 23, where the children were buried in wooden coffins whereas most of the adults were in lead/wood coffins. In even more sharp contrast to Vaults 9, 5 and 30 are Vaults 2, 4 and 21, where all the burials were in wood coffins. These are presumed to be family vaults although no burials within them could be identified (a consequence, probably, of the materials used for the coffins and coffin furniture), so neither the relative wealth of the families nor the date of the burials can be inferred.

In Vault 10, the large 'chambered vault', the proportion of lead/wood coffins to wood coffins is about half and half. However, this masks the fact that in two of the four chambers (Chambers A and D) all the burials were in wood coffins while in the other two chambers (B and C) they were all in lead/wood coffins. Chamber A contained only a single coffin but Chamber D contained nine wooden coffins. In the case of Vault 10, chronology is unlikely to be the key factor in the distinction. The burials of Samuel Wyer (d.1802) in Chamber A and Daniel Rowlinson (d.1801) in Chamber B are closely comparable in date but the former was buried in a wood coffin and the latter in a lead/wood coffin. In Vault 10, choice and possibly wealth seem to be the key factors and, in the case of the Cockle family in Chamber D, perhaps family tradition also.

It is unclear how the much smaller proportion of lead/ wood coffins used for burials in the brick-lined graves should be explained. Amongst the possibilities are cost/ status, practicality, choice and chronology. The nine or ten lead/wood coffins (one was found with only vestiges of lead) were found in just six of the 24 graves. The earliest dated burial, that of Sarah Parker (HB 625, V11), which dates no later than 1825, was in a coffin of lead/ wood construction, whilst the latest dated burial, of John Sansom (HB 189, V03), was in a coffin of wood. Because each grave was probably used over a shorter period than was often the case with the vaults, the more rapid decay of a wooden coffin was perhaps less of an issue. Furthermore, the vertical stacking of coffins inserted from above and often supported on timber beams possibly made the decay of earlier coffins less of a practical problem than it would have been in a family vault.

The coffins from the vaults could also be divided on the basis of shape, either 'fish-tail' or 'single-break' (Table 121). This distinction could only be made for the lead/wood coffins as the wood coffins were generally too decayed for their shape to be accurately determined. Furthermore, 10 of the 47 lead/wood coffins from the vaults were too fragmentary or crushed for their original shape to be determined.

Some examples of the shapes of coffins from St. Martin's are shown in Fig. 110. The 'fish-tail' coffins differ from the 'single-break' coffins in that rather than tapering in a straight line from the 'break' at the shoulder to the feet, they swell round the torso, taper in at the thighs, are narrow along the length of the lower legs and then splay out at the feet. It is this last characteristic that suggests the appellation 'fish-tail'. Another important

	Fish-tail	Single-break	Unclear	Total	Use range
Chambered Vault					
Vault 10	4	-	5	9	1801 – 1833
Family Vaults with identified individuals					
Vault 23	-	-	4	4	1811 – 1846
Vault 18	2	0	0	2	1816 – 1833
Vault 9	8	3	0	11	1816 – 1882
Vault 5	6	6	1	13	1842 – 1895
Vault 30	7	1	0	8	1831 – 1904
Totals	**27**	**10**	**10**	**47**	

Table 121: The shape of the lead/wood coffins in the vaults at St. Martin's.

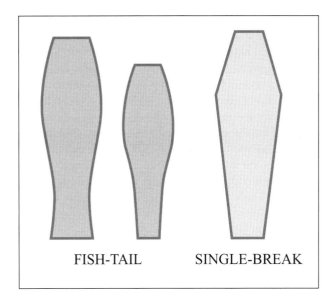

Fig. 110: Examples of the shapes of lead/wood coffins from St. Martin's.

characteristic of the fish-tail coffins is that they are sinuous or curvilinear; there are no sharp angles except at the ends. Perhaps the most significant point is that fish-tail coffins more closely follow the contours of the human form than do single-break coffins. However, although the lower legs are the narrowest part of the body, and thus the narrowest part of the coffin, the splaying to accommodate the feet, while anatomically appropriate, is sometimes exaggerated – this provides the 'true' fish-tail form. Many coffins do not show this exaggeration and although their designation as 'fish-tailed' may thus appear inaccurate, they are clearly a variant on the form. An illustration of this is provided by the well-preserved coffins of John Home (HB 575, d.1828) and Frances Home (HB 576, d.1833) in Vault 18 (Fig. 46, colour, Chapter 3). The larger coffin of John Home splays out at the foot to give the 'typical' fish-tail form while that of Frances Home, although sharing all the other characteristics of the form, barely splays out at the foot.

The fish-tail coffins from St. Martin's contrast with the chronologically overlapping group from Christ Church, Spitalfields (Reeve and Adams 1993, 78–83), where the great majority of the coffins were of single-break form and no fish-tail coffins were explicitly noted. The published photographs in Reeve and Adams (1993) do suggest that the shoulder of the coffins from the vaults in the crypt were sometimes markedly curved rather than having a sharp break. However, the narrowing at the thighs, which along with the splayed foot is an important characteristic of the fish-tail coffins, is not evident. At St. Martin's the contrast between the fish-tail form and the single-break form is clear cut. The single-break lead/wood coffins all have a sharp angle at the shoulder and straight sides. The distinction is clearly chronological.

This is well illustrated by the coffins from Vault 5 (Fig. 51, Chapter 3). Those on the lower two levels (Levels 1 and 2) are all of fish-tail shape while those on the upper two levels (Levels 3 and 4) are all of single-break shape. The transition takes place in the late 1860s/early 1870s (by which time burial in the crypt at Christ Church, Spitalfields had ceased). The transition is also clearly apparent in Table 122 below, which provides details of the coffins associated with the dated burials from St. Martin's.

The use of fish-tail shaped lead/wood coffins for vault burials at St. Martin's may perhaps be seen as a regional preference, and contributes to an overall impression that funerary fashions in the metropolis cannot be automatically generalised to the nation as a whole. It is tempting to view the transition to a single-break form at St. Martin's around 1870 as linked to a range of changes in attitudes which were taking place in the 1870s, influenced by the funerary reform movement (see Chapter 8) and ultimately giving rise to the growth of cremation (a practice in direct opposition to the Christian doctrine of the resurrection of the body).

Several of the lead/wood coffins from St. Martin's were preserved in good condition (e.g. Figs 111 and 112, colour). Some of them were very sturdy with the lead shell being up to 4mm thick. They all appeared to be manufactured in the same basic manner with the edges of the sides of the shell being folded over the lid and soldered down (see Stock 1998, 148–149). The wood used in their construction was predominantly elm, with oak only rarely noted (see Gale, this chapter). It is likely that the outer wooden cases of the coffins were in almost all cases covered with fabric, although often this did not survive. Coffin covers from eight coffins from the vaults and brick-lined graves were studied (Walton Rogers, this chapter) and were found to be made of a napped wool tabby dyed black. The covers were attached with copper-alloy studs (termed upholstery nails in the trade) arranged in a variety of patterns, although there is no evidence that any of them formed the initials of the deceased as has been noted at other sites (Boore 1998, 73). Cloth coverings to coffins are generally thought to have fallen out of fashion during the second quarter of the 19th century, following the introduction of french-polishing (Walton Rogers, this chapter). However, at St. Martin's it appears that the use of fabric covers continued until the early 1870s (see Table 122 below). A few of the coffins from St. Martin's preserved the remains of 'coffin-lace' (e.g. Figs 111 and 112, colour), a trim which is both an alternative means of fixing the fabric cover to the coffin and a form of decoration. 'White' coffin-lace was made from tinned metal, while 'black' coffin lace was made of thin rolled-out lead (see Chapter 8).

The outer surface of the lead shells were often wire-carded with a cross-hatched (or 'lozenge' or 'diaper') pattern. This practice was also common at Christ Church, Spitalfields (Reeve and Adams 1993, 82). As the lead shell was not a visible component of the completed coffin the purpose of this practice is obscure. Perhaps it was realised, from experience of vault burials, that once the outer wood case had rotted away the lead would exposed, and the pattern was, indeed, intended as a form of decoration.

Coffin Furniture

Plates were attached to the lid and sides of most of the coffins, usually one *depositum* or breastplate (giving the biographical details) and either six or eight handle or grip plates (three either side and, where these occur, one on each end). The grip plates from the vaults were made mostly of copper alloy, but also of iron, lead and tin/ nickel. In addition further purely decorative plates, called escutcheons, could be attached to the sides or lid of the coffin (when attached to the lid they are also called lid motifs).

Table 122 shows the occurrence of surviving coffin furniture on the dated coffins from the vaults and brick-lined graves.

There were several different styles and sizes of grips and some of them were highly decorated, again made mostly of copper alloy. One grip even had a date stamped on it (Vault 23 – 15th September 1842). Amongst the most popular motifs on the grip plates appeared to be the winged cherub (Fig. 113, colour) and a floral pattern, both very elaborate. Boore (1993, 73) states that the winged cherub motif is found in most post-medieval graveyards and is associated with all social classes. It dates from *c.*1740–1850 and was also found at St. Philip's Cathedral, Birmingham (Patrick 2001, 7). As Table 122 shows, it appeared on coffins at St. Martin's dating to the first third of the 19th century but not, insofar as the evidence is available, later. Also popular was an urn motif. Penny (1981, 25) refers to this as a 'pagan emblem' and a later style, appearing from the 1830s at various sites across the country and lasting until the 1860s. As reference to Table 122 indicates, this dating would appear to be closely followed at St. Martin's, with the earliest dated example being of 1834 (HB 779) and the latest occurrence probably 1870 (HB 334). The illustrated example (Fig. 114) is a lid motif of a flaming urn on the coffin of Capt. Adj. Benjamin Robinson (HB 779, d.1834).

Another popular design was a plain geometric shape, very different to the ornate flowered, cherub and urn designs. This simpler design may reflect the late Victorian trend towards less ornate funerals. However, only one coffin bearing this design was directly datable, that of Isaac Ainsworth (HB702) in Vault 23, which dated to 1837.

One coffin was very different to all the others, that of Ann Maria Browett (Vault 5, HB 297). This coffin, dated to 1894, was painted white rather than covered with fabric. The coffin furniture was of a unique design (Fig. 115), using a fleur-de-lys motif on the grip plates and the *depositum*, with the grips being straight pieces of copper

alloy with a twist pattern on them. The plates were all plain-shaped stamped copper-alloy sheets with no decoration on them.

The *depositum* plates (or breastplates) also came in a variety of styles. The text was mostly laid out in the same format, giving the name of the deceased, then the date of death (with the month, then the day and then the year), followed by the age of the person when they died. Two coffins had two plates giving the same information, a plain lead one attached to the inner lead lid and a more ornate copper-alloy one attached to the outer wooden lid (HB 702, Vault 23 and HB 840, Vault 30). This has also been noted at other sites, including St. Philip's, Birmingham (Patrick 2001).

The shape of the *depositum* should by heraldic convention indicate the sex and marital status of the person buried: a shield for a boy or young man, a lozenge for a girl or unmarried woman, rectangular with an oval

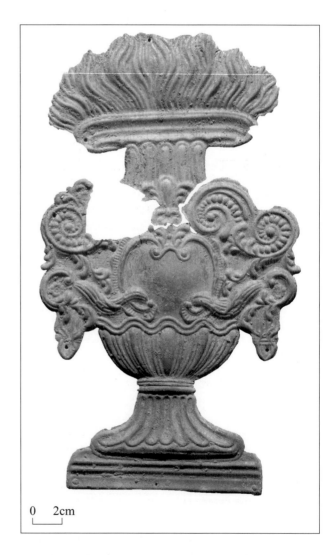

Fig. 114: Flaming urn lid motif on coffin of HB 779, Capt. Adj. Benjamin Robinson (d.1834), from brick-lined grave V33.

Date	Vlt	HB	Name	Coffin Type	Coffin Shape	Plate Mat.	Plate Type	Grips & Escutcheons	Cover
1801	10	382	Daniel Rowlinson	Lead/ oak	Fish-tail	Pb	Shield	-	Black wool
1815/ 1821	23	722	?Isaac or John Ainsworth	Lead/ elm	Fish-tail	Fe, gold paint	Shield, cherubs & crown	Cherub-motif grips	-
1815/ 1821	23	723	?Isaac or John Ainsworth	Lead/ elm	Fish-tail	Cu alloy	Shield, cherub	Cherub-motif grips	-
?1816	18	552 child	?Sophia Frances Home	Wood	-	-	-	Flower-motif grips	-
1827	9	861 infant	Vernon Jenkins	Lead/ wood	Fish-tail	Pb	Shield Type 1	-	-
1827	23	691	Hannah Ainsworth	Lead/ oak/elm	Fish-tail	Cu alloy	Rectan-gular	Angel/cherub-motif grips	Fabric, studded
1828	18	575	John Home	Lead/ elm	Fish-tail	Cu alloy	Rectan-gular	-	Fabric, brass studs
1833	10	543	James Cockle	Wood	-	Fe	Oval, cherubs & crown	Cherub-motif grips	-
1833	18	576	Frances Home	Lead/ elm	Fish-tail	Cu alloy	Shield Type 1	-	-
1834	33	779	Capt Benjamin Robinson	Wood	-	Cu alloy	Rectan-gular	Stamped fe urn	Fabric, studded
1837	23	702	Isaac Ainsworth	Lead/ elm	-	Cu alloy	Geo-metric shield	Patterned grips, geometric plates	Fabric
1842	5	574	Ann Maria Warden	Lead/ wood	Fish-tail	-	Shield Type 1	-	Fabric
1848	9	C 3087	Edmund Jenkins	Lead/ wood	Fish-tail	Cu alloy	Shield Type 1	-	-
1851	30	840	William Haines	Lead/ elm	Fish-tail	Cu alloy	'Ornate'	-	Fabric
1860	30	829	Frank Haines	Lead/ elm	Fish-tail	Pb	Rectan-gular	-	-
?1860	5	607	?Sophia Warden	Lead/ elm	Fish-tail	Fe, black paint	Rectan-gular with urn	Urn motif on grips and escutcheon	Black wool; coffin lace
?1861	5	597	?Edwin Warden	Lead/ wood	Fish-tail	Fe, black paint	Rectan-gular with urn	Urn motif on grips and escutcheon	Fabric; coffin lace
1861	9	N/A	Mary Jenkins	N/A	N/A	Cu alloy	Shield Type 1	N/A	N/A
1862	3	185 infant	Helen Mary Walker	Wood	-	Cu alloy	Shield Type 2	-	-
1862	9	C 1972	Leoline Jenkins	Lead/ wood	Fish-tail	Cu alloy	Shield Type 1	-	-
1863	5	587	George Warden	Lead/ elm	?Fish-tail	Cu alloy	Rectan-gular	-	Fabric
1864	30	841	Jane Lloyd Haines	Lead/ wood	?Fish-tail	Cu alloy	Shield Type 2	-	Fabric, studded
1866	5	598	Sarah Emma Warden	Lead/ elm	Fish-tail	Cu alloy	Shield Type 2	-	-
1869	5	336	Alfred Browett	Lead/ wood	Single-break	Fe, black paint	Casket-shaped	-	-
1869	30	794	William Tertius Haines	Lead/ elm/oak	Fish-tail	Cu alloy	Shield Type 2	-	-

Table 122: Details of coffins and coffin furniture from the dated burials in the vaults and brick-lined graves, arranged chronologically. For definition of 'Shield Type 1' and 'Shield Type 2' see Fig. 116. Continued overleaf.

Date	Vlt	HB	Name	Coffin Type	Coffin Shape	Plate Mat.	Plate Type	Grips & Escutcheons	Cover
?1870	5	334	?Frederick Browett	Lead/ wood	Single-break	Fe, black paint	-	Fe grips and escutcheon with urn motif	Fabric; coffin lace
?1871	5	304	?Mary Hannah Warden	Lead/ wood	Single-break	-	-	Plain	Fabric
1873	3	189	John Sansom	Wood	-	Cu alloy	Shield Type 2	-	-
1877	9	C 3089	Leonard Jenkins	Lead/ wood	Single-break	Cu alloy	Shield Type 2	-	-
1878	30	792	Campbell Lloyd Haines	Lead/ wood	?Fish-tail	Cu alloy	Shield Type 2	Fleur-de-lys and urn-motif escutcheons	-
1882	9	C 1975	Helen Jenkins	Lead/ oak	Single-break	Cu alloy	Shield Type 2	-	-
1894	5	297	Ann Maria Browett	Lead/ wood Painted white	?	Cu alloy	Rectangular with fleurs-de-lys on corners	Cu alloy grip plates with fleurs-de-lys on corners	-
1904	30	793	Eliza Haines	Lead/ wood	Single-break	Cu alloy	Shield Type 2	-	-

Table 122 continued.

Fig. 115: Depositum *and coffin grips from the coffin of HB 297, Ann Maria Browett (d.1894), Vault 5 (Warden family) Level 4. The* depositum *and grip plates employ a fleur-de-lys motif on the corners.*

panel for a married woman and rectangular with a square panel for a man (Litten 1991, 109). However, the use of heraldic convention in funerals appears to have waned from the beginning of the 18th century and Litten observes that in the 19th century coffin furniture manufacturers did not always follow the convention as they were unfamiliar with it. The *deposita* at St Martin's,

like those from Christ Church, Spitalfields (Reeve and Adams 1993), do not follow convention.

At St. Martin's the shield was the most popular shape for *depositum* plates, and most of the datable plates from the early 19th century through to the beginning of the 20th century were of this shape and used for men, women and children (see Table 122). The shield-shaped coffin

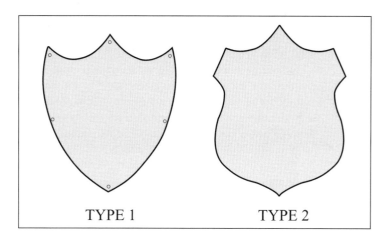

Fig. 116 (left): The two principal types of shield-shaped depositum *found at St. Martin's.*
Fig. 117 (right): A brass Type 2 shield-shaped depositum *from the coffin of HB 841, Jane Lloyd Haines (d.1864), Vault 30 (Haines family), Level 1.*

plates from St. Martin's came in two principal types, labelled for convenience Type 1 and Type 2 (Fig. 116). There is a clear chronological progression from Type 1 to Type 2 (Table 122). The earliest dated example of a Type 1 plate occurs in 1827 (HB 861, Vault 9) and the latest in 1862 (C 1972, Vault 9). The earliest Type 2 plate occurs in 1862 (HB 185, V03) and the latest in 1904 (HB 793, Vault 30), so there is virtually no overlap between the two types and what appears to be a very rapid transition around 1862. The example of a Type 2 shield-shaped coffin plate which is illustrated in Figure 117 is from the coffin of Jane Lloyd Haines (HB 841), who died in 1864.

From the remainder of the *deposita*, which were of very varied form, two examples have been illustrated. Figure 118 (colour) shows the coffin plate of James Cockle (HB 543), who died in 1833 and was buried in Vault 10. It is an elaborate iron coffin plate, with an oval centre surrounded by cherubs and surmounted with a crown. Figure 119 shows the *depositum* of Alfred Browett (HB 336, Vault 5) who died in 1869. It is also of iron but had been painted black (traces of the paint are visible) and was in the form of a casket.

When the metal from which the *depositum* plates were made is considered, an interesting contrast emerges between the largely contemporary burials in Vault 5 and Vault 9. In Vault 5 four of the seven coffin plates listed in Table 122 were made of iron and painted black. By contrast, in Vault 9 five of the six coffin plates listed were of copper alloy (probably brass). The table demonstrates that the contrast is not a chronological one, and it is possible that it relates to the occupation of the two 'founders' of these family vaults. Vault 5 was founded by Joseph Warden, an iron merchant, and Vault 9 by William Jenkins, a brassfounder. Could there be a symbolic significance to the favoured choice of metal and were the coffin plates manufactured in the workshops belonging to these two wealthy families? In both cases

0   10cm

Fig. 119: Iron depositum *from coffin of HB 336, Alfred Browett (d.1869), Vault 5 (Warden family) Level 3. The plate is in the form of a casket and had been painted black.*

coffin furniture may have been amongst the products of their respective works.

Coffin furniture catalogues

Comparison of the coffin furniture from St. Martin's with that illustrated in catalogues of the late 18th century, 19th century and early 20th century confirmed the overall date range of the assemblage and some of the general trends in fashion. Five catalogues were examined: the only surviving 18th-century catalogue, that of Tuesby and Cooper (1783), and examples of 19th- and early 20th-century catalogues from the Victoria and Albert Museum and the National Funeral Museum.

The 1783 catalogue has drawings of grips, grip plates and *depositum* plates. All are very elaborate, with the urn and flowers design, angels or cherubs on most plates. Some of the furniture from St. Martin's which is similar (for example from Vault 10) may date from around this time. Examples of upholstery studs are also shown. These are simple single or double rows around the edges of the coffin; there are no examples of elaborate patterns or coffin lace.

A pattern book from the Victoria and Albert Museum dating to *c.*1826 (no maker's name) also shows coffin furniture designs similar to those at St. Martin's. The choice of design is more varied here – rose and thistle motifs and plates showing the Masonic eye are available, as well as the angel, cherub and flower designs. The upholstery studs in this catalogue are more elaborate, being shown in single, double or triple rows of round or diamond-shaped studs. Coffin lace is also available. Only round studs were found at St. Martin's. Unfortunately the origin of this catalogue is unknown.

The late 19th-century catalogue housed at The National Funeral Museum (unknown date and maker) has much simpler designs than the earlier catalogues. There is little decoration on the plates and grips, and the angels, cherubs and flowers have all disappeared. The catalogue clearly shows the trend towards plainer designs approaching the end of the 19th century, although it is difficult to confirm this pattern at St. Martin's due to the patchy survival of the material and the relatively small number of burials of this date. The Dottridge Bros. coffin catalogue (*c.*1910–1915) shows a choice of coffins, all very simple in design, and includes both the Francis Seymour Hayden 'Earth to Earth' coffin (a biodegradable type) and a cremation box. Their furniture catalogue (1922) shows simple designs, which are different to those at St. Martin's.

Dr. Julian Litten kindly drew to the attention of the author the trade catalogue issued by CW&Sons of Birmingham in 1837. This little-known and unpublished catalogue is in the Linford-Bridgeman Collection at Lichfield. The catalogue includes a pattern for a *depositum* that is identical in almost every detail to the elaborate *depositum* (Fig. 118, colour) on the coffin of James Cockle (HB 543, d.1833) in Vault 10, Chamber D. The catalogue also includes a pattern (termed 'Urn') for an escutcheon very closely similar to the flaming urn lid motif found on the coffin of Capt. Adj. Benjamin Robinson (HB 779, d.1834) in brick-lined grave V33. The CW&Sons catalogue was issued only three to four years after the funerals of Benjamin Robinson and James Cockle, and the very close similarity of the patterns to

the excavated examples (they differ only in very minor details) must lead to the supposition that CW&Sons may well have been the supplier.

Other items in the CW&Sons catalogue include further patterns for escutcheons, termed 'Angel', 'Flower' and 'Glory'. The last of these, a flaming crown flanked by angels, is essentially the motif used for the *depositum* on James Cockle's coffin. The catalogue also includes a very wide range of patterns for coffin lace.

The catalogues thus confirm that the coffins and coffin furniture from St. Martin's mostly date from the nineteenth century and broadly follow national trends in design. However, despite the generally poor state of survival of the assemblage, several patterns have been observed which may be particular to the local scene as well as displaying individual idiosyncrasies. The funerary trade in Birmingham and the influence of the funerary reform movement are further explored in Chapter 8.

Wooden coffin remains
by Rowena Gale

Introduction

Most of the 857 burials were dated to the late 18th – 19th centuries, and were of unidentified individuals, interred in simple wooden coffins in earth-cut graves. Preservation in these contexts was poor and relatively few coffins survived. Wood samples were collected from 82 earth-cut graves, although only 28 of these were suitable for species identification. Further wood samples were recovered from 51 burials in vaults (Vaults 2, 4, 5, 9, 10, 18, 23 and 30) and brick-lined graves (V07, V08, V14, V15, V19, V20, V26, V32 and V36). Here the preservation was significantly better and it was possible to examine every sample.

Overall, the wood samples represent the mortuary or burial practices of a wide cross-section of the community. Species identification of the samples enabled the comparative study of coffin woods for both the poorer members of society and families of high social status and considerable wealth.

Materials and methods

The wood samples were mostly damp or waterlogged, although a few appeared to have dried out (probably after excavation). Structurally, the wood was very degraded, particularly when from earth-cut graves. Samples in association with HB 26, a burial in an earth-cut grave, HB 132 (Vault 2) and HB 269 (Vault 4) included wood preserved through partial mineralization (i.e. having undergone chemical changes brought about through contact with metal).

The samples were prepared for identification using standard methods (Gale and Cutler 2000). For waterlogged wood in reasonable condition, thin sections were removed from the transverse, tangential and radial surfaces and mounted on microscope slides. These were examined at magnifications up to ×400 using transmitted light on a Nikon Labophot-2 compound microscope. For desiccated and mineralized wood, fresh surfaces in the same orientations as above were exposed by fracturing and supported in sand; the samples were examined with the same microscope but using incident light illumination. The anatomical structures were matched to reference slides of modern wood.

Results

The taxa identified are presented on Table 1 (wooden coffins from earth-cut graves) and Table 2 (coffins from the chambered burial vault, the family vaults and the brick-lined graves) in Appendix 8 on the CD. Where a genus is represented by a single species in the British flora this is named as the most likely origin of the wood, given the provenance and period, but it should be noted that it is rarely possible to name individual species from wood features, and exotic species of trees and shrubs were introduced to Britain from an early period (Godwin 1956; Mitchell 1974). In degraded wood the identification of some unrelated taxa can be problematical, e.g. *Corylus* and *Alnus*. Classification follows that of *Flora Europaea* (Tutin, Heywood *et al* 1964–80). The taxa identified included:

– Betulaceae. *Alnus glutinos* (L.) Gaertner, European alder or Corylaceae. *Corylus avellana* L., hazel
– Fagaceae. *Quercus* spp., oak
– Ulmaceae. *Ulmus* spp., elm
– Pinaceae. *Pinus* spp., pine (Scots pine, *sylvestris* group)

An unidentified exotic timber was present amongst the coffin remains of HB 269, Vault 4. The wood was mineralized but too degraded to include sufficient diagnostic detail for identification. The wood structure included – Transverse surface (TS): *vessels* solitary, in radial pairs and chains; *parenchyma* confluent; *rays* up to 3 cells wide. Tangential surface (TLS): *rays* up to 3 cells wide, short. Radial surface (RLS): *rays* hetero-cellular, cells procumbent, marginal cells square.

Wooden coffins from earth-cut graves

Coffin woods were examined from a total of 28 burials in earth-cut graves (Table 1, Appendix 8, CD). In general, these coffins were less well preserved than those from the vaults. Nineteen samples were identified as elm (*Ulmus* sp.), six as oak (*Quercus* sp.), two as pine (*Pinus* sp.), and one as hazel (*Corylus avellana*) or alder (*Alnus glutinosa*).

Coffins from the chambered vault, family vaults and brick-lined graves

Wood samples from 50 coffins were examined (Table 2, Appendix 8, CD). The samples derived both from coffins made solely of wood and those incorporating a lead shell in their construction.

Chambered burial vault

This was the largest vault uncovered, comprising four individual chambers (labelled A to D) opening off an access corridor. Documentary research suggests that the vault was built in 1785, under a passage leading from the churchyard into the Bull Ring, and that the use of each chamber was purchased by a different family (see Chapter 3). Twenty burials were present using both plain wooden coffins (Chambers A and D) and lead and wood coffins (Chambers B and C). Fragments from 10 of the coffins (all for adults) were examined: HB 318 (Samuel Wyer, d.1802, Chamber A); HB 382 (Daniel Rowlinson, d.1801), HB 372 and HB 376 (Chamber B); HB 383, HB 390 and HB 391 (Chamber C); and HB 400, HB 544 and HB 545 (Chamber D). With the exception HB 382 and HB 383, which were identified as oak (*Quercus* sp.), the coffins were constructed from elm (*Ulmus* sp.).

Family vaults

Ten structures were classified as 'family vaults' (see Chapter 3). The families buried in these vaults could be identified in five cases and these were evidently high-status structures. Coffin woods were examined from seven of the ten vaults.

Vault 2 (family not identified)
The vault contained three adult burials and one child, all in wood coffins, from which the coffins of HB 121, HB 132 (child) and HB 151 were examined and identified as oak (*Quercus* sp.); HB 132 also included elm (*Ulmus* sp.).

Vault 4 (family not identified)
Coffins from two of the five adult burials, all in wood coffins, were examined. The sample from HB 270 proved to be non-wood. The coffin for HB 269 included both pine (*Pinus* sp.) and an unidentified exotic timber. The latter was preserved through mineralization (see above) but included insufficient diagnostic information for identification.

Vault 5 (Warden/Browett families)
This well-constructed vault contained 13 high-status burials of the Warden and Browett families, who were closely linked through marriage (see Chapter 6). Preservation of the coffin plates was good enough to indicate the names of the several of the individuals. The coffins were all of lead and wood construction. Coffin woods from adult burials HB 297 (Ann Maria Browett, d.1894), HB 587 (George Warden, d.1863), HB 598 (Sarah Emma Warden, d.1866) and HB 607 (possibly Sophia Warden, d.1860) indicated the use of elm (*Ulmus* sp.).

Vault 9 (Jenkins family)
Vault 9 was large and well constructed and contained eleven coffins, mostly relatively well preserved and all of composite lead and wood construction. However, as it was possible to preserve the structure *in situ* only three of the burials were excavated. These were the burials of infants (HB 861, HB 862 and HB 863) whose coffins had been badly damaged. The wood from the coffins of HB

862 and HB 863 was studied and both used elm (*Ulmus* sp.) in their construction. A piece of oak (*Quercus* sp.) was identified from C 1975, the coffin of Helen Jenkins (d.1882).

Vault 18 (Home family)

The vault contained four burials, two adults and two children. The two adult coffins, both constructed from lead and wood, were unusually well-preserved (HB 575 and HB 576). The wooden components were made from elm (*Ulmus* sp.). The coffin for HB 575 contained the remains of John Home who died in 1828, aged 50, while that for HB 576 related to Frances Home who died in 1833, aged 53.

Vault 23 (Ainsworth family)

There were nine burials, seven adults and two children, deposited in the vault. Wood was examined from seven of the coffins: HB 676, HB 681, HB 691, HB 697 (child), HB 702, HB 722 and HB 723. HB 681, a wood coffin, included oak (*Quercus* sp.); HB 691 included oak (*Quercus* sp.) on top of the lead lid, with elm (*Ulmus* sp.) wood used in the interior; the remaining five coffins included elm (*Ulmus* sp.).

Vault 30 (Haines family)

This well-built vault was constructed for a wealthy, professional family. Fragments from six of the eight coffins were submitted for species identification. These related to four adults, HB 794 (William Tertius Haines, d.1869), HB 829 (Frank Haines, d.1860), HB 840 (William Haines, d.1851) and HB 841 (Jane Lloyd Haines, d.1864), and two infants, HB 830 (William Haines, d.1831) and HB 831. The coffins were all constructed from lead and wood. Elm (*Ulmus* sp.) wood was used throughout, although in HB 830 oak (*Quercus* sp.) was used for some of the board wood lining.

Brick-lined graves

The brick-lined graves were typically of rectangular form and represented wealthier burials than those interred in earth-cut graves. Wood samples were examined from V07, V08, V14, V15, V19, V20, V26, V32 and V36. These mostly consisted of coffin fragments, although a pine (*Pinus* sp.) wood supporter was recovered from the top-soil layer in V07.

V08

The grave contained four burials, all in wood coffins. Coffin woods from all four burials, HB 221, HB 224 (child), HB 226 and HB 233 were identified as elm (*Ulmus* sp.).

V14

Three (HB 312, HB 330 and HB 342) of the four coffins (all adult's) were examined. The coffins, three of which also incorporated lead, were constructed from either oak (*Quercus* sp.) (HB 330) or elm (*Ulmus* sp.) (HB 342) or, for HB 312, from oak (*Quercus* sp.), elm (*Ulmus* sp.) and pine (*Pinus* sp.).

V15

The grave contained two lead/ wood coffins. Coffin wood from an adult burial, HB 255, was identified as elm (*Ulmus* sp.).

V19

The grave contained a single adult coffin for HB 262, constructed from elm (*Ulmus* sp.) and pine (*Pinus* sp.).

V20

The grave contained two burials, one unassigned and one of a child. The coffin of the child (HB 746), from the upper level of the grave, was made from elm (*Ulmus* sp.).

V26

A lead and elm (*Ulmus* sp.) wood coffin was recorded for adult burial HB 489.

V32

The grave contained a single adult burial, HB 724, in an elm (*Ulmus* sp.) wood coffin.

V36

A single adult, HB 868, was interred in a lead and elm (*Ulmus* sp.) wood coffin.

Discussion

Wood samples were examined from 28 earth-cut graves and 50 burials in brick-lined graves or vaults. All probably date to the late 18th – 19th centuries. The woods used for coffin construction included, predominantly, elm (*Ulmus* sp.) (61 coffins), but also oak (*Quercus* sp.) (18 coffins), pine (*Pinus* sp.) (6 coffins), hazel (*Corylus avellana*) or alder (*Alnus glutinosa*) (1 coffin) and possibly an unidentified exotic timber (1 coffin).

Although many of the coffins from the earth-cut graves had decomposed, leaving only tracer stains in the soil, these were mostly assessed to have been very basic in design (Hancox, this chapter). Coffins deposited in the various burial structures were generally more elaborate constructions. Many of the coffins from which timber samples were collected had collapsed, both in the earth-cut graves and vaults, and, as might be anticipated, the wood remains were very degraded. In addition, it was often not clear which part of the coffin the samples related to. It is probable that different woods were used for specific parts of the coffins, as suggested by samples from HB 312 in Vault 14, which indicated the use of oak, elm and pine. In triple-shell coffins different woods may have been used for the inner coffin and outer case. Wide planks would have been required to construct the main coffin cases and these were evidently supplied from mature elm and oak trees, and possibly, sometimes, pine. Beading, struts and other narrow wooden components probably employed timber or wood from trees of narrower dimensions, e.g. hazel or pine. Many coffins were adorned with decorative finishes on both the inner and outer surfaces – inner surfaces included textile linings and ribbons, while outer surfaces included metal (plaque, handles and other fittings), wood (perhaps exotic timbers, such as in HB 269, Vault 4) and sometimes textile coverings (e.g. the coffin of John Home, HB 575, which was covered with fabric and brass studs). Some wood samples may have derived from coffin supports (e.g. the pine timber recovered from the top-soil layer in brick-lined grave V07) or from furniture included either within the coffin itself or from within the vault.

Coffin-makers most probably obtained their materials from local timber merchants, although some may have procured their own timber from source. The greater proportion of the wood samples examined suggested an origin from wide planks that included heartwood – thus inferring the use of timber from well-established mature trees. The increase in demand for suitable timber for general construction work and numerous other purposes, in addition to coffin-making, would have correlated to the population explosion in the 19th century, bringing about sudden and significant pressures on extant wood resources. Economics dictates that local or home-grown supplies would have been the cheapest but, since both oak and elm are relatively slow-growing, it is difficult to assess how local woodlands (which were probably already comparatively sparse) could have sustained the increasing demand for mature timber. By the 18th and 19th centuries the timber trade was already well established, and quality timber was imported to Britain from many parts of the world (Stevenson 1920). Indeed, Baltic ports were supplying pine and oak to this country from the 12th century (Rackham 1976). It seems probable that by the mid-19th century some percentage of the coffins were made from imported timber.

Edlin (1949) notes that owing to the interlocking fibres and twisted grain of elm, the wood is very difficult to split and does not season well without warping. But, because it was cheap and plentiful in many areas, it was especially popular for everyday usage, particularly for coffins for the poor, and was sometimes sawn for that purpose directly after felling (i.e. while still green/ unseasoned). A high percentage of the coffins in the poorer quarters of the churchyard, in earth-cut graves, conform to this use. Evidence from the mid-19th century pauper burials in the Cross Bones burial ground in Southwark, London, however, demonstrates the extensive use of softwoods (pine and spruce or larch) as these were cheaper than elm (Brickley *et al.* 1999). Contemporary accounts relate that coffins were sometimes constructed of such low-grade wood that they were liable to fall apart before burial (*ibid.*, 26). Oak, on the other hand, provides a high-grade, durable timber that is easily cleft and worked and suited to an extremely wide range of purposes, including coffin-making (Edlin 1949). In the present day, oak is considered superior to elm for coffin-making.

In view of the demonstrable display of wealth and status afforded to family funerals during the mid-19th century, it is surprising to note the common use of elm (reputedly an inferior timber) for coffins associated with the prestigious burials in the vaults. It is possible that elm or some other cheap timbers were used for the inner coffin of triple-shelled coffins or for parts of the coffin that would remain unseen, for example, when hidden by fabric coverings. But elm also appears to have been used for many of the high-status burials where plain wooden coffins were interred, for example in Vault 10 (despite the generally preferred use of lead-lined coffins in vaults which reduced the smell of rotting flesh).

Comparatively few of the individuals exhumed from St. Martin's are known by name and consequently details of their personal status or wealth are unknown. It is possible that the choice of timber was influenced by family hardship, or that the less important family members failed to merit the addition of lead shells or the more expensive use of oak. In addition, there does not appear to be any particular distinction between the selection of coffin wood for adults and juveniles. From the evidence available, it is difficult to attribute the high incidence of elm coffins in high-status graves to any particular set of circumstances or social conditions. The dominant use of elm may even be directly linked to the timber supplies at any one time.

Conclusion

The analysis of wood samples from 78 coffins collected from burials in earth-cut graves and vaults indicated the predominant use of elm (*Ulmus* sp.) throughout. Oak (*Quercus* sp.), pine (*Pinus* sp.) and hazel (*Corylus avellana*) were also identified but relatively infrequently. Occasionally two or three species were identified from the same context – possibly representing different components of the coffin. There was no apparent distinction in the type of wood used by different social classes, despite the fact that elm is generally considered to be a lower grade wood than oak. The coffins examined mainly dated to the late 18th – 19th centuries, spanning a period of great commercial prosperity and consequent growth in the populace. This almost certainly would have had a significant knock-on effect for undertakers and coffin-makers, who, in turn, through the rapidly increasing demand for mature elm and oak timber, may have relied on foreign imports to supplement dwindling home supplies.

Textiles
by Penelope Walton Rogers
Textile Research (York, UK)

Introduction

The care 19th-century mourners lavished on their dead is especially revealed in the textiles used for burial. The austere linen shroud of the medieval period had long since disappeared and in its place were burial garments resembling night shirts and caps, and upholstered coffins with sheets, pillows and trimmings – all of which made the dead appear tucked up for sleep. In women's burials in particular (although also in some burials of men and children), ribbons and bows were added to shrouds and pillows, while both sexes might have ruffles on garments and pinked and punched edgings on sheets. Personal items, including pieces of daytime clothing, which were presumably placed in the coffin for sentimental reasons, also became more common in the 19th century.

Textiles of this kind have been recovered from 117 of the 857 St. Martin's burials. A full catalogue is provided in Appendix 9 on the CD. The largest and best preserved pieces are from 35 of the coffins found in the vaults and brick-lined graves, but many smaller fragments have been recovered from 82 of the 734 earth-cut graves in the churchyard, allowing a comparison between the two groups.

The speed with which the burials had to be excavated meant that it was difficult to record the exact location of the textiles in every case. The function of the fabrics has therefore been interpreted mostly by comparison with similar material from other sites. The large collection from Christ Church, Spitalfields, London, dated 1729–1852 (Janaway 1993), is well known, but there are less well-publicised groups of similar date from vaults and shafts inside churches at St. Mary-the-Less, Durham (Walton Rogers in Emery in prep), Wharram, Yorkshire (Crowfoot 1987), All Saints, Pavement, York (Walton Rogers forthcoming a), St. Martin-at-Palace, Norwich (Crowfoot unpublished a), St. Mary's, Little Ilford, Essex (Crowfoot unpublished b), and from churchyards at St. Mark's and St.Paul-in-the-Bail, Lincoln (Walton Rogers 1993, 18–23). There is a further collection from St. Peter's, Barton-on-Humber, Lincolnshire, which includes both churchyard and intramural burials (Walton Rogers forthcoming b). Further insight into the burial garments and costume details at St. Martin's has been generously provided by Josie Sheppard, Curator of Costume and Textiles, The Castle Museum, York, whose comments are acknowledged within the text as (JS).

Survival of textiles in burials

Despite the size of the St. Martin's collection, it probably represents only a small proportion of the amount originally buried. This partial survival can be explained by a review of the mechanisms by which plant and animal fibres survive. When buried in a sealed, anoxic environment, most textile fibres will last well, but where there is a damp oxygenated atmosphere, cellulosic plant fibres such as flax and cotton will tend to succumb to fungal attack (Sibley and Jakes 1983). Proteinaceous animal fibres such as wool and silk are more resistant to fungal damage and are especially protected where a decaying body provides the kind of mildly acidic environment which promotes survival of animal fibres at the expense of plant ones (Jakes and Sibley 1984, 25).

The textiles from St. Martin's are all made from wool and silk and there are no examples of the cottons which

were recovered from sealed lead coffins at Christ Church, Spitalfields (Janaway 1993, 96–100), and burials at St. Mark's, Lincoln (Walton Rogers 1993, 21–22). The most common fabric-type at St. Martin's is wool union, which has emerged from the burials as flat panels of parallel wool threads. A union is a fabric with two different fibres, one in the warp and the other in the weft, but in every case the second, non-wool fibre had disappeared. In three cases, HB 161(ii), HB 304 (Vault 5) textiles 1794 and 1795, it was possible to show by microscopy of stray fibre bundles caught into the wool that the missing system had been flax (linen). Since cotton decays more rapidly than flax (Sibley and Jakes 1983, 36), it is possible that some unions were once wool-cotton unions. At any rate, these half-textiles demonstrate the decay of cellulosic fibres at the site.

The frequency with which wool textiles have been recovered from St. Martin's is surprising, seeing that many of the burials are dated later than 1820. In the later 17th century a series of parliamentary acts, designed to promote the wool textile industry, demanded that only wool should be used in burials (Litten 1991, 74). These acts were repealed in 1814/15 and analysis of the datable Spitalfields textiles has shown wool falling away immediately after this date and being replaced by other fibres, especially cotton (Janaway 1993, 118). In contrast, the St. Martin's burials show that wool textiles, especially wool unions, continued in use in Birmingham for coffin linings and shrouds until the 1860s at least. They appear in coffins with dated *depositum* plates in burials HB 336 (Vault 5, d.1869), HB 574 (Vault 5, d.1842), HB 587 (Vault 5, d.1863), HB 575 (Vault 18, d.1828) and HB 576 (Vault 18, d.1833).

Coffin covers

The St. Martin's funerary textiles will be described from the outside in, starting with the external coffin covering. In the 18th and early 19th centuries, the body of the coffin was frequently covered with a black baize-like cloth (Litten 1991, 99–102). The cloth was fitted tightly against the coffin boards and fixed in place with rows of brass dome-headed tacks ('nails'), while handles ('grips') and coffin plates were applied on top. White metal 'lace' might also be added as a trim.

Remains of these coffin covers have been studied from eight of the burials from the vaults and brick-lined graves at St. Martin's (Table 123). The most obvious examples, HB 607 (Vault 5), HB 383 (Vault 10C), HB 390 (Vault 10C) and HB 262 (brick-lined grave V19), are still sandwiched between coffin board and metal lace, while the cloth from HB 382 (Vault 10B) has remains of wood on one face and imprints of coffin nails on the other. The cloths from HB 862 (Vault 9) and HB186 (V17) have no wood or metal present, but they have been dyed black, in contrast with internal fabrics which are undyed, and they are therefore assumed to be coffin covers. The construction of the best preserved examples is illustrated in

Figs 120–122 (colour). The piece from HB 607 (Fig. 120, colour) is probably from where the end board of the coffin joins the side, and the manner in which the cover tucks into the join implies that the cloth was applied to the boards before the coffin was assembled. The fragment from HB 382 (Fig. 121, colour) must be from a lid. HB 383 does not fit the standard coffin design, as it seems to have a second, raised, panel stepped away from the main board (Fig. 122, colour).

The fabrics are medium-weight wool tabby or wool union, dyed with natural tannin-based dyes which in some instances have been 'blued' with indigo and/or woad (Table 123; Fig. 123a). There were no examples of the more colourful silk velvets found on coffins of the upper ranks of society, such as the crimson silk-cotton velvet on the coffin of the 10th Earl of Strathmore (d.1820), in the Bowes family mausoleum at Gibside, Co. Durham (Walton Rogers in Emery in prep). The use of wool union for covers is unusual, but there is one other example from a burial at St. Peter's, Barton-on-Humber, which is a wool-cotton union and probably relatively late. The 29 coffin covers from St. Peter's proved to be more variable in weave, thread-count and general quality of manufacture in the early burials than in the later ones and dated coffins from other sites in the North support the view that coffin covers became more standardised through the course of the 18th century. Different qualities still existed in the later period, however, as indicated by a fine fabric on a coffin of the 1820s from All Saints, York (Walton Rogers forthcoming a) and a coffin-maker of 1838 drew attention to the 'superfine cloth' covering his best and most expensive oak coffins (Litten 1998, 9). The St. Martin's covers may be categorised as middling quality.

Only one of the coffin covers submitted for study was directly datable, that associated with the burial of Daniel Rowlinson (HB 382, Vault 10C), who died in 1801. HB 862 (Vault 9), an infant burial, is probably the burial of either Samuel Jenkins or Frances Jenkins, who died in 1816 and 1834 respectively (see Chapter 3). HB 607 (Vault 5) is likely to be the burial of Sophia Warden, who died in 1860 (Chapter 3). If this identification is correct, the late date is somewhat surprising as cloth covers are generally believed to have fallen out of use during the second quarter of the 19th century, following the introduction of french-polishing, and prior to the St. Martin's excavation no baize covers later than 1850 have been recorded. At St. Martin's the excavators noted the remains of fabric coffin covers on a total of 27 of the coffins from the vaults and brick-lined graves (see coffin tables in Chapter 3), although only eight samples were submitted for study. Of these, ten were directly datable from the *depositum* plate. While seven of the burials dated to before 1850, three were later: HB 840 (Vault 30, d.1851), HB 587 (Vault 5, d.1863) and HB 841 (Vault 30, d.1864). It is evident, therefore, that fabric coverings on coffins were still used occasionally in the 1860s, at any rate in Birmingham.

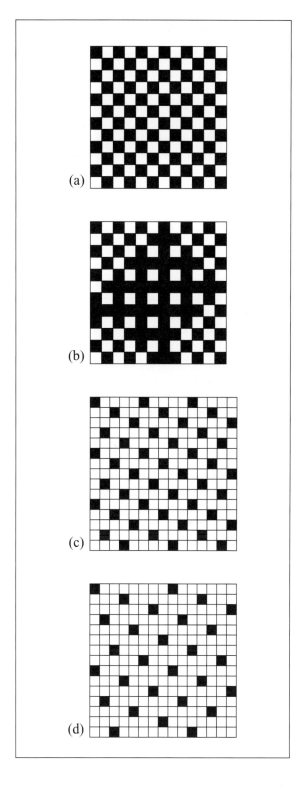

Fig. 123: Diagrams of the weaves of textiles from St. Martin's: (a) tabby; (b) tabby with weft-float pattern; (c) 5-end satin; (d) 8-end satin.

Lining the coffin

The coffin would be lined with fabric, although, when dealing with poorly preserved excavated fragments, it is often difficult to distinguish the lining from the winding sheet (see below). A fragment of undyed wool union from HB 573 (Vault 5) which has been folded concertina fashion and tacked in places with a close row of copper-alloy tacks (Fig. 124a) must be a lining and similar neat, parallel folds were noted in HB 862 (Vault 9). The large panes of wool tabby from HB 391 (Vault 10C) have marks of iron corrosion which suggest they were fixed to the coffin at the ends (Fig. 124b) and there were flat pieces of wool union adhering to the coffin boards in HB 372 (Vault 10B) and HB 576 (Vault 18). In HB 576 the coffin lining could be distinguished from another, finer, wool union arranged in thick loose folds in the same burial. Wool unions used for coffin linings were found in two burials at All Saints, York (Walton Rogers forthcoming a). No unions were recorded at Spitalfields, although only 31 of the 51 coffin linings were analysed (Janaway 1993, 102). As described above, undyed wool union was the most common textile type at St. Martin's, especially in the earth-cut burials (Table 124), and it is clear that sheets, shrouds and linings might all be made from similar fabrics.

Tufts of cattle hair, and occasionally horse hair, seem to have been used as an upholstery filling in the coffins. They were found adhering to the internal face of a coffin board in HB 128, adhering to wool unions in HB 10, HB

751 and HB 576 (Vault 18) and without association in HB 161, HB 230 and HB 858 (Table 125). They seem to have been inserted as loose tufts of fibre, unlike the flat panels of rabbit-fur felt used for the same purpose at St. Paul-in-the Bail, Lincoln (Walton Rogers 1993, 22). Well-preserved feathers were found with a type of strong ribbed fabric often used for bolsters in HB 255 (brick-lined grave V15), but no stuffing materials were recovered in the mattress and pillow described below. It is assumed that they were filled with plant materials, such as the hay used at Spitalfields (Litten 1998, 13), and have decayed during burial.

The coffin lining would sometimes be finished with a trimming which ran along the wooden beading inside the top edge of the coffin. The neatly tucked silk satin with pinked edges and punched decoration found in HB 574 (Vault 5) (Fig. 127a), a burial dated to 1842, is probably one of these top-edge decorations, since it matches a tucked cotton frill on a coffin at Spitalfields (Janaway 1993, microfiche 6.24 Burial 2257). The Spitalfields frill was arranged in two parallel rows, with the pinked edges pointing downwards. The Spitalfields coffin is undated, although the fact that the fibre is cotton suggests that it is later than 1815 and the presence of a wool coffin cover implies it may be earlier than 1850. A similar trim from HB 121 (Vault 2) lacks the tucks of HB 574, but it is made from a silk satin ribbon with pinked and punched decoration (Fig. 127b; Table 127) and it, and the wool union with it, were described by the excavator as 'coffin lining'.

(a)

0   2cm

(b)

0   10cm

Fig. 124: Probable coffin linings: (a) HB 573, Vault 5 (Warden family) Level 1; (b) HB 391, Vault 10C.

Mattress, pillow and sheets

A fragment of mattress cover was recovered from the burial of a child, HB 321 (Vault 5) (Fig. 125a). This has been made from a thick, densely woven tabby, felted, but without a pile of any sort (Table 126). Small rosettes mark the points where threads would hold front and back of the mattress together. The rosettes have been made by cutting a circle of the same fabric with pinking shears and then gathering it into a flower shape. A corner of a pillow made from a slightly coarser wool tabby was recovered from HB 391 (Vault 10C). This has simple scalloped ruffles made from the same fabric (Table 126, Fig. 125b).

Once the coffin had been fitted with lining and mattress, a winding sheet would be placed in the coffin, the body laid on it, and the sides of the sheet brought round and over the corpse. A full-size winding sheet required a substantial loom-width and, in order to economise, two narrow side sheets might instead be tacked to the base of the coffin and then folded over the body (Litten 1998, 13). The large flat sheets of undyed wool union from the vaults almost certainly represent either a winding sheet or a side sheet (Fig. 126a). Several of these sheets, such as those in HB 587 (Vault 5), HB 372 (Vault 10B) and HB 576 (Vault 18), have been finished with a silk ribbon folded lengthways around the raw edge, to make the sheet reversible (Fig. 126b–d). The wool union of these sheets often has a long brushed nap on one face, the pile being brushed across the line of the wool yarn, parallel to the missing system (Table 124). These fabrics may be a fore-runner of a brushed cotton fabric known as swansdown, which appears in late Victorian undertakers' catalogues (JS).

Fig. 125: Mattress cover and pillow: (a) a fragment of wool mattress cover from child burial HB 321, Vault 5 (Warden family) Level 4; (b) a fragment of a wool pillow from HB 391, Vault 10C.

There is another textile-type from St. Martin's which may also represent the winding sheet. This is represented by nine examples of a fine tabby-weave textile made from smooth Z-spun yarn, listed in Table 126 as 'linen-effect'. To the naked eye, they resemble linens, but under the microscope (×400–×620 magnification) it is evident that they are wool and the linen-like appearance is caused by damage to the fibre cuticle. This kind of damage can occur naturally in the archaeological environment, but in the cases described here the effect is uniform throughout large areas of the fabric. It seems likely that this was a deliberate attempt to emulate linen, by the use of some chemical or bleaching agent on the wool. The textile-type occurs in nine burials, all from the earth-cut graves, one of which is the earliest datable burial from the site, HB 408. The coffin plate identifies this burial as that of an 85-year-old who died in the 1720s – in other words,

someone old enough to remember when all shrouds were linen. These fabrics may have been an attempt to produce the appearance of linen while still complying with the terms of the Acts concerning the use of wool.

Shrouds and face cloths

The corpse itself would be dressed in a garment still called a 'shroud', because it had developed in stages from the sheet-like linen shroud of the medieval period (Litten 1991, 57–84). By the 18th century it was a full-length gown, worn by both sexes, with long sleeves gathered at the cuff, and a high neck often ornamented with ruffles running from the throat downwards. A large fragment of undyed wool tabby with a seam and hem from HB 304 (Vault 5) probably represents the lower part of a shroud of this nature (Fig. 128, colour, a) and other shaped pieces of wool tabby ornamented with ribbon bows from HB 321

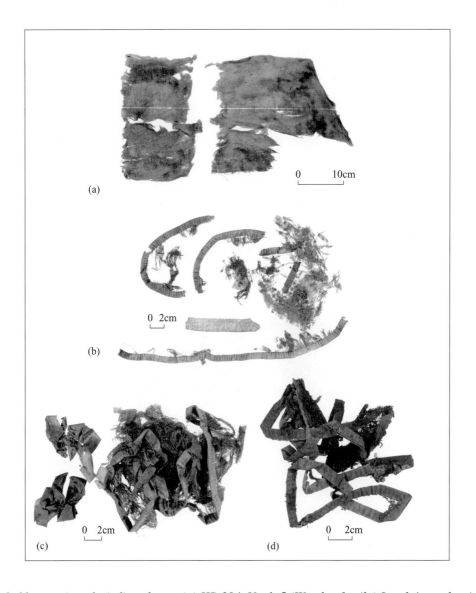

Fig. 126: Probable remains of winding sheets: (a) HB 304, Vault 5 (Warden family) Level 4, wool union; (b) HB 372, Vault 10B, wool union edged with silk ribbon; (c) HB 576, Frances Home (d.1833), Vault 18 (Home family), wool union edged with silk ribbon; (d) HB 681, Vault 23 (Ainsworth family) Level 3, a silk ribbon edging with a mitred corner.

(Table 126) may be the same. These wool tabbies, which are slightly felted but not properly napped, are likely to be the fabric known to the Victorians as 'shrouding flannel' (Litten 1991, 82). The long pieces of closely gathered gauze ribbons from HB 692 (Vault 23) and HB 698 (Vault 23) are probably ornamentation from the front of the shroud and the ribbons in HB 262 (brick-lined grave V19) seem to be ties from neck and cuff. No other fragments of shroud could be confidently identified, but it is likely that some of the wool unions, with remains of seams and loose folds (Table 124), originated in garments of this sort.

The face of the corpse was sometimes covered with an ornamented square of fabric. A pinked and punched square of wool tabby from HB 391 (Vault 10C) seems to be one of these face-cloths (Fig. 127c). The punched decoration incorporates hearts and circles of two different sizes which build up into a design of arcing flowers and leaves. One of the linen-effect textiles from the earth-cut graves, HB 850, also carries the remains of a punched decoration, although there the presence of stitching along a fold and several pins piercing the fabric may indicate a shroud.

Another rectangle of wool tabby decorated with a ribbon trim, from the child burial HB 321 (Vault 5) (Fig. 128, colour, b), was thought to be another example of a face cloth, until it was noticed that there were fragmentary remains of a second identical item in the same grave. It is possible that these are in fact an applied decoration from the shroud. Women's sleeves could be ornamented in a similar fashion in the mid-to-late Victorian period and the style may have transferred to burial garments (JS). The face cloth in this burial is more likely to be the simple rectangle of wool tabby, 185 × 150 mm, which has the imprint of a flat ribbon trim on all four edges (not illustrated).

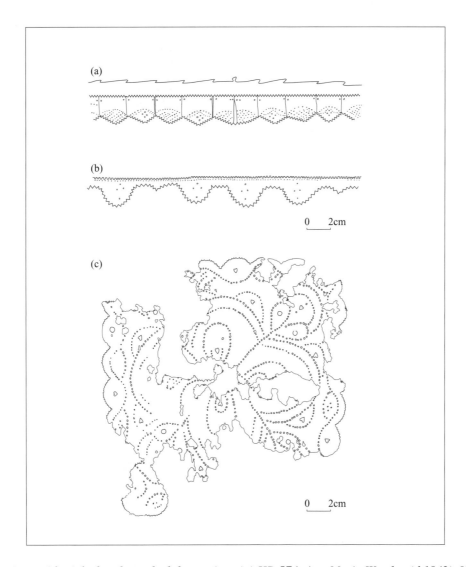

Fig. 127: Trimmings with pinked and punched decoration: (a) HB 574, Ann Maria Warden (d.1842), Vault 5 (Warden family) Level 1, made from silk satin; (b) HB 121, Vault 2, made from silk satin ribbon; (c) HB 391, Vault 10C, a pinked and punched wool face cloth.

Headgear

Human head hair has survived in several burials in both the vaults and the earth-cut graves (listed with other animal fibres in Table 125). In one instance, HB 598 (Vault 5), the textile associated with the hair was an open net-like wool tabby and in two cases, HB 112 and HB 529, a worsted (worsteds are lustrous textiles made from smoothly spun wool) (Table 126). These probably represent the remains of headdresses. Bonnet-like caps were worn by men, women and children and Janaway has shown that some were commercially produced caps made

for burial, while others were probably hats worn in life (Janaway 1993, 103–108). Ribbons which may be from caps were found in HB 297 (Ann Maria Browett, d.1894, Vault 5), HB 576 (Frances Home, d.1833, Vault 18) and HB 691 (Hannah Ainsworth, d.1827, Vault 23), but there were no examples comparable with the elaborate silk and wire bonnet worn by a woman buried in 1825/6 at All Saints, York (Walton Rogers forthcoming a).

The strings of the cap might be used to hold the jaw shut, but separate ribbon ties were sometimes used for the purpose. The knotted circle of ribbon from HB 691 (Hannah Ainsworth, Vault 23) may be just such a tie.

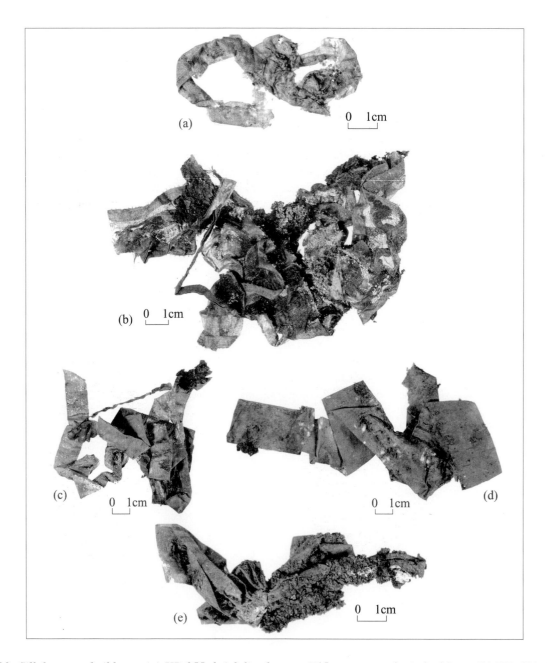

Fig. 130: Silk bows and ribbons: (a) HB 255, brick-lined grave V15, ornamental stitched bow; (b) HB 691, Hannah Ainsworth (d.1827), Vault 23 (Ainsworth family) Level 2, ruched ribbon; (c) HB 691 (as 'b'), probable jaw tie; (d) HB 692, Vault 23 Level 3, gathered ribbon; (e) HB 698, child, Vault 23 Level 1, ribbon bow.

Further ribbons from the child burial HB 321 (Vault 5), described as hair ribbons by the excavators, survived as two tied bows joined together in a festoon, with cut notches at the ends (Fig. 129, colour, c); similar ribbon rolled into a piped edging from the same part of the burial suggest some sort of silk-trimmed bonnet.

Ribbons, bows, covered buttons and rosettes

The silk ribbons from the vaults at St. Martin's come from the burials of both men and women, although predominantly the latter. The functions of these ribbons has already been described as trimmings on the edges of winding sheets, ruffles and bows on caps and shrouds, and ties for the jaw (Fig. 129, colour, and Fig. 130). Amongst the ribbon bows there is a distinction between the functional ones which are tied the way one would tie a shoe-lace, as in the child burials HB 321, Vault 5 (Fig. 129, colour, c) and HB 698, Vault 23 (Fig. 130e), and the ornamental bows made by folding the ribbon back-and-forth and then wrapping a second piece of ribbon around the middle, as in child burial HB 321, Vault 5 (Fig. 129, colour, a), or by stitching loops together, as in HB 255 from brick-lined grave V15 (Fig. 130a). Silk-covered buttons of different sizes were also found in association with the ribbons in HB 321 (Vault 5) with remains of silk rosettes. One well-preserved rosette was made from two strips of ribbon gathered around a covered button (Fig. 129, colour, b).

These ribbons were made in a range of widths and weaves, including tabby, 5-end and 8-end satin (Fig. 123a, c & d), and there are three examples of 'gauze ribbons', woven with vertical bands of satin weave alternating with bands of open-weave tabby. Some of the ribbons have looped selvedges, in which the weft yarn reaches out beyond the weave before returning. The structure of the different ribbons is summarised in Table 127 and a selection appears in Fig. 131 (colour). Charming as these are, they are not the best quality ribbons of the period and would represent the middle and lower end of the range available at the Victorian haberdasher's shop (JS). They were probably bought in bulk by the undertaker for the trimming of sheets and burial garments.

Silk dress trimmings

All the silk ribbons described so far were used undyed, as were the wool tabbies and wool unions from inside the coffins. Two fragments of silk from HB 297 (Vault 5), however, seem to have been dyed black and probably represent some form of ornament from a garment worn in life. The first is a small elliptical piece of ribbed silk with hemmed edges (Fig. 132a), which is a type of attachment which occurs on women's dress of *c.*1860–1880 (JS). The second is a fragment with a small angular motif worked in a weft-float technique (Fig. 132b). The burial is that of Ann Maria Browett, who died in 1894 at the age of 81, and she was probably wearing a garment that was a little out-of-fashion.

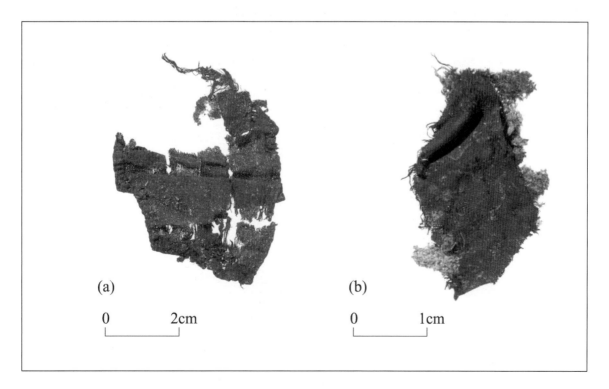

(a)

0   2cm

(b)

0   1cm

Fig. 132: Two black silk garment ornaments from HB 297, Ann Maria Browett (d.1894), Vault 5 (Warden family) Level 4: (a) possibly the remains of a ribbon bow; (b) the fragment of weft-patterned silk.

Wool stockings

One of the most curious finds from St. Martin's is a pair of wool stockings from the coffin of Campbell Lloyd Haines (HB 792, Vault 30), who died in 1878, aged 42 (Fig. 133 and Fig. 134, colour). They are a matching pair, knitted in stocking stitch from fine worsted (wool) yarn. The foot has been made in two separate segments, upper and lower, which are grafted together at the ankle before the work divides again for the leg, so that there is a seam up the back leg (Fig. 134, colour). The top has not been cast-off, but closed by binding the loops of the final row with a sewing thread. The different shades of colour in the toe were confirmed by dye analysis, which showed that the stockings were originally dark blue, with a red toe and a narrow band of green or blueish brown immediately above the red.

The stockings are heavily worn and stretched sideways as if to cover a very sturdy calf. At present, the feet are 200 mm long and the legs *c.*500 mm from heel to stocking top. There are two areas of heavy and irregular darning on both stockings, one at the front of the ankle and the other at the toe (Fig. 133b). This suggests some form of footwear with a high buckle or lacing, causing abrasion at the front ankle. Stockings of this style and technique were worn by both sexes in the Georgian and early Victorian period, and there are comparable examples from Spitalfields burials (Janaway 1993, 112; Janaway 1998, 31), but they would be highly unusual on a man by the 1870s (JS).

Conclusion

Trade catalogues of the 19th century show that the funeral industry was a major consumer of textiles, not just for burial garments and coffin sheets, but for clothing for the bereaved and drapes for their houses. Edward Baines in his *Account of the Woollen Manufacture of England*, published in 1875, gives statistics which show baize and flannel forming a significant part of the production of the English wool textile industry. Cottons from the burgeoning Lancashire cotton industry also formed a substantial part of the trade, and many of those burials at St. Martin's where no textiles have survived would almost

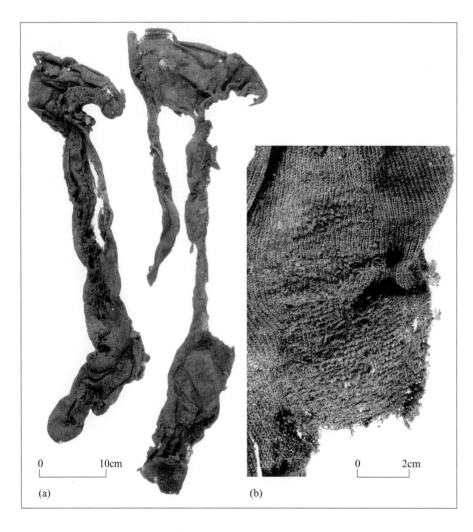

0   10cm

(a)

0   2cm

(b)

Fig. 133: The pair of darned stockings from HB 792, Campbell Lloyd Haines (d.1878), Vault 30 (Haines family) Level 2: (a) the pair of stockings; (b) a close up of a darned area.

certainly have been furnished with shrouds and winding sheets made of cotton.

Most of the fabrics used in the St. Martin's burials would have been bought in bulk by the undertaker and/or coffin maker, and this is reflected in the standardised nature of the materials recovered, here and at other sites. The presence of so many wool unions at St. Martin's is, however, noteworthy. Similar fabrics have been found in a small number of 19th-century burials in the north, but not, so far, in London and Essex. This suggests that there were still some regional differences, a view supported by evidence from Lincoln, where, in an area of rabbit-farming and felt-making, rabbit-fur felts were used to line coffins.

The fine linen-effect tabby weaves from earth-cut graves at St. Martin's are a new finding. A further difference between the earth-cut and the vault burials lies in the use of silks in the latter. The dense silk ruffles on shrouds and caps and pinked and punched trimmings inside coffins seem to reflect the higher status of the people buried inside the vaults. These extra trims would be an acknowledgement of social position. Such people would, however, still cover their coffins with the ordinary wool baize appropriate to their station, and, however wealthy, would not aspire to the velvets of higher ranks. Burials such as these speak eloquently on the stratification of 19th-century society.

Vault 5:

HB 607:2653/2654	tabby	14/Z × ?	Heavily napped on both faces. Dyed black: indigotin and tannins detected. Sandwiched between metal coffin lace and wood of coffin board (Fig. 120).

Vault 9:

HB 862:1975	tabby (union)	18/S × 12/?	Brushed nap on one face. Dyed black: indigotin and tannins. Fleece-type F.

Vault 10B:

HB 382: 1880/1881	tabby	16/S × 15/S	Heavily napped on both faces. Dyed black: tannins detected. Fleece-types SF x SF. Remains of wood on one face and imprints of coffin nails on other (Fig. 121).

Vault 10C:

HB 383: 1885/2085(S.156)	tabby	14/S × 12/S	Heavily napped on both faces. Dyed black: tannins detected. Fleece-types SF x M. Sandwiched between metal coffin lace and wood of coffin board (Fig. 122).
HB 390: 1882	tabby	14/S × 12/S	Napped on both faces. Dyed black: tannins detected. Sandwiched between metal coffin lace and wood of coffin board.

Vault 17

HB 186: 1513	tabby (union)	15/Z × 12	Brushed nap on one face. Dyed black (not tested).
HB 225: 1610/1612	tabby (union)	15/Z × 12	Brushed nap on one face. Dyed black: indigotin and tannins detected. Remains of white metal lace on one face.

Vault 19

HB 262: 1701/1702	tabby	14/Z × 10–12/S	Napped on both faces. Not tested for dye. Remains of wood on one face and white metal lace on other.

Table 123: Black wool coffin covers.
Notes: Dyes were identified by absorption spectrophotometry and thin-layer chromatography
Fleece-types: F = Fine, SF = Semi-Fine, M = Medium (longwool)

Textiles from earth-cut graves

Burial: find	Weave	Spin/thread-count	Notes
HB 007: 1019	?	14–18/S	
HB 010: 1024	?	18/S	cattle hair attached
HB 019: 1047	tabby	18–20/S × 16	
HB 046: 1124	tabby	16–18/S × 16	brushed nap on one face; folded
HB 047: 1127	tabby	18/S × 14	hair attached; much folded
HB 049: 1134	?	?/S	pierced by cu/a pin (>20 mm long)
HB 056: 1156	tabby	16/S ×x ?	patches of cu/a corrosion
HB 066: 1193	tabby	16/S × 16	'found by left mandible and right femur'
HB 084: 1230	tabby	16/S × 14	
HB 085: 1233	?	16/S × ?	with remains of cu/a pin
HB 091: 1250	?	18/S × ?	
HB 095: 1264	?	16/S × ?	
HB 097: 1270	tabby	16/S × ?	
HB 119: 1326	?	20/S × ?	from skull; human hair
HB 161: 1447	tabby	18–20/S × 14	ZS tabby and hair in association
	tabby	16/S/wool × 18/Z flax/hemp	
HB 175: 1488	?	22/S × ?	
HB 199: 1543	tabby	22/S ×x ?	
HB 228: 1619	?	?/S	crumpled; patches of cu/a corrosion
HB 234: 1635	tabby	20?S × 16	cu/a corrosion
HB 235: 1639	?	?/S	'pins and packing by skull'; hair in association
HB 244: 1674	tabby	16/S × 14	
HB 250: 1675	tabby	16/S × 12	crumpled folds
HB 289: 1801	?	14/S	crumpled pad; patches of cu/a corrosion
HB 295: 1823	tabby	22/S x 12	'found by hand/prox.femora L&R'; brushed nap on one face
HB 308: 1856	tabby	fine/S × ?	pierced by cu/a pin (>17 mm long)
HB 310: 1860	tabby	18/S × ?	crumpled pad
HB 351: 2014+2015	?	?/S	folded seam/hem
HB 353: 2025	tabby	18/S × ?	brushed nap on one face; cu/a corrosion
HB 361: 2043	?	20/S	imprint of cu/a pin
HB 394: 2109	tabby	16/S × 14	brushed nap on one face; imprint of cu/a pin
HB 509: 2411	?	20/S	
HB 539: 2471	tabby	16/S × 12–14	brushed nap on one face; black organics; cu/a pin
HB 540: 2475	?	?/S	thick cu/a pin
HB 727: 2924	tabby	16/S × 14	
HB 759: 3030	tabby	16/S × 12–14	much folded; pierced by several cu/a pins
HB 778: 3098	tabby	20/S × ?	
HB 805: 3173	tabby	24/S ×x ?	folded; cu/a corrosion
HB 806: 3177	?tabby	26/S × ?	folded; cu/a corrosion
HB 844: 3272	tabby	26/S × 12	brushed nap on one face

Textiles from vaults and brick-lined graves

Vault 2

HB 121: 1331/1332	?	12–14/S	adhering to SS tabby and pinked satin ribbon

Vault 5

HB 304: 1794/1795	tabby	15–18/S × 12–14	brushed nap on one face; several large flat fragments; remains of seam; in association with wool tabbies edged with ribbon
HB 321: 1979	?	fine/S	in association with wool tabbies and silk ribbons
HB 574: 2580	tabby	22/S × 18	adhering to pinked satin ribbon
HB 573: 2581	tabby	18/S × 14	brushed nap on one face; concertina folds and remains of cu/a tacks
HB 587: 2614	tabby	16/S × 15	edged by narrow silk tabby ribbon
HB 597: 2636	tabby	15/S × 15	
HB 607: 2653/2654	tabby	18/S × ?	'textile with bone'; also wool baize coffin cover

Table 124: Wool union textiles from burials. Continued overleaf.
Poorly preserved S-spun wool threads, probably the remains of wool unions, were also recovered from HB070: 1194
HB086: 1236   HB115: 1316   HB147: 1403 HB191: 1524   HB195: 1537   HB343: 1988   HB450: 2270+2272 HB751: 2975
HB845: 3275   HB336: 1958(V5)

Vault 9

| HB 862:1974/1975/3320 | (i)tabby | 22/S × 16 | brushed nap on one face; in crumpled folds; in association with worsted tabby |
| | (ii)tabby | 18/S × 12–14 | coarser than (i); brushed nap on one face; large flat fragments, some with neat folds, possibly seams |

Vault 10B

HB 372: 1874/1875/ S.146	(i) ?	15/S	adhering to coffin boards
	(ii)tabby	22–24/S × 18	brushed nap on one face; edged with silk tabby ribbon
HB 376: 1878/1879	tabby	40/S × ?	adhering to black organic material

V15

| HB 255: 1624/1682 | tabby | 20/S × 20 | brushed nap on one face; flat fragments in association with silk tabby ribbon and wool ZS tabby and feather |

Vault 18

HB 574: 2583	?	fine/S	'from skull'; hair in association
HB 575: 2582	tabby 16–18/S × 10–12		large area; crumpled folds; 'from skull'; cu/a corrosion
HB 576: 2097/2583	(i)tabby	20/S x 20	in folds, thick pads; hair adhering
	(ii)tabby	16/S × 14	Coarser than (i); adhering to coffin boards, S-spun wool across grain; silk ribbons and knitted wool fragment in same burial

V19

| HB 262: 1701/1702 | tabby | 18/S × 14 | in association with black organic matter and silk ribbon; black wool tabby (coffin cover?) in same burial |

Table 124 continued.

Burial: find	Identification	Notes
HB 010: 1024	cattle hair	in association with wool union
HB 044: 1120	probably human hair (PG), straight, dark brown	
HB 047: 1127	human hair, straight and blonde	in association with wool union
HB 112: 1308	human hair, straight, light brown	in assoc. with worsted tabby
HB 118: 1324	too decayed to identify	
HB 119: 1326	human hair, wavy, mid brown	in association with wool union
HB 128: 1347	possibly calf hair (PG)	adhering to wood
HB 135: 1371	too decayed to identify	
HB 161: 1447	horse mane hair (PG)	
HB 230: 1623	cattle hair	
HB 235: 1639	human hair, slightly wavy, light brown	in association with wool union
HB 288: 1800	too decayed to identify	
HB 408: 2150	too decayed to identify	
HB 529: 2450	human hair, straight, light brown	in assoc. with worsted tabby
HB 751: 2975	cattle hair	in association with wool union
HB 858: 3312	possibly calf hair (PG)	
V5:HB 297: 1827	human hair, light brown curls	in association with silk ribbons
V5:HB 598: 2635	human hair, straight, light brown	in association with net-like wool tabby
V17: HB 225: 1609	human hair, light brown/fair (PG)	
V18: HB 576: 2583	cattle hair	in association with wool union
	and human hair, straight, grey	in association with silk ribbons
V23: HB 691: 2817	human hair, fine, straight, light brown	in association with silk ribbon

Table 125: Burials with surviving human hair and other animal fibres.
PG = Phil Greaves. The remaining identifications are by the author

Textiles from earth-cut graves

Burial: find	Weave	Spin/thread-count	Notes
HB 109: 1301	tabby	15/Z × 11/Z	linen-effect
HB 112: 1308	tabby	20/Z × 15/Z	worsted; 'from top of skull' with hair
HB 129: 1351	?	?/S × ?	decayed remains of textile
HB 135: 1371	tabby	20/Z × 18/Z	linen-effect; 'found by skull' with hair
HB 142: 1390	tabby	18/Z × 16–18/Z	worsted; net-like; with hair and cu/a pin
HB 148: 1408	tabby	15/Z × 14/S	poorly preserved
HB 161: 1447	tabby	16/Z × 16/S	brushed nap on one face; crumpled; wool union and hair also in grave
HB 239: 1649	tabby	20/Z × 20/Z	linen-effect
HB 290: 1805	tabby	18/Z × 18/Z	linen-effect
HB 294: 1817	tabby	20/Z × 18/Z	linen-effect
HB 303: 1843	tabby	?/Z × ?/S	poorly preserved
HB 387/388: 2092	tabby	20/Z × 20/Z	linen-effect
HB 408: 2150	tabby	20/Z × 18/Z	linen-effect; hair and cu/a pin in association
HB 438: 2240	tabby	20/Z × 18/S	heavily napped on both faces; wood adhering to one face
HB 447: 2263	tabby	24/Z × 20/Z	worsted
HB 448: 2266	?	? × ?	wool fibres adhering to cu/a pins
HB 529: 2450	tabby	16/Z × 16/Z	worsted; hair present
HB 546: 2480	tabby	15/Z × 14/Z	linen-effect
HB 563: 2545	tabby	20/Z × 16/Z	linen-effect
HB 665: 2805	tabby	13/S × 12/S	pierced by cu/a pin
HB 668: 2810	tabby	20/Z × 16/Z	worsted; black organics and cu/a pin present
HB 764: 3061	tabby	20/Z × 18/Z	worsted
HB 857: 3309	tabby	19/Z × 17/Z	linen-effect; stitched; pierced by cu/a pins; single line of punched decoration

Textiles from vaults and brick-lined graves

Vault 2

HB 121: 1331/1332	tabby	?/S × ?/?S	decayed; adhering to wool union; satin ribbon in assoc.

Vault 4

HB 269: 1729	tabby	18/Z × 16/S	slightly felted
HB 270: 1732	tabby	14/Z × 20/S	slightly felted

Vault 5

HB 297: 1827	tabby	18–20/S × 16–20/S	slightly felted; silk ribbons, dyed silk textiles and hair also in grave
HB 304:1794/1795	(i)tabby	18/S × 15/S	light nap on both faces; seamed and hemmed
	(ii)tabby	24/Z × 16/S	light nap on both faces; silk ribbon and wool union also in grave
HB 321: 19341979	(i)tabby	18/S × 16–18/S	light nap on both faces; edged with silk ribbon;
	(ii)tabby	18/Z × 16/S	felted; seams, hem and applied rosettes made from same fabric; silk ribbon bows, silk covered buttons and wool union also in grave
HB 598: 2635	tabby	22/Z × 22/S	light nap on both faces; 'coffin fabric'

Vault 9

HB 862:1974/ 1975/3320	tabby	14/Z × 22/S	worsted; 'coffin fabric' in association with undyed wool union

Vault 10B

HB 382: 1880/1881	(i)tabby	15/S × 10/S	light, open fabric, undyed
	(ii)tabby	12/Z × 10/S	light nap

Vault 10C

HB 383: 1885/2085	?tabby	?/S × ?/S	fine fabric, poorly preserved
HB 391: 1886/1887	tabby	16/S × 12/S	light fabric; ruffled trim of same material
	tabby	18/Z × 12/Z	(i) large flat plain panels
			(ii) pinked and punched face cloth

V15

HB 255: 1624/1682	tabby	16/Z × 24/S	slightly ribbed; light nap; feather in assoc. and also black organics and bone; silk ribbon and wool union also in grave

Table 126: Wool textiles other than coffin covers (Table 123) and wool unions (Table 124).

Vault:burial: find	Width (selv–selv)	Weave	Twist/thread-count	Selvedge	Notes
V2:HB121: 1331/1332	≥22 mm	5-end satin	c.180/I × 40/I	tabby-woven selvedge has 2 looped weft returns alternating with 2 plain	scalloped edge; punched decoration; stitch holes along one edge; associated with wool union
V5:HB297: 1827	(i) 14 mm	5-end satin	110/I × 30/I	tabby-woven selvedge has weft entered in pairs; 3 looped weft returns alternating with 3 plain	stitch holes along one edge; other silk fabrics and wool tabby also in grave
	(ii) 18 mm	5-end satin	110/I × 30/I	exactly as (i)	stitch holes along both edges; some pieces folded lengthways
V5:HB304: 1794/1795	18 mm	satin, ?5-end	100/I × 40/Z	tabby-woven selvedge has weft entered in pairs; no loops	folded into square 265 × 320 mm; no stitch holes visible; in association with wool tabby; wool union also in grave
V5:HB321: 1934	(i) 21 mm	8-end satin	112/I × 44/Z	satin at edge, then a 1 mm wide band of tabby; no loops	several long pieces, one 0.64 m; one has V-shaped cuts with silk-covered button; another covered button has same ribbon frill around it, to make a rosette; also used as trim on two squares of SS wool tabby
	(ii) 27 mm	8-end satin	c.100/I × 40/Z	as (i)	folded bow; wool SS tabby on back
	15–16 mm	tabby	50/I × 32/I	simple	some lengths used flat and tied into bows others used as rolled piping ; in association with wool union
V5:HB574: 2580	420 mm	5-end satin	120/I × 40/I	simple	wide strip of satin cut from piece 0.42m wide; pinked edges, scalloped design; punched decoration; further lengths have regular tucks; in association with wool union
V5:HB587: 2614	8 mm	tabby	70/I × 44/I	simple	folded longitudinally as edging for wool union
V10B:HB372: 1874/1875/ S.146	18 mm	tabby	76/I × 32/I	simple	stitched to wool union, some flat, some folded longitudinally along edges

Table 127: Silk ribbons from burials (all from vaults and brick-lined graves). Continued overleaf.

Width Vault:burial: find	(selv-selv)	Weave	Twist/thread-count	Selvedge	Notes
V15: HB255: 1624/1682	13.5 mm	tabby	74/I × 40/I	simple, warp close-set	folded longitudinally or folded into a bow;
V18: HB576: 2097	17–18 mm	tabby	60–70/I × 44/I	simple	folded longitudinally around edges of wool union, or used flat for bows
V19: HB262: 1701/1702	25 mm	tabby	40–44/I × 40/I	simple, warp close-set	used flat or folded into a bow; in association with wool tabby
V23:HB681: 2844	16 mm	tabby	70–80/I × 40/I	simple	folded longitudinally in association with decayed wool textile
V23:HB691: 2817	13–14 mm	tabby	60–64/I × 40/I	simple	(i) arranged in circle or square with ends knotted; (ii) folded longitudinally and edging decayed wool textile
V23: HB692: 2129/2130	30 mm	5-end satin and open-weave tabby in vertical bands	c.100/I × 80 pairs and c.30/I × 80 pairs	tabby, weft in pairs; alternate weft returns are looped	gathered
	10 mm	tabby	68/I × 40/I	simple, warp close-set	fluted and wrapped around bone; on fragment folded longitudinally and stitched
	30 mm	5-end satin and open-weave tabby in vertical bands	c.160/I × 32/I and c.30/I × 32/I	tabby, weft in pairs; alternate weft returns are looped	arranged in regular tucks 8-12 mm wide
V23: HB698: 2904	26 mm 18 mm	tabby tabby	72/I × 40/I 60/I × 40/I	simple simple	loosely gathered tied bow
	27 mm	5-end satin and open-weave tabby in vertical bands	c.180/I × 26–28/I and c.50/I × 26–28/I	tabby, weft in pairs; alternate weft returns are looped	tightly gathered
V26: HB489: 2371	≥16 mm	tabby	60/I × 40/I	simple, warp close-set	
V30: HB841: 3265	19 mm	satin, ?5-end	c.100/I × 28/I	tabby-woven selvedge	selvedge is paler than rest

Table 127 continued.

Jewellery and other personal items
by Lynne Bevan

Introduction

The small finds assemblage is large and varied in its composition, containing a number of interesting and datable finds, particularly jewellery. The finds are discussed below, firstly in functional categories and, secondly, by material.

Jewellery

The small collection of jewellery is interesting for several reasons, particularly in view of the significance attached to the mourning ring, a very fine example of its type. The other gold rings, although less elaborate, are of no lesser importance in terms of their relationship with people who lived and died in Birmingham. The silver brooch and glass beads were also worthy of study. In the past such items might have been considered of little value in comparison to the aristocratic jewels found in catalogues of historical jewellery or in museum displays. Yet they are, perhaps, of far more interest, particularly on a local level, for what they reveal regarding the less expensive tastes of the inhabitants of 19th-century Birmingham.

Gold and copper alloy rings

Four gold rings and a copper alloy ring were recovered from human burials. The largest and most elaborate gold ring was a mourning ring from HB 372, dedicated to the memory of 'Mr THOS. (Thomas) MARTIN' who 'DIED 13 SEP 1808 AGED 53' (Fig. 135, colour, a). This was buried with a middle adult male in Chamber B of Vault 10, which is likely to be the vault of the Rowlinson family (see Chapter 3). Mourning rings were popular during the 18th and 19th centuries when they were commissioned in batches and given out at funerals to commemorate the deceased (Puckle 1926, 267, Plates 268, 270). There are published parallels for this early 19th-century style of ring, the outer face of which was usually enamelled (Becker 1980, Fig. 7.10, 93). A similar, but much earlier ring, dated to 1763 and inlaid with blue enamel, came from a female burial at Spitalfields, commemorating the death of the deceased's mother at the age of 29 (Reeve and Adams 1993, 89; Molleson and Cox 1993, Fig.15.4, 212).

The 'Thomas Martin' ring is of the early 19th-century style of mourning rings, which tended to be of more simple design, derived from neo-classical mourning jewellery of the late 18th-century, rather than the more elaborate Victorian mourning rings which became fashionable later (Becker 1980, 93). It is very unusual in having no extant traces of enamel, demonstrating that it had never actually been enamelled, although the outer banding is raised and could have supported enamelling. Could this have been a trial piece designed for the client to view before the batch of rings was made and distributed according to Mr Martin's will, or was the lack of enamel

a matter of personal preference? These questions cannot be answered on the available evidence.

Unsurprisingly, the hallmark 'N', dating to 1808-9, corresponds with the date of Mr Martin's death. The ring was of London manufacture and is almost certainly the work of Joseph Preedy who was active during the late 18th–early 19th century and is described as a 'good maker' (Pickford 2000, 62). This is not Preedy's standard stamp, since the 'I' and 'P' are enclosed in a waisted lozenge and separated by a small circle, but this form of stamp was also used by other contemporary makers during the late 18th–early 19th century (Pickford 2000, 63).

The other gold rings were all plain gold bands from the following human burials: HB 297 (Vault 5), HB 666 (Vault 21) and HB 793 (Vault 30). These all appear to have been women's wedding bands, although the ring from HB 666, which was particularly thin and worn and without a hallmark, accompanied a probable male adult. The ring from HB 297 belonged to Ann Maria Browett who died in 1894 aged 81 years (Fig. 135, colour, b). The hallmark on this ring denotes Birmingham manufacture and the letter 'm' with a curlicue across the central post attests to a date of 1835–36 (Pickford 2000, 84) when Ann Maria would have been about 22 years old. The amount of wear on this ring would accord with it having been worn, logically as a wedding ring, for nearly 60 years. The maker's mark, possibly 'W E' or 'W R', is less distinct than the rest of the hallmark and cannot be related to a known Birmingham goldsmith.

The ring from HB 793 was found on the left hand of Eliza Haines who died in 1904 at the age of 60. It was fairly worn and the hallmark was virtually illegible, although its arrangement might suggest an Exeter origin, in which case the letter 'F' indicates a date of 1842–43 (Pickford 2000, 128). However, at this date Eliza was not yet born (although the ring might be an heirloom) and the maker's mark, 'J R', does not correlate with the initials of any Exeter makers.

A small copper alloy ring recovered from HB 373, a burial in an earth-cut grave, had a decorated but very degraded surface and was in a very fragile condition (Fig. 135, colour, c).

Catalogue

1. Ring, gold, with external writing: 'Mr THOS. (Thomas) MARTIN. DIED 13 SEP 1808 AGED 53'. The writing is recessed within the raised outer edges of the ring. There is evidence of considerable wear on both the inner and outer faces. Diameter: 20mm, height: 7mm. HB 372 (Vault 10B), 1874, SF 26. Fig. 135 (colour) a.
2. Ring, gold, plain design. Diameter: 17mm, height: 2mm. HB 297 (Vault 5), SF 17. Fig. 135 (colour) b.
3. Ring, gold, plain design, slightly distorted. Diameter: 15mm, height: 3mm. HB 793 (Vault 30), SF 48.
4. Ring, gold, plain design. Diameter: 17mm, height: 1mm. HB 666 (Vault 21), 2820, SF 40.
5. Ring, copper alloy, with degraded surface showing signs of decoration. Diameter: 18mm height: 3mm. HB373, 2064, SF 27. Fig. 135 (colour) c.

Silver and copper alloy brooch

Of some interest in the collection was a small silver and copper alloy wire-work brooch in the form a cupid's arrow with a bird in the centre, and a foliate motif at the end inlaid with two turquoises or turquoise-coloured glass stones (Fig. 135, colour, d). The brooch was a stray find from the churchyard soil. The brooch is stylistically reminiscent of silver brooches of the late 19th century (Becker 1980, Fig. 5.6, 53). The mid-late 1880s saw the collapse of the silver jewellery market in Birmingham, partly as a result of fashion and partly due to silver becoming so cheap and mass-produced that it became regarded as vulgar (Becker 1980, 52–55). By the 1890s the trade had been revived, with the introduction of silver brooches, the design of which incorporated various motifs and symbols, including hearts, flowers and birds, as well as written names and messages (*ibid*, 55). Such items were relatively inexpensive and very popular among the urban working class, and it seems likely that this small, unpretentious piece was a love token or a keepsake of local Birmingham manufacture.

Catalogue

1. Brooch in the form of a cupid's arrow, with a bird in the centre, and a foliate motif, incorporating oak leaves, at the end, inlaid with two turquoises or turquoise-coloured glass stones. Length: 70mm, width at terminal: 25mm. 3008, SF 41. Fig 135 (colour) d.

Facetted glass inlay and beads

The remains of an almost complete necklace were recovered from HB 190 (brick-lined grave V03). This consisted of approximately 300 loose glass beads, opaque pink in colour, and a small copper alloy decorative fastener, inlaid with a pink cut-glass bead in the shape of a rose, to which four pink beads were attached (Fig. 135, colour, e). Each of the beads attached to the fastener appears to be the last bead *in situ* from a four-stranded necklace. That the opposite side of the fastener is fitted with a small loop implies that the other matching half of the fastener has been lost, along with many of the beads. Some of the threads used to string the beads had become fused to the copper alloy mount of the fastener. The remains of a second necklace consisting of a quantity of coloured beads of various sizes, with small pieces of remnant thread, some of which were found incorporated into a fragment of preserved textile fused to a piece of coffin wood, came from HB 16, a burial in an earth-cut grave. Other glass items consisted of a medium-sized, facetted turquoise glass inlay from an item of jewellery (SF 87), found in the churchyard soil, and a small blue-green bead from an earth-cut burial (HB 136). Very little is known of costume jewellery of this period, since most publications tend to be concerned with high status, valuable jewellery which is more likely to have survived through inheritance or resale. Popular publications for collectors or antique dealers tend to feature only expensive jewellery of the later Victorian period and the 20th

century, as comparatively few earlier pieces have survived in circulation.

The essential delicacy of necklaces like the pink one from HB 190 rendered such items particularly vulnerable to breakage and loss. Outside a burial context, re-stringing practices and standardised methods of bead manufacture through time would make it impossible to differentiate between beads like those found at St. Martin's and beads from much later periods. Apart from the simple style of these beads, which probably date to the early-mid Victorian period and would not have been greatly expensive at the time, perhaps the most interesting aspect is their deposition in the grave of a child. It seems likely that this necklace was the treasured possession of a young girl, or otherwise a distraught mother or other relative may have placed it in the coffin of a child of either sex. The former explanation seems more likely, since this is exactly the type of jewellery which would have appealed to a young girl.

Catalogue

1. The remains of a four-stranded bead necklace consisting of approximately 300 loose, glass beads, opaque pink in colour, and a small copper alloy decorative fastener, inlaid with a pink cut-glass bead in the shape of a rose, to which four pink beads were attached. Diameter of fastener: 11mm, average diameter of beads: 2mm. HB 190 (V03), 1530, SF 5. Fig. 135 (colour) e.
2. Multi-coloured beads of various sizes from a necklace, *c.*50 in total. Colours represented: clear, pink, opaque blue and translucent red. Diameter: largest beads: 2mm, smaller beads:1mm. HB 16, 1046.
3. Blue facetted glass inlay from jewellery. Diameter: 8mm, height: 6mm. 1648, SF 87.
4. Small blue-green bead. Diameter: 3mm. HB136, SF 70.

Hair accessories

Two main types of comb were recovered: simple combs and decorative hair combs, the majority of which were made from tortoiseshell. While the decorative tortoise-shell combs probably entered the grave in the hair of the deceased, which must have been dressed prior to burial, the simple grooming combs might have been pressed into service to arrange hair pre-burial or have entered the coffins in another way. It is possible that there was a reluctance to keep combs that had been used to groom the hair of corpses, which might explain why they were placed in the burials. Such grooming would logically have occurred in the home of the deceased and probably have involved the use of their own combs. The simple combs, which tended to be badly preserved, came from four burials: HB 266 (Vault 4), HB 270, (Vault 4), HB 370 (Vault 10B) and HB 692 (Vault 23). One burial also contained a poorly-preserved decorative bone comb (HB 266, Vault 4). Tortoiseshell hair combs consisted of two large examples (HB 304, Vault 5 and HB 868, V36), a medium-sized hair comb (SF 52, unstratified), a small hair comb, and a fragment from a tortoiseshell comb (HB 607, Vault 5).

Tortoiseshell combs were particularly subject to breakage and discard, and it is unusual to see so well-preserved and intact an assemblage as that from St. Martin's. In the 19th century, particularly during the 1860s-1880s, tortoiseshell and metal combs were used to support elaborate coiffures, often supplemented by additions of false hair (Keyes 1967; de Courtais 1973). These combs tended to be of a 'coronet' style (de Courtais 1973, 124–125, Fig. 269a and b), a broader, more angular comb with shorter teeth, and as such, are unlike the combs from St. Martin's, which are earlier. However, very few early or pre-Victorian hair combs have survived, although they are known to have been used in hairdressing as early as the 18th century and also during the earlier 19th century. Apart from a brief trend for cropping hair *à la guillotine* (de Courtais 1973, 96), hair fashions of the 1780s and 1790s tended to be elaborate. Hair was curled and pinned up, using combs and padded 'cushions', to add height under the equally elaborate hats of the time, while some curls were left to hang loosely over the shoulders (Willett and Cunnington 1957, 378–384). Combs were worn as ornaments and used to secure chignons (*ibid.*, 379). In 1797 *The Times* lamented that, 'our ladies cannot make an appearance without a dozen combs in their heads, and as many false curls and cushions' (*ibid.*, 386).

During the early 19th century hairstyles were subject to classical influences and a number of elegant but complex styles were created, including the unpowdered 'Grecian style...fastened with combs of diamonds, gold etc', as well as other ornaments, as described in *The Lady's Magazine* of 1800 (de Courtais 1973, 96). As the 1800s progressed, braiding and plaiting were incorporated in complex styles in which most of the hair tended to be 'dressed towards the crown of the head' and by 1820 were worn in a large 'top knot' (*ibid.,* 104–105, Fig. 223). Many of the high styles of the 1820s were achieved with the use of long pins and 'high combs of tortoiseshell and gilt metal set with jewels' (*ibid.,* 104–105).

On the present evidence, a post-1800 date, possibly as late as the 1820s or 1830s, seems most likely for the tortoiseshell combs at St. Martin's, post-dating the late 18th-century floruit of elaborate hairstyles involving multiple combs and other ornaments. That most of the tortoiseshell combs from St. Martin's were particularly large and long and only occurred singly in burials suggests that a fairly simple coiffure, perhaps involving a single chignon, was preferred, at least for mortuary attire. The larger examples would have secured a substantial coil or plait of hair. On the other hand, it seems unlikely that the extravagant hairstyles of London society, festooned with feathers, flowers, ribbons and golden combs, would have influenced the more conservative middle classes of Birmingham to any great extent. Such elaborate styles might even have been considered vulgar and indicative of low morality by the church-going middle classes of Birmingham. Were

golden, jewelled hair ornaments ever worn by the ladies buried at St. Martin's, and there is no evidence to suggest that they were, such items are more likely to have been passed on to relatives of the deceased, than the more utilitarian tortoiseshell combs found in the graves.

The main question here is whether hairstyles in death accurately reflected hairstyles worn by the living, or was their simplicity, ornamented by these simple combs, considered proper in a mortuary context, as befitting a girl or woman going forth to meet with her maker? Other factors, such as the age of the deceased and her marital or social status, as well as considerations of fashion, would have influenced the type of clothing and hairstyle in which the deceased was buried. It is interesting that two of the combs came from the burials of middle adult women (HB 304 and HB 86) and another came from an old adult woman (HB 607). Was a chignon or other upswept style, favoured by mature, probably married women? On the other hand, were the two grooming combs, one of tortoiseshell and one of bone, from the burial of a young adult female (HB 370), used for a different hairstyle? A younger, possibly single, woman might have had her hair pinned back from her face, with long tresses arranged over the shoulders, rather than worn in an upswept style. Such a style would have emphasised her youth and untimely death at such a young age. On the other hand, the hairstyle of a much older woman with sparser hair, for example, might have been more formal, conservative or even old fashioned, than that of a younger woman. She might even have worn a cap of the kind seen at Spitalfields (Reeve and Adams 1993, 105, Fig. 6.9) rather than have had her hair dressed with combs.

While there is a great deal of published work on mortuary apparel for mourners, particularly from the Victorian period, very little is known regarding fashions in dressing the body and hair of the deceased. It is apparent, however, that the deceased were being carefully prepared for burial to the extent of having their hair deliberately dressed in a certain way with these elegant combs. This attention to detail might be explained by the common practice during the 18th and 19th centuries for the coffin to be left open at home for two or three days for the deceased to be viewed by family and friends prior to burial (Reeve and Adams 1993, 95). It seems likely that none of the women with dressed hair had died of a contagious disease that might hasten burial, precluding careful washing and preparation of the corpse, as well as it being laid out in an open coffin.

Other finds comprised a small probable hairpin from HB 598 (Sarah Emma Warden, d.1866, Vault 5) and a well-preserved fragment from a decorative bone plate with a floral motif executed in cut-work. This item is of probable later Victorian date and might be part of a hair ornament or a carved panel from a box.

Catalogue

Combs

1. Complete tortoiseshell hair comb, with strands of long

blonde hair attached. Length: 102mm, width: 90mm, thickness: 2mm. HB 304 (Vault 5), 1795, SF 28.

2. Tortoiseshell hair comb, with slight breakage to one side and a fragment of fine textile attached to the front, possibly from a shroud or headdress. Length: 100mm, width: 79mm, thickness: 1–2mm. HB 868 (V36), 3338, SF 49.

3. Complete tortoiseshell hair comb, with some damage to surface. Length: 62mm, width: 45mm, thickness: 2mm. SF 52, unstratified.

4. Complete bone hair comb, very degraded surface, and poorly-preserved bone grooming comb. Decorative comb: Length: 70mm, width: 66mm, thickness: 1.5mm. Grooming comb: Length: 27mm, width: 86mm, thickness: 1.5mm. HB 266 (Vault 4), 1718, SF 53.

5. Small tortoiseshell hair comb and fragment from tortoiseshell grooming comb. Hair comb: Length: 40mm, width: 40mm, thickness: 1mm. Grooming comb: Length: 25mm, surviving width: 44mm, thickness: 1–2mm. HB 607 (Vault 5), 2654, SF 51.

6. Small tortoiseshell hair comb, broken at one end. Length: 35mm, width: 46mm, thickness: 1mm. HB 692 (Vault 23), 2130, SF 54.

7. Two grooming combs, one of tortoiseshell and one of degraded bone. Tortoiseshell: Length: 29mm, surviving width: 53mm, thickness: 1mm. Bone: Length: 28mm, surviving width: 60mm, thickness: 1mm. HB 370 (Vault 10B), 1873, SF 25.

Possible hairpin

8. Possible hairpin, probably iron, with textile fragments attached, broken. Length: 45mm, width: 9mm, thickness: 3mm. HB 598 (Vault 5), 2021, SF 35.

Bone plate

9. Fragment of bone plate, with floral cut-work motif reminiscent of a sunflower. The fragment is curved and there are two copper rivets on the reverse and a patch of iron corrosion on the front. Length: 56mm, width: 21mm, thickness: 2mm. 1727, SF 55.

Coins and tokens

A total of nine coins and tokens and a metal disc was recovered, the generally poor condition of which precluded identification in some cases. The earliest identifiable coins comprised: a very worn George II penny dated to the 1750s (SF 42, 3008) and a farthing dated 1814, with 'Hamilton' and 'Retailer's Token' stamped on the reverse, from earth-cut burial HB 353 (SF 72). A 1792 'Coventry Halfpenny', with an elephant and castle motif on one side and Lady Godiva mounted on horseback on the other, was recovered from earth-cut burial HB 314 (SF 74, 1919).

Trade tokens like SF 72 and SF 74 were introduced to alleviate the chronic shortage of small change during the late 18th and early 19th century (Whiting 1971). Birmingham, particularly the Matthew Boulton manufactory, was a major producer of these tokens. The Coventry Halfpenny was a token issued in 1792 by the ribbon manufacturers Reynolds and Company of Coventry, and produced by Lutwyche, a Birmingham coining firm.

In addition, four very degraded, unidentifiable coins

(SF 1, HB129, 1353; SF 30, 2158; SF 3, 1523 and unstratified) and a plain metal disc, possibly a token (SF 71, 1381), were found. The size of two of the coins suggests that they might have been halfpennies of possible 18th-19th-century date, but their poor condition precludes positive identification.

It is possible that some of the coins broadly contemporary with burials entered the graves on the eyelids of the deceased according to past funerary custom.

Other copper alloy items (excluding buttons)

A total of 60 complete pins and *c*.80 pin fragments was recovered, the vast majority of which were found in burials, where they had been used to pin shrouds around bodies. A few had become fused to skulls, following the decomposition of hair and soft tissue. Several of the pins and pin fragments had retained textile fragments. The pins tended to be plain, with rounded heads, the complete examples being of a fairly standard size. These simple, dressmaking pins, examples of which have been found elsewhere in Birmingham (Bevan forthcoming), were the most common type of pin. They would have been used to secure shrouds and winding sheets (Walton Rogers, this chapter), hence their occurrence around the head area of some of the bodies. There were a few examples of a pin with a horizontal line around the head and some small, flat-headed tacks, the latter probably from coffin lining rather than from funerary attire. Other finds possibly connected with wrapping or dressing the body, included a needle, two small rings with textile fragments attached, a fragment from a similar ring (HB 773, 3078), and four clothing hooks, the latter from the burial of an adolescent (HB 334, Vault 5).

Three buckles were recovered, including a complete, decorated rectangular buckle from an earth-cut grave with some fibres of a woven fabric attached (HB 701, 2878, SF 77), the form of which is suggestive of a knee buckle from breeches dating to *c*.1720–*c*.1790 (Whitehead 1996, Nos. 709–710, 111). Another complete buckle frame was probably from a shoe (SF 78, unstratified) and a small fragment from a buckle with ridged decoration, found in an earth-cut grave, was probably from a boot or garter (HB 261, SF 11). Both of buckles are of probable later 18th-century date. One further possible buckle fragment was recovered (SF 76, unstratified), but its small size precluded further identification and dating. Other finds from clothing included three lace ends, two of which came from HB 237, a burial in an earth-cut grave, and a fragment of a third from HB 694, a burial of a middle adult female in an earth-cut grave, where it was found near the skull (2870). Lace ends were used for various dress functions from the 15th century onwards, with later examples dating to the 17th century (Margeson 1993, 22–24). In later centuries clothing was more likely to have been secured with buttons, although lace ends might still have been used on shoelaces or purse strings. These three examples could be residual finds, pre-dating the burials.

The majority of this material was in a poor condition. Other identifiable finds, all from earth-cut graves or the churchyard soil, included a small hinge with a maker's mark, probably 'T.A.', on one side (HB 315, 1910, SF 83) and a possible brooch pin (HB 595, 2631, SF 82). The remainder of the collection consisted of fragmentary items, including a leaded copper alloy disc with textile survival on each side (HB 439, SF 32), a fragment of circular plate (3172, SF 46), and a small hook-like object (HB 322, 1925). Other fragmentary items comprised a fragment of twisted wire (1009, SF 81), a ring (SF 85, unstratified), two rod fragments (HB 237, 1642, SF10 and SF 85, unstratified) and a strip fragment (HB 23, 1064, SF 86).

Catalogue

1. Round-headed pin. Length: 42mm, diameter of head: 2mm. Unstratified.
2. Pin with horizontal indentation around head. Length: 42mm, diameter of head: 2mm. HB 215, 1586.
3. Three small, flat-headed tacks. Length: 11mm, diameter of head: 3mm. HB 215, 1586.
4. Needle, broken. Length: 26mm, width of head: 2mm. HB 48, 1130.
5. Two rings. Diameter: 12mm, thickness: 1mm. HB 576 (Vault 18), 2097, SF 34.
6. Four clothing hooks. Length: 14mm, width: 9mm, thickness:1mm. HB 334 (Vault 5), 1965, SF 20.
7. Two lace ends, one of which is broken. Length of complete lace end: 34mm, width: 1–1.5mm. HB 237, 1642, SF 10.
8. Complete rectangular buckle, probably a knee buckle from breeches, with a corroded iron anchor chape with two, or possibly three, tongues, attached to fragments of a woven fabric, possibly wool. The surface of the frame appears to have been decorated with raised floriform motifs. Length: 35mm, width: 32mm, thickness: 3mm. HB 701, 2878, SF 77.
9. Rectangular buckle frame, probably from a shoe. Length: 38mm, width: 27mm, thickness: 5mm. SF 78, unstratified.
10. Small fragment from a buckle with ridged decoration, probably from a boot or garter. Surviving width: *c*.25mm, thickness: 1mm. HB 261, SF 11.

Iron items

The only iron object found was a corroded pair of scissors from an earth-cut grave (HB 771, 3081, SF 45). Based upon published parallels, this item is of probable mid-late 17th century date (e.g. Goodall 1993, Fig. 101: 924, 136; Noël Hume 1969, Fig. 87:3–6, 268).

Catalogue

1. Pair of scissors, very corroded. Length: 155mm, maximum width of blades: 11mm. SF 45, HB 771, 3081.

Lead items

Lead finds, other than the lead shells of coffins and *depositum* plates, comprised a small length of window leading from an earth-cut grave (HB 408, 2148, SF 79) and two small balls, possibly lead shot (SF 75, unstratified).

Bone and copper alloy buttons

Eighteen buttons were recovered from a number of burials. The most decorative of the buttons, from HB 490, a burial in an earth-cut grave, has a floral motif and a tinned surface. Two small bone buttons, with single central holes and surface scratching, were recovered from earth-cut burial HB 35 (1099, SF 60) and HB 264 (V14, 1708, SF 69). SF 60 had been stained green, probably from contact with copper alloy, and SF 69, the smaller of the two, had taken on a brown colouration. They are both probably contemporary with the burials, and from the clothing of the deceased. Five small bone buttons of regular size, with single large central holes and green staining, were recovered, and seemed to originate from the same garment (1386, SF 67), possibly a shroud. Two other bone buttons were recovered, a small four-holed, probable shroud, button from HB 794 (Vault 30, William Tertius Haines, d.1869, 3143, SF 47), and a degraded, broken button from HB 318 (Vault 10A, Samuel Wyer, d.1802, 1870, SF 64).

Most of the other buttons were of copper alloy, with attachments loops, the kinds of buttons that might have originated from day clothes rather than funerary attire. They ranged from 17mm to 22mm in diameter. Five of these came from the following human burials: HB 51 (1140, SF 51), HB 71 (1198, SF 71), HB 148 (1408, SF 65), HB 157 (1438, SF 12), all in earth-cut graves, and HB 330 (V14, 1947, SF 68). Another three copper-alloy buttons, including a four-holed button, came from context 2976 (SF 57).

Catalogue

1. Tinned button, with floral motif. Diameter: 14mm, thickness: 1mm. HB 490, 2375, SF 33.
2. Small bone button, with a single central hole, surface scratching and green staining. Diameter: 11mm, thickness: 1mm. HB 35,1099, SF 60.
3. Small bone button, with a single central hole, surface scratching and brown staining. Diameter: 9mm, thickness: 1mm. HB 264 (V14),1708, SF 69.
4. Five small bone buttons, with large central holes and green staining. Diameter: 11mm, thickness: 2mm. 1386, SF 67.
5. Small bone button, with four central holes. Diameter: 7mm, thickness: 2mm. HB 794 (Vault 30), 3143, SF 47.
6. Bone button, with a single central hole, broken. Diameter: 12mm, thickness: 2mm. HB 318 (Vault 10A), 1870, SF 64.

Pipeclay wig-curlers

Three broken wig-curlers were recovered, two of which came from earth-cut burials (HB 343, SF 88 and HB 355, SF 21), and the third of which was an unstratified find (SF 89). Wig-curlers were used by both men and women at different times from the 16th century to the very early 19th century (Crummy 1988, 24). The main period of male usage of these items covered the 18th century up to *c*.1790, and female usage was from *c*.1795-1810 (*ibid.*, 24). The style of the unstratified wig-curler is reminiscent of a type from Colchester dated to *c*.1700–1760 (Crummy

1988, Fig. 28: 1869, 25–26). The second wig-curler is similarly-shaped and the third is larger and more bulbous.

Wig-curlers were used to curl the wig, with the application of rags and heat from an oven, prior to being worn (Noël Hume 1969, 322–323), so it is unlikely that either of the two from the burials entered the grave in a wig worn by the deceased. Like the unstratified example it is probable that the wig-curlers entered the burials as re-deposited refuse, pre-dating most of the burials studied here.

Catalogue
1. Half of a wig-curler, with a bevelled end. Length: 33mm, maximum width: 12mm. Unstratified.
2. Half of a wig-curler, with a bevelled end. Length: 29mm, maximum width: 13mm. HB 343, 1988, SF 88.
3. Half of a wig-curler, with a bulbous end. Length: 35mm, maximum width: 14mm. HB 355, 1985, SF 21.

Clay tobacco pipes

A total of 14 complete bowls, 27 bowl fragments, and 257 stem fragments from clay tobacco pipes were found. Nine stamps were identified, three of which occurred on pipe stems and the others on bowls. The complete bowls, and some of the larger bowl fragments, were related to Oswald's dated typology of clay pipes (1975). Most of the dated bowls conformed to mid-late 18th-century to mid-19th-century types, although at least four of the bowls might date to the earlier-mid 17th-century. Details of the contexts of these items can be found in the site archive.

Wooden item

A small, turned wooden ball, with a diameter of 14mm, was found (1985, SF 22), and was probably used in a game.

Glass

A total of 302 small fragments of glass was recovered. The majority comprised 111 small fragments from 18th–19th-century wine and beer bottles, and 180 small fragments of window glass. There were five fragments from clear bottles of recent appearance, a fragment of pale blue glass, three necks and a base from 19th-century medicine bottles, and a clear glass rod of uncertain purpose, though it might be an apothecary's tool (HB 810, 3173).

Worked stone

Two circular worked stones with square-shaped central perforations were recovered, both of which came from Vault 10B. These stones, which were of a similar size, had been used to support a coffin (HB 372), containing a middle adult male wearing the ring commemorating the death of Thomas Martin in 1808.

The morphology of the stones is suggestive of an industrial use, that they were used in some kind of grinding or pressing process, perhaps in brewing or metal production. Moreover, the reason for their presence in the vault, where they had been deliberately placed to support a coffin, one at each end, is problematic. Was their placement an opportunistic use of available materials, perhaps from an abandoned workshop nearby, or did it hold some symbolic significance, being perhaps emblematic of the business of the person in question? Similar stones were recovered at the Park Street site, which is almost adjacent to St. Martin's churchyard (Bevan and Ixer forthcoming).

Conclusions

The small finds assemblage from St. Martin's, which includes a number of items of jewellery and hair accessories, is significantly larger and more varied than that recorded at Spitalfields (Reeve and Adams 1993, 89). There are numerous published studies regarding past burial ritual (e.g. Llewellyn 1951; Litten 1991; Jupp and Manchester 1999), particularly with regard to the pre-Victorian and Victorian periods, and the finds from St. Martin's allow us to reconstruct funerary practices of the time. These artefacts are also important in terms of gender and funerary ritual, a field of research which has recently attracted attention (Arnold and Lanham 2002). The hair combs, in particular, are of interest, both as artefacts, since so few pre-Victorian and early Victorian examples have survived intact, as well as aids in the reconstruction of pre-burial hairdressing techniques.

The study of this small finds assemblage provides an insight into middle-class tastes and aesthetics at the time of the emergence of this class as the driving force behind the economic growth and prosperity of towns like Birmingham at this period. The assemblage also contributes towards the broad study of the products of a number of industrialised crafts of the town in the Victorian era, a significant theme emerging from the study of finds assemblages from other, non-burial sites recently excavated in the city centre at Edgbaston Street and Park Street. While the contexts of most of the artefacts and their relationship with their deceased owners are a poignant reminder of the fragility of human life, they also present an interesting and unusual record of life in Birmingham during the 18th and 19th centuries. Not only do they offer some insight into contemporary burial ritual (Llewellyn 1951; Litten 1991), including the preparation and grooming of the corpse for laying out, and the accoutrements of mourning (Bury 1985), but also into fashions in jewellery and hair accessories of the earlier 19th century (Becker 1980; Keyes 1967; de Courtais 1973).

Plant offerings
by Marina Ciaraldi

The taphonomic conditions present in many of the burials excavated at St. Martin's have allowed the preservation of different types of biological remains. Anoxic conditions and favourable pH values slow down the degradation of the biological remains. Well-preserved botanical remains were present in some of the burials.

Identification criteria

The plant remains, easily recognisable by the naked eye during the excavation, were systematically sampled by the excavators. The plant remains were preserved as dry and none of the samples required further processing. Their identification was achieved using a low-power microscope and with the help of the author's reference collection.

Most of the preserved plant remains consisted of leaves. This is unsurprising, considering that leaves tend to be tougher than other anatomical parts, such as flowers or soft fruits. The leaves were exceptionally well-preserved and therefore it was possible to identify them on the basis of their shape, vein pattern or other macroscopic details.

Box leaves (*Buxus sempervirens* L.) were identified on the basis of their shape and by the position of the leaves on the sprig. The juniper twig (*Juniperus communis* L.) was identified by the characteristic needle-shape of the foliage and by the position and shape of the female cone. The cherry leaves (*Prunus avium* L.) had an oval shape and a rather pointed tip; the leaf margin was pronouncedly toothed. Finally, the privet leaf (*Ligustrum* sp.) had and elongated oval shape, entire leaf margin and stomata on the underside of the leaf.

Discussion

Box (Buxus sempervirens L.) (HB 233, HB 226 and HB 681)

Box is not only the commonest species amongst those identified at St. Martin's, but it is also the one that is traditionally associated with burial rituals. In the Roman period box was used to line coffins (Godwin 1956). It has been found in three burials, brick-lined grave V08 – HB 233 (leaves only), V08 – HB 226 (sprig) and Vault 23 – HB 681 (sprig).

Box is an evergreen plant, native to England and present nowadays only in restricted areas of southern England, on chalk and limestone (Stace 1997). The inclusion of the word 'box' in place names, however, suggests that it was more widespread in the past (Mabey 1996). It is often planted in gardens, in hedges or used in topiary. The association of box with burials is long and well documented. Young shoots were commonly used in wreaths as far back as the middle ages. A thicket of box, yew and snowdrops surround the memorial cross which marks the site of the execution of Piers Gaveston (1312) at Blacklow Hill, Warwickshire (Mabey 1996). Wordsworth describes how box was traditionally used in death rituals and his words are also confirmed by the following report that appeared in the *Daily Telegraph* in 1868 (cited in Mabey 1996, 256):

I find an old Lancashire custom observed in the case of this funeral. By the side of the dead man, the relatives, as they took their last look at the corpse, have formed a tray or plate, upon which lay a heap of sprigs of box. Each relative has taken one of these sprigs, and will carry it to the grave, many of them dropping it upon the coffin. Ordinarily the tray contains sprigs of rosemary or thyme: but these poor Hindley people not being able to obtain poetical plants, have, rather than give up an old custom, contented themselves with stripping several trees of boxwood.

The presence of flower buds on the box sprigs from HB 226 and HB 681 gives some hint of the time of deposition; this must have occurred during the spring, when the buds are in blossom.

Juniper (Juniperus communis L.) (HB 304)

Juniper too, like box, is a native evergreen plant. Unlike box, however, there seems to be no record of the practice of offering juniper twigs to the deceased. It is however worth mentioning the fact that juniper oil was used in the past as abortifacient and, in the medieval period, 'giving birth under a savin tree' was an euphemism for a miscarriage (Mabey 1996). It is interesting in this respect that HB 304 was a middle adult female buried in Vault 5, the Warden/Browett family vault.

It is known from other archaeological cases (Zias *et al.*1993) that medicinal plants, possibly associated with the final illness of the dead person, were placed in their burial. Juniper also produces a strongly scented resin whose smell is pronounced when burnt. Juniper twigs might have been burnt while the coffin lay open.

Cherry (Prunus avium/cerasus) (HB 333)

Five well-preserved leaves of cherry were found in burial HB 333. Cherry is a deciduous tree and the presence of its leaves in the burial gives a clear indication of the period of their deposition, between March and September when the leaves are still on the trees. In Chapter 3 burial HB 333 in Vault 5 is tentatively identified as Mary Elizabeth Warden, who died on 17th August 1867 at the age of 20 or 21.

Wild/garden privet (Ligustrum vulgare/ovalifolium.) (HB 749)

Leaves of privet were found in burial HB 749, a burial of a young adult female in an earth-cut grave. Though well preserved (one was still green), they were rather fragmented.

Privet is an evergreen plant and the wild species grows on calcareous soils (Stace 1997). The garden species is of Japanese origin. It has been used as hedging shrub since the 16th century (Mabberley 1989). It is possible that privet was used, like box, to make wreaths. It is also possible that its honey-scented flowers were offered, in which case they must have been placed in the burial between June and August.

Other botanical remains

Leaves of a grass plant were found in HB 297, the burial

of Ann Maria Browett in Vault 5, and HB 277, an earth-cut burial. They could represent the remains of a filling material for a pillow, mattress or coffin lining.

Conclusion

Although plant remains were recovered from only a small number of the burials at St. Martin's they add an interesting and little-explored dimension to funerary practice. All of the 'offerings' studied appear to represent plants placed in (rather than on top of) the coffin and to have had a symbolic or practical function. According to Litten (1991, 70), floral tributes, such as those we are familiar with today, only made their appearance in English burials in the late 1860s, and most of the burials at St. Martin's are earlier than this date. Traces of two wreaths, for instance, were noted by the excavators on the coffin of Eliza Haines (Vault 30), who was one of the last burials at St. Martin's, buried in 1904. It is of course, difficult to judge whether the absence of the traces of such tributes on other coffins is to be attributed to a real absence or whether it is a question of date or preservation or a combination of the two.

6 The Families: Documentary Research

Josephine Adams

This chapter is concerned with describing something of the lives of the individuals and families who were buried in the large chambered vault (Vault 10), the family vaults and the brick-lined graves. The information is incomplete. For five of the ten family vaults the name of the family is known, together with the names of many of those who were, or probably were, buried in the vault. For the other five family vaults nothing is known about who was buried in them. Information on the identity of those buried in the brick-lined graves is available for only three of the twenty-four graves excavated.

Despite the fragmentary nature of the evidence, sufficient can be learned from this sample to characterise what sort of people were buried in the vaults, what careers they pursued, and to sketch aspects of their family life. A major bias is that no individuals who were buried in the simple earth-cut graves are described, despite the fact that those buried in these graves formed the majority (86%) of the excavated burials at St. Martin's. This omission arises simply because there was not a single example amongst the burials in the earth-cut graves where the identity of the individual could be determined. Of course in general terms we do know who these people were – their names are listed in the parish burial register – but we cannot link a specific name to a specific grave. One group who certainly had the simplest of burials were those who could not afford to pay (or their families could not afford to pay) for a funeral. These people were given a 'parish funeral', that is a funeral paid for by the parish. In the late 18th century this stigma was preserved for ever in the parish records, where 'pauper' was recorded against the person's entry.

In an attempt to correct this bias, in the next chapter an outline is provided of aspects of the lives of Birmingham's working classes – the sort of men, women and children who are likely to have been buried in the earth-cut graves. This both complements and is informed by the analysis of the human remains from these graves described in Chapter 4. In Chapter 9, the likely character of the funeral of one individual who was probably buried

in an earth-cut grave, a butcher's wife called Ann Cockayne, is contrasted with what can be reconstructed of the funeral of the iron merchant Joseph Warden (Vault 5), whose life is briefly described in this chapter.

Following an outline of the methodology employed in undertaking the research on the 'named' individuals from the vaults, the results are given in the order in which the vaults were described in Chapter 3.

Methodology

The documentary research on the named individuals in the churchyard began with the original source of the information, which in most cases was the *depositum* (coffin plate). Their condition varied greatly, making the information often very difficult to decipher. Most were completely illegible, whilst others crumbled when touched and were impossible to salvage. In some cases the wooden coffin had completely decayed and the plate was lying on the individual's ribs. The information on the majority of the plates which were legible consisted of the individual's name, age and date of death, although one included birth date, place of residence and parents' names. In one case additional information was obtained from an associated grave memorial, and in Vault 10 the inscriptions over the entrance to two of the four chambers provided valuable extra information. The only other source was a mourning ring associated with (but not identifying) HB 372 in Vault 10.

The name and date of death provided a starting point from which the research could developed using a variety of sources. The amount of information that could be obtained in any particular case depended upon several different factors. The date of death was particularly important because tracing families before the introduction in 1837 of Civil Registration (St. Catherine's Index – SCI), the procedure whereby all births, deaths and marriages are recorded centrally, was more difficult.

As a first step, the church burial registers were consulted to confirm the details on the coffin plate, which were sometimes difficult to read unambiguously. The registers often also revealed further information about the individual's address or family relationships (e.g. 'son of ...' or 'daughter of...', especially for children). However, the hand-written registers were themselves often difficult to read and the information was not always complete. If an address was available this could be used in some cases for research in the census records, which are available from 1841. The value of these varies as the early ones are not always complete. The 1851 and 1881 census returns for Birmingham were particularly useful in that they include a surname index, whilst the others can only be used if the correct address is known.

Sometimes further information could be obtained from the International Genealogical Index (IGI). This is a county index of parish registers compiled by the Church of Jesus Christ of Latter Day Saints, and is available on fiche and online. It was particularly useful for the pre-1837 period, but could not always be considered to be completely accurate. There are sometimes sections of records missing including, unfortunately, a large part of the St. Martin's record for the second part of the 19th century.

The National Burial Index (NBI), available on CD, lists all burials in England and Wales from 1538 until 2000, although coverage is not comprehensive. It was however invaluable in locating burials at the church prior to 1826.

The trade directories and Post Office listings, which catalogue people either alphabetically or by their profession, provided valuable information about an individual's occupation and business or residential address, and are available from the late 18th century, although again the coverage is not complete. There are a range of directories and different editions of several of them, but the main ones used were Holden's Triennial Directory (HTD), Chapman's Birmingham Directory (CBD), Wrightson & Webb (WW), and Pigot's Directory (PD).

Obituaries published in *Aris's Gazette* (AG), the Birmingham weekly newspaper of the time, published between 1741 and 1856, provided useful information on some individuals, and occasionally the account was quite long. In some cases also a will had been lodged that confirmed family relationships and gave some indication of the material wealth of the individual towards the time of their death. The wills also supplied valuable factual information and provided interesting insights into family and social history. If a will was lodged prior to 1858 it was held at Lichfield Diocesan Office, and some were available online.

At Birmingham Central Library (BCL) there were items held in the Birmingham Archives and Local History sections that were invaluable. These consisted of various forms of documentary evidence, such as details of property or business deals, photographs, invoices, receipts, other types of business or personal papers, and trade catalogues.

Other sources that were consulted at the BCL included:

Electoral Records
Land Registry
Rate Books
National Burial Index (NBI)
Service Records
Existing Birmingham histories
Coroners' Records
Poor House Registers
Monumental Inscriptions (MI)
Local History Society Journals
Probate Records
Maps

Internet sources were also used.

Sometimes librarians, archivists and others were able to help open up further avenues of research that were less immediately obvious than the main sources listed above. These aspects of research are difficult to quantify, but often provided valuable information.

Where possible, the documentary research was used to construct family trees. It must be stressed that the information presented in these trees is often incomplete. As the research was heavily reliant on burial records, family members who were not buried at St. Martin's, or whose birth, death or marriage were otherwise difficult to trace, may have been over-looked. The extent of these omissions cannot be quantified.

In the accounts given below, a brief introduction to each vault is provided for orientation, followed by the results of the documentary research undertaken. More detailed descriptions of each vault are provided in the corresponding sections of Chapter 3. In Chapter 3 extensive use was made of the documentary research described in this chapter in order to identify – or attempt to identify – the individuals buried in the vaults. This was necessary in the effort to date and interpret the vaults. While some overlap and repetition is inevitable, the focus of this chapter is different, and its main aim is to reconstruct something of the lives of those buried in the vaults.

Documentary research is an open-ended process and with more time and resources it is probable that much more could have been uncovered about many of the individuals and families researched. Given the practical limitations the research had to be targeted. A minimum was to identify who the individuals were, who their immediate relatives were (who might also be buried in the vault), where they lived and worked, and what their profession was. At an early stage it was decided to focus in particular on Vault 5, the Warden family vault, because here the quality of the archaeological, anthropological and documentary evidence best converged. Of necessity, the other vaults have been dealt with in a more summary fashion.

Vault 10 – Chambered vault

This was a large 'chambered' vault comprising four vaulted chambers (labelled A-D) leading off from an access corridor. It was built in or shortly before 1785 in a passage that led through the houses and shops which surrounded the churchyard at that time and out into the Bull Ring. It is probably an example of a 'parish vault', built by the church. A charge of £10, a substantial sum, was made for the use of each of the four chambers.

These historical inferences concerning Vault 10 derive from an entry in The Town Book, a volume that contains minutes of parish meetings from 1676. An extract from The Town Book, reproduced in Bunce (1875, 50), quotes the minutes of a vestry meeting on June 28th 1785, when it was resolved that "Ten pounds be paid for every new vault situated in the Passage leading to the Bull Ring". Then follows a note: "In consequence of this resolution Mr Edmd Tompkins paid Ten Pounds."

The evidence that the 'vaults' to which the minutes refer should be identified with the four chambers of Vault 10 is discussed in detail in Chapter 3. The cartographic evidence in particular (Fig. 21) would appear conclusive.

Mr Tompkins would seem to have been planning ahead as he was about 18 when he paid for his vault. He lived locally and may have been associated with Tompkins & Co, who are listed in Holden's Triennial Directory (1908–11, Vol. 1) as makers of ink-stands, cruet and liquor-frames in Lichfield Street. On March 18th 1804 he married Sarah Brettal at the church (IGI) and died aged 57 on July 30th 1824 (NBI) when he was no doubt interred in 'his' vault.

It is possible, by a process of elimination, that the Tompkins' family vault may have been Chamber C, as three other families can be associated with the other three chambers.

Chamber A

Above the entrance to this chamber there was an inscription that read 'SmL + Wy9r' (see Chapter 3). There was only one burial in the chamber so despite the absence of a legible coffin plate this suggests that the burial was of one Samuel Wyer, who was buried at St. Martin's on 20th August 1802, having died the day before (NBI). Whilst this cannot be a definite identification, it is one of the earliest references we have to a vault burial.

Samuel Wyer had lived in the area for many years, having married Sarah Freeth at the church on 29th May 1787 (IGI). He is listed in Pye's Birmingham Directory as living in Old Meeting Street in 1788, and then 1791 he is described as a Coach Proprietor. Chapman's Birmingham Directory of 1801 describes him as the Master of the Dog Inn in Spiceal Street, a position he held until he died. In this capacity he must still have overseen coaches since the Dog Inn was a departure point for daily mail coaches to London and Shrewsbury. The Birmingham Post coach arrived from London every day at 10am and departed again at 7pm. The Stourbridge and Dudley coach used the inn as a pick up point every Tuesday, Thursday and Saturday.

Chamber B

This chamber had an 'R' inscribed over the entrance in a similar manner to the inscription over Chamber A. There were six adult burials in the chamber. The *depositum* associated with one of these (HB 382) was partially legible and read 'Daniel Rowlin... died 30th March....'. Investigations into contemporary obituaries in *Aris's Gazette* suggested that this was Daniel Rowlinson of Smallbrook Street who died on 30th March 1801, the earliest confirmed burial in a vault in St. Martin's churchyard.

At the time of his death he was listed in Chapman's Birmingham Directory (1801) as trading as a brass and cockfounder with his son. The business had been established since as least 1788, and he had also been described as a candlestick-maker. His wife, Ann Lewis, whom he married in the church on 16th January 1772 (IGI), carried on this role until her death on 31st January 1817 (AG), and his son maintained the family tradition of making brass candlesticks until his death on 19th June 1831 (AG). The skeletal analysis lists another burial in the chamber, HB 376, as an 'old adult female'. This was perhaps Daniel's wife Ann. HB 372 is listed as a 'middle adult male', and this may be Daniel's son John, who was 56 when he died in 1831 (AG).

This last burial was wearing a gold mourning ring inscribed 'Mr THOS. MARTIN DIED 13 SEP 1808 AGED 53' (Fig.135, colour; see Bevan, this volume, Chapter 5). The ring does not identify the burial but commemorates a relation or friend. Mourning rings were popular in the 18th and 19th centuries, when they were commissioned in batches and given out at funerals as a form of commemoration and remembrance. As to the identity of Mr Martin, there is no record of his death in the St. Martin's parish burial records or the National Burial Index, nor of his birth or death in the International Genealogical Index. The latter two sources cannot be considered completely comprehensive but they are the only national sources available. Chapman's Birmingham Directory (1801) lists two Thomas Martins, one a boot and shoe maker living at 94 Bull Street and the other a caster living on Little Charles Street, but neither can be linked to the ring.

There are two other possible female adults in the chamber unaccounted for. A Daniel Taylor Rowlinson was also listed in the obituaries in *Aris's Gazette* and could have been another son. However, his death was registered in Geneva where he may have gone to try and cure the consumption that he died of, so it is unlikely that his body was returned to the family vault.

Chamber C

There were four adult burials in this chamber but there was no information available for research. However it is possible, as noted above, that this chamber was the vault of the Tompkins family. Edmund Tompkins and his wife Sarah may have been two of the burials.

Chamber D

This chamber contained nine burials, six adult and three children. One coffin plate associated with HB 543 was partially legible and read '[J]ames Cockl... Died Feby 20th 18?3 Aged 83 Years' The National Burial Index records a James Cockle, aged 83, who was buried at St. Martin's on 25th February 1833, five days after his death. He had married Mary Chapman at the church on 28th October 1781 (IGI) and is listed in Holden's Triennial Directory (1809-11, Vol. 2) as a leatherdresser in Bradford Street. Mary died in 1822 at the age of 65 and is likely also to have been buried in the chamber.

Research using the National Burial Index, the International Genealogical Index and the parish burial records for St. Martin's revealed the names of six children of James and Mary, five daughters and a son, who were also buried in St. Martin's churchyard. This information is shown in Table 6, Chapter 3. Although the age at death of the children is not given, the dates of their deaths suggest, when compared to the date of James and Mary's marriage, that few if any will have reached adulthood. That they were still infants or children at the time of death is also indicated by them being described in the burial records as 'son of James and Mary' or 'daughter or James and Mary', a usage usually reserved for children. As there were only three child burials identified in the chamber, and no infants, not all of the children appear to have been buried in the vault (it is most likely that those dying very young would be the ones buried elsewhere). The two children with the latest burial dates (Catherine d.1805 and Caroline d.1807), who may have been the oldest, were both buried in a vault however, as the burial register specifically records this.

Vault 23 – Ainsworth family

This family vault was located towards the northwestern corner of the graveyard, against the boundary wall. It was probably built by Isaac Ainsworth, perhaps in partnership with two of his brothers, Benjamin Ainsworth and John M. Ainsworth, in 1810–11 (Chapter 3). It contained nine burials on three levels. The two burials in the middle level were identifiable from legible *deposita*. They were Isaac Ainsworth (HB 702), who died on 11th December 1837 aged 80, and Hannah Ainsworth (HB 691), who died on 1st January 1827 aged 68.

Isaac and Hannah Ainsworth, a married couple, lived on St. Martin's Lane, one of the boundary roads around the church, where they had married on 17th February 1782 (IGI). Hannah had moved to the town from Inkberrow in Worcestershire, where she was born in 1757 or 1759. Isaac was a saddler, a profession that was vital at this time to maintain the large number of horse drawn

carts and carriages that formed part of daily life (Fig. 136). By the 1840s Birmingham had the second largest concentration of saddlers and harness makers in the country, after London (Thomson 1976, 60–81). It has been suggested that the number of carts, vans and wagons grew by 75%, to over 200,000 between 1811 and 1851, and the number of horses to two million nationwide, resulting in a huge potential market for saddlery and associated trades (*ibid.*). There were many leatherworking establishments in the streets around St. Martin's, usually small domestic workshops employing two or three people to supply local demand. Some made just saddles, while other more specialist shops made whips, whip thongs and collars.

It is possible, since they lived and worked at the same address, that Hannah and other family members contributed to the business, since the Second Report of the Children's Employment Commission (1843) records that women and children were often employed to cut, stitch and plait the leather. However, the fact that the family could afford burial in a vault, and Hannah was buried in what must have been an expensive coffin (Chapter 3), suggests that the Ainsworth's business was one of the larger establishments and Hannah may not have had to

Fig. 136: A 19th-century saddler at work.

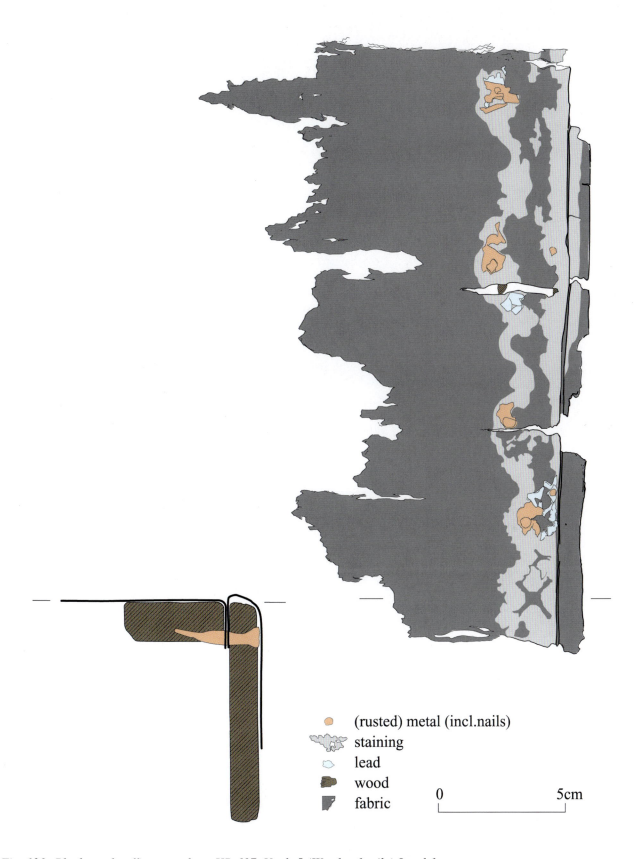

(rusted) metal (incl.nails)
staining
lead
wood
fabric

0   5cm

Fig. 120: Black wool coffin cover from HB 607, Vault 5 (Warden family) Level 1.

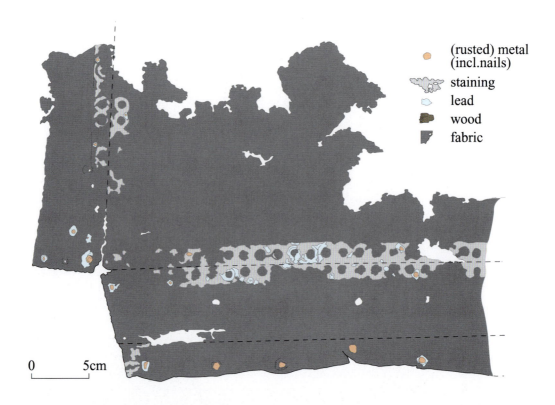

Fig. 121: Black wool coffin cover from HB 382, Daniel Rowlinson (d.1801), Vault 10B.

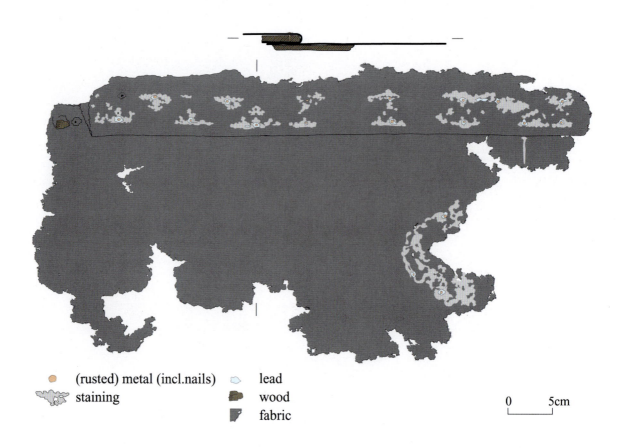

Fig. 122: Black wool coffin cover from HB 383, Vault 10C.

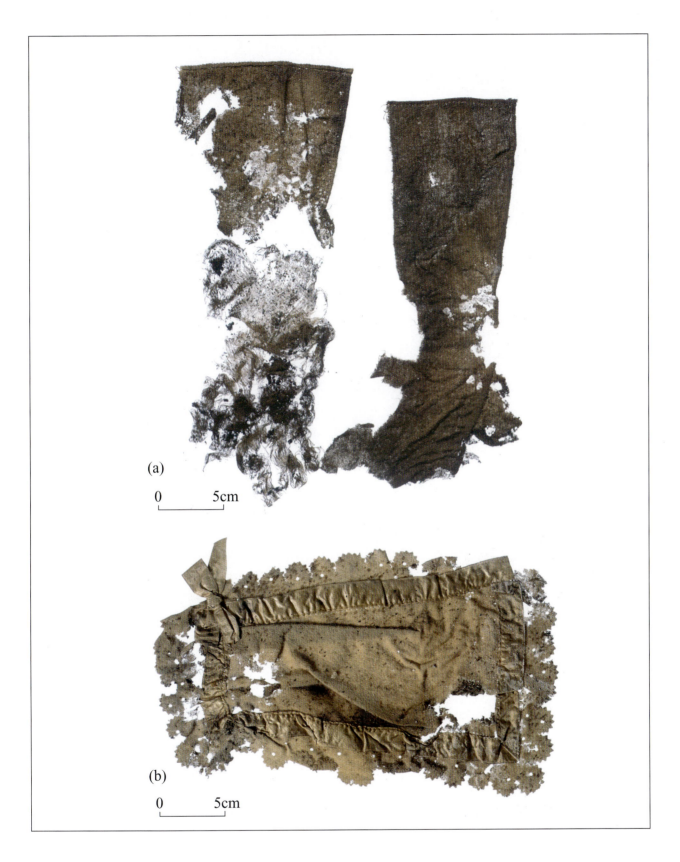

Fig. 128: Wool burial garments: (a) a seamed and hemmed wool textile from HB 304, Vault 5 (Warden family) Level 4; (b) one of a pair of wool and silk items, possibly sleeve ornaments, from child burial HB 321, Vault 5 (Warden family) Level 4.

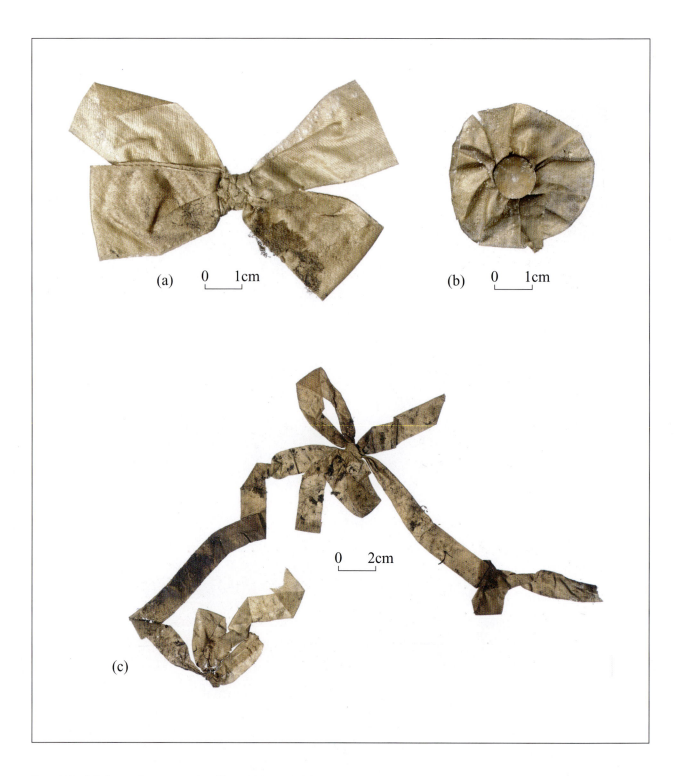

(a) 0 1cm

(b) 0 1cm

(c) 0 2cm

Fig. 129: Silk bows, buttons and ruffles, all from child burial HB 321, Vault 5 (Warden family) Level 4: (a) ornamental bow; (b) covered button rosette; (c) festoon of tied ribbon bows.

Fig. 131: Silk ribbons from burials in vaults: (a) HB 297, Ann Maria Browett (d.1894), Vault 5 (Warden family) Level 4, 5-end satin 14mm wide; (b) HB 304, Vault 5 (Warden family) Level 4, 5-end satin 18mm wide; (c) HB 262, brick-lined grave V19, tabby 25mm wide; (d) HB 691, Hannah Ainsworth (d.1827), Vault 23 (Ainsworth family) Level 2, gauze ribbon; (e) HB 692, Vault 23 (Ainsworth family) Level 3, gauze ribbon; (f) HB 698, child, Vault 23 (Ainsworth family) Level 1, gauze ribbon.

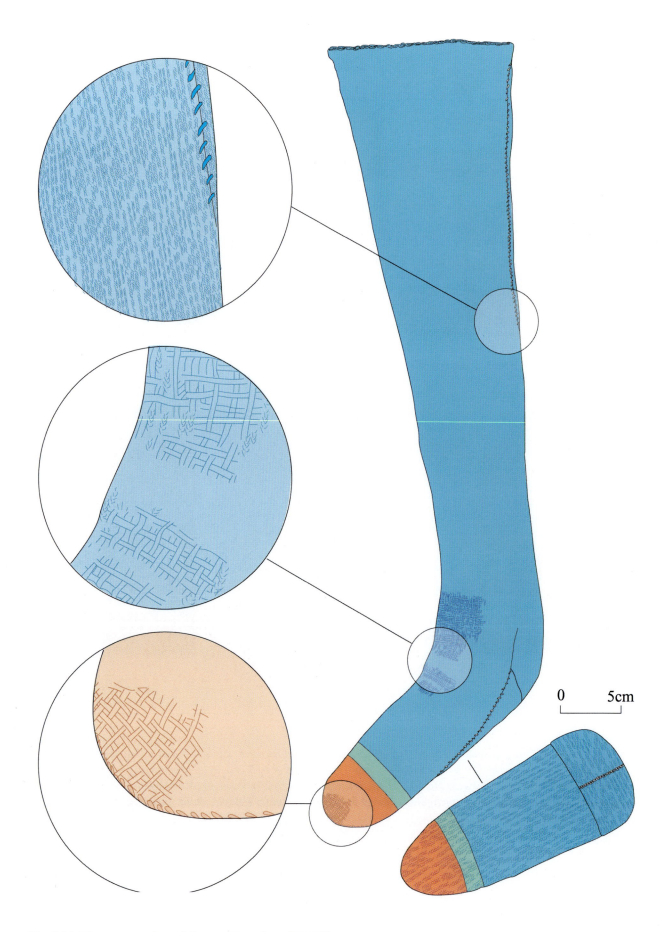

Fig. 134: The construction of the stockings from HB 792.

Fig. 135: Jewellery: (a) gold mourning ring, HB 372, Vault 10C (SF26); (b) gold wedding ring, HB 297, Ann Maria Browett (d.1894), Vault 5 (Warden family) Level 4 (SF17); (c) copper alloy ring, HB 373, earth-cut grave (SF27); (d) brooch in form of cupid's arrow, unstratified (SF41); (e) necklace comprising pink cut-glass bead in the shape of a rose with four pink beads attached, HB 190, child, brick-lined grave V03 (SF5).

Fig 153: Soldiers of the 6th or Royal 1st Warwickshire Regiment of Foot in 1838, shortly after the death of Captain Adjutant Benjamin Robinson.

Fig 154: The colours of the 6th or Royal 1st Warwickshire Regiment of Foot. The colours bear the names of important campaigns or battles, including 'Peninsula' and 'Corunna' in which Benjamin Robinson participated.

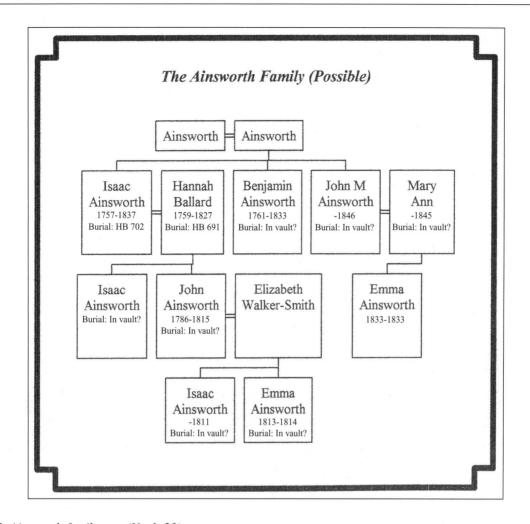

Fig. 137: Ainsworth family tree (Vault 23).

work. In the bell room at St. Martin's a plaque on the wall lists an Isaac Ainsworth as a churchwarden in 1820. From the date, this could be either Isaac or one of his sons, also called Isaac, but it serves to illustrate the close ties the family evidently had with the church.

Using various documentary sources (NBI, IGI and obituaries) together with the skeletal evidence it is possible to provide tentative identifications of the remaining individuals in the vault (Fig. 137). The two adult burials in the lowest level (HB 722 and HB 723) could be Isaac and John, sons of Isaac and Hannah, who died aged 28 and 29 respectively. Isaac was also a saddler and is listed in the obituaries as living with his parents, but in the National Burial Index as living on nearby Moseley Street. His brother John was a whipmaker in Digbeth who had married Elizabeth Walker Smith at the church on 3rd August 1808 (IGI). In 1812 John is listed as living at the Moat, the ancient seat of the de Birmingham lords but by then occupied by manufacturers and their premises (Watts 1980, 25). John and Elizabeth had two children, Isaac and Emma, who died very young and could be the two child burials in the lowest level of the vault (HB 697 and HB 698).

On the top level of the vault, two of the three later burials, all adults, could be John M. Ainsworth, who died in 1845, and his wife Mary Ann, who died in 1846. The third burial could Benjamin Ainsworth who died in 1833 aged 72. The relationship of John and Benjamin to Isaac (senior) is not known for certain, but it is likely that they were his brothers.

Vault 18 – Home family

This vault was located near to the northern churchyard wall and was probably built for John Home in the period 1810–1816 (Chapter 3). Although of average size it contained only four burials, all on the floor, comprising two adults and two children. The adult coffins and their brass *deposita* were particularly well preserved. These two adults were John Home (HB 575), who died on 27th October 1828 aged 50, and Frances Home (HB 576), who died on 20th November 1833 aged 53.

John Home was a 'chemist and apothecary' or 'chemist and druggist' from 1803 to 1825. For the majority of this time his place of business was 70 High Street, in the centre of the town, although briefly, in 1816, he moved to

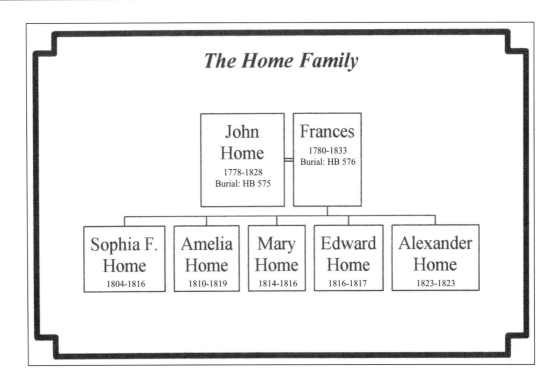

Fig. 138: Home family tree (Vault 18).

Union Street, before returning to High Street in 1818. It is possible that the Homes lived above the shop in the High Street but subsequently moved to the Bristol Road, where Frances lived alone after her husband died (HTD 1809-11; CBD 1803-1808; WW 1821-1830).

Their deaths are both listed in *Aris's Gazette*, together with two of their children, Sophia Frances, aged 12 when she died on 31st December 1816 and Edward who died at only 8 months old on 15th March the following year. The National Burial Index shows that John and Mary also lost Mary, aged 1 year 7 months on 8th May 1816, Amelia, aged 9 on 23rd February 1819 and Alexander, aged 5 months on 12th December 1823. Their family life vividly illustrates the reality of high child mortality in early 19th century Birmingham; five of John and Frances Home's children did not survive beyond 12 years (Fig. 138).

The two child burials in the vault (HB 552 and HB 901) were separated from the adult burials by a brick dividing wall. From the estimated ages of the skeletons provided by anthropological analysis it is likely that these were Sophia Frances and Amelia respectively.

The local chemist and druggist provided a valuable service in the community since many people could not afford to visit the doctors.. The profession had evolved during the 18th century from the chemist who dealt with chemicals, and the druggist, who used drugs of animal and vegetable origin (Jackson 1981, 3). An Act of Parliament in 1815 gave them the right to buy, compound and sell drugs and medicines, resulting in the establishment of chemist and druggists, or apothecaries, serving the needs of the growing parish.

Vault 9 – Jenkins family

This vault was the largest of the family vaults at St. Martin's, situated close to the northern boundary wall of the churchyard. It was built for William Jenkins between 1810 and 1816 (Chapter 3). The vault contained eleven burials, eight adults and three infants, arranged on two levels. However, as it was decided that the vault could be preserved intact only the infant burials were analysed anthropologically as their lead coffins had been damaged. The remaining coffins were recorded *in situ*.

There were six legible coffin plates amongst them, upon which the documentary research on the Jenkins family was based (Table 128).

These plates were the most legible found in the vaults and indeed the one that related to Mary Jenkins, although detached from its coffin, contained more information than any of the others from the churchyard.

It stated that this was

Mary Jenkins,
wife of William Walker Jenkins
late of Digbeth House
and second daughter of Thomas and Mary Scudamore
late of Spiceal Street
Birmingham
Born 1788
Died April 20th 1861.

Mary had lived near the church all her life, coming from a family of cutlers in Spiceal Street (HTD 1809-1811, Vol. 2). On 3rd January 1809 she married William Walker Jenkins, a brassfounder from Digbeth, at the

Burial	Name	Age	Date of birth	Date of death
HB 861	Vernon Jenkins	3 mths	-	14th November 1827
N/A	Edmund Jenkins	25	-	2nd January 1848
N/A	Mary Jenkins	73	1788	20th April 1861
N/A	Leoline Jenkins	37	-	21st March 1862
N/A	Leonard Jenkins	59	-	19th November 1877
N/A	Helen Jenkins	72	-	25th April 1882

Table 128: Vault 9, burials identified from coffin plates.

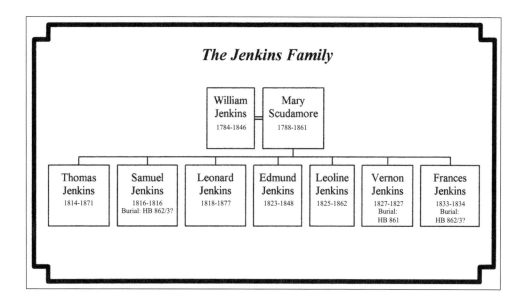

Fig. 139: Jenkins family tree (Vault 9).

church. It is not known where they started their married life but by 1816 on the death of their son Samuel, aged 11 months, they were listed in the parish records as living at Lombard House, Deritend. They later moved to Digbeth House, which may have been the home of William's parents.

In the 1812 Wrightson and Webb Directory, William's father (also called William) is described as a brassfounder in Digbeth, so it would seem that his son William Walker followed the family trade. It is not known when the business began but it is likely that its origins were relatively modest, centred initially on a fairly small workshop in Digbeth where brass objects were produced. Theirs may have been one of many similar establishments in the area that produced the small 'toys' (objects of all kinds) that Birmingham was renowned for. By the 1830s the skilled workforce together with the enterprise of men such as William Jenkins had made Birmingham the centre of the brass industry in the country. As William's company grew, larger premises were required, so he moved his business to Summer Row near Broad Street (WW 1846) where there was space for expansion and the nearby canals made transportation of raw materials

quicker and cheaper. An indication of the size of his business can be gained from a deposition he made to the Factory Enquiry Commission in 1833, recorded in the British Parliamentary Papers. Here it is stated that his brassfoundry utilised mechanical power in the form of a 100 horse-power steam engine (a large engine) and employed 250 people. The same report provided an insight into the working conditions of the day in an establishment that must have been one of the larger ones in the town (see Chapter 7).

William and Mary had at least five sons and two daughters, but like many contemporaries suffered the misfortune to lose three children under one year old (Fig. 139). There were three infant burials in the vault. One *depositum* confirmed the identity of Vernon (HB 861), and it is likely that Samuel, mentioned above, and a daughter Frances, who died in 1834 aged 10 months, were the other two burials (HB 862 and HB 863).

As the family became more prosperous they, like others, moved away from the crowded streets and polluted atmosphere of the town and choose to live at Elsecar House in Water Orton, a small village nearby (AG). William died in 1846 aged 62 and is almost certainly one of the unidentified adult burials in the vault. Mary's will informs us that in her later years, possibly after William had died, she moved to Clent Cottage in the same village but went back to Elsecar House to be nursed by her family up to her death.

William and Mary's other sons lived longer, although Edmund, whose coffin was identified, was only 25 when he died in 1848. As a contemporary advertisement shows, Thomas and Leonard became successful wire manufacturers in the town (Fig. 140). The manufacture of steel wire grew dramatically in mid century with the number of wire workers increasing from 380 in 1841 to 2,630 in 1871 (Skipp 1983, 57); this may be partly attributed to the fact that it was one of the most extensively mechanised trades in the town. The industry supplied the piano wire trade, the needle and fish hook industry in nearby Redditch, and heavier steel wires which were used for engineering, machinery, colliery winding ropes and ships' rigging (*ibid*).

The coffin of Leonard, who died on November 24th 1877 aged 59, was amongst those identified in the vault. It is likely that Thomas, who died on October 3rd 1871 aged 57, occupied one of the unidentified coffins.

Leoline, who died on March 21st 1862 aged 37, and whose coffin was identified in the vault, was a nailmaker who traded from 208/209 Ashted Row (Kelly's Directory 1861). However his obituary in the *Aris's Gazette* states that he later lived in Milton, Yorkshire, but was at his brother's house in Water Orton when he died. This is a similar scenario to that of the Haines and Warden families (below), where one of the sons died elsewhere and was then brought back to be buried in the family vault. In this case Leoline may have come home to die amongst his family, so he too could be laid to rest in the vault.

The coffin of Helen Jenkins was one of those identified in the vault. She was 72 when she died in 1882 and may have been one of William and Mary's daughters-in-law. The identity of the remaining burial in the vault remains unknown.

The Jenkins family is an example of a successful Birmingham family who, like the Wardens, made their money in the metal-related industries in the town. As they became increasingly prosperous they moved away from their place of work to more pleasant and affluent surroundings, but the family still retained their loyalty to St. Martin's.

Vault 5 – Warden/Browett families

Vault 5 was a standard-sized family vault situated to the north of the church in the 'old' part of the churchyard. Its construction must have involved the disturbance of several earlier burials. It was built for Joseph Warden at some time in the period 1812 to 1842 (Chapter 3). There was a total of 14 burials in the vault – twelve adults, an adolescent and a child – arranged on four levels. Five of those buried in the vault were identified from *deposita* (Table 129).

There was also a memorial stone found near the vault and presumably associated with it. The stone commemorated Sophia Warden 'second wife of late Joseph', who died in 1860 aged 68, and Edwin Warden, 'son of Joseph and Ann Maria' who died in 1861 aged 41.

The fact that there appeared to be two distinct family groups in the vault initially seemed unusual since investigation of the other vaults had suggested that a vault would be purchased for one family's use only. However, the documentary research revealed that the

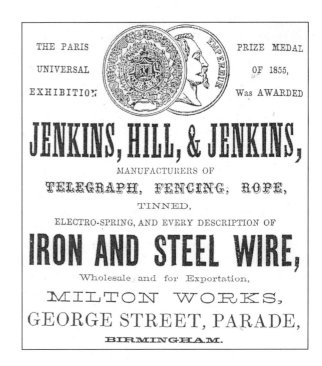

Fig. 140: Advertisement for the firm of Jenkins, Hill & Jenkins.

Burial	Name	Age	Date of death
HB 574	Ann Maria Warden	52	17th February 184?
HB 587	George Warden	33	26th November 1863
HB 598	Sarah Emma Warden	47	14th December 1866
HB 336	A(lfred) Browett	-	186?
HB 297	Ann Maria Browett	81	8th April 1894

Table 129: Vault 5, individuals identified from coffin plates.

Wardens and the Browetts were related by marriage, and various branches of the two families remained close on a business and personal level throughout most of the 19th century. This explained why some of them were buried together in the same vault.

It would appear that in the late 18th century members of both the Warden and Browett families moved from small villages in the Coventry area to Birmingham. This is an illustration of the migration that occurred at that time as people moved from rural communities into the expanding industrial centres. Both families had their origins in small shops and as they became more prosperous they and their descendents diversified into related industries in the town. They could both be considered to be part of the newly emerging middle classes that aspired to better themselves as their businesses grew. This was clearly illustrated by their place of residence that changed from 'living over the shop' to the more fashionable suburbs of Edgbaston, and even the acquisition of property in the developing spa town of Leamington.

The Warden family

Joseph Warden, the central figure in the family tree (Fig. 141), came from Bulkington, to the north east of Coventry. He was born in 1787 to Joseph Warden and Ann Whetstone, who had married in 1772. Joseph moved to Birmingham and subsequently married Ann Maria Marston (HB 574) on April 28th 1812 (IGI). On the birth of their first daughter, Ann Maria, in 1813 Joseph was described in the parish records as an 'Ironmonger'.

In the early 19th century an ironmonger's shop was a vital part of the community, supplying a huge variety of goods from screws and latches to lighting and heating fixtures, cooking appliances, cycles and sports goods (Meadows 2000, 6–7). They often had workshops on the same premises as the shop, where some manufacturing and repair of goods would take place. Consequently tinware, copper and japanned ware, along with many small household items like saucepans and kettles, may have been produced. In some shops the manufacturing aspect of the business became more important. It would seem that Joseph progressed from being a shopkeeper because in 1816 he is described in the Commercial Directory of Birmingham as an 'ironmaster' trading as Warden & Marston, at 14 Smallbrook Street. This was apparently a partnership between Joseph and his wife's family, which was initially described as 'iron merchants', but changed shortly afterwards to 'iron and steel merchants' (WW 1821). In 1829 Joseph is listed as the sole trader (WW 1829), and from 1835 the description included tin plating and the firm had business premises at 5 & 6 Edgbaston Street in addition to Smallbrook Street (PD 1835, Part II). This illustrates diversification and expansion as Joseph adapted to the changing market that occurred as industrialisation in the town increased. In 1842, the business name changed to 'Joseph Warden & Son' to include William (PD 1842) and in 1846 it was

'Joseph Warden & Sons', as Thomas joined the family firm (WW 1846; Fig. 142). The family firm was further strengthened in 1854 as sons Joseph and Thomas formed a partnership with Benjamin Williams (Birmingham Archives, Lee Crowder 562). This lasted for 21 years at the Oak Farm Ironworks, illustrating something of the enduring quality of a firm that started as an ironmonger's shop at the beginning of the century.

While Joseph's businesses were prospering, he and his wife brought up twelve children. To accommodate this growing family and reflect his increasing wealth, Joseph and his wife first moved to 87 Bristol Road (Triennial Birmingham Directory 1825) and then to a terraced house at 169 Bristol Road (Fig. 143) (WW 1846), before finally moving to a large detached house at 14 Wellington Road, Edgbaston (Fig. 144) (History and General Directory of Borough of Birmingham 1849). A family of twelve children would be considered unusual nowadays but in the early 19th century infant mortality was high and methods of contraception were still scarce and often unreliable. Condoms were available but were used mainly by prostitutes as prevention against venereal disease, so the more 'respectable' members of society were reluctant to be associated with them (Bartley 1996, 20–21). The fact that all twelve children survived to adulthood was remarkable for this period.

After Ann Maria died in 1842, aged 52, Joseph married Sophia (probably HB 607 in the vault), who lived with him at Wellington Road until his death on 25th January 1856 aged 68. Sophia died four years later, in 1860, also aged 68.

Joseph had during his lifetime risen from running a small ironmonger's shop quite close to St. Martin's Church in Smallbrook Street, to owning a large iron workshop in Edgbaston Street, nail shops in Gloucester Street and other property in the town. He remained the astute businessman all his life and on 15th January 1849 drew up a detailed will, held in the Birmingham Archives (Lee Crowder 564), in which he left very specific instructions about how his estate should be divided up after his death. The trustees were to be his sons, Thomas and William. To his second wife, Sophia, he left "the use of my household furniture, plate, linen, china and all other household effects during her widowhood". An inventory of all these goods had to be drawn up after his death and signed by Sophia and the trustees. This privilege was only until "her decease or second marriage, whichever event shall first happen", then the goods would be sold and converted into capital for his estate. His share of the business in Edgbaston Street was to be valued and then offered to his sons and partners, William and Thomas. The rest of the estate was divided between the twelve children, with additional bequests of £50 to two nephews, and £19 19s to his three sisters. He must have had some doubts about the ability of his son James to look after his money since he stated that the legacy left to him and his future wife and children should cease if he

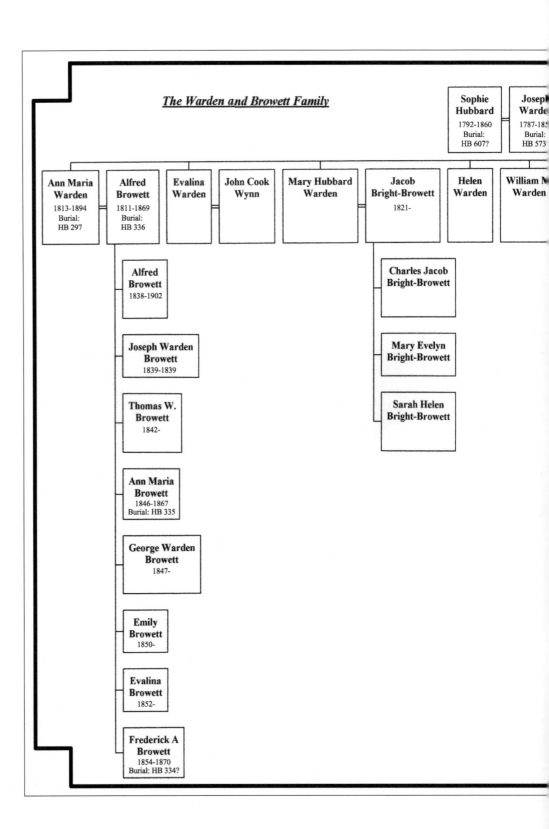

Fig. 141: Warden and Browett family tree (Vault 5).

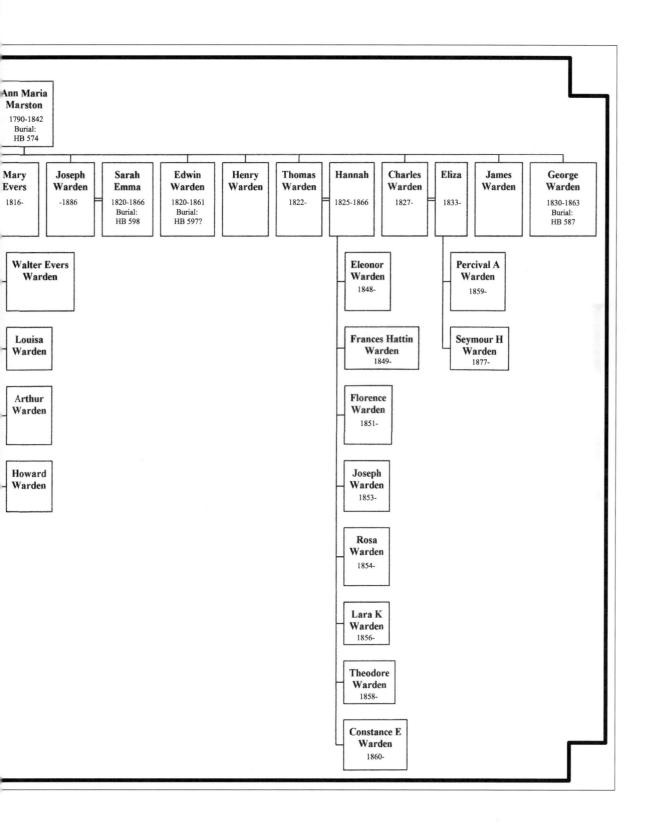

became "bankrupt or insolvent". If this should happen, he "empowered the Trustees at their discretion to transfer to James more money in the future if he shall change his habits and course of his life".

The bequest to his daughter Helen was to be kept until she reached the age of majority, and George, the youngest son, had his money invested until he reached the age of 22, to pay for his maintenance, support, clothing and education. George later went on to study at Worcester College, Oxford.

Subsequently, various codicils were issued to alter the will, the first of which revoked Edwin's legacy and

Fig. 142: Advertisement for the firm of Joseph Warden & Sons.

Fig. 143: Joseph Warden's house on the Bristol Road.

Fig. 144: Joseph Warden's house on Wellington Road, Edgbaston.

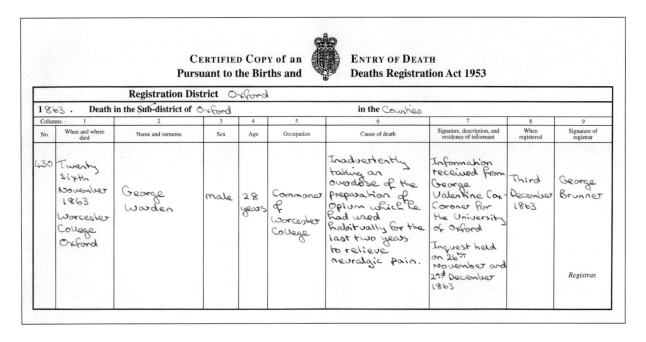

Fig. 145: George Warden's death certificate.

substituted it with a single bequest of £250. Alfred Browett, Joseph's son-in-law, also became one of the trustees. No explanation is given for these changes, but it is clear that the behaviour of some of Joseph's sons did not always please him, and that he looked upon his son-in-law favourably – Alfred was later to be buried in the Warden family vault.

In 1850 another codicil made an additional bequest dividing a piece of land in the Parish of St. Martin's between sons James and Joseph and his brother-in-law Edward Penn. This land comprised a factory on Gas Street, a foundry and some shops that had also been used as a wharf, another indication of Joseph Warden's wealth and status in the parish. This codicil also contained a similar proviso to that in the original will, to the effect that if James did not manage his money properly the bequest would lapse.

Amongst the male children, William and Thomas joined the family firm. However, by 1851, William must have died since in the 1851 Census his wife Mary is described as 'head of the household and iron merchant', an interesting designation for a woman at this time, suggesting that she had taken over her husband's role.

The younger Joseph Warden's career mirrored his father's, in that he too began life as an ironmonger and then diversified. In 1839, his business was based at 3 St. Martin's Lane but by 1842 it had developed into a spring, axle and cart arm manufactory (PD 1842). By 1845 he was described as an agricultural implement maker at 25 Jamaica Row, Edgbaston Street (PD 1845). However, just a year later in 1846, in addition to the above he was now making coach and cart axletrees, springs, hames, chains and shovels (WW 1846). In 1864 Joseph's business had

moved to 1 High Street, Deritend and by 1871 he was listed as having two premises on Cheapside and Balsall Street.

Joseph married Sarah Emma Fortesene (HB 598) in 1844 at St. Philip's Church (IGI), and according to the 1851 Census lived first in Hob Lane, before moving to Green Lane, Small Heath (Corporation Directory of Birmingham 1861, Pt. 1). His will, held in the Birmingham Archives, shows that afterwards they moved to 80 Francis Road, Edgbaston.

Edwin Warden (probably HB 597 in the vault) was a builder and was listed in the Post Office Directory of Birmingham (1845) as living at 169 Bristol Road, the home of his father, for a while, with business premises in Benacre Street. He later moved to 3 Mary Street (Corporation Directory of Birmingham 1861). As we have seen, Edwin was included in his father's will but a later codicil changed the bequest.

George Warden (HB 587), Joseph and Ann Maria's last child, was unusual in that when he died in 1863, aged 33, he was not in trade but was studying at Worcester College, Oxford, as his death certificate reveals (Fig. 145). He was originally admitted to the University at Magdalen Hall on 4th June 1861 (Alumni Oxonienses) but at some point changed to Worcester College. In 1863 the University Calendar lists him amongst the 51 Commoners of the college.

George's death certificate states that he died from "inadvertently taking an overdose of the preparation of opium which he had used habitually for the last two years to relieve neuralgic pain". This conclusion was the result of the two post-mortem examinations carried out by George Valentine Cox, the University of Oxford Coroner. The

Fig. 146: Portrait of Charles Warden.

skull of George Warden preserved evidence of the cranial autopsy performed (see Chapter 4). The taking of opium was common practice at the time. An earlier student at Worcester College, the essayist Thomas de Quincey, also took opium, both as a remedy for neuralgia and because "here was the secret of happiness about which philosophers had disputed for so many ages" (Gribble 1910, 297).

Joseph and Ann Maria's remaining sons were Henry, of whom nothing is known, James, who was an iron merchant at 89 Snow Hill (Corporation Directory of Birmingham 1861, Pt. 1), and Charles, who became a surgeon (Fig. 146). The 1881 Census reveals that Charles then lived with his wife and children at 44 Calthorpe Road, Edgbaston, and in 1894, in his official capacity, he signed the death certificate of his sister, Ann Maria Browett. It is noteworthy that Joseph's youngest sons, George and Charles, did not go into trade but pursued academic and professional careers.

The Browett family

The connection between the Warden and Browett families began when two of Joseph and Ann Maria's daughters married into the Browett family.

Ann Maria, the eldest daughter, married Alfred Browett in 1836 (parish records). He was the son of William Browett, who ran a chandler's shop in Smallbrook Street, close to where Joseph Warden's ironmonger's shop was situated (WW 1835).

Ann Maria Browett

Ann Maria (HB 297) was born in February 1813 to Joseph and Ann Maria Warden, who then lived on Bristol Street (parish records). She was named after her mother, suggesting that she was their first daughter and, 33 years later, was to follow the same tradition and call her own first daughter by the same name.

On 26th July 1836, Ann Maria married Alfred Browett (HB 336), the son of William Browett, who was a draper and had moved from Stoke, a small village in the Coventry area (census). Alfred worked with his father in a shop at 47 Smallbrook Street. This was described as a 'grocer, tea dealer and chandler' (WW 1833). Over the ensuing years this description varied. In 1842, the business is listed as a 'chymist and druggist' in Jamaica Row (PD); in 1849 the History and General Directory of the Borough records that the business returned to Smallbrook Street, with the added description of 'cheesemonger and maltster'. This shop, like the ironmonger's that Ann Maria grew up in, was situated close to St. Martin's in an area of small crowded streets, full of a variety of shops. These shops included butcher's, nail maker's, umbrella maker's and jeweller's, all very close to the markets from where supplies would have been readily available. Many shops also had the facility for small-scale manufacturing. Joseph Warden may have had a small forge and foundry in his ironmongers; Alfred may have had facilities for processing cheese. However, Alfred was described primarily as a 'tallow chandler' and would also have made candles and soap, both vital commodities in the Victorian household. He would, therefore, have been subject to the same taxes and excise restrictions as a soap boiler, who had to inform the excise officers twenty-four hours before making soap (Walters 2000, 211, 225).

It is impossible to know whether Ann Maria helped Alfred in the shop. However, women were more actively engaged in the retail trade than any other (Davidoff & Hall 1987, 304), so it may have been a possibility at the beginning of their married life.

In 1849 the History and General Directory of the Borough shows that William Browett's name has disappeared from the shop title. This suggests that either he had died or had retired from the business, leaving his son in charge. The family may have lived over the shop during the first part of their married life, as the lock-up shop was still unusual in 1850 (Alexander 1970, 11). However, in the 1851 Census they are listed as living on Bristol Road, once again illustrating the growing trend to move away from the place of work into nearby suburbs.

Also in the 1851 Census, Alfred and Ann Maria are listed as having five children. Alfred, aged 13, and

Thomas, aged 9, are described as 'scholars', while George, aged 4, is listed as a 'scholar at home'. In contrast young Ann Maria, aged 5, has no such description.

The family employed a nursemaid and cook, who were born in Westbury on Severn and Bromsgrove respectively. This again illustrates the migration which was occurring at the time, as people moved from rural areas into the town to find employment. In Birmingham, as nationally, domestic service was by far the largest occupation, and as the 1851 Census shows employed double the number of people to any other form of employment (Hopkins 1998, 53). The family's ability to employ two servants also gives some indication of their level of income.

Further proof of this financial stability is indicated in the Corporation Directory of 1861 (Pt. 1), where although Alfred is still described as a 'tallow chandler' at 47 Smallbrook Street, he is now listed as living at 9 Yew Tree Road in the nearby suburb of Edgbaston (Fig. 147). The two eldest boys are now at Commercial College and the 15 year-old daughter (Ann Maria) and the 14 year-old son (George) are described as 'scholars'. There are now three other children, Emily, aged 11, Evalina, aged 9, and Frederick, aged 7. The family still had help in the house with two domestic servants, aged 16 and 19. By this time the couple had seven surviving children (1861 Census), Joseph having died in 1839, aged 3 months. The move to Yew Tree Road illustrates the aspiration of many people at that time to move away from their place of business and live in a house with a garden, not far away from but, "insulated from all view of the town and its annoyances" (Davidoff & Hall 1987, 17).

The house the Browetts lived in was not one of the biggest in Edgbaston but had a garden back and front and was close to neighbouring streets where the more affluent Birmingham families lived, in rather larger properties. Although other areas developed, Edgbaston was the most popular because it overlooked the countryside and was only 10 minutes carriage drive – or a brisk walk – away from the town centre (Davidoff & Hall 1987, 368). It was described by H. H. Horton in a poem about Birmingham thus:

See Edgbaston, the bed of prosperous trade,
Where they recline who have their fortunes made (*ibid*).

In 1867, Ann Maria's daughter, her namesake, died. On 16th March 1869 her husband Alfred (HB 336) died at home after being ill for a month, according to his death certificate, with Phthisis, a term used at the time for pulmonary tuberculosis (Johnstone 1999, 1062). DNA analysis has confirmed that he suffered from tuberculosis (see Chapter 4). He had probably worked long hours in the shop all his life. Opening times varied but often they stayed open 12 to 16 hours per day and longer on Fridays and Saturdays. Hours were extended in the summer and those shops catering for the working classes, as Alfred's would have done, would also have been open longer. The

shop may have been small and badly ventilated, all of which could have contributed to the cause of Alfred's death (Alexander 1970, 191); despite a relatively high standard of living, the fear of fever, cholera and consumption (tuberculosis) was ever present in the growing industrial cities (Davidoff & Hall 1987, 22).

It would seem that none of Alfred's sons took over the shop since the eldest, also called Alfred, became a manufacturer in Dean Street, as his will shows, and George and Thomas became 'coal and brick manufacturers' in the town (1881 Census). The family still lived in Yew Tree Road in 1870, but sometime after Frederick (possibly HB 334 in the vault) died there on 16th September, aged 16, they moved. By 1881 Ann Maria was living in a house in Greenfield Crescent, Edgbaston, where she and her daughter Evalina are listed in the 1881 Census as lodgers, with an income from a house in Leamington.

By 1894, Ann Maria had moved again, to 185 Bristol Road (Fig. 148). This is near to where she had lived as a child, and she died there on 8th April, aged 81. On her death certificate, her death was attributed to chronic bronchitis, that she had suffered from for some years, and senile decay. At the time of her death she still had the leasehold of a property in Leamington, three of her sons were businessmen in the town, her daughters Emily and Evalina were married and three of her children had pre-deceased her. She was buried in a vault at St. Martin's along with other members of the Browett and Warden families that had been first united by her marriage to Alfred 58 years before, in 1836. Ann Maria (HB 297) was buried wearing what was perhaps a somewhat out of date dress (Walton Rogers, this volume, Chapter 5), her wedding ring (Bevan, this volume, Chapter 5) and false teeth (Hancocks, this volume, Chapter 4). Stable isotope analysis of her hair (Richards, this volume, Chapter 4) suggests that she may have been on a non-meat diet for the last months of her life.

The Bright Browett family

Mary, Joseph and Ann Maria Warden's third daughter, married Jacob Bright Browett, a draper, who was probably the son of William and Ann, a draper and his wife from Stoke, a village to the east of Coventry. William and Ann were also the parents of Alfred, who had married the Ann Maria just described in the previous section, so two Warden daughters had married two Browett sons. Although drapers sold a few articles of ready-made clothing, their primary role at that time was to sell materials for people to make clothes at home. They often stocked a large range of materials and small items of haberdashery like pins, ribbons and threads, and some 'fancy goods' (Alexander 1970, 125–129).

Children of the Browett/Warden marriages

Some of the children of Browett/Warden marriages stayed in the locality and began businesses of their own. Alfred,

Fig. 147: Alfred and Ann Maria Browett's house on Yew Tree Road, Edgbaston.

Fig. 148: Ann Maria Browett's last house, on the Bristol Road.

the eldest son of Ann Maria and Alfred Browett, became a silversmith and manufacturer of electro-plated silver ware with his works at 14 Dean Street. His trade catalogue (Fig. 149), held in the Local Studies section of the Birmingham Central Library, vividly illustrates the ornate items that were fashionable at the time. His brothers, Thomas and George, as already mentioned were 'coal & brick manufacturers', working in the town but living at a different address, 84 Ryland Street, Edgbaston (1881 Census). These occupations, together with the iron and steel connections of the Warden children, illustrate how closely both families were involved in some of the most important aspects of Birmingham industry in the 19th century.

The connection between the families continued up to 1883 when Joseph W. Browett, a solicitor of Messrs Powell & Browett, signed the younger Joseph Warden's will. Thus some members of the Browett family went into the legal profession, suggesting that the increased fortunes of the Browett family allowed later generations to follow a profession rather than a trade, as had also occurred in the Warden family.

Vault 30 – Haines family

This well-built vault was located on the western side of the church, in a prominent position near the church entrance. Illustrations and photographs suggest that it

had been surmounted by a large chest-tomb and surrounded by high iron railings. The vault was built for William Haines in the period 1826–1831 (Chapter 3). It contained eight burials, comprising six adults and two infants, arranged on two levels. Six of the burials could be identified from legible *deposita* (Table 130).

Details of the other burials in the vault have been obtained from a Vault Record Book held in Birmingham Archives (MS943/13/1). This lists vaults and gravestones in the churchyard in 1879 and is associated with a plan of the churchyard, drawn at the time. These other burials were all of infants (Table 131).

There is a discrepancy in that eight burials were excavated but the documentary evidence indicates that

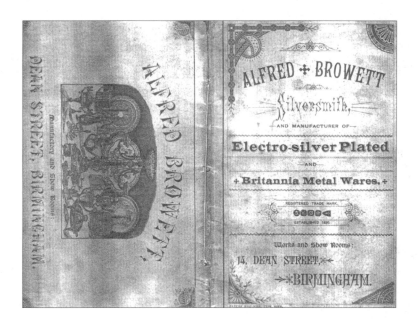

Fig. 149: Alfred Browett's trade catalogue.

Burial	Name	Age	Date of birth	Date of death
HB 840	William Haines	54	-	2nd July 1851
HB 829	Frank Haines	-	10th October 1840	16th September 1860
HB 841	Jane Lloyd Haines	64	-	21st January 1864
HB 794	William Tertius Haines	-	5th November 1831	30th August 1869
HB 792	Campbell Lloyd Haines	42	-	18th June 1878
HB 793	Eliza Haines	60	-	3rd August 1904

Table 130: Vault 30, individuals identified from coffin plates.

Burial	Name	Date of birth	Date of death
N/A	James Haines	13th July 1830	25th April 1831
N/A	William Haines	10th November 1828	8th July 1831
N/A	Alfred Haines	30th October 1838	1st September 1839

Table 131: Vault 30, burials of Haines family recorded in the Vault Record Book but not identified from coffin plates.

nine people were interred in the vault. It is possible that one of the two infants who died at less that one year of age was not recovered amongst the skeletal assemblage, or was erroneously described as buried in the vault when in fact he was buried elsewhere.

The life of William Haines

William Haines (HB 840), his wife Jane (HB 841) and six or seven of their children were buried in the vault (Fig. 150). Both William and Jane had a strong connection with St. Martin's Church, and both were christened there, in 1797 and 1804 respectively (IGI).

William, described as a 'Gentleman' in his will and 'Solicitor of this town' in the Vault Record Book, was born on 13th January 1797, the son of William and Ann, while Jane's parents were James Busby and Lucy Lloyd, who also married in the church on 29th December 1785. Jane's maternal grandparents were Sampson and Ann Lloyd, who possibly belonged to the wealthy Lloyd family (IGI) that with John Taylor, the wealthy button maker, started Taylor & Lloyds Bank (later Lloyds Bank) in the town in 1765.

William and Jane married at St. Bartholomew's Church, a Chapel of Ease to St. Martin's Church, on 13th April 1826 (IGI) and began their married life living at 48 Lower Hurst Street, near the centre of the town (WW 1831). By this time, William was already practising as a solicitor, having been first mentioned in The Law List in 1820.

He began practising at a time when the profession was undergoing considerable change as it sought to improve the reputation of the solicitor who, in previous centuries, had been often considered corrupt and of ill repute. The aspiration of the profession was to ensure that its practioners were all 'gentlemen', and so knew how to conduct themselves. However, the recurring problem was how to define the term and then how to substantiate the claim (Kirk 1976, 49). This together with the contemporary climate that prevailed after Queen Victoria came to the throne in 1837 – "to end all of the degradations and scandals of the previous seventy years and to cleanse the air of public and private life" (*ibid.*, 208) – led to more stringent regulations being introduced by The Law Society to regulate their members. William Haines, however, began practising before these regulations were enforced so was either considered a 'gentleman' at the outset of his career, or had earned it by his death when it was inscribed on his grave memorial.

William was described in the Law List as an 'Attorney & Solicitor', and in 1821 worked in a partnership with John Arnold and W. Smith, which was based in Lower Hurst Street, where William had his home. The firm evolved and moved to 2 Cannon Street in the centre of the town where it was known as 'Arnold and Haines' before moving to 86 New Street, when John Arnold (junior) joined his father.

The firm was also listed as Clerks to the Commissioners of the Birmingham Streets Act, which meant they acted on behalf of the Street Commissioners. This body was formed in the late 18th century when it became apparent that the increase in population necessitated some form of central body to establish law and order and improve public health. In the early 18th century, when Birmingham was still a relatively small community, the Manor and Parish provided the necessary local government. However as the town grew a body with greater powers was required. In 1769 the 'Improvement' or 'Lamp' Act was passed, which initially nominated 50 Town Commissioners who had the power to levy a rate on local inhabitants, so that conditions in the town could

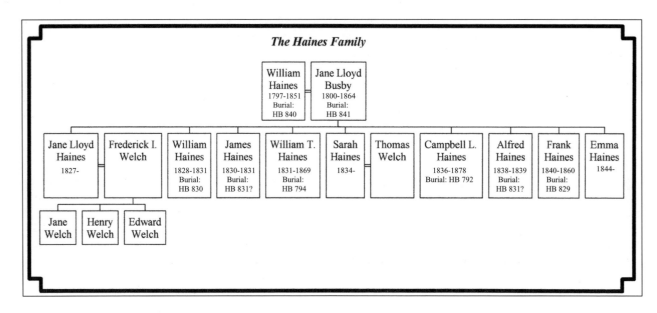

Fig. 150: Haines family tree (Vault 30).

be improved (Skipp 1980, 75). Its jurisdiction initially covered regulation of traffic, street cleaning and lighting. However, the powers of the Commissioners were soon increased to include policing and road maintenance. They initiated the first scheme to reduce smoke pollution. They were also instrumental, as described in Chapter 2, in the demolition of the old buildings that choked the market place (including the buildings that surrounded St. Martin's churchyard), and the provision of new markets, including the Market Hall. They also instigated the building of the Public Record Office in Moor Street and the Town Hall (Skipp 1983, 105–107).

The Commissioners were not a democratically elected body but consisted of wealthy, public-spirited citizens whose primary aim was to improve the town in which they lived. They were not accountable to the people they served. They nominated their own members, fixed their own taxes and decided amongst themselves on how the money should be spent. They attracted criticism from some of the working and middle classes who, although benefiting from the improved environment, felt the money should be administered along more democratic lines (*ibid.*, 100). As the town grew in size, concern about public health in particular increased, and the Street Commissioners requested greater powers. However the growing unease about their work prompted calls for change and in 1838 the Privy Council granted a Charter of Incorporation to Birmingham. This meant that all town services would be regulated by a municipal body and was to signal the demise of the Street Commissioners. This, however, took some years to implement and it was not until the 1851 Improvement Act was passed that their work was finally ended (*ibid.*, 100).

In his capacity of Clerk to the Commissioners, William Haines helped to implement some of their policies. In 1828 he was involved in the plans for the proposed new Market Hall (Birmingham Archives, Local History section D/S 62704), opened in 1835, and in 1844 he was involved in a court case concerning air pollution (Birmingham Archives MS 4/222). On this occasion, a Mr Cadbury had complained to the Commissioners about smoke coming from a steam engine that belonged to a Mr James Hughes in Broad Street. Mr Hughes had to appear at Warwick Assizes and was subsequently fined £500 plus £10 damages, and told to rectify the problem. He did not do so immediately and, after another report from the Inspectors, Mr Haines had to write again threatening him with more legal action. Mr Hughes eventually agreed to fit a new boiler and adapt the chimney, so the problem was solved.

In 1849, William Haines was involved in preparing the evidence to put before the Inspectors for the enquiry into the sewerage, drainage, supply of water and the sanitary condition of the town (Birmingham Archives, Local History Section, Lp 45 64263).

As William's professional life progressed his private family circumstances changed too. As the 1851 Census

illustrates, he and his wife had more children and as he became more prosperous the family, like many others, moved out of the centre of the town to more picturesque surroundings in Harborne. They lived at 57 Lodge Road, which became known as Harborne Lodge. William and his wife had nine children but sadly William, James and Alfred died before their second birthday. They had a staff of a housemaid, an underhouse-maid, a cook and a groom.

Towards the end of his life, another indication of William's growing wealth was the acquisition of property in Small Heath and Kings Norton (Birmingham Archives MS1386/10, MS 12/2/8, MS 39/42). His death certificate records that he died in July 1851 aged 54, having suffered from general debility with *atrophia cordis* (heart problems) for nearly four years. His will, held in the Public Record Office in London, is a comprehensive document that illustrates not only his considerable wealth, but also his attitude towards his family. It would appear to be a second will, revoking a previous one written in haste during an illness. His legal expertise is evident as he went into great detail about how the executors should administer his estate for the benefit of his children, paying particular attention to the welfare of his daughters. His plate, china, goods, wine and household effects were left to his wife and youngest child until she reached 21. This would ensure that she would have somewhere to live if her mother died before her. The main bequest, however, is that £15,000 is to be invested to provide for his wife, Jane, during her natural life and while she remains his widow. This was a fairly common clause in contemporary wills. However, William added his own caveat stating that if she remarried the investment should be reduced to £5,000. He explains this by saying, "I have not the remotest idea that my wife would marry again. I know well her affection for me and the children but I have seen so often the offensive importunities of designing men upon widows well provided for, that I am determined to prevent as much as may be the occurrence of such annoyances to my wife and children".

The Haines family

Following William's death the family moved to 9 Vicarage Road in Harborne, where, ten years later, his widow Jane still lived with three of her children (1861 Census).

The eldest of these was Jane Welch, a married daughter who lived there with her three young children. It is conceivable that her husband had died young since the children had been born elsewhere, and she had brought her family back to live with her mother.

Campbell Lloyd Haines (HB 792), unmarried at 25, was an architect and surveyor and in the Corporation Directory of Birmingham (1861) is working at 70 New Street. In 1864 he diversified and invested in one of the growth industries of the day. Despite a period of economic depression in the town, the brass trade was still expanding, and in particular the production of brass bedsteads (Fig. 151). Between 1885 and 1886 production rose from 5000 to 20,000 (Hopkins 2001, 35). This sudden rise in output could be accounted for by peoples' desire to have a bed that did not harbour bed bugs, as the more traditional wooden frames did, or just because it was a new fashion trend. Campbell Lloyd Haines must have realised the potential because in 1864 became a partner in 'Hulse and Haines', a company that made brass and iron bedsteads in Icknield Street West, as an advert in the Corporation Directory for Birmingham 1864 shows (Fig. 152). His death certificate states that he died aged 42 at 31 Birley Street, Blackpool, although the parish records list his place of death as nearby Southport. His cause of death was *morbus cordis et pulmonum myelitis paralysis* (heart and lung problems). He had suffered from rickets as a child, had a broken nose like his father and appears to have suffered from gout in his later years (Chapter 4).

The third child at home at that time was Emma, who was 17 and unmarried.

William Tertius Haines (HB 794), another of William and Jane's sons who was buried in the family vault, lived longer than his young siblings. However, his was not a long life, dying aged 38 in 1869. He, like his father, was described as a 'Gentleman' in his will, and when he died he was living on the Bristol Road. The will suggested that he had not married since he left his estate to be divided up between his brothers and sisters and their spouses. He instructed that his personal articles were to be divided up by ballot. The will also indicates that his sister Sarah married Thomas Welch, and since another sister, Jane, married Frederick Welch, then it would appear that two sisters married two brothers.

Frank Haines (HB 829), the only other son to survive childhood, died at 20. DNA analysis undertaken on his skeleton indicated that he had suffered from tuberculosis, which is a likely cause of his death (Chapter 4).

The other occupant of the vault was Eliza Haines (HB 793), who was living in Lechmere Crescent, Hallow Road, Worcester when she died in 1904, aged 60, of sciatica

Fig. 151: Bedstead manufacture, Lionel Street, 1902.

HULSE AND HAINES,

MANUFACTURERS OF ALL KINDS OF

BRASS AND IRON BEDSTEADS,

ICKNIELD METALLIC BEDSTEAD WORKS,

ICKNIELD STREET WEST, BIRMINGHAM.

Fig. 152: Advertisement for the firm of Hulse and Haines.

and spinal myelitis (inflammation of the spine), according to her death certificate. She had lived all her life in Worcester but her link with the Haines family was through her husband Ernest Montague Haines. He was described in the 1881 Census as living on "income from interest of money".

Eliza Haines was interred 26 years after Campbell Lloyd Haines, and was one of the last people to be buried in the churchyard.

Brick-lined graves

V11 – Parker

This was a 'shouldered' (i.e. coffin-shaped) brick-lined grave of 'dual-chamber' construction. The gently-curved vaulted roof of the lower chamber formed the floor for the upper chamber. It was situated just to the north of the church, forming part of a distinct cluster of brick-lined graves and a family vault (Vault Group IV).

The *depositum* associated with the burial in the lower chamber (HB 625) was partially legible. The coffin plate disintegrated on touch and was impossible to salvage. The only details that could be deciphered before it crumbled were the name and month of death. The plate read '*Sarah Parker...Died November...*'. The National Burial Index lists three Sarah Parkers buried in St. Martin's during November, in 1777, 1790 and 1825. Given the dating evidence from the other brick-lined graves and the family vaults, the latest of these three dates might be considered the most likely. However as this could not be confirmed no further research was carried out.

V33 – Robinson

This was a rectangular brick-lined grave with a barrel roof, located just to the southwest of the modern church, in association with two other closely similar brick-lined graves, V31 and V32 (Vault Group I). The grave contained two coffins, one above the other. The burial containing the legible *depositum* (HB 779) was above the earlier coffin (HB 789).

The coffin plate associated with HB 779 read '*Captain Adjutant Benjamin Robinson Died June 5th 1834 Aged 60 Years'*.

Captain Adjutant Benjamin Robinson was the son of Jonathan Robinson and Rebecca Harfield, a local couple who had married in 1769 in neighbouring Aston (IGI). He was christened in St. Martin's on 23rd August 1773 (IGI) and sixty years later was buried there.

He was a soldier who rose to the rank of Captain Adjutant in the 6th or Royal 1st Warwickshire Infantry regiment (Fig. 153, colour). Some details of his military achievements were given in his obituary published in the *Aris's Gazette* on 9th June 1834. Captain Robinson was involved in the Peninsula War, landing with his regiment in August 1808, and became part of the famous retreat of

Sir John Moore to Corunna (Fig. 154, colour). During this latter campaign 6,000 soldiers died and many others returned to England, wasted and ill from the hardships they had had to endure. Then in 1809, when he was 35, he took part in the expedition to Walcheren, a small island off the Dutch coast. The objective of this campaign was to capture Antwerp in order to prevent Napoleon using it as a base for a future invasion of England. The expedition was not successful as the army became marooned on the island with 218 dying in action, 4000 dying of malaria and another 11,000 ill when they were evacuated (Glover 1974, 86).

In his will, which is held at the Public Record Office in London, Captain Robinson instructs that he should be "decently interred in the same grave with my dear wife". This identifies HB 789 as Elizabeth Robinson, who died on 14th March 1831 aged 55, and who was buried below her husband in the brick-lined grave.

The will does not name any children of the marriage, but his estate is divided between his brothers, Jonathan and Thomas, and various other couples that could include his sisters, since he names the woman first. One of these couples, Martha and James Onions, were recorded on a grave memorial (ST 30, Appendix 2, CD) recovered unassociated with any grave during the excavations, but showing that they too were buried in the churchyard. In conclusion, the will states that he will clear all debts and demands against his brother Thomas that are outstanding at the time of his death.

When Captain Robinson died he was living at Cheapside, very close to St. Martin's. His obituary in the *Aris's Gazette* cited his military achievements and described him as "filling the arduous position of Quarter Master to the 6th Regiment of Foot as part of the rear division" during Moore's retreat from Corunna.

V03 – Sansom

This was a rectangular brick-lined grave, butting onto an earlier family vault (Vault 4), in the old part of the northern churchyard. It contained three burials. The lower two burials were of an infant (HB 185) and a child (HB 190). Above this was the burial of an old adult male (HB 189). The *deposita* associated with two of the burials were legible (Table 132).

John Sansom (HB 189) was born in 1808 in Bilston, Staffordshire and married Eleonor Evans from Perry Barr, Birmingham, on 26th July 1830 at St. Philip's Church (IGI). In the 1864 Corporation Directory of Birmingham he is listed as retail brewer in Sherbourne Road. The number of these small retail outlets selling beer had increased dramatically in the town after the 1830 Beerhouse Act (Monckton 1969, 79). This Act abolished beer duty and allowed any householder assessed on the poor rate to obtain an Excise Licence for 2 guineas, to sell beer from his own house, either as an on or off sale. The householder did not have to make any application to the Justices but was subject to restricted opening hours. The

Burial	Name	Age	Date of death
HB 185	Helen Mary Walker	18 mths	23rd December 1862
HB 189	John Sansom	65	3rd March 1873

Table 132: Brick-lined grave V03, identified burials.

reason behind the act was an attempt to control the growing problem of spirit drinking. It was thought that these small establishments would draw people away from the alehouses and inns where spirits and beer were both sold. However, the act had the reverse effect as more and more of these small drinking houses appeared and drunken behaviour increased. In subsequent years the government introduced further Acts of Parliament to control the problem (*ibid.,* 81), and by 1871, when he was listed in the census for Leamington Spa as a Licensed Victualler at 95 Brunswick Street, John would have had to adhere to much more stringent rules. This was the address of the Queen's Head, which was possibly a family concern as in the Inns and Taverns list of 1874 (F. White & Co of Warwickshire), the year after John's death, it was run by George L. Sansom, another member of the family.

The parish burial records state that John died in Leamington, and he was brought back to St. Martin's Church to be buried, possibly because there was a family grave available. His will (held in the Birmingham Archives) was written in 1870, three years before he died, and was extremely thorough. He had stocks and shares and various trusts, with a total value under £1000. His beneficiaries were his wife and his daughter Ann, who married Samuel Walker and lived in Balsall Heath (Fig. 155). The provisions made for his daughter are interesting. He states that the bequest should be "for her own and absolute use and benefit free from the debts power or control of her present or any future husband she may happen to have". He also made provision for the education and maintenance for any grandchildren she may have, and if Ann, his daughter, should die then it is the grandchildren, not her husband, that should have the money, when they reach 21.

Of the remaining two occupants of the grave, HB 185 has been identified as Helen Mary Walker, John's 18-month old granddaughter. Skeletal analysis (Chapter 4) suggests that the other burial (HB 190) was a child of about 11 or 12, who was buried together a necklace of pink glass beads (Bevan, this volume, Chapter 5). It is a possibility that this was another of John's grandchildren but research in the registers, which was not however in depth, did not reveal any possible names.

John's wife Eleonor, aged 77 at death, was buried in the churchyard in 1887 and the burial is almost certain, because of the late date of the interment, to have been in a brick-lined grave or a vault (see Chapter 2). After John died in Leamington, it is probable that she left the town and returned to Birmingham to live with her married daughter, because at the time of her death in 1887 the

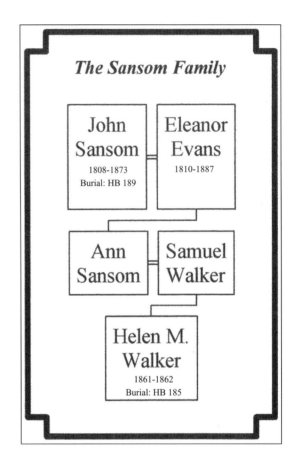

Fig. 155: Sansom family tree (brick-lined grave V03).

parish records list her as living in Balsall Heath.

It is curious that Eleonor's coffin was not in the same brick-lined grave as her husband. There was certainly space for it, and the grave was provided with putlocks to support three levels of burials.

Conclusions

The research into the 'named individuals' from the vaults at St. Martin's provides an insight into aspects of the lives of a few of the families from the area in the 19th century. While the history of the area has been the subject of much research, this analysis of individual's lives provides an alternative, and more intimate, perspective.

The study of these people reflects the social history of the day, and shows how interesting ordinary people's lives are, as they work to earn a living, look after their families and better themselves.

The study of each family illustrates much about the

19th-century family unit, including the large number of children, the high child mortality rate that seemed to occur whatever the socio-economic status of the family, and the closeness of siblings as they lived and worked together. It illustrates too the entrepreneurial spirit that inspired people to take risks and diversify as the markets changed. As the families became wealthier some moved away from their place of work to nearby suburbs. Others aspired to greater things and moved to pleasant rural villages such as Water Orton, fashionable spas like Leamington, or further afield to Southport. All retained a loyalty to St. Martin's, however, returning to the church to be buried in the family vault.

The occupations of those buried in the family vaults and brick-lined graves also provides an illustration of the range of trades upon which Birmingham's wealth was built – the iron merchant, brassfounder, saddler, chemist, publican, etc.

However, whilst the study does illustrate a great deal about these families, it must be remembered that they are just a subset of the people of the parish – people who, for whatever reason, could afford a vault or brick-lined grave in the churchyard. In the next chapter, an attempt is made to put these people into their wider social context, and to consider in more general terms the lives of the majority of the people, those buried in the earth-cut graves.

7   St. Martin's in Context: Life in the Parish

Josephine Adams, Megan Brickley and Simon Buteux

The purpose of this chapter is to provide a sketch of the economic and social conditions of the people of St. Martin's Parish in the 19th century. This sketch is intended to provide some broader context for the interpretation of the archaeological results (Chapter 3), the anthropological analyses (Chapter 4) and the documentary research into individuals and families (Chapter 6).

A second aim of the chapter is to use the archaeological discoveries, anthropological analyses and documentary research arising from the project to illuminate aspects of social and economic conditions. In particular, the anthropological analysis provides a completely new source of data on aspects of the health and lifestyle of the population of Birmingham, which has not been exploited before.

The account is necessarily very brief and cannot be comprehensive; changes through time, which were of course substantial, are given scant attention. The focus is on those aspects which are most relevant to the inter-pretation of the results of the anthropological analyses of the human remains – the range of occupations of the population, working and living conditions, and some aspects of culture. As some impression of the lives of the middle classes was given in the previous chapter, most attention is paid here to the working classes, who are presumed to have been buried in the simple earth-cut graves. Of the 505 skeletons that were fully analysed, 406 (80%) were from the earth-cut graves.

Another aspect of life briefly explored in this chapter is the importance of the family. Here, equal attention is paid to the middle classes. The phenomenon of middle-class family vaults, which were built in the churchyard from the early 19th century, must be related to how the individual, the family and family relationships were perceived. Some comments on the possible social and symbolic significance of these vaults are offered.

Of course, the mode of burial does not just reflect ideas about the role of the individual or family in society, but reflects religious beliefs, broader cultural perceptions and the practicalities of the 'disposal of the dead' (all these factors being entwined in a complex manner). Consideration of the role of the church, funerals and the funerary industry are reserved for Chapters 8 and 9.

The people of Birmingham

Throughout this volume a broad distinction has been made between the people who were buried in St. Martin's churchyard in simple earth-cut graves and those who were buried in brick-lined graves or family vaults. The two modes of burial have been taken to represent, very broadly, the 'working classes' and the 'middle classes'. This is certain to be an oversimplification, although the analyses described in Chapter 4 do show several dis-tinctions between the two groups.

In socioeconomic terms, the distinction between unskilled labourers and skilled craftsmen could be of equal if not greater significance than that between the working class and the middle class, although both might be defined as 'working class'. Depending on circum-stances, the latter could earn six times as much or more than the former (Hopkins 1998, 152). This would make a huge difference in the kind of housing which could be afforded, and in lifestyle and diet, all of which will have contributed to overall levels of health. Furthermore, throughout the period covered by the burials investigated from St. Martin's levels of employment and wages were uneven. Broadly speaking, these tracked the demand for Birmingham's products and the fortunes of the local and national economy. For most of the period from 1793 to 1815 England was at war with France and this caused a severe setback to Birmingham's prosperity (which had been buoyant and growing in the decades leading up to 1793) as much of this was dependent on foreign exports (Hopkins 1998, 70–75). The years following the French Wars were marked by depression, then there were various ups and downs until, in the late 1830s and early 1840s, the whole nation entered a depression which was one of the most severe of the 19th century (the 'Hungry Forties'). Other factors, such as poor harvests leading to high bread prices, affected the purchasing power of one's income.

These variations in the economy and in labour demand, with direct consequences for employment and wages, are an important factor when considering the patterns of health discussed in Chapter 4. In lean times it was the poorest who were worst affected, with malnutrition and starvation leading to raised susceptibility to disease for all members of the family, in a kind of vicious spiral which must be reflected in the patterns of morbidity and mortality described in Chapter 4. For example the potato blight, which caused the famine in Ireland (1846–50), also destroyed crops around Birmingham; potatoes are an important source of vitamin C, and the blight may be linked to the level of scurvy in juveniles detected from the analysis of the skeletons from the earth-cut graves (Brickley and Ives in press). Furthermore, the poorest people would neither have had the money (nor perhaps the inclination) to subscribe to the 'provident and friendly societies' which provided an insurance for the more affluent worker against times of unemployment or distress. By the 1840s there was a wide range of such societies, the name of one, the 'Rational Sick and Burial Society' (Report to the General Board of Health 1849), being a reminder that there was a need to provide for the costs of sickness and death as well as unemployment.

The range of trades pursued by the people of Birmingham was very varied (Figs. 156 and 157). Some reflection of this is to be found in the occupations of those who were buried in the vaults at St. Martin's and their families (see Chapter 6), although some of the most important trades, such as button-making and gun-making are not reflected.

A more balanced impression of the range and relative importance of the various occupations is to be found in the census returns for 1851 (when the population of Birmingham was around 230,000), where the principal occupations listed are as follows (Hopkins 2001, 17):

Blacksmiths	1,091
Brassfounders	4,914
Bricklayers	1,694
Button makers	4,980
Carpenters, joiners	1,851
Cabinet makers	1,027
Cooks, housemaids, nurses	1,113
Domestic servants (general)	8,359
Glass manufacturers	1,117
Other workers in gold & silver	1,153
Gunsmiths	2,867
Goldsmiths, silversmiths	2,494
Iron manufacture	2,015
Other workers & dealers in iron and steel	3,864
Labourers	3,909
Painters, plumbers, glaziers	1,097
Messengers, porters	2,283
Milliners	3,597
Shoemakers	3,153
Tailors	2,009
Tool-makers	1,011
Washerwomen	1,965
Workers in mixed metals	3,778

The centrality in Birmingham's economy of metal-working of all types and occupations involved with it is readily apparent from these figures. However, in terms of numbers employed by far the most important single occupation was domestic service. All of the 8,359 'domestic servants (general)' listed above were women; a mere 711 men were also listed under this occupation. The predominance of domestic service as an occupation in Birmingham reflects the national scene.

Other occupations represented in smaller numbers in the 1851 census figures include the professions and associated types of work, of which the following is a sample:

Solicitors	107
Law clerks	170
Accountants	130
Commercial clerks	1,037
Commercial travellers	327
Surgeons	169
Druggists	233
Schoolmasters	149
Schoolmistresses	475
Police officers	353

For the service trades, some examples of those involved in food and drink are:

Grocers	787
Butchers	799

Fig. 156: An unknown smith, archetype of industrial Birmingham, c.1895.

Fig. 157: Rag sorters at the paper mills, Landor Street, c.1895

Fishmongers	141
Cowkeepers and milk sellers	258
Malsters	169
Brewers	717
Licensed victuallers and beershop keepers	718

From these figures the importance of alcoholic drink in the working class culture of Birmingham is evident, and there was certainly a number of unlicensed beershops, or 'wobble shops', too which did not figure in the official statistics. Drinking was the principal leisure activity of the working classes, and some of the consequences, in terms of violence and injury, are no doubt reflected in the patterns of trauma described in Chapter 4 (see below).

Taken together, the figures presented above (which are just a sample and may not be entirely accurate) also indicate the extent to which working-class women were in employment. That domestic servants were overwhelmingly women has already been noted, and other occupations, such as washerwoman, were obviously women's work. Women (as well as children) were also extensively employed in manufacturing. Some figures are provided by Allen (1929); those shown below present the percentage of females to the total amount of employment for a sample of trades in 1861:

Brass and non- ferrous metals	24%
Buttons	58%
Saddlery and harness	28%
Pens	94%
Tinplate ware	18%
Jewellery (excluding electro-platers)	28%
Brush	22%

Clearly, the numbers of women employed in different

trades was variable, with some industries, such a pen-making, dominated by women. Button-making and pin-making also employed large numbers of women and children.

The various figures presented above are only intended to provide a flavour of the character of employment in Birmingham in the 19th century. Obviously, the importance of different trades changed greatly throughout the course of the century as did the patterns of employment. Nevertheless, in broad terms the people buried in St. Martin's churchyard must present a cross-section of the people of Birmingham as a whole.

The organisation of industry

One commentator (Allen 1929) observed that as late as 1860 work premises in Birmingham

might be divided up into the large factory with 150 workers and above; the small factory, with thirty to forty workers up to 150; the workshop, employing thirty or forty workers; and the workshop of the garret master, employing only his family and an occasional journeyman or apprentice. It was usually only for the largest workplace that premises were specially built. The small factory often simply consisted of a chain of converted dwelling houses, and the workshop and garret master were commonly dependent upon a factor for the supply of raw material and the marketing of their goods (Allen 1929, paraphrased in Hopkins 2001, 20).

It was enterprises at the lower end of this scale – that is the workshops – that were dominant in Birmingham's economy from the 18th century through to well into the second half of the 19th century (Fig. 158). Larger factories, such as that of William Jenkins (Vault 9), which employed 250 hands, were comparatively rare. One reason for the essentially small-scale nature of industry in Birmingham is that, unlike textile production in the north of England, it was not highly mechanised. Widespread use was made of small hand-operated machines, such as the stamp, the press, the lathe and the drawbench, but before about 1830 the employment of steam power appears to have been very limited, and most of the engines were small, with a notional average of 16 horse power in 1835 (Hopkins 1998, 34). At 100 horse power the steam engine employed by William Jenkins in 1833 (see Chapter 6) was therefore a very large engine. Mr Jenkins was a brassfounder, and such large engines were only useful in the primary metal industries, for hammering, rolling and blowing purposes (Hopkins 1998, 35).

The essentially small scale of industry in Birmingham and the predominance of small businesses has numerous ramifications for issues such as working conditions, working hours and labour relations. (The economic power of Birmingham, which earned it the appellation of 'the first manufacturing town in the world', came in the aggregate). At root, in a small business the social gulf between employer and employee is reduced, and the employee is correspondingly more powerful as an individual. For example, there is much evidence to suggest that in Birmingham traditional working practices, such as the practice, inherited from the 18th century and beyond, that Monday was an unofficial day off ('St. Monday' as it was called) continued well into the 19th century (Hopkins 1998). This does not mean that the Birmingham worker did not have to work hard to make a living – many people were paid by results ('piecework') instead of a regular wage – but rather that it was often they, not the employer, who dictated the pattern of work, putting in very long hours towards the end of the week to make ends meet.

Another ramification of the small scale of most businesses was that it both permitted and encouraged economic and social mobility (something that will be touched on again below when considering family backgrounds). In many businesses, including the smaller metal-working trades, little capital was needed to get an enterprise going. From this point onward expansion was possible in favourable circumstances:

> Beginning as a small master, often working in his own house with his wife and children to help him, the Birmingham workman has become a master, his trade has extended, his buildings have increased. He has used his house as a workshop, has annexed another, has built upon the garden or the yard, and consequently a large number of the manufactories are most irregular in size (Timmins 1866, quoted in Hopkins 2001, 20).

There are, of course, many other aspects to the organisation of industry and employment in Birmingham, but the few aspects that have been mentioned here are sufficient to emphasise a point made earlier: Birmingham society was much more varied and textured than a simple

Fig. 158: Regent Row about 1900, a typical example of Birmingham's infinite variety of small workshops. The following trades were crammed together in this narrow passage: paperbox maker, gas fitting manufacturer, press tool makers, brass founders, coal merchant, jewellery and glass cutters, lapidary and crate makers.

division into two monolithic groups, the 'working classes' and the 'middle classes', would suggest.

Working conditions

A variety of sources provide information on working conditions and on the employment of women and children. Of particular interest in the present context is a government investigation of 1833, the main purpose of which was to look into the conditions of child workers (Factory Enquiry Commission 1833).

Whilst the majority of the problems were found in the textiles factories of the North, representatives of the commission also visited Birmingham to check on factories in the area for similar problems. They found that a large proportion of the work was piecework, carried out in the workers' own houses or in small local workshops (as already noted). However, they did visit a pin factory, a cut-nail factory and a button factory, together with two brassfoundaries where children were employed, to interview their owners about working conditions. One of those interviewed was William Walker Jenkins, the brassfounder and builder of Vault 9 at St. Martin's (see Chapters 3 and 6), and his answers provide a fascinating insight into the working conditions of the day.

Jenkins employed about 250 people of whom 30 were between the ages of 9 and 14. He did not employ any younger children, as the work was "generally laborious". Both children and adults had the same working day, 13 hours in the summer and 12 in the winter, with 2 hours off per day for meals and rest. They worked Monday to Saturday, although on Saturdays they worked one hour less. No children worked at night or slept in the factory overnight. Mr Jenkins seemed aware of the Ten Hour Labour Bill (a measure that the Earl of Shaftesbury was trying to implement in the early 1830s) but did not believe that it applied to him. He considered that the children were safe at work, well clothed and generally in good health. The rooms where they worked were not heated, although a few might experience higher temperatures in the lacquering room. He took precautions to avoid accidents involving heavy machinery (recall that his factory employed a large 100 horse power steam engine), and reported that he had never had any fatal or serious accidents. He did not authorise any employees to inflict corporal punishment on the children, and if he did receive any complaints of the children being beaten by others he investigated it himself. He did say, however, that on rare occasions he "had to chastise them with a light whip".

Mr Jenkins was questioned about the education and living conditions of his child employees and whilst he thought that in the past many of them could not read, the majority now could, a fact he attributed to their increased attendance at Sunday Schools. He had no direct know-ledge of the children's houses but his opinion was that if families were in full employment their houses were "healthy and comfortable". He paid the adults between 15s and 24s and the children between 1s 3d and 4s per week.

In common with most of the other Birmingham employers interviewed for the report, the conditions in Mr Jenkins' brassfoundary do not seem to have given cause for concern at the time, although it is not clear whether it actually received a visit from the inspectors. The report concluded that the evidence gathered presented "a very favourable impression ...of the present general condition of the working classes in Birmingham".

To the modern observer, the reliance placed on the testimony of an employer might seem suspect. Although Mr Jenkins did not report any serious or fatal injuries, what does 'serious' mean and what less serious injuries took place? Quite what did the chastisement administered by Mr Jenkins with a 'light whip' signify?

An independent line of evidence on injury in the workplace and violence in society in general is provided by the human bone analysis described in Chapter 4. The differences in fracture patterns reported between men and women, and also between middle and working class women, are almost certainly related to different patterns of work and family life. When all types of trauma that affect the skeleton were considered, not just fractures, individuals from the working classes were far more likely to have sustained such injuries. Research undertaken during the writing of Chapter 4 on medical reports produced by a surgeon working in Birmingham at this period demonstrated that in men many of the fractures sustained were from work-related injuries. Although it is impossible to be sure, many of the fractures reported on in Chapter 4 probably came from this type of accident.

It has been emphasised that large establishments like that of Mr Jenkins were atypical, and that on the whole industry in Birmingham was not centred upon large custom-built, steam-powered factories but was mostly dependant on the workshop system with many small units using intensive labour and hand-held technology. This enabled both men and women to work, often alongside each other, in workshops close to their homes; their sons and daughters often followed them in to the same employment (Terry-Chandler 1995, 259; Pinchbeck 1977, 272). Many women and children worked at home making hairpins, safety pins, hooks and eyes or carding buttons. Children as young as six were often expected to contribute to the family income in some way (Barnsby 1989,192).

The conditions in these workshops, however, were often grim. A government report of 1843 summed up the situation as follows:

> In general the buildings are very old, and many of them are in a dilapidated, ruinous, and even dangerous condition. Nothing is more common than to find many of the windows broken .... The shops are often dark and narrow; many of them, especially those used for stamping, are from 4 to 7 feet below the level of the ground; these latter, which are cold and damp, are justly complained of by the workers. From defective construction, all these old shops are liable to become 'suffocatingly hot in summer (and also at night when the gas is lighted) and very cold in winter' (Children's Employment Commission 1843, quoted in Hopkins 1998, 111).

A range of the illnesses and medical conditions described in Chapter 4 may be attributable in part to working conditions such as these, and it must be remembered that diseases and conditions which leave their mark on the skeleton (many do not) will greatly under represent actual prevalence. In almost all cases the prevalence of a pathological conditions recognised through analysis of human bone represents a minimum level of occurrence. Understanding the full significance of the results presented in Chapter 4 is dependent upon appreciation of this point.

All the cases of osteomalacia (adult vitamin D deficiency) recorded during the skeletal analysis were recorded in working class individuals (i.e. individuals buried in earth-cut graves). Vitamin D is essential to ensure that newly formed bone is properly mineralised,

Fig. 159: Typical Birmingham slum housing of the 19th century. One of many unsanitary courts, c.1875.

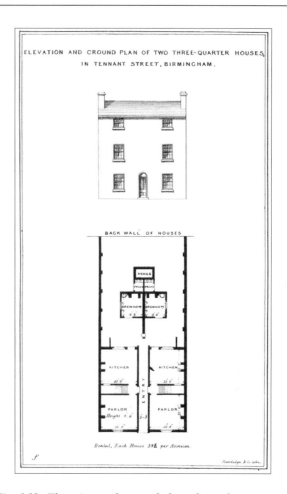

Fig. 160: Elevation and ground plan of two three-quarter houses in Tennant Street (from Chadwick's Report of 1842).

and a deficiency results in inadequate materialization of the skeleton and frequent fractures from very slight causes. In most of the cases recorded, low light levels received by the affected individual due to their working environment probably caused the condition.

Living conditions

A popular perception is that all 19th-century working-class urban housing was slum-like in character. In reality the situation was much more variable, and the skilled craftsman could afford accommodation that was considered by the standards of the day to be of good quality. A generally favourable comparison between Birmingham and other major towns emerges from four major inquiries into sanitary conditions that were carried out in the 1840s: the *Report on the Health of Towns Select Committee* (1840); the *Report on the Sanitary Condition of the Labouring Population of Great Britain*, 'Chadwick's Report' (1842); the *Report of the Commission of Inquiry into the State of Large Towns and Populous Districts* (1844); and the *Report to the General Board of Health on the Borough of Birmingham*, 'Rawlinson's Report' (1849).

Despite the fact that much giving a favourable impression emerges from these reports, that they were considered necessary at such frequency is a measure of the level of concern at the time, and many of the findings confirm that the concern was not misplaced (Fig. 159).

According to Chadwick's Report, at the top end of the working class range were the so-called 'three-quarters houses' (Fig. 160). With a high rent of 7s per week these

were only available to the skilled workman. Two houses shared a central tunnel entrance with the front doors opening off either side of the passage. Each house had a parlour and kitchen on the ground floor, with two bedrooms each on the first and second floors. There was a privy and brewhouse for each house at the back.

Another type of working-class housing, common in Birmingham, was the 'back-to-back'. These houses were only one-room deep and each house was built literally back-to-back to another. The houses were two or three stories high and outside was a yard with about one privy and a brewhouse for each four houses. These houses were cheap to build and generally of poor quality but the committee of physicians and surgeons which compiled the 1842 report did not find them necessarily bad.

At the bottom end of the range were the 'court houses', which could be rented for between about 2s 6d and 4s 6d per week, depending upon size, location and condition. These consisted of closed courts, approached by a narrow passage, surrounded by several small houses, some of just two rooms (Fig. 161). In the small central court were communal privies and brewhouses.

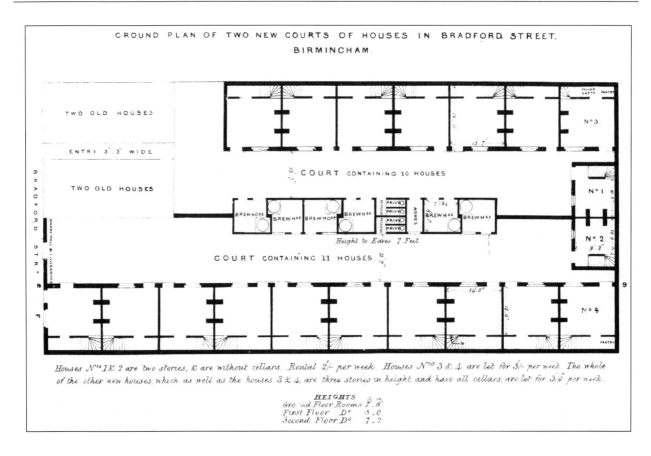

Fig. 161: Court housing in Bradford Street. Note that 21 houses are served by just four privies (lavatories).

Universally condemned as the worst form of accommodation were the lodging houses.

The sanitary conditions, particularly in the older courts, could be appalling. They were filthy, claustrophobic, poorly lit, badly drained and ill-ventilated. The privies (earth closets) were disgusting and covered in excrement. The practice was to empty the contents of the ash pits and privies into the street at night for collection in the morning. In Rawlinson's report of 1849 it was noted that there were about 2,000 close courts without proper drainage, and that many were unpaved.

In terms of the overall conditions of life and work, it should be noted that conditions varied in different parts of the town, with conditions in the older parts, including the areas around St. Martin's, generally worse than in the newer parts. Earlier in this chapter it was noted how as a business expanded the demand for workshop and domestic accommodation was such that many of the gardens were lost. The buildings around St. Martin's had become densely packed as many small courts and alleyways were built between the main roads (Skipp 1980, 48). The very high prevalence of vitamin D deficiency related conditions found in the individuals buried at St. Martin's undoubtedly relates to the nature of the built environment in the town as well as atmospheric pollution.

It was noted in the previous chapter, with several examples drawn from the families who had built vaults at St. Martin's, that as their businesses developed the middle classes escaped the squalor of the centre of town for the suburbs, typically Edgbaston, or beyond. The housing here was, of course, of a much higher standard (much of it survives today whereas only a handful of back-to-backs have been preserved as a museum), and several examples were illustrated (Figs 143, 144 and 148). Nevertheless sanitary conditions were far from perfect, as is noted in Rawlinson's Report of 1849:

> In the Hagley Road [Edgbaston] the gutters are receptacles of drains and filth till they become in the most putrid state, reeking with the contents of water closets in the finest neighbourhood of Birmingham.

Family backgrounds

As industrialisation gathered momentum in Birmingham during the 19th century the population of the town rapidly increased. Much of the growth was a consequence of immigration, usually from the rural areas surrounding Birmingham. The move away from small rural communities to the towns in search of employment changed the framework of people's lives. Families whose ancestors had perhaps lived in one locality for generations became fragmented as sons and daughters decided to move to the towns. There was undoubtedly a degree of dislocation and 'culture shock' for many, with the transition from the seasonal of the rhythms of agricultural work to the new patterns of industrial work, for example, or from the traditional authority structures of squire and parson to the more varied and flexible social structures of the town.

The diverse opportunities that Birmingham offered provided the motivation for people to migrate; some people were skilled in particular crafts that could be utilised in the town, while others learnt new skills as new types of industry evolved. Many became involved in the retail trade in the Bull Ring markets and in the neighbouring streets, where the number of shops was increasing. For a great many women, domestic service became an option as the expanding middle class employed growing numbers to help them run their homes.

Some people became more successful than others. The entrepreneur with an eye for business could succeed and prosper, building a successful enterprise from small beginnings. Birmingham had few resident aristocratic families but as the number of these enterprising individuals increased they became the *nouveaux riches* of the day and began to emulate the aristocratic leisured classes that had long existed in cities like Bath and York (Davidoff & Hall 1987, 39).

The families buried in the vaults in St. Martin's churchyard illustrate some of these patterns. The ancestors of the Wardens and Browetts (Vault 5) were immigrants, having moved from rural villages near Coventry. Hannah Ainsworth (Vault 23) moved from Inkberrow in Worcestershire, while the Haines family had servants who had moved from Hereford, Malvern and Easthorpe in Shropshire. While some of these immigrants remained craftsmen or traders serving the local community, others illustrate the transition from shopkeeper to businessman. Joseph Warden's family, for example, lived over their ironmonger's shop in Smallbrook Street in the early years, before moving to a large house in Edgbaston as his business interests in the town diversified and became more successful.

That the transition from agricultural employment to work in the towns had an adverse affect on health was widely recognised at the time. The testimony of Mr E. T. Cox, a surgeon involved in the recruitment of marines, is recorded in Chadwick's Report of 1842:

> Has examined the results of marines for 30 years, during 10 years he examined all the recruits enlisted in Birmingham. Has great experience of the physical state of the men who have been employed in manufacturers and agriculture. Those of the latter class are much stronger and more hale in most respects than those of the former. They are generally taller. The mechanics are shorter, more puny, and altogether inferior in their physical powers. Many of the men presented for examination are distorted in the spine and chest, which witness attributes to the confined position in which they work.

Family life

Despite the amount of migration that took place, once an individual had become established in the town and married, the importance of the family became paramount. The economic survival of the family was fundamental, and amongst many in the working classes a contribution from both husband and wife (and later the children) was essential for its viability. For the more successful, some could subsequently afford to dispense with the productive labour of the wife and children, and the man became the sole provider for his family.

The emotional reasons for marriage are impossible to quantify but in practical terms "it made sexual relationships permissible, ensured the legitimacy of children and provided a framework of support for the family" (Bartley 1996, 8). Amongst the middle classes it was often considered as the "beginning of a new enterprise" (Tilly & Scott 1978, 41), a new kinship group that would provide support not only for the expected children, but also for the wider family group both in business and social spheres.

The importance of the family group as a unit is, of course, given material expression in the family vaults that were built in St. Martin's churchyard by some of the more successful businessmen and professionals from the community in the early decades of the 19th century. The decision by a man to build a vault for himself and his family was a strong symbolic statement of his values and aspirations, while the matter of who was – and who was not – given burial in the vault provides a more subtle insight into family values.

Amongst the middle classes the different roles of men and women were clearly defined, with husbands assuming overall responsibility for their wives and the expected children, while the woman's role was to establish and maintain the home. The overall maintenance of an acceptable life style amongst the newly emerging middle classes was, however, dependent upon the success of the husband's business, since few had the financial security of a substantial inheritance behind them. In some cases a wife's inheritance may have provided capital for a business venture, while in others a marriage produced links with other families that integrated sons, brothers and uncles into the enterprise. This was especially prevalent in Birmingham, where strong religious beliefs often linked families, providing both moral and financial support for the formation of many successful business enterprises in the town (Davidoff & Hall 1987, 321–323). A good example of this from St. Martin's is provided by the career of Joseph Warden (Vault 5). In the early stages of his career he is found trading as 'Warden & Marston', which indicates a partnership with his wife's family, while later on the Warden family formed strong links with the Browetts, when two of Joseph's daughters married into the Browett family (Chapter 6). Joseph's son-in-law Alfred Browett was sufficiently trusted and close not only to be named in Joseph's will as one of the trustees of his estate, but also to be buried in the Warden family vault. In his will Joseph also divided property comprising a factory, a foundry and some shops between two of his sons and his brother-in-law Edward Penn.

Increasingly for the middle classes the home was seen as a place of sanctuary, separate from the husband's place of work, where he could return to at the end of the day and find respite amongst his family. This domestic idyll was to become a classic Victorian ideal that the rising middle classes aspired to (Davidoff & Hall 1987, 364–369). Again, the symbolic significance of the family vault is apparent. Here the husband would again find sanctuary in the bosom of his family, and the vault structure itself separated him and his family from the 'common herd' in death, mirroring the way that his house did in life. Surrounding the tomb above the vault with high iron railings, as was done in the case of the Haines family vault (Vault 30), further expressed both privacy and social separation.

The care of children within a marriage was a source of major concern, as child mortality was high. The threat of disease and death was ever-present in the towns and struck all classes of people regardless of status. The most common killers were measles, whooping cough, scarlet fever and tuberculosis, although the latter gradually declined as the century progressed. The Jenkins family (Vault 9) suffered the loss of three infants under the age of one, and the Haines family (Vault 30) lost three sons under three, despite the wealth and position in society of these two families. Likewise John Home (Vault 18), a chemist and apothecary who lived on High Street, was unable to use his skills to save five of his children, who died between 1817 and 1823 (Chapter 6).

Nevertheless the analysis of the human bone, reported on in Chapter 4, did reveal a number of differences between the health of children who died and were buried in earth-cut graves compared to those buried in vaults. The relative prosperity of middle-class families, which would have enabled them to buy a wider range of fresh foodstuffs, seems to have provided some protection against scurvy (vitamin C deficiency). No cases of scurvy were observed in middle class children, but the prevalence of this condition was quite high (10.5%) amongst those from working-class backgrounds. However as we have seen, this prosperity did not remove all risks to the children from middle-class families. The children of the affluent were still affected by rickets (vitamin D deficiency, which is strongly linked to light levels and pollution). Although many of these families had moved out from the overcrowded and very polluted centre of town, pollution levels were probably still quite high and socio-cultural ideas on the extent to which children should be allowed outside to play may have had a role in the development of rickets. When levels of Cribra orbitalia (lesions seen in the orbits, possibly linked to anaemia) were examined, the middle class children were more frequently affected than those from poorer backgrounds.

It is possible that fashionable new ideas on infant feeding practice adopted by middle-class families actually had a detrimental effect on the health of their children. Although the research undertaken on burial in the vaults (Chapter 3) suggests that not all children from middle-class families may have been given a vault burial, it is still clear from the age at death data presented in Chapter 4 that infant mortality was very high in both groups.

Despite high infant mortality, families were often large – the Jenkins (Vault 9), Warden (Vault 5) and Haines (Vault 30) families all demonstrate this as far as the middle classes are concerned. Ann Maria Warden, for example, had 13 children between 1813 and 1830, and her daughter had seven in 16 years; both had servants to help (Chapter 6).

The working-class mother, on the other hand, was often expected, in addition to bearing and raising the children, to work (up to 13 hours a day), run the household and control the family income (Terry-Chandler 1995, 244). In contrast to the sheltered life of wealthier women, working class mothers often worked right up to the birth of their children and returned to work soon afterwards. The ongoing problem of childcare then had to be accommodated around the demands of the workplace. Initially the young baby might be taken to work with the mother, then the other children in the family would be expected to help. As the children grew they would be sent out to work, both to earn much needed income and as a form of childcare.

For the working-classes, family life could be extremely precarious. Over and above the fluctuations in employment and the cost of living caused by such factors as the French Wars or the success of the harvest, the illness or death of a wage earner, or even the burden of a large number of children, could result in destitution for the rest of the family. As was noted earlier, some of the families that were able invested a few pence each week in the many provident or friendly societies that were being formed, to insure against these hard times. However, if disaster struck and the benefit had run out, and everything possible taken to the pawnshop, the only alternative was to apply to the Poor Law authorities for 'outdoor relief' or admission into the workhouse. This was considered by most to be the last resort and the social stigma attached to the workhouse was to be avoided at all costs. In 1812 Thomas Attwood observed that the "multitudes would rather perish than apply for parochial aid" (Hopkins 1989, 156). The spectre of old age was also horrifying since few had accumulated any savings to care for themselves when they could no longer work, so by the end of the 19th century the largest single group of paupers in the workhouse was the old, followed by children whose families had, for whatever reason, been unable to support them (Walvin 1987, 21). At the beginning of the century, as was noted in Chapter 2, those who had had to suffer the ignominy of a pauper's funeral were duly noted in the parish burial records.

The ideal of mutual love and support within the family is well expressed in one man's grave epitaph found in St. Martin's churchyard, that reads:

Farewell dear wife my life is past
my love was true while life did last
therefore for me no sorrow make
but love our children for my sake.

The reality, however, could be different. The dominant position of the man within the family, and the authority he held over wife and children, could easily lead to abuse. Research on records from the Birmingham Police Courts, undertaken in relation to the investigation of trauma recorded in the human skeletal remains reported in Chapter 4, revealed that domestic violence was relatively common. At least some of the fractures recorded on female skeletons, to the ribs for example, could have been the result of domestic violence, although there is of course no way to be sure.

Working class culture

When there was employment to be had, the working classes in Birmingham spent most of their waking life at work. As has been seen, this applied to women and children as well as men. Provision for working-class education in Birmingham was very limited until well into the second half of the 19th century. At the time of the 1851 census one in 11.02 children in Birmingham attended school, which was slightly lower than the national average (one in 8.36) (Hopkins 2001, 30). Furthermore, it was typical for a child only to attend school for about two years, until they were ready to start

earning a wage. When Mr Jenkins, the brassfounder and builder of Vault 9 in St. Martin's churchyard, was interviewed in 1833 about conditions in his factory (see above), one part of the rosy picture which he painted was that, although things had been different in the past, he now believed that the majority of the children in his employ could read. He attributed this to increased attendance at Sunday Schools. Mr Jenkins' statement is very unlikely to be true. While Sunday Schools were an important addition or alternative to day schools, and taught reading skills (much more rarely writing), by 1841 only 35% of working-class children were attending them (*ibid*). As a consequence, literacy levels were very low.

At the end of the 18th century and in the earlier part of the 19th century, amongst the most popular leisure activities of the working classes appear to have been various violent sports such as dog-fighting, cockfighting, bull- and badger-baiting, street football and boxing (Rule 1986, 214). Popular too were the wakes and fairs. Wakes, which had started out as church festivals, were local holidays lasting three or four days, and were characterised by heavy drinking and brutal sports. William Hutton (1809, 205) described them as "a church festival turned into riot, drunkenness, and mischief".

Of course there were more high-minded pastimes, some of which are mentioned in the next chapter, although they never seem to have attracted large numbers. That drinking was probably the principal leisure activity of the working classes may be deduced from any number of sources: the numbers employed in various aspects of the trade, the numbers of inns and beerhouses (Fig. 162), the testimony of commentators and newspapers, and so forth. The heaviest drinkers are likely to have been young skilled

Fig. 162: The Old Leather Bottle public house, Digbeth, c.1885.

men, who could command the highest wages. In Chadwick's Report of 1842 it is suggested that drunkenness

> most generally prevails among that class of workmen who obtain the highest wages, but who are often found in the most deplorable and abject condition. The improvidence of which we are speaking is to be traced in very many instances to extreme ignorance on the part of the wives of these people. The females are from necessity bred up from their youth in the workshops, as the earnings of the younger members contribute to the support of the family.

Analysis of the human skeletal remains, outlined in Chapter 4, produced evidence on a range of fractures and other skeletal trauma that was almost certainly linked to interpersonal violence. There was one possible case of a healed blade injury to the skull on one of the men buried in the vaults, and a number of cases of fractures in the hands and facial region that could be linked to violence. Whilst some of these injuries could have been the result of sporting activities, such as boxing (which would have been 'bare-knuckle fighting' for most of the period), many were probably sustained in fights following drinking. As

discussed in Chapter 4, there are numerous accounts in Birmingham newspapers from this period of violence, particularly following drinking in the town's inns and public houses.

During analysis of the human skeletal remains it was also noticed that a number of males had patterns of injury that fitted with what would be expected in individuals that have been termed 'injury recidivists'. As discussed in Chapter 4, these individuals were nearly always male, normally young when their first injury occurred, often of low socio-economic status and/or unemployed, and frequently involved in illegal activities.

Addressing what were perceived as the moral and religious failings of the poor, and the very real deprivations and iniquities suffered by the working classes, was a matter of growing concern as the 19th century progressed. In the following chapter, aspects of the role of the church in the life of St. Martin's parish are explored, together with the growth of the funerary trade – a profession much blamed for the exploitation of the poor – and the consequent growth of a funerary and mourning reform movement.

8 St. Martin's in Context: the Church and Funerals

Josephine Adams, Simon Buteux and Richard Cherrington

The religious dimension to death and burial is funda-mental. A funeral at St. Martin's was a Christian ceremony – more specifically an Anglican ceremony – filled with meaning, captured most succinctly in the words, 'earth to earth; ashes to ashes; dust to dust; in sure and certain hope of the Resurrection to eternal life'. How much did the religious dimension matter to the people who were buried in St. Martin's churchyard?

The significance of religion

The significance of religion in the lives of people in 19th-century Birmingham is almost impossible to quantify. At the beginning of the century it was the Dissenters, not those adhering to the Church of England, that made up the majority of the worshippers in the town. These included Baptists, Methodists, Roman Catholics and, notably, Quakers and Unitarians. It was from the latter two groups that many of the strong businesses that were to underpin the growth of the town began to emerge. However, the growth of the evangelical movement at the end of the 18th century meant that religion became a fundamental part of the lives of the emerging middle classes, and by the 1830s and 1840s the Anglican Church became more active in the town (Hopkins 1989, 140).

This growing religious zeal resulted in an increase in the publication of religious literature, a growth of charities and the establishment of Sunday Schools (Davidoff & Hall 1987, 78). The realisation that the existing number of religious establishments was inadequate for the rapidly growing population led to more churches and chapels being built in the earlier part of the century. However, despite the fact that some of these new churches, notably Christchurch and St. Peter's, were built specifically for the working classes, it was the middle classes that attended church much more frequently (Davidoff & Hall 1987, 79). For them, attendance at church became a social obligation. In a town with no structured aristocracy, membership of a religious community provided a frame-work, in both the public and private spheres, in which position, status and a sense of identity could be acquired. The constant round of Christian meetings, events and societies provided a social calendar for both men and women. In a wider sense, the close association of like-minded people led to networks growing within the town and beyond, providing support for both family and business connections (Davidoff & Hall 1987, 99–103).

The only reasonably comprehensive statistics available on religious observance are provided by the 1851 Religious Census that, however, records church atten-dance on just one Sunday in that year. The overall figure for attendance at any sort of religious establishment in Birmingham was 36.1%, a substantially lower proportion than in other Midlands towns. Unfortunately it is not known what proportion of those attending were middle class or working class, but one speculative estimate puts working-class attendance at between 12% and 24% (Hopkins 1989, 162). However the figures are interpreted, the majority of the working classes and the majority of Birmingham's population were not regular church attendees. The reasons for this are unclear but could be attributed to a variety of factors. Recent migrants from the country may have simply lost the habit of regular church attendance that had previously governed their lives in a small village. Some churches, including St. Martin's (see Chapter 2), levied a pew rent that would have been prohibitive to the less well off. Separate 'free pews' may have been provided but this segregation together with the lack of a 'Sunday best' outfit may have increased working class feelings of social isolation, further dissuading them from attending. Some churches held separate services for working men, sometimes outside the church building, that may have exacerbated their feelings of social segregation, and visits from well-meaning clergy and missionaries amongst the poor were often considered "patronising and interfering" (Hopkins 1989, 163).

However, allegiance to the church should not just be

measured by attendance at services. There was in Birmingham a relatively high number of church schools that gave a few children some degree of Christian education. There was, for some, weekday contact as churches and chapels supported charities that provided food, clothing and fuel in times of hardship, and ran savings clubs that met in church vestries and church halls. Thus contact with the Church increased in times of distress (Hopkins 1989, 163–165).

At the beginning of the 19th century there was little leadership from the Rector of St. Martin's, who spent most of his time away from Birmingham. However, in 1829 the appointment of Thomas Moseley to St. Martin's brought a "deepening sense of spiritual life to the Parish" (Mole 1965, 97), and subsequently in 1846 the arrival of John Cale Miller heralded the beginning of a revival for the church (Fig. 163). He became "a leading personality in the neighbourhood, preaching and speaking widely, publishing a variety of sermons and pamphlets, and taking part in movements for educational and social reform" (Mole 1965, 97). His charismatic approach resulted in a huge increase in the congregation that packed into the church while he preached, often for an hour or more. This meant services often went on for some time, immortalised locally by the rhyme (Mole 1965, 98):

Cookery, cookery, kissery cook,
Bobbie's in the kitchen;
Sunday beef's a-baking hard,
While the Miller's preaching,
Twelve o'clock, one o'clock, half past two,
Sunday beef's as black as my shoe.
Hey the Miller! Ho the Miller!
This won't do.

Miller increased the number of services, organised special meetings for different age groups and advocated the use of the open air pulpit (Fig. 164), which he felt encouraged working men to come to church.

His influence was to spread beyond the parish into civic life. His awareness of contemporary social conditions and his organisational skills led him to form the St. Martin's Black Shoe Brigade to encourage street urchins to earn some money by cleaning shoes. This scheme eventually failed but his Hospital Sunday Fund, where collections were made in all churches and chapels throughout the town on the same Sunday every year, was more successful.

Miller realised that the established Church was out of touch with working class men and women and constantly tried to address this problem. This manifested itself in a liberal outlook that advocated social reform through municipal activity and better working conditions for the working classes. In 1854 he founded a working-men's association at St. Martin's. This held lectures, classes and discussions, and ran tea and music parties and a savings club. The Rector believed, in contrast to some of his contemporaries, that the working class were best

Fig. 163: Two influential rectors of St. Martin's. Dr. Miller (left), Rector 1846–66, and Dr. Wilkinson, Rector 1866–1897.

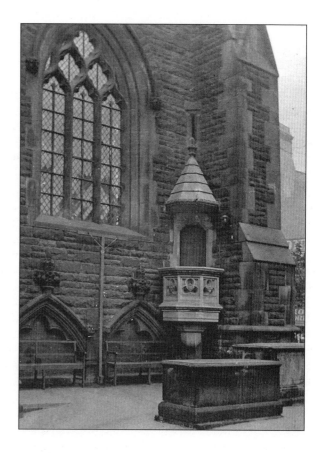

Fig. 164: The outside pulpit at St. Martin's, where Dr. Miller used to preach.

approached by members of their own class and so encouraged scripture readers and missionaries from the group to go out and minister to their workmates (Mole 1965, 102).

The effectiveness of these initiatives is difficult to gauge, although the fact remains that while the Church was of central importance to the middle classes the majority of the working classes remained indifferent. If we take into account the very low levels of school attendance, including Sunday School attendance, amongst the working-classes, mentioned in the previous chapter, then the level of understanding of Christian doctrines may have been very low. A reasonable generalisation might be that levels of awareness of Christian teachings grew throughout the course of the 19th century as a consequence of the evangelical movement and charismatic preachers such as John Cale Miller, the Sunday School movement and the growth of education in general.

The level of knowledge of Christian teachings, and the degree of relevance which different individuals felt they had for them, must have been reflected in the significance which was attached to burial in St. Martin's churchyard. Along with marriages (which up to 1836 had by law to take place in the parish church), funerals may well have been the main contact that many people had with the Church in the form of attending a religious ceremony. The funeral service, however, encapsulated the central doctrine of Christianity, which is the possibility of resurrection through Jesus Christ and of eternal life in Heaven, and the belief that death is a deliverance out of the miseries of a sinful world (see Chapter 9). However shaky one's grasp of the doctrines of Christianity, it is likely that everybody understood the concept of resurrection and a life everlasting, whether they believed in it or not. Quite how people viewed the role of the physical body laid in the grave – the 'earthly remains' – in resurrection may well have been variable (and perhaps confused), irrespective of the theological position on the matter, and of course the dead are surrounded with a range of popular superstitions. This would have affected attitudes to the mode of burial, the type of coffin and the disturbance of human remains.

It was noted in the previous chapter how the construction and use of family vaults reflected both concepts of family values and privacy, and the sense of social distinction between the middle and working classes. As allegiance to the Church was much stronger in general amongst the middle classes than amongst the working classes, the sense of social distinction may well have had a strong religious dimension to it; the vaults were erected amongst the graves of both the 'deserving' and the 'undeserving' poor. Certainly, there are a number of indications of the strength of allegiance of some of the families buried in the vaults to St. Martin's. For example, Isaac Ainsworth (Vault 23) was a church warden (see Chapter 6) and members of both the Jenkins (Vault 9) and Warden (Vault 5) families were subscribers to the book on the *History of Old St. Martin's, Birmingham* published by Bunce in 1875. Furthermore, these families retained their loyalty to St. Martin's even after they had moved out of the parish. As was noted above, the church provided a focus for social solidarity amongst the middle classes, as well as a mechanism for social and business networking. It may not be a coincidence that most of the family vaults at St. Martin's were probably built in the period 1810-1830: the men who built them are very likely

to have known each other well and to have shared a particular religious outlook.

The funerary trade in Birmingham

Coffins

The undertaking trade in Birmingham grew out of the coffin and coffin-furniture manufacturing industry, believed to have been introduced to Birmingham from London around 1760 (Aitken 1866, 193). Anyone could set up as an undertaker or coffin-maker, but the majority had already been involved in the cabinet-making and upholstery trades. It seems, however, that few earned a living purely by making coffins. Some tradesmen in the timber, textile and tin-plate industries saw coffin-making and funeral furnishing as a lucrative sideline. Most preferred to supply the trade, while others merely advertised their ability to make coffins while still carrying out their daily trade (Fig. 165).

The coffin has always been a highly visible indicator of status, both actual and aspired to. The quality of the wood, coffin furniture and workmanship played a decisive role in communicating the importance of both the deceased and those who survived them. In its visual importance, the coffin only shares the stage with funerary monuments. The main coffin types in use in the 18th and 19th centuries were the single-case, double-case and triple-case. All of these coffin types were present at St. Martin's, although in varying degrees of preservation (see Hancox, this volume, Chapter 5).

A single-case coffin was standard for an earth-cut burial and was by far the most common type, patronised by the lower-classes. It did not go unadorned. As one Birmingham observer noted, "the most economical of companies in the 'black business', whose advertisements appear immediately after the announcements of death in our newspapers, find it necessary to nail a groat's-worth of pathetic sham-finery even on a pauper's coffin" (Aitken 1866, 193). The purely wooden construction enabled the coffin to decay along with the body. This allowed for the deposition of further burials. Although the single-case

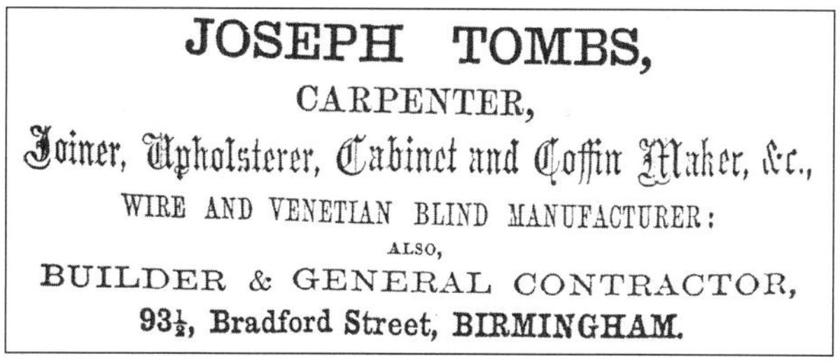

JOSEPH TOMBS,
CARPENTER,
Joiner, Upholsterer, Cabinet and Coffin Maker, &c.,
WIRE AND VENETIAN BLIND MANUFACTURER:
ALSO,
BUILDER & GENERAL CONTRACTOR,
93½, Bradford Street, BIRMINGHAM.

Fig. 165: An advertisement in the Directory of Birmingham of 1858 for Joseph Tombs, who appropriately included coffins amongst his diverse range of products.

coffin was unsuitable for deposition in burial vaults and brick-lined graves, some examples were present in these structures at St. Martin's. The triple-case coffin comprised three elements: an inner wooden coffin, a lead shell, and an outer wooden case. These took much longer to break down. This exclusive coffin-type was the choice of the wealthy, and was most commonly used for deposition in burial vaults and, less often, in brick-lined graves. Orders for lead shells would often go out to those with lead-working skills, a local plumber or roofer, perhaps. In 1852, Slater's Directory of Birmingham lists John Horton as 'Builder and Coffin Maker'; his associate and probable relative, Frederick Horton, is described as a 'Paper Hanger, Painter, Plumber and Glazier'.

As the 19th century progressed concern about the sanitary aspects of coffins increased, leading to much innovation in coffin design. For example, the Corporation Directory of 1846 includes an advertisement for an 'air tight metallic coffin', amongst the claimed benefits of which were:

> In addition to the economy of these coffins their great advantage is that no matter what the cause of death, or however infectious the disease there can be no possibility of danger to relatives or inmates of the house from the escape of any noxious effluvia.

At the bottom of the advert was a list of people seemingly endorsing the product and including 'C. Warden M.D.', one of the sons of Joseph Warden (Vault 5).

Coffin furniture

A writer in 1781 commented on the arrival and subsequent development of the coffin-furniture trade in Birmingham:

> The manufacture of these articles, till very lately, was confined principally to the metropolis …. their introduction into this town, (but a very few years ago) has been attended with singular advantages …. Artists of inventive minds and unwearied application, have called in the aid of dyes, presses and stamps. These have given an expedition to the execution of business, unknown, and unthought of before" (The Birmingham Directory 1781).

Apparently, the growth of cheap mass-produced coffin furniture led to the expansion of other markets:

> The great demand for the Coffin Furniture above mentioned, from its reduced price, encouraged an attempt to manufacture a new species of ornament, of the same composition, for rooms, picture frames, girandoles, chimney pieces, looking glasses, door and wainscot pannels, &c. (*ibid.*).

James Yates & Co., of Bradford Street, Birmingham, is an early example of such 'multi-tasking'. In the Pye's Birmingham Directory of 1797 the firm is described as:

> Brass-Founders, and Platers of Coach and Coach Harness Furniture, Manufacturers of Coffin Furniture of all Sorts, also Looking Glasses, Picture Frames, Composition Ornaments, &c..

It would seem that innovation, one of the defining characteristics of the Birmingham industrial experience in the 18th and 19th centuries, was not so readily appreciated elsewhere. Aitken (1866, 193), writing about the 18th century, believed that:

> A strong prejudice existed in the mind of the London undertaker of the period against any article not 'town-made', and the Messrs. Wagstaffe at first declined even to look at the 'Brummagem' patterns.

A glance through the Birmingham trade directories and other literature demonstrates the growth and development of the funerary trade in the 19th century (Fig. 166). In 1800, Bisset's survey of Birmingham lists five firms involved in the production of coffin furniture, secondary to other products. One of the firms, 'Jones and Baker' had simply been listed as brassfounders in 1781. As the Napoleonic Wars drew to a close in 1815 this number had risen to 20 and are now referred to as 'Coffin Furniture and Picture Frame Makers'. However, in 1829 the Birmingham Directory lists only 10 firms as being 'Coffin Furniture Manufacturers'. From this decline in numbers, one could be forgiven for thinking that the boom in coffin-furniture manufacturing demonstrated by the 1815 listings was over. However, the 1829 listings may in fact represent the vitality of the industry, demonstrated by the departure of coffin-furniture manufacture from allied trades. The fact that 'Yates, Hamper and Perry', a Birmingham firm, are now also trading in 'Mercer's Street, Long Acre, London' illustrates the growing confidence of the industry in Birmingham.

Another aspect of the coffin-furnishing trade in Birmingham was the production of 'coffin-lace', which was applied to the outside of fabric-covered coffins as an ornament and as an alternative to upholstery nails. Despite its name coffin-lace was made from metal. It was available in two colours, white, made from tinned metal, or black, from very thin rolled-out lead. Coffin lace was present in association with several of the coffins in the vaults at St. Martin's. The appearance in 1804 of mass-produced coffin-lace made from 'Albion metal' is attributed to one Thomas Dobbs, its inventor (Aitkin 1866, 196). Dobbs, obviously a colourful character, is described as 'a fellow of infinite jest' and of 'most excellent fancy', who did 'the comic business' on the boards of the Birmingham Theatre Royal (*ibid.*). By 1866 it was claimed that as much as 60 to 80 tons of block tin were consumed annually in Birmingham for the manufacture of coffin-lace (Aitken 1866, 197).

Undertaking

By 1845 the funerary trade appears to have separated into its constituent elements. The Post Office Directory of that year lists 16 coffin-furniture manufacturers, 22 coffin-makers, and 11 newly appeared undertakers trading in Birmingham. By 1875 the number of undertakers had risen to 46, supplied by 9 coffin-furniture manufacturers.

Undertakers now clearly dominated the funerary industry.

Howarth (1997, 121) argues that the creation of a separate undertaking business occurred for a variety of reasons, which would have affected Birmingham in the same way that they did the nation as a whole. First, the Protestant rejection of the doctrine of Purgatory led to funerals focusing more on the feelings of the bereaved and less on the salvation of the deceased, and time that would have been spent praying for the souls of the dead was now directed towards care of the corpse. Second, the dying process was becoming the responsibility of the doctor rather than the clergy, leading to the undertaker taking control of the corpse. Third, the rise of individualism and of the importance of the nuclear family led to death becoming a more private matter, with a consequent need to mark loss through mourning.

As funerals became more complex and ostentatious, the work practices of the industrial age meant that there was less time to organise them. Handing over the organisation of the rituals to a professional saved time and took pressure off the family. As a result, demand for a specialist service rose dramatically (*ibid*). These factors, combined with the increasing wealth and numbers of the middle classes, explain rising expenditure on funerals and mourning dress, especially in the first half of the 19th century. Furthermore, as more of the decision-making was handed over to undertakers, they increasingly exerted their influence over funerary rituals.

This manipulatory policy, coupled with the increasing extravagance and cost of funerals, shed a poor light on the industry. Ostentatious display at funerals became a fashion that was to peak in the 1850s. For the working classes, burial clubs were established to provide a saving scheme for funerals; it was also hoped that some of the money saved would go toward supporting the family after the death of a household earner, especially the father, although this was often not the case. The establishment of burial clubs might appear at first to be a force for good: in return for weekly payments, the clubs guaranteed an appropriate funeral. However, undertakers invested heavily in burial clubs, which they also often administered. Many others felt that the clubs encouraged funeral extravagance and that the pressure to provide a 'good send-off' impoverished the lower-classes. This led to the creation of a burial and mourning reform movement.

Before giving consideration to this movement, which was well represented in Birmingham, something should be said about the threat of 'body snatching', which undertakers were expected to help protect their clients from. Security from this threat may have been one of the motivations behind the construction of brick-lined graves and family vaults.

The 'Resurrectionist' threat

Interment in a burial structure acted as a safeguard against

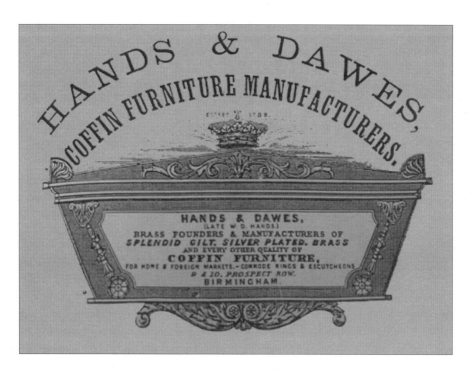

Fig. 166: An advertisement for Hands & Dawes, coffin furniture manufacturers (from the Post Office Directory of Birmingham 1875).

the perceived, or perhaps quite often real, threat posed by grave robbers, the so-called 'resurrection men' of the early 19th century. The growth of medical science encouraged a lucrative trade in the illegal supply of cadavers to medical schools for anatomical study. Cadavers had to be fresh, and a resurrectionist could expect to be well paid for a body in good condition. This was set to continue until the Anatomy Act of 1832, which legalised the dissection of paupers' corpses. The much publicised accounts of grave robbing, such as the infamous case of Edinburgh's 'Burke and Hare', did much to heighten existing fears surrounding the security of corpses buried in churchyards up and down the country. It was not unknown for those entrusted with the care of the deceased to be involved in grave robbing activities. Sextons, undertakers, and other funerary personnel were often viewed with suspicion in body-snatching cases. It appears that such people could be bribed into selling corpses and then filling the coffin with a substitute weighty material.

The threat of body-snatching for dissection and the theft of body parts and personal items was greatest out in the open churchyard, where very little could be done to defend against the activities of the 'resurrectionists'. To afford some protection, on occasion long straw was placed in the grave over the coffin (McKenna 1992, 17). The straw was placed lengthways and crossways between layers of earth until the grave was filled. This would make the hasty excavation of the grave slow and laborious. This practice has been recorded in Birmingham (*ibid.*).

McKenna (1992, 17–19) provides information on several recorded instances of grave robbing in Birmingham. The jaw was removed from the body of a young woman buried at St. Bartholomew's churchyard for the making of false teeth. The perpetrator received six months hard labour (*ibid.*, 18). When a 19th-century grave at the Baptist Chapel in Cannon Street was opened for reinterment at Witton Cemetery, no coffin or body was present. Bricks had been placed in the grave in the dimensions of a coffin. As this was an enclosed graveyard, the complicity of the chapel keeper was suspected (*ibid.*, 18–19). Although there is no evidence for this type of activity at St. Martin's there is the distinct possibility that it did take place.

A number of schools of anatomy and surgery appeared in the provinces during the period 1800-1830, including in Birmingham (Poynter 1966, 121). Richardson (1987, 83) asserts that all burial grounds within the vicinity of an anatomy school were under constant threat from resurrectionists.

Among the more portable items of value to be obtained from a corpse were the teeth. Innovations in dentistry provided a financially worthwhile sideline for the resurrectionists. Human teeth were supplied to dentists for the manufacture of false teeth, as the case of the young woman buried in St. Bartholomew's churchyard, mentioned above, illustrates.

The cost of funerals and the reform movement

A movement for the reform of burial, to limit extravagance and expenditure, gathered pace from as early as the 1830s (Howarth 1997, 122). The Birmingham Funeral and Mourning Reform Association was established in 1876 and became an important player in the movement. Although the Birmingham association was formed nearly 30 years after the last earth-cut burial took place at St. Martin's, the information contained in their annual reports is still relevant as it not only reveals the plight of the lower classes, but also gives a valuable insight into the workings and impact of the funerary industry during the period as a whole. The account below is based largely on the reports of the Birmingham Funeral and Mourning Reform Association for 1876 and 1884 (B. F. M. R. A. 1876; 1884).

The Birmingham association sought to:

abolish unnecessary show and useless expenditure on the occasion of funerals, in the hope that by common consent a more simple and less gloomy ceremonial may be substituted [and argued that] the present system is extremely burdensome and oppressive to poor people (B. M. F. R. A. 1876 – 'specially addressed to the working classes').

The trend for lavish displays of mourning at middle- and upper-class funerals put pressure on the lower classes to follow suit. The association realised that this often precluded the poor from adopting reform "from fear that they might be thought – by the ignorant and prejudiced – as wanting in respect to their deceased friends" (*ibid.*). The underlying principle of funeral and mourning reform was "that simplicity is not shabbiness, and that economy (for the sake of the living) is no dishonour to the dead" (*ibid.*). The accounts of reformers reveal the social impact of burial expense on the poor. The Bishop of Sodor and Man outlined his reasons for joining the movement:

a reason for supporting this movement was the expense in which the survivors were involved. They would often find that a poor widow, left with hardly enough to put bread into the mouths of her children, was obliged to go to a great expense in order to bury her husband or a relative in (what is called) a decent way (*ibid.*).

Extravagant funerals did at least provide periodic opportunities to make a little extra cash and engage in other distractions:

He remembered once visiting a poor shoemaker's family in London, whose children he had missed from school, and on enquiring where the man was he was told that he had gone to be a "Mute", for which he was paid 3s 6d and spirits (*ibid.*).

Funerals were thought to contribute to insobriety, a recognised social ill of the day (see Chapter 7). There are many references to excessive drinking at funerals, and the association wholeheartedly embraced "the abolition of the custom of employing Hired Mourners and Mutes, and the discontinuance of Feasting and Drinking at funerals" (*ibid.*).

Undertakers were viewed with suspicion by many, beyond their possible complicity in grave robbing. Agents and touts for the undertakers were accused of preying on the grieving poor, inducing poor women to employ them to undertake funerals with a view to making large profits out of the transaction. The reformers complained that it was "a great pity that these *widow robbers* cannot be discovered and punished for their nefarious traffic" (B. F. M. R. A. 1884, 8). On occasion the association intervened on behalf of individuals who felt undertakers had overcharged them, apparently with some success. A letter from one complainant reads: "We are glad to tell you that we have satisfactorily settled the matter with Messrs —. Please accept our thanks for the trouble you have taken in this matter" (*ibid.*).

The Birmingham reformers were prepared to give the names of undertakers willing to perform funerals in an economical and orderly manner. Unfortunately we do not know who these enlightened Birmingham undertakers were as this information was only available upon request (B. F. M. R. A. 1876 – 'specially addressed to the working classes').

The Birmingham association recorded the effect of expensive funerals on the finances of the poor. In their 1884 report the association provided specimen charges for funerals performed for those who had subscribed to burial clubs. Table 133 provides the charges incurred for a working man's funeral – the family were soon destitute.

Table 134 shows the costs to 'E. B.', a widow aged 27 years, of burying her husband who died on 5th August 1883. She had three children to support, aged 7, 5, and 3 years, and had to apply for relief 31st August 1883.

Table 135 shows the costs of burying 'J. P.', a 45-year-old man with three children, whose wife was in an asylum. He had been in receipt of 5s per week relief, and when he died he was buried by the burial club of which he was a member, the (pitiful) balance from the costs of the funeral being handed over for the maintenance of the children.

The reformers sought to reduce these expenses and suggested limitations on the number of coaches, no ornaments on horses, no elaborate funerary apparel, no gifts of hatbands, scarves or gloves, no hired mourners or mutes, plain coffins, and simple refreshments (B. F. M. R. A. 1876 – 'specially addressed to the working classes').

The Guardians of the Poor knew that often widows who had received £10 or £15 from a burial club spent it all on a lavish funeral and mourning, and then went to the Guardians as paupers to ask for poor relief (*ibid.*). The association spoke in terms of "absolute pauperism, which indirectly affects the whole community" (B. F. M. R. A. 1884, 2).

Reform was also aimed at the upper and middle classes who should set an example for the lower classes and "should adopt the reforms and make simple funeral fashions". The 1843 report on 'Interment in Towns' found that the average funeral expenses of titled people varied from £800 to £1,500, and those of the upper gentry from £200 to £400.

Of particular interest in the present context are the charges levied at St. Martin's for different types of burial (burial in an earth-cut grave, burial in a vault, etc.) and associated monuments and grave stones. Bunce reproduced a table of the charges in 1848 in his *History of Old St. Martin's, Birmingham* (1875, 35) (Table 136).

Funeral Items	£	s.	d.
Coffin	2	10	0
Register	0	1	3
The Road	0	7	6
Grave	0	12	6
Hearse and 3 Coaches	4	4	0
Bearers	0	12	6
Tea and Refreshments	2	8	0
Six pairs Gloves	0	18	0
Coachmen (Gift)	0	2	0
Band and Sashes	0	3	0
TOTAL	**£11**	**18**	**9**

Table 133: Specimen charges for working man's funeral in 1884.

	£	s.	d.
Amount due from club	£10	0	0
Funeral expenses	£9	6	3
Balance for maintenance of children	£0	13	9

Table 135: Funeral expenses paid by burial club.

Insurance	£	s.	d.	Funeral Expenses	£	s.	d
Insurance	17	0	0	Funeral Charges	6	18	4
Burial club	8	0	0	Mourning Apparel	10	11	5
				Refreshments	1	2	5
				Sundries	0	7	9
TOTAL	**£25**	**0**	**0**	**TOTAL**	**£18**	**19**	**11**

Table 134: Costs to a widow of burying her husband in 1883.

Of course, these charges represent only a small proportion of the costs of a funeral, but they presumably reflect the different order of expenditure made by the middle classes and the working classes. For example the charge for a 'vault in yard' (which would not include the cost of its construction) was £5 1s, or sixteen times the cost of a 'grave' (6s 4d) , while each 'fresh interment' in a vault cost £1 15s 6d, or nearly six times the cost of burial in a grave.

Members of the Birmingham Funeral and Mourning Reform Association were encouraged to set an example by leaving written instructions as to the manner of their own funerals:

> I direct my Executors to conduct my funeral in a simple and unostentatious manner, and that no plumes, velvet cloths, or trappings be used for the carriages or horses. And I request that those who attend the funeral wear no scarf, cloak, or long hatband, and that if any mourning apparel be worn after my decease, it be of the simplest kind (B. F. M .R. A. 1884, 9).

The Birmingham reformers evangelised about funeral and mourning reform but apparently did not always practise what they preached. The same report contained the following note: "No rules are made as to the conduct of Members' Funerals. Each one being perfectly free as to adopting or rejecting any of the Association's suggestions. Membership merely implies approval of Funeral and Mourning Reform" (*ibid.*, 4). Interestingly,

with regard to double standards, two members of the Browett family and two of Warden family are listed as members of the association during the period 1876–1884. Several members of these families were buried in the Warden family vault (Vault 5), both before and after this period, but there is little evidence from the coffins of the later burials (Level 4), which were in lead coffins with elaborate fixtures (see Chapter 3 Table 14), that any expense was spared.

The expense incurred by a death did not end with the funeral itself. In the 19th century one was expected to adopt mourning dress for a period of time, and this was aimed almost exclusively at women. The Birmingham Daily Mail remarked that "there still lingers a not inconsiderable amount of the senseless, but well-meaning belief, that respect for the deceased must be measured by yards of crape and silk, and that grief increases in proportion to the undertaker's bill" (quoted in B. F. M. R. A. 1876). Such etiquette was often not an option for the urban poor whose choice of funeral arrangements was constrained by family finances. In the concluding chapter an attempt is made, using the range of archaeological and historical evidence presented thus far, to reconstruct the main features of two funerals that took place at St. Martin's, one of a member of the middle classes, the other of the working classes, in 1856, before the influence of the reform movement had taken hold.

	Rector			Clerk			Sexton			Total		
	£	s.	d.	£	s.	d.	£	s.	d.	£	s.	d.
Grave not exceeding 6 feet	0	1	4	0	1	0	0	4	0	0	6	4
Ditto, per every additional foot extra	''	''	''	''	''	''	0	1	0	0	1	0
Vault in Church	5	5	0	0	5	0	''	''	''	5	10	0
Fresh interment in ditto	2	2	0	0	2	6	''	''	''	2	4	6
Vault in yard	4	4	0	0	5	0	0	12	0	5	1	0
Fresh interment in ditto	1	1	0	0	2	6	0	12	0	1	15	6
Tomb with railings, without vault	4	0	0	0	5	0	''	''	''	4	5	0
Fresh interment in ditto	1	1	0	0	2	6	0	12	0	1	15	6
Tomb over vault, extra to vault	1	0	0	0	2	6	''	''	''	1	2	6
Ditto, higher than 3 feet	2	0	0	0	5	0	''	''	''	2	5	0
Brick Grave	1	1	0	0	2	6	0	12	0	1	15	6
Fresh interment in ditto	1	1	0	0	2	6	0	12	0	1	15	6
Flat Stone	1	1	0	0	1	0	''	''	''	1	2	0
Head or foot stone	0	5	0	0	0	6	''	''	''	0	5	6
Tablet outside Church	3	3	0	''	''	''	''	''	''	3	3	0
Tablet inside Church	5	5	0	''	''	''	''	''	''	5	5	0

Table 136: Charges for burials at St. Martin's in 1848; from Bunce 1875.

9   Two Funerals at St. Martin's

Josephine Adams

In this final chapter two funerals which took place at St. Martin's in 1856 are reconstructed. Although there is necessarily speculation in the account, the findings of the archaeological excavations in the churchyard, and the documentary research which has been undertaken to place these findings in context, have provided sufficient information to ground most of the reconstruction, including many of the details, on firm evidence.

January 1856

January 1856 was unusually mild with drizzly rain rather than snow falling most days. The whole country waited for the outcome of the peace talks in Paris aimed at ending the Crimean War. In Birmingham, as the local newspaper *Aris's Gazette* reveals, there was the usual concern with the domestic issues of the day. There was a meeting of the Guardians of the Poor, and in the Town Hall a talk on Income Tax reform. There was great interest in the Rugeley poisonings too, a court case that dominated local news. However in two Birmingham households much attention must have been focussed not on the foreign or local news but on the decline and death of two elderly family members. These were Joseph Warden, who died on January 25th, and Ann Cockayne who died nine days before, on 16th January.

According to one source, in the Victorian era the objective of the time after death that culminated in the funeral, and of the following period of mourning, was

to show that love toward the deceased part which Nature requireth; then to do him that honour which is fit both generally for men, and particularly for the honour of his person; last of all, to testify the care which the Church hath to comfort the living, and the hope which we all have concerning the resurrection of the dead *(Ecclesiastical Art Review*, quoted in Morley 1971, 22).

Whilst the care of the Church and the hope of resurrection could be considered a personal and private ethos, the way to show the love and respect for the deceased was in the very public ceremony of the funeral, which in class-conscious Victorian society had to be seen to follow correct conventions. A funeral was an event considered vital to preserve social status. The fear in death of a 'parish funeral', when the deceased person's family was unable to pay for the ceremony and was reliant on the local parish for burial, was akin to the social stigma in life of having to enter the workhouse. Having enough money to pay for an appropriate funeral was therefore an ongoing worry for many people. The style of the funeral depended upon one's status in society, one's desire to be seen to be adhering to social convention, and upon one's ability to pay. People often made elaborate and detailed provisions for their funeral. The danger was that, in a desire to emulate the rich, the working classes would arrange a funeral that was considered too ostentatious for their station in life, would be in bad taste or might result in destitution (Litten 1991, 165; see also Chapter 8).

Joseph Warden and Ann Cockayne

Something of the life of Joseph Warden, of 14 Wellington Road in the prosperous suburb of Edgbaston, and of the lives of members of his family, has already been described in Chapter 6. The wealthy iron merchant died on Friday 25th January 1856 at the age of 68. His death certificate states that he died of kidney disease, and that his daughter Helen was at his bedside (Fig. 167). He was buried at St. Martin's Church on 1st February. From a material point of view the later years of Joseph's life would have been comfortable, with his second wife, Sophia, and family around him, together with a housekeeper and servants to look after the house. He would probably have had a servant to care for his personal needs and, in such an affluent household, a trained nurse may have been engaged during his illness. His son Charles Warden was a doctor and lived very close by, so it is likely that he would have been a regular visitor.

Some days earlier, on January 20th, Ann Cockayne, a widow aged 76, was also buried at St. Martin's, having

CERTIFIED COPY of an ENTRY
Pursuant to the Births and Deaths Registration Act 1953

DEATH

1856 DEATHS in the District of Edgbaston in the Counties of Warwick & Worcester

No.	When Died.	Name and Surname.	Sex.	Age.	Rank or Profession.	Cause of Death.	Signature, Description, and Residence of Informant.	When Registered.	Signature of Registrar.
421	Twenty fifth January 1856 44 Wellington Road Edgbaston	Joseph Warden	Male	68 years	Iron Merchant	Disease of the Kidnies Certified	Helen Warden present at the Death 44 Wellington Road Edgbaston	Thirtieth January 1856	Edward Baker Registrar

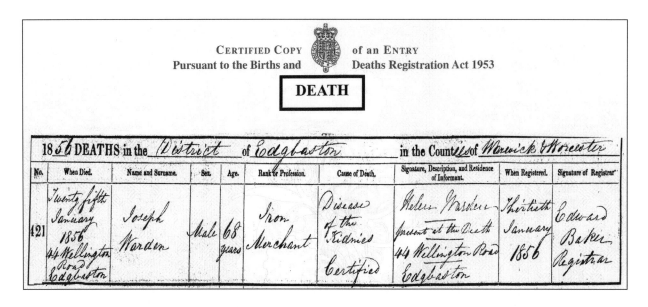

Fig. 167: Joseph Warden's death certificate.

CERTIFIED COPY of an ENTRY
Pursuant to the Births and Deaths Registration Act 1953

DEATH

1856. DEATHS in the District of St Martin Birmingham in the County of Warwick

No.	When Died	Name and Surname	Sex	Age	Rank or Profession	Cause of Death	Signature, Description, and Residence of Informant	When Registered	Signature of Registrar
399	Sixteenth January 1856 105 Digbeth	Ann Cockayne	Female	76 Years	Widow of John Cockayne Butcher (Master)	Decay of Nature Certified	Thomas Cockayne In Attendance 105 Digbeth Birmingham	Seventeenth January 1856	John White Registrar

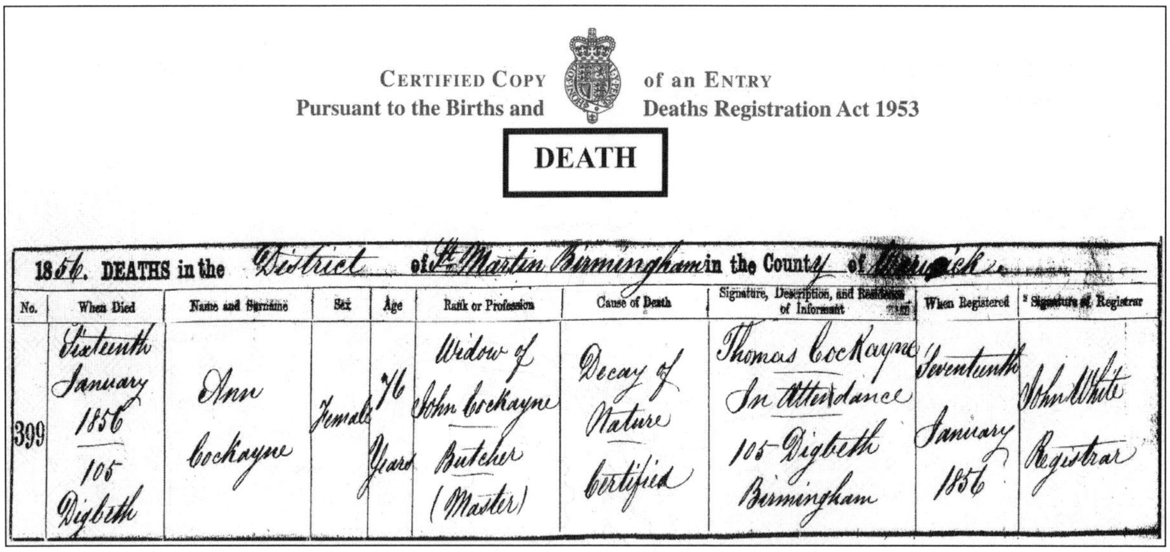

Fig. 168: Ann Cockayne's death certificate.

died on 16th January with her son Thomas at her bedside (Fig. 168). Like Joseph Warden, Ann and her husband John had moved to Birmingham in their youth, hoping that the rapidly expanding industrial town would provide them and their family with a secure future. In contrast to Joseph, however, whose career went from strength to strength, Ann was to remain at 105 Digbeth all her life, where John and subsequently son Thomas ran a butcher's shop. Despite being described as a *Master Butcher* in contemporary trade directories, John's income evidently did not enable the family to move away from the crowded town streets of St. Martin's to the leafy suburbs of Edgbaston. Another son, Walter, was also a butcher at 31 Digbeth. Ann's death certificate suggests that she died simply of 'decay of nature', and it is probable that she was cared for by just her immediate family and local friends.

Preparations for the funerals

While it is not known exactly how these two families commemorated the deaths of their relatives, there is plenty of evidence to suggest that the difference between the funeral of a rich member of the newly emerging middle classes and the wife of a butcher would have been considerable.

Fig. 169: An advertisement for Messers. Brookes & Oakes, who in this advertisement for their funeral carriages attempted to appeal to both the 'Working Classes' and 'Gentlemen and Professional Men'.

It can be safely assumed that Joseph Warden, father of twelve, entrepreneur, owner of foundries and nailshops in the town, had a funeral that demonstrated the measure of his success. The trend for limiting lavish display at funerals had not yet begun in the town (Chapter 8), so it is probable that little expense was spared on his funeral.

Ann Cockayne's commemoration on the other hand is likely to have been more modest (or, at least, less expensive). However, she too would have wanted a funeral that illustrated her position in society and one that the family could be proud of. She may well have contributed to a burial club throughout her life to ensure that adequate funds were available.

Both families would have hired the services of a local undertaker, a trade that was becoming lucrative at that time (Chapter 8), but it is probable that the Warden family would have chosen one of the high-class establishments, such as Brookes & Oakes at Warwick Mews, Lower Hurst Street. Brookes & Oakes advertised funeral carriages and cabs, richly trimmed hearses and splendid mourning coaches with long-tailed black Flemish horses, all trimmed with rich velvets and ostrich plumes. The Cockayne family, meanwhile, may have turned to one of the small local establishments, such as B. Smith at 19 Court, Bromsgrove Street, listed in contemporary trade directories. However, Brookes & Oakes also tried to appeal to the working-class market, as one of their advertisements shows (Fig. 169).

In the days that followed the deaths of Joseph Warden and Ann Cockayne there would have been many similarities between the two families as they prepared for their respective funerals. Both Joseph and Ann died at home and their bodies would have remained in the house until the funeral. As a mark of respect and to indicate to the outside world that a death had occurred, the curtains or blinds would have remained drawn until the funeral cortege left the house (Curl 1972, 7).

Joseph's body would probably been laid out by his nurse or a trusted family servant, while a female member of the family or a hired local woman who specialised in both midwifery and laying out would have attended to Ann. Nurses received instruction on how to lay out a body during their training, but a sister or daughter would equally do their best to treat the body with respect (Jalland 1996, 212).

Members of the family may have visited to pay their respects and to view the body, which would have been placed in an open coffin. In the 17th century a funeral feast may have been held before the funeral, with the body as the guest of honour. This was partly to confirm to the mourners that the person was indeed dead, and partly to ensure that the person was still part of their lives. The visitors were all identified by their relationship to the deceased (Curl 1972, 13).

In both cases, the death would have been notified to the registrar of the district, within five days, by one of those present. As well as the name, sex, age and profession of the deceased, the date and cause of death had to be notified before a certificate of registry could be issued. This was then shown to the minister before the interment could take place (Jalland 1996, 213). It was at this point that the differences between the classes began to show.

It is likely that, as a mark of respect, Joseph Warden's businesses would have closed for the day of the funeral. The working class Cockayne family, on the other hand, chose a traditional Sunday ceremony, probably so that no trading days were lost (Morley 1971, 26). They would have used St. Martin's because they lived within the parish, so close in fact that they could probably have seen the church from their house. While the Warden family had by this time moved away to nearby Edgbaston, they retained strong links with the church – they are even listed as subscribers to an early history of St. Martin's (Bunce 1875) – and probably still worshipped there. Moreover, the Warden family vault had been built in St. Martin's churchyard.

The Warden family vault is Vault 5, and it is described in detail in Chapter 3. It is argued there that Joseph Warden is likely to have built the family vault not long after his marriage, at the age of 25, to Ann Maria Marston in 1812 and the birth of their first daughter, whom the couple also called Ann Maria, in 1813. At that time Joseph was still living locally. As well as paying for the cost of building the vault and erecting a tomb over it, there was also a fee to pay to the church. Although Joseph built his vault earlier than this date, a scale of charges is available for 1848 (see Chapter 8) and at that time the total fee for a vault in the churchyard with a tomb above was £9 6s, a considerable sum. Joseph began incurring the steep costs of his funeral many years before his death.

Although Joseph may have built the vault many years earlier, the first burial in it appears to have been that of his first wife, Ann Maria (HB 574), who died in 1842; he was fortunate, unlike many of his contemporaries, that all of his twelve children survived through to adulthood. While Joseph Warden's coffin was not among those in the vault with a legible coffin plate, he is tentatively identified as HB 573, interred beside Ann Maria.

Thus Joseph's place of burial had been decided long before his death and preparations would have been made before the funeral to dig down beside the vault on its western side and dismantle the brickwork of the (non load-bearing) western wall to admit his coffin. There was a charge for this too; in 1848 it was £1 15s 6d for a new interment in an existing vault.

No such long-term provisions are likely to have been made for Ann Cockayne's place of burial, which is likely to have been a simple earth cut grave, either in the churchyard or perhaps the detached burial ground in nearby Park Street. By 1856 the churchyard was very crowded (see Chapter 2). For women of Ann's class, if they could not be buried with their husband, the sexton would have selected a suitable spot using his (approximate) knowledge of the date and location of earlier

burials, supplemented by probing with a rod – the aim being to avoid areas with the most recent burials. Nevertheless, disturbance of earlier burials was almost inevitable, as the large amount of inter-cutting of graves revealed by the excavations shows. The charge for an earth-cut grave was much less than that for interment in an existing vault – the total fee to the rector, clerk and sexton being 6s 4d in 1848.

An announcement of Joseph Warden's death was placed in the Obituary column of the local weekly newspaper, *Aris's Gazette*. Memorial cards, with a suitable text, would be ordered and sent out to all his business associates and wide circle of friends (Fig. 170). Some of these would include an invitation to his funeral (Curl 2000, 202–203). In contrast, in the crowded streets of St. Martin's, word of mouth would soon tell of a death in the butcher's family of Digbeth.

In any Victorian household the period of mourning was important and there were strict codes of etiquette that had to be adhered to in some levels of society (Jalland 1996, 300–307). These customs inevitably waned during the century, and the influence of the royal court procedure would have lessened in the provinces, but amongst the *nouveaux riches* of Edgbaston, Sophia, Joseph's second wife would have wanted to be seen to behave in the correct manner. So, in the seven days that elapsed between death and burial, mourning clothes would have been ordered (Fig. 171). The widow was the main focus of the mourning and would be expected to wear full black for two years. Traditionally, during the first year of 'deep' mourning this consisted of black dresses made of paramatta and crape (the former being a combined fabric of silk and wool or cotton, and the latter a harsh black silk fabric with a crimped finish produced by heat). These particular fabrics were chosen for their dull, lustreless qualities that produced a 'dead' appearance. After a year and a day, this material could be replaced by fabrics of a slightly lighter texture, then during the last six months colours of half mourning such as grey, violet, and black and white could be introduced. The daughters and daughters-in-law would also have been expected to wear full black at the time of the funeral, while for the men the dress code was easier as their normal sombre suit was sufficient, although black cloaks, gloves, hat bands and cravats may have been added.

Unless a long illness had given the family sufficient forewarning of death, the purchase of all these articles could be problematic as different shops had to be visited for each article. However by the 1840s there was a growth in 'mourning warehouses' that sold the whole range of mourning attire, making life easier for the recently bereaved (Morley 1971, 73). The Warden family may have visited one such establishment, 'The Birmingham Mourning and Funeral Warehouse' of Bach & Barker at 42 New Street, whose advertisement is illustrated (Fig. 172). In a more comprehensive notice in *Aris's Gazette* of 28th January 1856, the same company advertised

Fig. 170: Examples of memorial cards.

"black lace, tulle and tarletan dresses, jackets and pelerins" (women's long narrow capes), together with every conceivable accessory.

The financial outlay on all this would have been considerable and for the Cockayne family in Digbeth improvisation would have been required (Flanders 2003, 341). If the ladies of the family could have afforded it, new black dresses would have been bought, but in many cases mourning clothes were handed on between family and friends after a period of mourning had ended. Alternatively, existing day dresses were dyed for the

occasion, either by the owner themself or by specialised dyers whose entire business may have depended on dying clothes for mourning.

Despite the large outlay on mourning dresses, Sophia Warden and Joseph's daughters and daughters-in-law may not have attended his funeral. It was considered that women, especially the widow, might not be able to contain their grief, and public displays of grief were considered unseemly (Jalland 1996, 221). If they did attend, however, they would probably have stayed in the church while the actual burial was taking place. It is more likely that the

Fig. 171: A selection of ladies' mourning dress from 'The Queen', a ladies' newspaper, August 27th 1881.

Fig. 172: An advertisement for Bach & Barker, a warehouse selling a range of mourning attire (Corporation Directory of Birmingham 1861).

female members of Ann's family, together with friends and associates from the local community, attended her funeral.

The funerals

On the day of Joseph's funeral, 1st February 1856, the doorknockers and doorknobs of his house would have been draped with black crape and two mutes employed by the undertaker would have stood either side of the front door (Fig. 173). These mutes were men dressed in black frock coats and top hats who carried crape covered wands to symbolise the visitation of death (Curl 1972, 7). An elaborate box-type hearse with solid sides drawn by four black horses would have arrived at the house to collect the coffin, together with two or more horse-drawn mourning coaches to accommodate Joseph's large family. Each coach and horses would have been decorated with velvet coverings and black ostrich feathers (Fig. 174).

Some of the details of Joseph's coffin can be recon-

structed from the three coffins found in the bottom level of the Warden family vault, which include not only the coffin which was probably his, but either side of this those of his first wife Ann Maria and (very likely) his second wife Sophia. It was of the triple-shell wood/lead/wood type (probably elm), shaped in the fish-tail style with a cover of black baize-like woollen cloth held in place by brass domed tacks. His body would have been dressed in a shroud made of undyed tabby or 'shrouding flannel' with a bonnet-like cap on his head. He would have been placed on a mattress made of thick, more densely woven material stuffed with plant materials and covered with a winding sheet made of wool union. A man of his wealth would probably have had a full-size winding sheet on which the body was placed in the coffin before the sides were brought up and over to cover him.

The coffin would have been placed in the hearse and covered by a silk velvet pall. The hearse was preceded by mutes and flanked by attendants, all with gowns, silk hat bands and gloves, who headed the procession. There is unlikely to have been the colourful floral tributes associated with funerals today, with everything from the plumes and plush velvets to the coach and horses being black to create the impression of sombre opulence and formality that befitted the occasion.

In contrast, the procession for Ann Cockayne's funeral held on January 20th, a few days before Joseph's, would have been more modest. It was a much shorter distance from her house to the church but it is likely she still had a hearse, albeit much smaller, less elaborate and drawn by just two horses, with only one mute preceding. Like Joseph's coffin, the wood used for Ann's coffin would probably also have been elm, but it is likely it would have been of single-case design with no lead shell. It is

Fig. 174: Advertisement for John Marston & Co., a Birmingham firm of hearse and cab builders (Undertaker and Funeral Directors' Journal, 22nd July 1887).

Fig. 173: Two mutes employed to stand outside the deceased person's house on the day of the funeral and accompany the hearse to the church.

probable, although not certain, that she had an iron-stamped *depositum*, and the coffin would have had six or eight iron grip plates (see Hancox, Chapter 5). It would have been covered by a cloth for the actual funeral. She too would have been dressed in a shroud and bonnet but with none of the silk ruffles and ribbons of a higher-status female. To economise, her winding sheet may have consisted of two narrow side sheets tacked to the sides of the coffin, rather than the whole one that probably covered Joseph. The coffin linings too would have been simpler.

In contrast to the grand horse-drawn procession for Joseph Warden, Ann's family and friends would have walked the short distance to the church. The people of the busy streets around St. Martin's were used to the sight of a funeral. There was at least one a day at that time, and while they may have stopped for a few moments as Joseph's grand procession passed, either as a mark of respect or just out of curiosity, they may not have spared a glance towards Ann's, unless of course they saw it as an excuse to join in the wake, a practice common at the time (Morley 1971, 26).

The service for the burial of the dead was the same for all – in theory wealth or poverty made no difference, although it could not be used for anyone who was not baptized or had committed suicide. Nevertheless, there were many subtle and not-so-subtle ways that differences could be marked in the conduct of the service depending on the status of the deceased – for example, the appearance and deportment of the mourners, or the length, solemnity and elaboration of the service.

The priest would meet the coffin at the entrance to the churchyard and walk in front of it into the church singing or saying specific verses from the Gospel of John, the Book of Job and the Book of Timothy:

I am the resurrection and the life, saith the Lord: he that believeth in me, though he were dead, yet shall he live: and whosoever liveth and believeth in me shall never die (John 11.25.26).

And though after my skin worms destroy this body, yet in my flesh shall I see God (Job 19.26).

We brought nothing into this world, and it is certain we can carry nothing out (Timothy 6.7).

Once inside, psalms would be sung followed by a Lesson from the 15th Chapter of the former Epistle of Saint Paul to the Corinthians:

O death, where is thy sting? O grave, where is thy victory? The sting of death is sin, and the strength of sin is the law. But thanks be to God, which giveth us the victory through our Lord Jesus Christ.

Following the service in the church, at the graveside specific verses would be said or sung as the coffin was being prepared for burial and then put into the grave:

We give thee hearty thanks, for that it hath pleased thee to deliver this our brother out of the miseries of this sinful world… (The Book of Common Prayer 1662).

Here again the class differences would emerge because while Joseph's coffin was lifted into his family vault (something that, in practical terms, must have been difficult to achieve with dignity), Ann's would have been lowered into her simple earth-cut grave.

After the funerals

It seemed to vary amongst the middle classes as to whether a funeral wake was held. In some cases mourners were expected to leave after the carriages had returned to the family home, unless they had travelled some distance when they would be offered a meal. Others may have just returned to the house to hear the will read (Jalland 1996, 223–224). In Joseph Warden's case this may have caused some family consternation as he had added various codicils amending his bequests when his sons' behaviour had upset him (see Chapter 6).

It is likely, though, that the Warden family, being large and well known in the area, invited people back to the house where a large meal was waiting. This could have been prepared by the household staff or laid on as part of the service offered by the undertaker. It would have included sherry, to warm the mourners after the cold damp funeral service, together with ham, pies, port and cakes, with jelly and trifle being especially popular (Curl 1972, 12).

In the streets of Digbeth it is more likely that some sort of wake took place after Ann's funeral. It was more a point of honour to feed the mourners, so a large meal would be prepared with large quantities of ham – readily available in this family – and plenty of ale and cider to drink (Curl 1972, 12). It was a Sunday so the shops and local businesses were shut but the pubs were open – it is possible that neighbours and friends used the occasion not only to commemorate Ann's life, but as an excuse to enjoy themselves.

After the funeral a stonemason would have been employed to mark Joseph's death on the chest tomb above the vault, while Ann may have had a memorial stone to mark her place of rest (further costs and fees for both families). Joseph's legacy was to live on until 2001 with the discovery of his family vault, while Ann's stone was lost forever as the churchyard was altered and landscaped over the years.

References

Abernethy (1826) Mr Abernethy's physiological, pathological and surgical observations. *Lancet* 7, 97–105.

Aitken, W. C. (1866) Coffin Furniture. In W. C. Aitkin *The Early History of Brass and the Brass Manufacturers of Birmingham*. Birmingham, Billingson & Co.

Albright, F. and Riefenstein, E. (1948) *The Parathyroid Glands and Metabolic Bone Disease*. Baltimore, Williams and Wilkins.

Alexander, D. (1970) *Retailing in England during the Industrial Revolution*. London, Athlone Press.

Allen, G. C. (1929) *The Industrial Development of Birmingham and the Black Country, 1860–1927*.

Allen, J. (1849) *A Pictorial Guide to Birmingham*. Birmingham.

Anderson, T. (2000) Congenital conditions and neoplastic disease in British palaeopathology. In M. Cox and S. Mays (eds.) *Human Osteology in Archaeology and Forensic Science*, 199–226. London, Greenwich Medical Media.

Armstrong (1825) Lectures on the principles and practice of physic, Lecture 21, the gout. *Lancet* 7, 33–40.

Arnold, B. and Lanham, M. D. (2002) *Gender and the Archaeology of Death*. AltaMira Press.

Aufderheide, A. C. and Rodríguez-Martín, C. (1998) *The Cambridge Encyclopaedia of Human Paleopathology*. Cambridge, Cambridge University Press.

Azmi, I., Razak, M. and Hyzan, Y. (1998) The results of treatment of dislocation and fracture-dislocation of the elbow – a review of 41 patients. *Medical Journal of Malaysia* 53 Supplement A, 59–70.

Baines, E. (1875) *Account of the Woollen Manufacture of England*, originally printed in T. Baines, *Yorkshire Past and present*, reprinted separately with a new introduction, 1970, Newton Abbott.

Barnes, E. (1994) *Developmental Defects of the Axial Skeleton in Paleopathology*. Colorado, The University Press of Colorado.

Barnsby, G. J. (1989) *Birmingham Working People: A History of the Labour Movement in Birmingham 1850–1914*. Wolverhampton, Integrated Publishing Services.

Bartley, P. (1996) *The Changing Role of Women 1815–1915*. London, Hodder & Stoughton.

Bass, W. M. (1995) *Human Osteology. A Laboratory and Field Manual*. Columbia, Mo., Missouri Archaeological Society.

Bassett, S. (2001) Birmingham before the Bull Ring. *Midland History* 26, 1–33.

Becker, V. (1980) *Antique and Twentieth Century Jewellery*. London, NAG Press.

Behrensmayer, A. K. (1978) Taphonomic and ecologic information from bone weathering. *Paleobiology* 4, 150–162.

Bevan, L. (forthcoming) The Medieval and Post-Medieval Small Finds. In S. Buteux and S. Rátkai (eds.) *The Bull Ring Uncovered: Archaeological Excavations at Edgbaston Street, Moor Street and Park Street, Birmingham City Centre, 1997–2001*. Oxford, Oxbow Books.

Bevan, L. and Ixer, R. (forthcoming) The Worked Stone. In S. Buteux and S. Rátkai (eds.) *The Bull Ring Uncovered: Archaeological Excavations at Edgbaston Street, Moor Street and Park Street, Birmingham City Centre, 1997–2001*. Oxford, Oxbow Books.

B. F .M. R. A. (1876) *Report of the Birmingham Funeral and Mourning Reform Association for 1876*.

B. F. M. R. A. (1884) *Report of the Birmingham Funeral and Mourning Reform Association for 1884*.

Black, M. (1985) *Food and Cooking in 19th Century Britain: History and Recipes*. London, English Heritage.

B. M. J. (1908) England and Wales, from our special correspondents, Birmingham. *British Medical Journal* 48.

Boore, E. (1998) Burial vaults and coffin furniture in the West Country. In M. Cox (ed.) *Grave Concerns: Death and Burial in England 1700–1850* (Council for British Archaeology Research Report 113). York, Council for British Archaeology.

Booth, P. (2001) The Archaeology of the M6 Toll (Birmingham Northern Relief). *West Midlands Archaeology* 44, 37–54.

Boulter, S., Robertson, D. J. and Start, H. (1998) The Newcastle infirmary at the Fourth, Newcastle upon Tyne. ARCUS Report, Unpublished skeletal report, University of Sheffield.

Boyle, A. and Keevill, G. (1998) 'To the Praise of the Dead, and Anatomy': the Analysis of Post-Medieval Burials at St. Nicholas, Sevenoaks, Kent. In M. Cox (ed.) *Grave Concerns: Death and Burial in England 1700–1850* (Council for British Archaeology Research Report 113). York, Council for British Archaeology.

Boylston, A. (2000) Evidence for weapon-related trauma in British archaeological samples. In M. Cox and S. Mays (eds.) *Human Osteology in Archaeology and Forensic Science*, 357–380. London, Greenwich Medical Media.

Brickley, M. (2000) The diagnosis of metabolic disease in

archaeological bone. In M. Cox and S. Mays (eds.) *Human Osteology in Archaeology and Forensic Science*, 183–198. London, Greenwich Medical Media.

Brickley, M. (2001) The Human Bone. In C. Patrick *The Churchyard of St. Philip's Cathedral, Birmingham: An Archaeological Watching Brief*. Unpublished report, Birmingham University Field Archaeology Unit.

Brickley, M. (2002a) Recognition and understanding of age-related bone loss and osteoporosis-related fractures in the eighteenth and nineteenth centuries. In R. Arnott (ed.) *The Archaeology of Medicine*, 125–128. Oxford, British Archaeological Reports.

Brickley, M. (2002b) An investigation of historical and archaeological evidence for age-related bone loss and osteoporosis. *International Journal of Osteoarchaeology* 12, 364–371.

Brickley, M. (in press) Rib fractures in the archaeological record: a useful source of sociocultural information? *International Journal of Osteoarchaeology*.

Brickley, M. and Ives, R. (in press) Skeletal manifestations of infantile scurvy. *American Journal of Physical Anthropology*.

Brickley, M. and McKinley, J. (eds.) (2004) *Guidance and Standards for Recording Human Skeletal Remains*. Institute of Field Archaeologists/British Association of Biological Anthropology and Osteoarchaeology, University of Reading.

Brickley, M., Mays, S. and Ives, R. (in press) Skeletal modifications of vitamin D deficiency osteomalacia in documented historical collections. *International Journal of Osteoarchaeology*.

Brickley, M., Miles, A. and Stainer, H. (1999). *The Cross-Bones Burial Ground, Redcross Way Southwark, London. Archaeological Excavations (1991–1998) for the London Underground Limited Jubilee Line Extension Project*. MoLAS Monograph 3. London, Museum of London Archaeological Service.

Brothwell, D. R. (1981) *Digging up Bones*. London, British Museum (Natural History).

Buhr, A. J. and Cook, A. M. (1959) Fracture patterns. *Lancet* 1, 531–536.

Buikstra, J. E. and Ubelaker, D. H. (eds.) (1994) *Standards for Data Collection from Human Skeletal Remains. Proceedings of a Seminar at the Field Museum of Natural History*. Arkansas Archaeological Survey Research Seminar Series No. 44.

Bulger, E. M., Arneson, M. A., Mock, C. N. and Jurkovick, G. J. (2000) Rib fractures in the elderly. *The Journal of Trauma, Injury, Infection and Critical Care* 48, 1040–1047.

Bunce, J. T. (1871) St. Martin's Church. *Birmingham and Midland Institute, Archaeological Section, Transactions for 1870*, 7–19.

Bunce, J. T. (1873) *St. Martin's Church: notes from Church Books*. Birmingham, Cornish Brothers.

Bunce, J. T. (1875) *History of Old St. Martin's, Birmingham*. Birmingham, Cornish Brothers.

Burrows, H. (1908) Punch fractures. *British Medical Journal* March 28, 740–742.

Bury, S. (1985) *An Introduction to Sentimental Jewellery*. London, H. M. S. O.

Buteux, S. (2003) *Beneath the Bull Ring: the Archaeology of Life and Death in Early Birmingham*. Studley, Brewin Books.

Buteux, S. and Rátkai, S. (eds.) (forthcoming) *The Bull Ring Uncovered: Archaeological Excavations at Edgbaston Street, Moor Street and Park Street, Birmingham City Centre, 1997–2001*. Oxford, Oxbow Books.

Conheeney, J. and Waldron, T. (in press). *The Human Bone from St. Bride's Lower Churchyard, Farringdon Street (FAO90), London*. Museum of London Archaeological Services Monograph.

Cooper, A. (1824a) Surgical lectures. *The Lancet* 3(4), 97–113.

Cooper, A. (1824b) Surgical lectures. *The Lancet* 3(12), 353–369.

Cooper, A. (1824c) *Treatise on Dislocations and on Fractures of the Joints* (3rd edition). London.

Cooper, A. (1824d) Surgical lectures No. 68. *The Lancet* 4(5), 127–140.

Cox, J. (1892) *Public Parks and Pleasure Grounds*. City of Birmingham.

Cox, M. (1996) *Life and Death in Spitalfields 1700 to 1850*. York, Council for British Archaeology.

Cox, M. (ed.) (1998) *Grave Concerns: Death & Burial in England 1700–1850* (Council for British Archaeology Research Report 113). York, Council for British Archaeology.

Cox, M. (2000) Ageing adults from the skeleton. In M. Cox and S. Mays (eds.) *Human Osteology in Archaeology and Forensic Science*, 183–198, pp 61–82. London, Greenwich Medical Media.

Crowe, P. (1975) *St. Martin's in the Bull Ring, a story of seven centuries*. Birmingham, St. Martin's PCC.

Crowfoot, E. (1987) Coffin Coverings. In R. D. Bell and M. W. Beresford (eds.) *Wharram III* (Society of Medieval Archaeology Monograph Series No.11), 149–150 and fiche 5 (Chapter 6, section E).

Crowfoot, E. (unpublished a) St. Martin-at-Palace, Norwich: Textiles (Typescript).

Crowfoot, E. (unpublished b) Textiles from Essex Burials (Typescript).

Crummy, N. (1988) *Colchester Archaeological Report 5: The Roman and Post-Roman finds from the Excavations in Colchester 1971–85*. Colchester Archaeological Trust Ltd.

Curl, J. S. (1972) *The Victorian Celebration of Death*. Newton Abbott, David & Charles Ltd.

Curl, J. S. (2000) *The Victorian Celebration of Death*. Stroud, Sutton Publishing Limited.

Davidoff, L. and Hall, C. (1987) *Family Fortunes: Men and Women of the English Middle Class 1780–1850*. London, Routledge.

De Courtais, G. (1973) *Women's Headdress and Hairstyles in England from A.D. 600 to the Present day*. London, Batsford.

Dent, R. K. (1894) *The Making of Birmingham*. Birmingham.

Dent, R. K. (1916) *Public parks and gardens of Birmingham*. Birmingham, Parks Committee.

Divelbiss, B. J. (2004). Phalangeal fractures. *eMedicine* http://www.emedicine.com/orthoped/topic258.htm. 02/01/2005.

Dolman, A. H. (1860) Transactions of branches, Midlands branch, two cases of gangrene after injury, in which amputation was successfully performed. *British Medical Journal* April 7, 765–266.

Dottridge Brothers Ltd. (1922) *General Catalogue of Coffins, Coffin Furniture and Drapery*. London.

Edlin, H. L. (1949) *Woodland crafts in Britain*. London, Batsford.

Fahey, V., Opeskin, K., Silberstein, M., Anderson, R. and Riggs, C. (1998) The pathogenesis of schmorl's nodes in relation to acute trauma. An autopsy study. *Spine* 23, 2272–5.

Flanders, J. (2003) *The Victorian House*. London, Harper Collins.

Fletcher (1853) Birmingham Pathology Society Report. *British Medical Journal* 20, 443–444.

Gale, R. and Cutler, D. (2000) *Plants in Archaeology*. Westbury and Royal Botanical Gardens, Kew.

Glason, M. (n.d.) *The Origins and Early History of the Walsall Leather Trades*. Walsall Leather Museum.

Glencross, B. and Stuart-Macadam, P. (2000) Childhood trauma in the archaeological record. *International Journal of Osteoarchaeology* 10, 198–209.

Glover, M. (1974) *The Peninsula War 1806–1814: A Concise Military History*. London, David and Charles.

Godwin, H. (1956) *The History of the British Flora*. Cambridge.

Goodall, I. H. (1993) Iron Scissors. In S. Margeson *Norwich Households: The Medieval and Post-Medieval Finds from Norwich Survey Excavations 1971–1978* (East Anglian Archaeology Report No. 58), 135–136. The Norwich Survey/Norfolk Museums Service, University of East Anglia.

Gribble, F. (1910) *The Romance of the Oxford Colleges*. London, Mills and Boon Ltd.

Gupta, K. (2004). Rheumatoid arthritis. *eMedicine* http://www.emedicine.com/pmr/topic124.htm. 22/12/2004.

Hasluck, P. (1905) *Coffin Making and Undertaking, a Manual*. London, Cassell and Co.

Hershkovitz, I., Greenwald, C. M., Latimer, B., Wish-Baratz, S., Eshed, V., Dutour, O. and Rothschild, B. M. (2002) Serpens endocrania symmeetrica (SES): a new term and a possible clue for identifying intrathoracid disease in skeletal populations. *American Journal of Physical Anthropology* 118, 201–216.

Hillson, S. (1996) *Dental Anthropology*. Cambridge, Cambridge University Press.

Hillson, S. (2000) Dental Pathology. In M. A. Katzenberg and S. R. Saunders (eds.) *Biological Anthropology of the Human Skeleton*, 287–302. New York, Wiley-Liss.

Hodder, M. A. (1992) Excavations in Wednesbury 1988 and 1989: The Medieval and Post-Medieval settlement and the Seventeenth Century Pottery Industry. *Transactions of the South Staffordshire Archaeological and Historical Society*, Volume XXXII (for 1990–91) 1992, 95–115.

Hodder, M. A. (2004) *Birmingham: The Hidden History*. Stroud, Tempus Publishing.

Holcomb, J. B., McMullin, N. R., Kozar, R. A., Lygas, M. H. and Moore, F. A. (2003) Morbidity from rib fractures increases after age 45. *Journal of the American College of Surgeons* 196, 549–555.

Holick, M. F. (2003) Vitamin D: A millennium perspective. *Journal of Cellular Biochemistry* 88, 296–307.

Holliday, J. R. (1873) Notes on St. Martin's church and the discoveries made during its restoration. *Transactions of the Birmingham Archaeological Society* 4, 1–26.

Hopkins, E. (1989) *Birmingham: the First Manufacturing Town in the World 1760–1840*. London, Weidenfeld & Nicholson.

Hopkins, E. (1998) *The Rise of the Manufacturing Town: Birmingham and the Industrial Revolution*. Stroud, Alan Sutton. (A 2nd edition of Hopkins 1989)

Hopkins, E. (2001) *Birmingham: The making of the second city 1850–1939*. Gloucester, Tempus Publishing.

Howarth, G. (1997) Professionalising the Funeral Industry in England 1700–1960. In P. C. Jupp and G. Howarth (eds.) *The Changing Face of Death*, 120–134. Basingstoke, Macmillan.

Hunt, B. (1855a) The modern treatment of fractures. *British Medical Journal* 119, 341–343.

Hunt, B. (1855b) The modern treatment of fractures. *British Medical Journal* 131, 622–624.

Hunt, B. (1855c) The modern treatment of fractures. *British Medical Journal* 134, 699–701.

Hunt, B. (1855d) The modern treatment of fractures. *British Medical Journal* 140, 836–838.

Hutton, W. (1781) *History of Birmingham* (2nd edition 1783; 3rd edition 1795; 4th edition 1809; 6th edition 1835). Birmingham.

Ives, R. and Brickley, M. (2004) A procedural guide to metacarpal radiogrammetry in archaeology. *International Journal of Osteoarchaeology* 14, 7–17.

Jackes, M. (2000) Building the bases for paleodemographic analysis: adult age determination. In M. A. Katzenbert and S. R. Saunders (eds.) *Biological Anthropology of the Human Skeleton*, 417–466. New York, Wiley-Liss.

Jackson, W. A. (1981) *The Victorian Chemist and Druggist*. Princes Risborough, Shire Publications.

Jakes, K. A. and Sibley, L. R. (1984) Survival of protein fibres in archaeological contexts. *Science in Archaeology* 26, 17–27.

Jalland, P. (1996) *Death in the Victorian family*. Oxford, Oxford University Press.

Janaway, R. C. (1993) The Textiles. In J. Reeve and M. Adams *The Spitalfields Project, Volume I: Across the Styx* (Council for British Archaeology Research Report 85), 93–119. London, Council for British Archaeology.

Janaway, R. C. (1998) An introductory guide to textiles from 18th and 19th century burials. In M.Cox (ed.) *Grave Concerns: Death and Burial in England 1700–1850* (Council for British Archaeology Research Report 113), 17–36. York, Council for British Archaeology.

Jenkins, Rev. A. T. (1925) *The Story of St. Martin's, Birmingham Parish Church*. Midland Educational Company.

Johnstone, W. D. (1999) Tuberculosis VIII 147. In K. F. Kiple (ed.) *The Cambridge World History of Human Disease*, 1059–1068. Cambridge, Cambridge University Press.

Judd, M. (2002) Ancient injury recidivism: an example from the Kerma period of Nubia. *International Journal of Osteoarchaeology* 12, 89–106.

Jupp, P. C. and Howarth, G. (eds.) (1997) *The Changing Face of Death*. Basingstoke, Macmillan.

Jupp, P. and Manchester, C. G. (1999) *Death in England: An Illustrated History*. Manchester, Manchester University Press.

Jurmain, R. (1989) Trauma, degenerative disease and other pathologies among the Gombe chimpanzees. *American Journal of Physical Anthropology* 80, 229–237.

Jurmain, R. (1999) *Stories from the Skeleton: Behavioural Reconstruction in Human Osteology*. Amsterdam, Gordon and Breach Publishers.

Jurmain, R. and Kilgore, L. (1998) Sex-related patterns of trauma in humans and African apes. In A. L. Grauer and P.

Stuart-Macadam (eds.) *Sex and Gender In Paleopathological Perspective*, 11–26. Cambridge, Cambridge University Press.

Karmaker, M. J. and Ho, A. M. (2003) Acute pain management of patients with multiple fracture ribs. *The Journal of Trauma, Injury, Infection and Critical Care* 54, 615–625.

Kerr-Valentic, M. A., Arthur, M., Mullis, R. J., Pearson, T. E. and Mayberry, J. C. (2003) Rib fracture pain and disability: can we do better? *The Journal of Trauma, Injury, Infection and Critical Care* 54, 1058–1064.

Keyes, J. (1967) *A History of Women's Hairstyles 1500–1965*. London, Methuen.

Kirk, H. (1976) *Portrait of a Profession – A History of the Solicitors' Profession 1100 to the Present Day*. London, Oyez Publishing.

Krakowicz, R. and Rudge, A. (2004) *Masshouse Circus, Birmingham City Centre: Archaeological Recording 2002*. Unpublished report, Birmingham Archaeology Report 923.

Le, B. T., Dierks, E. J., Ueeck, B. A., Homer, L. D. and Potter, B. F. (2001) Maxillofacial injuries associated with domestic violence. *Journal of Oral Maxillofacial Surgery* 59, 1277–1283.

Leach, P. and Sterenberg, J. (1992) *Holy Trinity Churchyard, Sutton Coldfield: an archaeological evaluation*. Unpublished report, Birmingham Archaeology Report 204.

Liman, S. T., Kuzuca, A., Taştepe, A. I., Ulasan, G. N. and Topçu, S. (2003) Chest injury due to blunt trauma. *European Journal of Cardio-Thoracic Surgery* 23, 374–378.

Litten, J. (1991) *The English Way of Death: The Common Funeral Since 1450*. London, Robert Hale.

Litten, J. (1998) The English Funeral 1700–1850. In M. Cox (ed.) *Grave Concerns: Death and Burial in England 1700–1850* (Council for British Archaeology Research Report 113), 3–16. York, Council for British Archaeology.

Llewellyn, N. (1951) *The Art of Death: Visual Culture in the English Death Ritual c.1500–1800*. London, Reakton Books.

Mabberley, D. J. (1989) *The Plant Book*. Cambridge, Cambridge University Press.

Mabey, R. (1996) *Flora Britannica*. London, Sinclair-Stevenson.

Margeson, S. (1993) *Norwich Households: The Medieval and Post-Medieval Finds from Norwich Survey Excavations 1971–1978* (East Anglian Archaeology Report No.58). The Norwich Survey/Norfolk Museums Service, University of East Anglia.

May, T. (2000) *The Victorian Undertaker*. Princes Risborough, Shire Publications.

Mays, S., Brickley, M. and Dodwell, N. (2002) *Human Bones from Archaeological Sites. Guidelines for Producing Assessment Documents and Analytical Reports*. English Heritage/BABAO.

Mays, S., Brickley, M. and Ives, R. (in press) Skeletal manifestations of rickets in infants and young children in a historic population from England. *American Journal of Physical Anthropology*.

McKenna, J. (1986) *Birmingham Street Names*. Birmingham Public Libraries.

McKenna, J. (1992) *In the midst of life: a history of the burial grounds of Birmingham*. Birmingham, Birmingham Library Service.

McKinley, J. I. and Roberts, C. (1993) *Excavation and Post-Excavation Treatment of Cremated and Inhumed Human Remains*. Institute of Field Archaeologists Technical Paper no. 13.

McTimothy, C. A. and Micheli, L. J. (2003) Current evaluation and management of spondylolysis and spondylolisthesis. *Current Sports Medicine Report* 2, 41–6.

Meadows, C. A. (2000) *The Victorian Ironmonger*. Princes Risborough, Shire Publications.

Michell, B. R. and Deane, H. (1962) *Abstract of British Historical Statistics*. Cambridge, Cambridge University Press.

Mitchell, A. (1974) *A Field Guide to the Trees of Britain and Northern Europe*. London, Collins.

Mole, D. E. H. (1965) John Cale Miller: a Victorian Rector of Birmingham. *The Journal of Ecclesiastical History* Vol XVII. No.1, 95–103.

Molleson, T. and Cox, M. (1993) *The Spitalfields Project Volume 2. The Anthropology: The Middling Sort*. (Council for British Archaeology Research Report 86). York, Council for British Archaeology.

Monckton, H. A. (1969) *A History of the English public house*. London, Bodley Head.

Morley, J. (1971) *Death, Heaven and the Victorians*. GB, Studio Vista.

Mould, C. (2001) *St. Martin's Church, Birmingham City Centre. Desktop Study of Burials*. Unpublished CgMs Report.

Müldner, G. and Richards, M. P. (2005) Fast or Feast: reconstructing diet in later medieval England by stable isotope analysis. *Journal of Archaeological Science* 32, 39–48.

Neilson, C. and Duncan, M. (2001) *Masshouse Circus, Birmingham City Centre: an archaeological watching brief*. Unpublished report, Birmingham University Field Archaeology Unit Report 773.

Noël Hume, I. (1969) *A Guide to Artifacts of Colonial America*. New York, Alfred A. Knopf.

O'Connell, T. C. and Hedges, R. E. M. (1999a) Investigations into the effect of diet on modern human hair isotopic values. *American Journal of Physical Anthropology* 108, 409–425.

O'Connell, T. C. and Hedges, R. E. M. (1999b) Isotopic comparison of hair and bone: archaeological analyses. *Journal of Archaeological Science* 26, 661–665.

Ortner, D. J. (1999) Paleopathology: Implications for the history and evolution of tuberculosis. In G. Pálfi, O. Dutour, J. Deák and I. Hutás (eds.) *Tuberculosis Past and Present*, 255–261. Hungary, Golden Book Publisher Ltd, Tuberculosis Foundation.

Ortner, D. J. (2003) *Identification of Pathological Conditions in Human Skeletal Remains* (2nd edition). Amsterdam, Academic Press.

Ortner, D. J. and Ericksen, M. (1997) Bone changes in infancy in the human skull probably resulting from scurvy in infancy and childhood. *International Journal of Osteoarchaeology* 7, 212–20.

Ortner, D. J. and Mays, S. (1998) Dry-bone manifestations of rickets in infancy and early childhood. *International Journal of Osteoarchaeology* 8, 45–55.

Ortner, D. J. and Putschar, W. G. J. (1981) *Identification of Pathological Conditions in Human Skeletal Remains*. Washington, Smithsonian Institution Press.

Oswald, A. (1975) *Clay pipes for the Archaeologist.* Oxford, BAR British Series 14.

Owens, I. (1889) Reports of the collective investigation committee of the British Medical Association. Geographical distribution of rickets, acute and subacute rheumatism, chorea, cancer and urinary calculus. *The British Medical Journal* Jan. 19, 113–116.

Palm, T. A. (1890) The geographical distribution and etiology of rickets. *Practitioner* 45, 270–4.

Parker, L. (1855) Clinical lectures on surgery now in course of delivery at Queen's College, Birmingham. *British Medical Journal* June 15, 557–558.

Patrick, C. (2001) *The Churchyard of St. Philip's Cathedral, Birmingham: an archaeological watching brief.* Unpublished Report, Birmingham University Field Archaeology Unit Report 701.

Peh, W. C. G. (2002) Ankylosing spondylitis. *eMedicine*, http://www.emdicine.com/radio/topic41.htm, 22/12/2004.

Pemberton, O. (1853) Report of the Birmingham Pathological Society, Thursday April 14th, 1853. *British Medical Journal*, 433–4.

Peng, B., Wu, W., Hou, S., Shang, W., Wang, X. and Yang, Y. (2003) The pathogenesis of Schmorl's nodes. *The Journal of Bone and Joint Surgery (Br)* 85, 879–882.

Penny, N. (1981) *Mourning.* London, Victoria and Albert Museum.

Periscopic Review, March 9 (1855) Discussion on cancer in the French Academy of Medicine: merits of the microscope as compared with clinical examination. *British Medical Journal*, 232–233.

Pickford, I. (ed.) (2000) *Pocket Edition Jackson's Hallmarks.* Suffolk, Antique Collectors' Club.

Pinchbeck, I. (1977) *Women Workers and the Industrial Revolution 1750–1850.* Frank Cass.

Plehwe, W. E. (2003) Vitamin D deficiency in the 21st century: an unnecessary pandemic? *Clinical Endocrinology* 59, 22–24.

Pope, T. (1855) On cancer. *British Medical Journal* Sept. 14, 859–860.

Poynter, F. N. L. (ed.) (1966) *The Evolution of Medical Education in Britain.* London, Pitman Medical Publishing Co.

Puckle, B. S. (1926) *Funeral Customs, Their Origin and Development.* London, T. Werner Laurie.

Purvis, J. (ed.) (1995) *Women's History of Britain 1850–1945.* London, UCL Press.

Quain, R. (1855) Some observations on osteoid cancer. *British Medical Journal* October 26, 970–973.

Rackham, O. (1976) *Trees and Woodland in the British Landscape* (1990 edition). London, Dent.

Rátkai, S. (2000) *Excavations at 3–4 Walsall Street, Wednesbury (WSW 00A).* In Wainwright, J. Marches Archaeology Internal Report.

Reeve, J. and Adams, M. (1993) *The Spitalfields Project. Volume 1: The Archaeology. Across the Styx* (Council for British Archaeology Research Report 85). York, Council for British Archaeology.

Resnick, D. and Niwayama G. (1988) *Diagnosis of Bone and Joint Disorders* (2nd edition). Philadelphia, W. B. Saunders.

Richards, M. P. (2002) Isotope analysis of hair samples. In J. Adams and R. Cherrington *Excavations at St. Martin's Churchyard 2001: Post-Excavation Assessment and Updated Project Design.* Unpublished report, Birmingham University Field Archaeology Unit Report No. 798.

Richardson, R. (1987) *Death, Dissection and the Destitute.* London, Routledge & Kegan Paul.

Roberts, C. (2000) Trauma in biocultural perspective: Past, present and future work in Britain. In M. Cox and S. Mays (eds.) *Human Osteology in Archaeology and Forensic Science*, 337–356. London, Greenwich Medical Media.

Roberts, C. (in prep) Lower respiratory disease in archaeologically derived skeletal material: a survey from a variety of contexts. To be submitted to American Journal of Physical Anthropology.

Roberts, C. and Buikstra, J. E. (2003) *The Bioarchaeology of Tuberculosis: A Global View on a Reemerging Disease.* Gainsville, University Press of Florida.

Roberts, C. and Cox, M. (2003) *Health and Disease in Britain from Prehistory to the Present Day.* Stroud, Sutton Publishing.

Roberts, C. and Lewis, M. (1994) A comparative study of the prevalence of maxillary sinusitis in medieval urban and rural populations in Northern England. Unpublished report to NERC, University of Bradford.

Roberts, C. and Manchester, K. (1995) *The Archaeology of Disease* (2nd edition). Stroud, Sutton Publishing Limited.

Robinson Hill, W. (1860) Cases of tubercular meningitis: with remarks. *British Medical Journal* 27 Oct., 836–838.

Rogers, J. (2000) The paleopathology of joint disease. In M. Cox and S. Mays (eds.) *Human Osteology in Archaeology and Forensic Science*, 163–182. London, Greenwich Medical Media.

Rogers, J. and Waldron, T. (1995) *A Field Guide to Joint Disease.* Chichester, John Wiley and Sons.

Rule, J. (1986) *The Labouring Classes in Early Industrial England 1750–1850.* London, Longmans.

Russell, J. (1860) Transactions of the branches, Birmingham and Midland counties branch. Cases of syphilitic disease of the cranium. *British Medical Journal* March 3, 165–168.

Salter, R. B. (1999) *Textbook of Disorders and Injuries of the Musculoskeletal System* (3rd edition). Philadelphia, Lipincott Williams and Williams.

Saunders, S. R., De Vito, C. and Katzenberg, M. A. (1997) Dental caries in nineteenth century upper Canada. *American Journal of Physical Anthropology* 104, 71–87.

Schultz, M. (2003) Light microscopic analysis in skeletal paleopathology. In D. J. Otner *Identification of Pathological Conditions in Human Skeletal Remains* (2nd edition), 73–108. Amsterdam, Academic Press.

Showell's Dictionary of Birmingham (1885). Birmingham, Cornish Brothers.

Sibley, L. R. and Jakes, K. A. (1983) Survival of cellulosic fibres in the archaeological context. *Science in Archaeology* 25, 31–38.

Sirmali, M., Türüt, H., Topçu, S., Gülhan, E., Yazici, U., Kaya, S. and Taştepe, I. (2003) *European Journal of Cardiothoracic Surgery* 24, 133–138.

Skipp, V. (1980) *A History of Greater Birmingham, down to 1830.* Birmingham, privately published.

Skipp, V. (1983) *The Making of Victorian Birmingham.* Birmingham, privately published.

Stace, C. (1997) *New flora of the British Isles.* Cambridge, Cambridge University Press.

Start, H. and Kirk. L. (1998) 'The bodies of friends' – the osteological analysis of a Quaker burial ground. In M. Cox (ed.) *Grave Concerns: Death and Burial in England 1700 to 1850* (Council for British Archaeology Research Report 113), 167–177. York, Council for British Archaeology.

Steinbock, R. T. (1993) Rickets and osteomalacia. In K. F. Kiple (ed.) *The Cambridge World History of Human Disease,* 978–980.

Stevenson, J. C. (1991) The epidemiology of osteoporosis. In J. C. Stevenson (ed.) *Osteoporosis.* Guildford, Reed Healthcare.

Stevenson, W. (1920) *Trees of Commerce.* London, William Rider and Son.

Stock, G. (1998) The 18th and early 19th century Quaker burial ground at Bathford, Bath and North-East Somerset. In Cox, M (ed.) *Grave Concerns: Death and Burial in England 1700–1850* (Council for British Archaeology Research Report 113), 144–153. York, Council for British Archaeology.

Stuart-Macadam, P. (1991) Anaemia in Roman Britain: Poundbury Camp. In H. Bush and M. Zvelebil (eds.) *Health in Past Societies: Biocultural Interpretations of Human Skeletal Remains in Archaeological Contexts,* 101–114. BAR International Series No. 567.

Studley, M. (2003) Septic arthritis. *eMedicine* http://www.emedicine.com/radio/topic629.htm 22/12/2004.

Terry-Chandler, F. (1995) *Women, Work and the Family: Birmingham 1800–1870.* Unpublished Thesis, DISSA2895. University of Birmingham.

Thomson, F. M. L. (1976) Nineteenth century horse sense. *Economic History Review* 29, 60–81.

Thursfield, R. (1854) Artificial teeth swallowed, and ejected by the bowels. *British Medical Journal,* 923.

Tilly, L. A. and Scott, J. W. (1978) *Women, Work and Family.* Methuen.

Timmins, S. (ed.) (1866) *Birmingham and the Midland Hardware District.*

Trott, A. (1992) *No Place for Fop or Idler.* London, James and James.

Trotter, M. (1970) Estimation of stature from intact limb bones. In T. D. Stewart (ed.) *Personal Identification in Mass Disasters,* 71–83. Washington DC, Smithsonian Institution.

Tutin, T. G., Heywood, V. H. *et al.* (1964–80) *Flora Europaea,* 1–5. Cambridge.

Upton, C. (1993) *A History of Birmingham.* Chichester, Phillimore.

Upton, C. (2003) From Bull Ring to Bullring. In M. Hallett and P. James *Bullring: the heart of Birmingham,* 14–21. Stroud, Tempus Publishing.

V. C. H. (1965) *The Victoria History of the Counties of England: A History of Warwickshire.* Oxford, Oxford University Press.

Von Endt, D. W. and Ortner, D. J. (1984) Experimental effects of bone size and temperature on bone diagenesis. *Journal of Archaeological Science* 11, 247–253.

Waldron, T. (1993) The health of the adults. In T. Molleson and M. Cox *The Spitalfields Project, Volume 2 – The Anthropology. The Middling Sort* (Council for British Archaeology Research Report 86), 67–87. York, Council for British Archaeology.

Waldron, T. and Rogers, J. (1988) Iatrogenic palaeopathology. *Journal of Palaeopathology* 1(3), 117–29.

Walker, P. (1995) Problems of preservation and sexism in sexing: some lessons from historical collections for palaeodemographers. In S. Saunders and A. Herring (eds.) *Grave Reflections: Portraying the Past through Cemetery Studies,* 31–48. Toronto, Canadian Scholars Press.

Walker, P. L. (1997) Wife beating, boxing and broken noses. In D. L. Martin, D. W. Frayer (eds.) *Troubled Times: Violence and Warfare in the Past,* 145–179. Amsterdam, Gordon and Breach.

Walker, P. L., Dean, G. and Shapiro, P. (1991) Estimating age from tooth wear in archaeological populations. In M. A. Kelly and C. S. Larsen (eds.) *Advances in Dental Anthropology,* 169–178. New York, Wiley-Liss.

Walters, C. (2000) *A Dictionary of Old Trades, Titles and Occupations.* Newbury, Countryside Books.

Walton Rogers, P. (1993) *Textiles from the City of Lincoln 1972–1989.* Report privately published by City of Lincoln Archaeology Unit.

Walton Rogers, P. (forthcoming a) Texts on burial textiles from All Saints, Pavement, York. In H. E. M. Cool (in prep).

Walton Rogers, P. (forthcoming b) Text on burial textiles from St. Peter's, Barton-on-Humber, Lincs. In C. Atkins and W. Rodwell (in prep)

Walton Rogers in Emery (in prep) No title yet (A report on the textiles on the coffins in the Bowes vault at St. Mary-the-Less, Durham).

Walvin, J. (1987) *Victorian Values.* Andre Deutsch Ltd.

Watts, L. (1980) Birmingham Moat: its history, topography and destruction. *Transactions of the Birmingham & Warwickshire Archaeological Society* 89, 1–77.

Whitehead, R. (1996) *Buckles 1250–1800.* Greenlight Publishing.

Whiting, J. R. S. (1971) *Trade Tokens: A Social and Economic History.* Newton Abbott, David and Charles.

Whittaker, D. (1993) Oral Health. In T. Molleson and M. Cox *The Spitalfields Project Volume 2 – The Anthropology. The Middling Sort* (Council for British Archaeology Research Report 86), 49–65. York, Council for British Archaeology.

Willett, C. and Cunnington, P. (1957) *Handbook of English Costume in the 18th Century.* London, Faber and Faber Ltd.

Wood, J. W., Milner, G. R., Harpending, H. C. and Weiss, K. M. (1992) The osteological paradox. Problems of inferring prehistoric health from skeletal samples. *Current Anthropology* 33, 343–70.

Zias *et al.* (1993) Early use of cannabis. *Nature* 363, 2156.

Official Publications

Factory Enquiry Commission 1833 (Parliamentary Papers 1833, XX), 1st Report, Report on Birmingham by Mr Horner, Depositions.

Report of the Commissioners on the State of Large Towns and Populous Districts 1839.

Report on the Health of Towns Select Committee 1840 (Parliamentary Papers 1840, XI).

Report on the Sanitary Condition of the Labouring Population of Great Britain 1842 ('Chadwick's Report'; Parliamentary Papers 1842, XXVII), Report on the State of the Public Health in the Borough of Birmingham.

Report of the Children's Employment Commission 1843 (Parliamentary Papers 1843, XIV).

Report of the Commissioners of Enquiry into the State of Large Towns and Populous Districts 1844 (Parliamentary Papers 1844, XVII).

Report of the Commissioners on the State of Large Towns and Populous Districts 1845.

Report to the General Board of Health on the Borough of Birmingham 1849 (Rawlinson's Report).

Trade Directories

The Birmingham Directory 1781. Pearson & Rollason.

Birmingham Directory 1829–1830, 1847.

Bisset, The Magnificent Directory 1800.

Chapman's Birmingham Directory 1801.

Commercial Directory of Birmingham 1816–1817.

Corporation Directory of Birmingham 1846, 1861, 1864.

Directory of Birmingham 1846. Wrightson & Webb.

History & General Directory of the Borough of Birmingham 1849. White.

Holden's Triennial Directory of Birmingham, Vol 2 1809–1811.

Kelly's Directory of Birmingham 1861, 1876–1877.

Pigot's Directory of Birmingham Pt 2 1835, 1842.

Pigot's National and Commercial Directory of Warwickshire 1835, 1842.

Post Office Directory of Birmingham 1845, 1854, 1864, 1856, 1871, 1875.

Post Office Directory of Birmingham 1875 – Trades and Adverts.

Pye's Birmingham Directory 1797.

Slater's Directory of Birmingham 1852–1855.

Triennial Birmingham Directory 1825. Wrightson.

Wrightson's Directory of Birmingham 1815, 1823, 1825, 1831, 1835, 1839.

Index

personal items, 180–4
  buckles, 182
  buttons, 183
  hair combs and pins, 35, 42, 51, 61, 86, 88, 100, 180–2
  lace ends, 182
  leather shoes, 61
  pins, 182
  scissors, 183
  wig curlers, 183–4
  see also clay pipes
  see also jewellery
plague, 15–16
planning process, xv–xvi, 5
  Diocesan Registrar, 5
  Disused Burial Ground Act 1884, 5
  Home Office application, 5
  Town and Country Planning Act 1990, 5, 23
  see also Bullring development
plant remains, 184–6
  box, 185
  cherry, 185
  juniper, 185
  privet, 185
poliomyelitis, *see* infectious disease
public health, 12, 22, 90–1, 115, 118, 119, 128–9, 131, 138, 153, 204–5, 211, 216
  diet and lifestyle, 91, 131–2, 136
  reports on, 113, 117, 118, 128–9, 214, 215, 216, 217
  spread of disease, 91, 113, 115, 118
  vaccination, 113
  see also dental health
  see also St. Martin's churchyard, public health concerns
pyogenic arthritis (PyA), *see* joint disease

Quinton Cemetery, Birmingham, 5

re-interment of remains, xvi, 5
recording methods, 24–25
religion, 221–3
  Anglican Church, 221
  attendance, 221
  Baptists, 221
  Church schools, 222
  Dissenters, 221
  evangelical movements, 221, 223
  Methodists, 221
  pew rents, 12–13, 221
  Quakers, 221
  Roman Catholics, 221
  Sunday Schools, 214, 219, 221, 223
  Unitarians, 221
  see also charity
  see also funerals and funerary practices
'resurrection men', *see* funerary industry, body snatching
rheumatoid arthritis (RA), *see* joint disease
rickets, *see* metabolic disease
Rivenhall, Essex, 141
Robinson family,
  Captain Adjutant Benjamin, 74, 75, 87, 88, 126, 160
    coffin, 74–5, 156, 160; military career, 207; obituary, 207; residence, 207; will, 86, 207
  Elizabeth, 74, 75, 87, 88, 207

  see also brick-lined graves, V33
Rotunda, The, 1
Roundabout House, 9
Rowlinson family, 34–35, 38, 179
  Ann, 34
  Daniel, 31, 34, 35, 154, 165, 189
    marriage to Ann Lewis, 189; obituary, 34, 189; occupation, 34, 189
  John, 34, 189
  see also Vault 10

Salt, Thomas, 12
sanitary conditions, *see* public health
Sansom family
  Ann, 208
  Eleonor, 207, 208
  John, 75–6, 86, 87–8, 154
    marriage to Eleonor Evans, 207; occupation, 207; will, 208
  see also brick-lined graves, V03
Scheuermann's disease, *see* congenital disease
Schmorl's nodes, *see* joint disease
schools, *see* social issues, education
scoliosis, 103, 104–5, 106
scrofula, 117
scurvy, *see* metabolic disease
Serpens Endocrainia Symmetrics (SES), *see* joint disease
Shambles, 9
sinusitis, *see* infectious disease
Smallbrook Street, 195, 200, 217
smallpox, *see* infectious disease
Smith, Elizabeth Walker, 191
social issues, 90–1, 208–9
  childcare, 218
  contraception, 195
  education, 214, 219
    see also Church schools
  family life, 217–19
  family size, 195, 218
  famine, 211
  health and diet, 90, 91, 117, 131, 134–5, 136, 138, 145, 147–51, 210
  housing, 8, 12, 117, 193, 195, 200, 201, 210, 214, 215–6
  living conditions, 115, 117, 135, 131–2, 204–5, 214, 215–6
  marriage, 217
  pollution, 118, 131–2, 134, 136, 138, 205, 216, 218
  poor, 211, 218, 220, 221, 226, 227
  prostitution, 195
  rise of the middle classes, 3, 91, 184, 195, 210, 216, 217, 218
  unemployment, 211
  workhouses, 127, 218, 229
  see also leisure
  see also public health
Soho Manufactory, Handsworth, 6
Spiceal Street, 34, 58
  Dog Inn, 17, 189
spina bifida cystica, *see* congenital disease
spina bifida occulta, *see* congenital disease
spondylolysis, *see* joint disease
St. Bartholomew's chapel, Birmingham, xvi